Marketing and Football

Marketing and Football

An international perspective

Edited by

Michel Desbordes

AMSTERDAM • BOSTON • HEIDELBERG • LONDON • NEW YORK • OXFORD
PARIS • SAN DIEGO • SAN FRANCISCO • SINGAPORE • SYDNEY • TOKYO
Butterworth-Heinemann is an imprint of Elsevier

ELSEVIER

Butterworth-Heinemann is an imprint of Elsevier
Linacre House, Jordan Hill, Oxford OX2 8DP, UK
30 Corporate Drive, Suite 400, Burlington, MA 01803, USA

First edition 2007

Much of this book was originally published as *Marketing et football: une perspective internationale*, by Presses universitaire du sport

British Library Cataloguing in Publication Data
A catalogue record for this book is available from the British Library

Library of Congress Cataloguing in Publication Data
A catalogue record for this book is available from the Library of Congress

ISBN–13: 978-0-7506-8204-6
ISBN–10: 0-7506-8204-3

For information on all Butterworth-Heinemann publications
visit our web site at http://books.elsevier.com

Typeset by Charon Tec Ltd (A Macmillan Company), Chennai, India
www.charontec.com
Printed and bound in Great Britain

07 08 09 10   10 9 8 7 6 5 4 3 2 1

Contents

Contents

List of figures

List of tables

Contributors

Francisco Aguiar has worked for over nine years in the sports and entertainment businesses in Argentina and Latin America. He has worked for Grupo Clarín, the Argentina Rugby Union, and is now the Licensing Manager for Global Brands Group Argentina. He is also Professor of the Executive Program of Sports Business Management at ESEADE, and teaches the Masters degree course in Entertainment and Media at the University of Palermo. He is co-author, with Gerardo Molina, of the book *Sports Marketing* (*Marketing Deportivo: El Negocio del deporte y sus claves*) published by Norma, 2003.

Carlos P. Barros is Auxiliary Professor of Economics at the Instituto Superior de Economia e Gestao, Technical University of Lisbon. He has published more than fifty papers in several areas of economics and management, and his work has also appeared in *The Journal of Sport Economics, European Sport Management Review, Applied Economics, Applied Economic Letters* and *Sport Management Review*. He has co-written (with M. Ibrahimo and S. Szymanski) a book on sports, *Transatlantic Sport* (published by Edward Elgar) and has served as guest editor for a special issue of *The International Journal of Sport Management and Marketing*.

Catarina de Barros is studying a Masters in Sport Management at the Institute of Sport Sciences at the Technical University of Lisbon. She is currently finishing a thesis on Sport Management, and is planning to start a PhD on Sport Management. She has published in the *European Sport Management Quarterly* and *The International Journal of Sport Management and Marketing*.

Anne Bourke is currently Head of Teaching and Learning at University College Dublin (UCD) Business School. She lectures in International Business and Services Management. Her main research interests include services management in the hospitality and leisure sector, governance issues for sports organizations (professional and non-professional), course design and development for adult learners, and examining career and educational options for elite sports participants. She has presented at many international conferences and organized workshops for professional development, and is presently a board member of the European Association of Sport Management (EASM).

Simon Chadwick is Programme Director of the MSc in Sport Management and the Business of Football, and the MSc module manager for Strategic Sport Marketing and the Football Industry, at the University of London, where he is also a Director of the Birkbeck Sport Business Centre. He is Editor of *The International Journal of Sports Marketing and Sponsorship* and an editorial board member for *Sport Marketing Europe, The International Journal of Sport Marketing and Management*, *The International Journal of Sport Management*, *The Journal of Leisure, Sport and Tourism Education* and *The International Journal of Coaching Science*. Simon is the founder and Chair of the Academy of Marketing's Sport Marketing Special Interest Group, and is a lead examiner for the Chartered Institute of Marketing's Sport Marketing Certificate programme. He is co-editor of the books *The Business of Sport Management* and *The Marketing of Sport* (both published by Financial Times Prentice Hall).

Dae Ryun Chang is a Professor of Marketing at Yonsei University, where he is currently the Director of the Business Research Institute. He holds an MBA from Columbia University and a Doctorate of Business from Harvard University. He has held visiting teaching positions at the Helsinki School of Economics and Business, the Australian National University, the Hong Kong University of Science and Technology, and the Singapore Management University. He has published numerous journal articles in outlets such as *Management Science*, the *Journal of Marketing*, and *Decision Science*. Dr Chang's primary research interests lie in integrated marketing communication, business-to-business marketing, sports sponsorship, and marketing in the entertainment industry. He has been an advisor and lecturer to many of the major corporations in Korea, including Samsung, LG, Hyundai, Daewoo, SK Telecom, Doosan, Amore Pacific, On Media and Boryung.

Sergio Cherubini is Director of the MBA in Sport Management at the University of Roma Tor Vergata, Italy. He is a very well-known specialist in sport marketing in Europe, and has published several important books in this research field. He is also a consultant for Italian soccer clubs.

Michel Desbordes is a Professor at the University of Strasbourg, France. He is also Associate Professor at the ISC Business School in Paris. He is a specialist in sport marketing; his research focuses on the management of sport events, sports sponsorship, and marketing applied to football. He has published fourteen books, and also fourteen academic articles in the *International Journal of Sport Marketing and Sponsorship* and *European Sport Management Quarterly*. He is a consultant in sport marketing, and Associate Director of the company MX Sport (http://www.mxsports.net).

Jaime Gil-Lafuente has been a Professor at the Universitat de Barcelona, Spain, since 1993. He is a specialist in sport marketing and in new decision-making tools for marketing and sport management. He has published fourteen books, more than thirty articles from national and international conferences, and has presented at thirty-seven seminar and conferences in this field. He organized the 'I World-Wide Congress of Economic Management of Sports' in Barcelona in 2003, and is at present organizing the 'II World-Wide Congress of Economic Management of Sports' (Mérida, Venezuela, 2007). He is also responsible for the courses 'Strategic marketing management in sport organizations' and 'Financial and fiscal management in sports organizations' at the University of Barcelona.

Paolo Guenzi is an Assistant Professor of Marketing at the Università Commerciale 'Luigi Bocconi' and SDA Bocconi Graduate School of Management, Milan, Italy. He is programme coordinator of the Marketing module of the FIFA Masters in Management, Law and Humanities of Sport. His main research interests are relationship marketing and sales management, and his research has been published in the *European Journal of Marketing, Journal of Marketing Management*, and *International Journal of Service Industry Management*.

Knut Helland is a Professor at the Department for Information Science and Media Studies at the University of Bergen, Norway. His main research areas are news, journalism and news production, as well as relations between sport and the media, with a particular focus on sports rights and sports journalism. He has published books and articles in these and other areas.

Matthew Holt is a Researcher at the Football Governance Research Centre at Birkbeck, University of London. He is a specialist on the governance and regulation of English and European football, and is a recipient of the João Havelange Research Scholarship, awarded by FIFA. He is co-author of the annual *State of the Game* survey of corporate governance in English football, and has a particular interest in the organization and control of club competition in Europe.

Timo Huttunen is the Director of Grassroots at the Football Association of Finland. He gained a Masters degree in Educational Sciences at the University of Joenssu, Finland, in 1993, and holds a UEFA A-licence. He has been working for the Football Association of Finland since 1998, and a member of the UEFA Grassroots Expert's Panel since 2003.

Mark S. Nagel is an Associate Professor at the University of South Carolina. He is a specialist in sport finance. He has also served as a consultant for the Atlanta Beat and has published numerous articles and presented at various conferences.

Yoshinori Okubo is a graduate of the MBA in Football Industries (2001–2002) at the University of Liverpool, UK. His first degree was in Human Science with Media and Communication Studies at the Tokiwa University in Japan. Recent work has included researching and compiling the *Sports Media Directory* for the Sport Services Group in London. His published work so far includes an article about the Japanese TV overview in *Sports Media*, three articles about the Japanese football business in *Football Insider*, and a chapter in *Marketing et Football* (Presses universitaires du sport).

Frank Pons is an Assistant Professor of Marketing at the University of San Diego. His research interests include sports marketing, consumer behaviour, cross-cultural studies and services marketing. His work has been published in journals including *Sport Marketing Quarterly*, *The International Journal of Sport Marketing and Sponsorship*, *The Journal of Service Research*, *The Journal of Business Research* and *The International Journal of Advertising*. Dr Pons is also a member of the editorial board of *The International Journal of Sport Marketing and Sponsorship*. His latest research focuses on fans' motives, and branding issues in professional soccer and hockey. He has been quoted as an expert in several publications for his work on the National Hockey League. He was born in France, and has travelled extensively for research and consulting purposes in Hong Kong, the United States, Lebanon, France, Spain and Mexico.

Kari Puronaho started as a Research and Development Director in the Sport Institute of Finland, Vierumäki, at the beginning of 2006, before which he was a senior researcher at the University of

Jyväskylä. He is Secretary General of the European Association for Sport Management (EASM). He is a specialist in sport economics and marketing, and his current research interests are related to sport club activities, financing and marketing, as well as national sport federations, sport management in general and the economic impact of sport. He has been a visiting lecturer in most European countries, and has published prolifically. He has been a chairman or member of various scientific committees of international congresses, and is also a member of the editorial board of *European Sport Management Quarterly*.

Santiago Ramallo is the Marketing Director of San Isidro Club (Rugby) in Argentina. He is also Associate Professor at ESEADE for the Executive Program of Sports Business Management. He has worked for a sports events marketing company, and his research focuses on sports sponsorship and management as applied to football.

André Richelieu is an Associate Professor at the Faculty of Business Administration, Université Laval, Canada. He is a specialist in sports marketing. His research interests relate to: how professional sports teams can leverage their brand equity by capitalizing on the emotional connection they share with their fans, thus generating new streams of revenues (e.g. merchandising); how professional sports teams can internationalize their brand; how sports teams can improve fans' experience at the sport venue and increase fans' attachment to both the game and the team; and how sports teams and equipment makers can capitalize on the Hip Hop/Urban movement, which has led to a recovery in sports teams' symbols. His work has been published in different journals and presented at various conferences. He also works with sports organizations to help them define the identity and positioning of their brand and launch marketing actions in order to leverage the latter.

Abel Santos is Adjunct Professor in the Department of Sport Social Sciences and Psychology at the Higher School of Sport Sciences of Rio Maior. His major field is sport management; he also teaches sport marketing and the human resources of sport. He studied for his PhD in Methodologies of Research in Sport Sciences at INEFC – University of Leida, Spain, and has an MSc in Sport Management from the Technical University of Lisbon. His major research interests are in the areas of organizational performance, strategy and sport sponsorship. He has published in *European Sport Management Quarterly* and *The International Journal of Sport Management and Marketing*.

Guido Schafmeister is a research assistant at the Department of Services Management, University of Bayreuth. His research focuses on value creation of organizations, controlling, price management and sport management.

Harry Arne Solberg is Associate Professor at Trondheim Business School at Sør-Trøndelag University College, Norway. In 2003 he earned his PhD with a thesis entitled *The Economics of Major Sporting Events – a European perspective*. He is about to publish a book, *The Economics of Sport Broadcasting*, with Professor Chris Gratton from Sheffield Hallam University. He has published a number of articles about the economic impacts of sport and sporting activities, with special attention on sport broadcasting and major sporting events. Solberg is a member of the editorial boards of *European Sport Management Quarterly* and *The International Journal of Sport Finance*.

Amir Somoggi works as a sport marketing and management consultant for an accounting firm, specializing in sport business and plans, creating, executing and controlling sport marketing projects for clubs, sponsors, agencies and media. He also teaches sport marketing and management, has written a number of articles and creates special sports business events. His research focuses on sport marketing, strategic planning, football club management, sponsors' strategies and media relationships.

Richard M. Southall is an Assistant Professor of Sport and Leisure Commerce and Assistant Director of the Bureau of Sport and Leisure Commerce at The University of Memphis. He is a specialist in sport market research, sport law, and organizational culture in sport settings. He served as a consultant for the WUSA's Atlanta Beat for three years during the league's existence. His work has been published in various journals and presented at numerous international conferences.

Stephen Standifird is an Assistant Professor of Management at the University of San Diego (USA). He teaches primarily in the area of strategic management. Prior to joining USD, he taught at the Western Washington University and was a visiting lecturer at the Academy of Entrepreneurship and Management in Warsaw. His current research interests include international institutional influences and organizational reputation. He has published in a variety of journals, and currently serves on the executive committee of the Western Academy of Management and on the editorial boards of *The Journal of Management Inquiry* and *Corporate Reputation Review*. He holds a PhD in Organization Studies from the University of

Oregon, an MBA from Northwestern University and a BS in Chemical Engineering from Purdue University.

Tim Ströbel is a research assistant in the Department of Services Management at the University of Bayreuth. His research focuses on value creation of organizations, brand management, and sport management.

Herbert Woratschek holds the Chair of the Department of Services Management at the University of Bayreuth, Germany. His research focuses, among other things, on measuring service quality, price theories for services, destination management in tourism, and services management applied to several fields of sport management. In these areas of research, he has authored three books and made seventy contributions to books and academic articles in journals such as *The European Journal for Sport Management* and *The Journal of Relationship Marketing*. He is also a member of the board of the European Association for Sport Management.

Sport Marketing Series Preface

The **Sport Marketing Series** provides a superb range of texts for students and practitioners covering all aspects of marketing within sports. Structured in three tiers, the series addresses:

1. Sub-disciplines within sports marketing – for example, branding, marketing communications, consumer behaviour

2. Sports and sporting properties to which marketing is applied – for example, the marketing of football, motor sports, the Olympic Games

3. Philosophy, method and research in sports marketing – for example, research methods for sports marketing students, theoretical perspectives in sports marketing, undertaking successful research in sports marketing.

International in scope, they provide essential resources for academics, students and managers alike. Written by renowned experts worldwide and supported by excellent case studies and pedagogic tools to accelerate learning, the texts available in the series provide:

- a high-quality, accessible and affordable portfolio of titles which match development needs through various stages

- cutting-edge research and important developments in key areas of importance
- a portfolio of both practical and stimulating texts in all areas of sport marketing.

The **Sport Marketing Series** is the first of its kind, and as such is recognized as being of consistent high quality and will quickly become the series of first choice for academics, students and managers.

Series Editor Information

Simon Chadwick is a Director of the Birkbeck Sport Business Centre, and Programme Director for the MSc in Sport Management and the Business of Football at the University of London. His research interests are based around sport marketing, in particular sponsorship, advertising and marketing communications, relationship marketing, branding, fan behaviour and segmentation strategies. He has published extensively in various areas of sport marketing and sport management, and has worked with various organizations across sport. Simon has also served as a consultant to sport businesses on projects relating to sponsorship management, spectator behaviour, service quality in sport, the international development of sports markets and the use of the Internet.

Amongst Simon's other responsibilities, he is Editor of the *International Journal of Sports Marketing and Sponsorship*, and is an Editorial Board member for *Sport Marketing Europe*, the *International Journal of Sports Marketing and Management*, the *Journal of Leisure, Sport and Tourism Education*, the *International Journal of Sport Management*, the *Journal of Coaching Science* and the *Journal of Sport and Tourism*. He also serves as a national correspondent for the European Association of *Sport Management and Sport Marketing Quarterly*.

Simon is the founder and Chair of both the Academy of Marketing's Sport Marketing Special Interest Group and the European Sport Marketing Network, is a lead examiner for and contributor to the Chartered Institute of Marketing's Sports Marketing Certificate programme, and is an external examiner at a number of other UK universities. He is an Associate Member of faculty at IESE (University of Navarra) in Madrid, an Honorary Research Fellow of Coventry Business School, and a member of the Advisory Panel for Sport und Markt's European Sport Sponsorship award.

Simon is co-editor of the following books: *The Business of Sport Management*; *The Marketing of Sports* and *The Business of Tourism Management* (all Financial Times Prentice Hall). He has also contributed chapters to books on football marketing, commercial sport, sport management and sport tourism.

Acknowledgements

by Michel Desbordes

This project was conceived in discussions with Francesca Ford (Butterworth-Heinemann–Elsevier) and Simon Chadwick (Birbeck College, University of London, UK) in November 2005. It is an adaptation of a book that was first published in French with the publisher PUS (*Presses Universitaires du Sport*). However, this version is much improved because twenty-six co-authors participated in the writing of seventeen chapters, giving a unique insight into the relationship between football and marketing. Numerous people have contributed in various ways to the production of this book, and it would have been impossible to complete it without their help.

I am immensely grateful for the professionalism and support of the authors who contributed original work to this book: Francisco Aguiar, Carlos Barros, Catarina de Barros, Ann Bourke, Simon Chadwick, Dae Ryun Chang, Sergio Cherubini, Jaime Gil-Lafuente, Paolo Guenzi, Knut Helland, Matthew Holt, Timo Huttunen, Mark S. Nagel, Yoshinori Okubo, Frank Pons, Kari Puronaho, Santiago Ramallo, André Richelieu, Abel Santos, Guido Schafmeister, Harry Arne Solberg, Amir Somoggi, Richard M. Southall, Stephen Standifird, Tim Ströbel and Herbert Woratschek.

This book has a particular purpose, which is to build a bridge between academic research and the 'real' world of marketing as it is applied in the field of football. Almost every chapter involved interviewing at least one practitioner who provided insights into their field of expertise; some chapters involved several practitioners revealing information regarding the way in which they manage marketing in clubs or leagues in their own country. Without them the book would never have existed, and thus I am very grateful to the twenty-seven experts who collaborated with the authors in the production of this book. They are listed here in order of appearance; some wished to remain anonymous and are therefore identified only as M1, M2, A and B:

Bjørn Taalesen, sports editor, TV2 (Norway)
Øyvind Lund, sports editor, NRK (Norway)
Tor Aune, Head of Sports Rights, NRK (Norway)
Hallbjørn Saunes, News editor, TVNorge (Norway)
Morten Aass, Managing Director, TVNorge (Norway)
François Ponthieu, Lawyer and President of the DNCG
    (Direction Nationale du Contrôle de Gestion), Paris (France)
Giuseppe Rizzello, FC Internazionale (Italy)
Practitioner M1 (sport manager of a premier-league club,
    Germany)
Practitioner M2 (sport manager of a second-league club,
    Germany)
Esteve Calzada, Marketing Director of the Barcelona FC (Spain)
Fernando Gomes, Chief Executive of FC Porto (Portugal)
A and B (Ireland)
Timo Huttunen, Director of the All Stars Programme, the
    Football Association of Finland (FAF)
Luciano Kleinman, Marketing Director, adidas, Brazil
Sadao Suzuki, CEO, Kashima Antlers (Japan)
Takaaki Shimazu, Senior Managing Director, Sapporo Dome
    (Japan)
Eddie Rockwell, Vice President Operations, Columbus Crew
    (MLS, USA), and former General Manager, Atlanta Beat
    (WUSA, USA)
Steve Pastorino, General Manager, Real Salt Lake (MLS, USA)
Kevan Pipe, Chief Operating Officer, Canadian Soccer
    Association (CSA) (Canada)
Joey Saputo, President, and Stéphane Banfi, Communications
    and Marketing Director, Montreal Impact (Canada)
José María Aguilar, President, Club Atlético River Plate
    (Argentina)
Mauricio Macri, President, Boca Juniors (Argentina)
Joonhyoung Park, Executive Director, Brand Marketing
    Consulting, TBWA/Korea
Sung Jin Kwon, Director of Marketing, Inchon United (Korea)
Jae Hoon Lee, Sponsorship Marketing Manager, Samsung
    Electronics (Korea)

I also owe thanks to my friend, Remi Duchemin, for his help with the section on 'The sports business in Asia' in the Introduction.

Finally, and very importantly, I have been lucky enough to enjoy the support of my family – my wife, Sylvie, my son, Antoine, and my two daughters, Camille and Amélie Desbordes.

Introduction: new directions for marketing in football

The context of international professional football largely evolved during the 1990s. In the past ten years or so, football has moved from being a national culture to real internationalization. This has created a huge business with several dimensions, and thus football has become a unique example of merchandising in sport – the only similar case perhaps being the Olympics, which are also universal but occur less frequently.

The internationalization of sport in the world

Sport has now become globalized, including even the traditional professional American leagues (the so-called 'closed leagues'). As national markets are small, sport managers in various fields began to realize that the development of their turnover required more globalized politics, but that this would only be possible if the whole world felt involved with sport. The National Baseball Association (NBA) therefore gradually integrated foreign high-level players (see Table I.1), and this made the diffusion of TV rights or NBA products in their countries much easier. For example, 20 per cent of merchandising and 15 per cent of TV rights were sold outside the US in 2004 (source: www.nba.com).

Table I.1
Number of foreign players in the NBA, 1984–2003

Season	Number of foreign players
1984–85	1
1988–89	11
1992–93	14
1996–97	27
2000–2001	36
2002–2003	65

Source: Desbordes (2004).

In football, the same tendency was observed and the Bosman and Malaja cases (see Box I.1) contributed to increasing the cosmopolitan character of the biggest European teams (the London clubs Arsenal and Chelsea sometimes play with no British team members!). This has led to a particular ridiculous situation, where some Japanese players are used as a foil to create interest among Japanese consumers (see, for example, Chapter 12 in this book).

Box I.1: Handball goalkeeper Kolpak wins court case (9 May 2003)

Yesterday the Slovakian handball goalkeeper, Maros Kolpak, won a court case at the European Court that will have great consequences for a number of football countries within the EU. Kolpak, who has since 1997 played in the German handball league, has been in dispute for many years with the German handball union, which considered him – unjustly, it now seems – to be a non-EU player.

The German handball league followed the rule that a club was allowed to have under contract a maximum of two players from outside the EU. As a result of Kolpak being considered a non-EU player, his club, TSV Ostringen (later SG Kronau/Ostringen) could not engage another player from outside the EU for years.

Kolpak fought the decision of the German handball league because Slovakia is one of the twenty-four countries that participated, in 1994, in a so-called 'association agreement' with the Community. On the basis of this agreement, Kolpak should have the same rights as a player from one of the EU countries.

Since the Bosman judgment of 1995, there has been free movement of workers within the fifteen EU countries. A limitation on the number of professional players from these countries is therefore no longer allowed. Following the verdict of the European Court in the

Kolpak case, the same will now apply for the twenty-four countries that participated in the association agreement with the Community.

In December 2002, the French courts pronounced a comparable verdict in the Malaja judgment. Lilia Malaja, a Polish basketball player in Strasbourg, stated the same legal case as did Kolpak. Now the European Court, the highest legal instrument within Europe, has pronounced an identical verdict, the fifteen EU countries will no longer be allowed to limit the number of professional players from the twenty-four countries involved in the association agreement.

Until now, seventeen countries have fallen under the Bosman judgment – the fifteen EU countries of Austria, Belgium, Denmark, Germany, Finland, France, Great Britain, Greece, Holland, Ireland, Italy, Luxembourg, Portugal, Spain and Sweden – and the two countries from the so-called European Economic Area, Iceland and Norway. After the the Kolpak judgment, the same rights will be extended to the following twenty-four countries: Algeria, Armenia, Azerbaijan, Belarus, Bulgaria, Czech Republic, Estonia, Georgia, Hungary, Kazakhstan, Kyrgyzstan, Latvia, Lithuania, Moldova, Morocco, Poland, Romania, Russia, Slovakia, Slovenia, Tunisia, Turkey, Ukraine and Uzbekistan.

(*Source*: http://fifpro.org/index.php?mod=one&id=11097)

This globalization has much in common with traditional industries. Nowadays, big clubs such as Real Madrid, Juventus Turin or Manchester United consider their marketing and financial strategies at a world level, and on a theoretical basis the product lifecycle (PLC, Figure I.1) is a very useful tool from industrial economics that helps to direct this global distribution.

Looking at the product lifecycle, it appears that companies try to export their products at the beginning of the decline stage: globalization is a way to curb this decrease in sales.

The sport business in Asia

(Readers are directed to Duchemin (2003) for further information regarding the sport business in Asia.)

The sport business has reached the maturity phase of the lifecycle in the traditional markets of Occidental Europe and North America (Nys, 1999). The slackening of growth in TV rights, sponsoring investments and players' salaries over the past few years has proved that the market is heading towards saturation or stability. For example, in Europe, we think that it will be a long time before a football club agrees to pay more than the 78 million euros Real Madrid spent on Zinedine Zidane. So what should professional

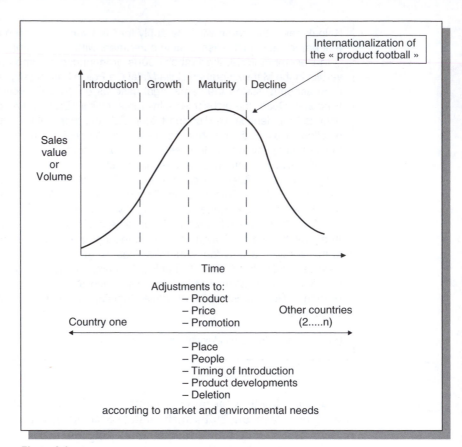

Figure I.1
The product lifecycle
(*Source*: http://www.fao.org/docrep/W5973E/w5973e0a.gif)

sports promoters (federations, leagues, clubs, etc.) do to manage the maturity phase of their product?

Three main strategies are possible. The first is mixed a marketing-modification strategy (prizes, advertising, promotions, etc.), but this does not appear to be well-adapted to sport. The second is a product-modification strategy (new attributes, new rules, new sports, new competitions, etc.), although this would be difficult to implement in the short term. However, it is an option. The third strategy – market modification – is the best one in this case. World-wide, the sport business has to restart its lifecycle and thus increase its income again. How can it do this?

Remembering that

Sales volume = Number of consumers × Utilization rate,

sport business promoters have to think about stretching their market by:

1. Increasing the number of consumers via new marketing targets, such as
   - new populations (women, young children, the disabled, etc.)
   - new geographic territories with high development potential

2. Increasing the utilization rate by
   - multiplying the consumption opportunities
   - improving the consumption level for each opportunity.

As European and American markets are becoming increasingly saturated and economic systems more and more global, sport business has to win new markets, particularly in Asian countries, to prolong its development. A geographic opening strategy aimed at South-east Asia could allow the lifecycle of worldwide sport business to begin again, because these markets are:

1. Emergent, with a very high potentiality of commercial development

2. Highly populated (for example, there are 1.3 billion inhabitants in China)

3. Solvent, with increasing levels of purchasing power

4. Passionate about sport, especially football

5. Super-consumers of merchandising and media.

To illustrate this non-exhaustive list of characteristics, we quote David Stern (Commissioner of the NBA):

> The Chinese adolescent has a computer, goes shopping in supermarkets, drinks Sprite and watches NBA games on TV.

Another illustration is provided by the Asian Football Confederation (AFC), which in 2001 had more than 105 million players – around 44 per cent of the total worldwide (Football 2000 Worldwide; FIFA official survey, April 2001). In comparison, although football is considered the 'king of sports' in Europe, UEFA has only 52 million players – 50 per cent less than in Asia. There are 7.2 million players in China (0.6 per cent of the population) and 3.3 million in Japan (2.6 per cent), versus 2.9 million in France (4.9 per cent) and 2.5 million in Spain (6.4 per cent). These figures support what Mohamed Bin Hammam (the President of the AFC) said recently:

> We truly believe that the future of world football is to be found in Asia.

Some experts think that Asia represents the future of all sport business.

The major European football clubs' search for new solvent markets

In Europe, three of the five main football markets are very dependent on television rights (these represent more than 50 per cent of the French, Italian and Spanish professional clubs' income; see Table I.2). This situation is quite delicate because the broadcasting rights decrease for a couple of months.

Football business has reached the maturity phase of the life-cycle in traditional areas (Europe, South America), and export is one of the few possible development possibilities. Professional clubs are trying to diversify their incomes by finding new potential markets. They have begun to understand the importance of being less dependent on exogenous incomes (difficult-to-estimate incomes, like TV rights when they are negotiated collectively, or ticket incomes when sporting results are not very good) and of developing endogenous incomes (easier-to-estimate incomes, such as from merchandising or sponsorship). To prolong growth, the marketing plans of European football clubs are increasingly including more South-east Asian countries – markets with a high purchasing power, where the population is very passionate about football and the people are super-consumers of merchandise.

So what is the strategy of these clubs? What are they doing to increase their merchandising income in Asia, on the other side of the world?

Table I.2
Breakdown of European football clubs' income in 2003, by percentage

	Germany	England	Spain	Italy	France
TV rights	29	31	51	56	56
Sponsorship & merchandising	44	35	25	25	28
Tickets & PR	27	34	24	19	16
Total	100	100	100	100	100

The main objective is to target and to reach new markets by opening media windows in theses countries. This strategy will:

- allow clubs to develop merchandising sales
- increase media rights income (TV and Internet)
- facilitate sponsoring contracts
- reinforce international awareness of the major clubs.

For the past two or three years, there has been an increasing number of Asian players in the different European professional championships, especially in England, Italy and Germany (see Table I.3). By recruiting Asian players, European clubs have attracted the Asian media – especially TV channels. For example, the first games of Lie Tie and Sun Jihai in the English Premier League were broadcast in more than 700 million Chinese homes (La Lettre de l'Economie du Sport, 27 November 2002). Football clubs want to exploit the positive image their Asian players have in

Table I.3
Asian players in the European football championships, 2003

Player	Nationality	Club	Country
Hidetoshi Nakata	Japanese	Parma AC	Italy
Shunshuke Nakamura	Japanese	Reggina	Italy
Atsushi Yanagisawa	Japanese	Perugia AC	Italy
Shinji Ono	Japanese	Feyenoord Rotterdam	Netherlands
Naohiro Takahara	Japanese	Hamburg SV	Germany
Junichi Inamoto	Japanese	Fulham	England
Takayuki Suzuki	Japanese	RC Genk	England
Kazuyuki Toda	Japanese	Tottenham Hotspur	England
Fan Zhiyi	Chinese	Dundee FC	England
Sun Jihai	Chinese	Manchester City	England
Li Tie	Chinese	Everton	England
Li Weifeng	Chinese	Everton	England
Qu Bo	Chinese	Tottenham Hotspur	England
Shao Jiayi	Chinese	Munich 1860	Germany
Yang Chen	Chinese	Eintracht Frankfort	Germany
Seol Ki-Hyeon	South-Korean	Anderlecht	Belgium
Park Ji-Sung	South-Korean	PSV Eindhoven	Netherlands
Ahn Jung-Hwan*	South-Korean	Perugia AC	Italy

*The marketing potential of Jung-Hwan seems to have been secondary to Italian pride: his club, Perugia AC, dismissed him after his 'golden goal' during the match between Italy and Korea in the World Cup, 2002.

China, South Korea and Japan. In the major clubs, all sportsmen are profitable marketing tools and every player is supposed to facilitate commercial relations with a precise market. Thanks to Hidetoshi Nakata, Parma became the second Italian travel destination for Japanese tourists after Rome, and before Florence, Venice, Naples and Milan (see Box I.2).

Box I.2:   Hidetoshi Nakata, a marketing player

Hidetoshi Nakata, the Japanese international midfielder, arrived in Europe after his recruiting by the Italian club Roma. During the summer of 2001, Nakata was bought by Parma AC for 30 million euros – a record for an Asian sportsman. Even though he initially rarely played whole games, Nakata soon became the best-paid player of his team and the sixth best-paid player in the world (9.36 million euros in 2003; *France Football*, 6 May 2003). With his 'boy-band' looks, Nakata has become the most popular player in Japan, with significant media-marketing potential – especially in terms of merchandising (T-shirts, etc.) and Asian TV channels. When Nakata appears on a game list, coverage of the game always interests two or three Japanese broadcasters. Nakata has also had different endorsement contracts with international brands as Nike, Canon, MasterCard, J-Phones, Subaru and Sky Perfect TV.

Today, many clubs are trying to improve their visibility in Asia. They want to develop a strong base of consumers who will spend a great deal of money on caps, shirts or scarves. During the 2002 World Cup, the high purchasing power and the 'discipline' of Asian fans generated some incredible merchandising sales (each fan spent 70 euros on buying the national team shirt, which is not the case in Europe). The major football clubs (Juventus Turin, Real Madrid, Manchester United, etc.) have developed fan clubs in Hong Kong, Singapore and Tokyo, and have opened specialist shops in various cities where Asian fans can find all the products relevant to their favourite European club.

As an example, let us focus our attention briefly on Manchester United – the richest football club in the world. Whereas commercial income (sponsorship and merchandising) represents 16 per cent of the French clubs' global turnover (19 per cent in Italy, 24 per cent in Spain, 27 per cent in Germany and 34 per cent in England), it represents around 43 per cent of Manchester United's turnover. In an increasingly saturated European market, the club decided to develop different products to reach its estimated 14 million fans throughout the world (over and above the 3.9 million fans in England), especially in Singapore, Hong Kong, Tokyo and

Bangkok. Manchester United has opened several merchandising shops, and is also trying to sell Internet rights on a pay-per-view basis.

To reinforce the attachment of their foreign fans, the major European teams organize occasional international tours that combine sporting games and marketing operations. Whereas they have played in North America for few years, the concept is now extending to Asia. In 2003 the inaugural 'Peace Tournament' took place in South Korea, with various European clubs such as Lyon (France), Chelsea (England), PSV Eindhoven (Netherlands) and Roma (Italy) taking part. As another example, Newcastle United signed a marketing alliance with Dalian Shide (China) and participated in the inaugural English Premier League Asian Cup in July 2003 in Malaysia.

In Europe, major professional clubs try to reach their Asian fans all year long, and not only through Asian media. They are developing some interactive services of interest to the target market, allowing fans to follow the season of their favourite players (especially Chinese, Korean and Japanese) – for example, Dundee FC and Borussia Dortmund's websites have a Chinese version, and PRT Asia Company (based in England) signed a contract with the Chinese Internet portal Sino.com and China Link to provide an interactive premium service for Asian fans of Premier League club Everton and its Chinese international midfielder Li Tie.

Since the arrival of Asian players in the different European championships, football business promoters (federations, leagues and clubs) have realized that such a marketing opening is also a real opportunity to sell media rights in new territories, which might balance the expected decrease in TV rights in Europe. This trend concerns mainly Internet rights: 'When the pay per view is real in Japan, we think that with 10 per cent of the 40 million Japanese football fans, we will be able to earn in one day what we earn in Spain in one year' said a Real Madrid manager in 2002 (Roger, 2002). Moreover, Asian broadcasters are increasingly buying European football TV rights:

- China Central Television signed a deal with ESPN (the international rights holder) for the live rights to thirty-one English Premier League games for the 2002–2003 season. The Premier League is the third most popular foreign league behind Serie A and Bundesliga.

- Hong-Kong free-to-air channel Television Broadcasts Ltd, acquired broadcast rights to Serie A, which is the second most popular league in Hong Kong, behind the Premier League.

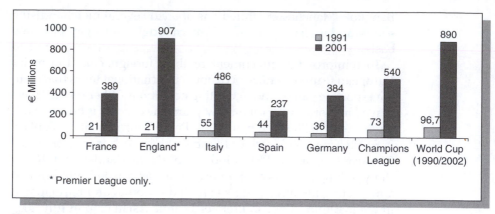

Figure I.2
The increase in TV rights in European football between 1991 and 2001
(*Source*: Eurostaf and KirchMedia)

By extending their visibility in new solvent markets, European football clubs hope that they may also reinforce sponsorship income. Many companies could be interested, especially international brands which want to increase their awareness or to improve their image in Asia. Following finalization of the deal between Reebok and Liverpool in 2003, Reebok's CEO Martin Coles declared that: 'Our goal is to build Liverpool FC into the premier football brand in the world. Much of this focus will be towards Asia, which Liverpool toured in 2001 and is planning to visit again'. Sponsorship of European football clubs is also of interest to some Asian brands – for example, the mobile phone manufacturer Kejian agreed to sponsor Everton, although its products are only available in the Chinese market.

This introduction illustrates how football has become a worldwide sport. The uncertain future of TV rights has been a major factor in the 'Asian temptation', because the continent could prove to be a new Eldorado for broadcasters. Figure I.2 illustrates the explosion of TV rights in European football between 1991 and 2001.

The financial difficulties of broadcasters since 2000 (ITV Digital in England, Canal+ in France, Stream and Telepiu in Italy) in reaching profitability reinforced their desire to export football throughout the world. The Internet will make segmentation almost infinite for marketers.

The structure of the book

Football is played all over the world, and universal marketing tools are necessary in order for it to be profitable. However, it is interesting to wonder whether marketing is the same in every country or whether there are cultural differences that imply the need to adapt the marketing policies of the clubs and leagues. This is the key question of this book, which gathers seventeen contributions from first-class researchers involved in soccer marketing in Europe, North America, South America and Asia. A detailed description of the structure of the book follows.

Part 1: Marketing football in Europe

It is logical to begin the book with a large section concerning the development of soccer marketing in Europe, as Europe has always been the region of the world where this sport has had the most important place in the field of sport, and in sport marketing in general. England invented football, and it became a professional sport very early on (the beginning of the twentieth century in France; even earlier in England). Part 1 therefore contains ten chapters and is divided in three sub-parts.

Sub-part A, 'The general state of football marketing in Europe', contains two chapters that deal with UEFA and TV rights. Chapter 1 concerns the marketing of the UEFA Champions League. In 1992 the European Cup was transformed into the UEFA Champions League (UCL), around which a new marketing strategy and brand identity were developed and implemented by UEFA in partnership with TEAM Marketing. This chapter analyses the phenomena that completely transformed the approach of national and European competitions.

Chapter 2 concentrates on journalism as an instrument in promoting TV sports rights. The nature of TV sports broadcasting has changed dramatically in recent years, and today TV channels will pay expensive fees to broadcast the most attractive events. The focus of the chapter is on football, and it raises the following question: what consequences do sports media rights – and in particular football rights – have for broadcast journalism regarding sports?

Sub-part B deals with the 'Big Five' market. Managers use this expression when they talk about England, Germany, France, Italy and Spain, which are the five biggest markets in the economics of football in Europe. Each chapter was written by a native specialist of each country. Chapter 3 describes the original model of financial control that has been implemented in France since the 1990s. Its declared aim is to ensure that clubs which begin the championship will be able to finish it without having to file for bankruptcy – which would, of course, distort the competition. Today this consists more of coming up with a business plan than strictly controlling bankruptcy. If clubs' accounts are not in accordance with what was agreed, they are punished seriously – for example, by being relegated. The key point of this chapter is to discuss whether this model can be exported all over Europe, considering the increasing power of the G14 (an organization of European football clubs founded in 2000, initially by fourteen members, with another four clubs added in 2002).

Chapter 4 deals with co-marketing (cooperative marketing) activities. These are often carried out in other industries, and they can be very useful for soccer managers. Co-marketing is different from sponsorship because the partners play a more active role rather than simply being financial contributors. The co-marketing concept has been applied in many cases by Italian football clubs of different sizes; some of the examples in this chapter have been chosen for their originality or significance.

Chapter 5 discusses a market research technique that managers may use to support decision-making processes concerning the transformation of football stadiums into multipurpose recreational facilities. Paolo Guenzi analyses the prospects of transforming stadiums into multipurpose leisure centres which provide a wide range of services. A resumé of empirical research based on conjoint analysis and applied to the biggest clubs in Italy ends the chapter.

Chapter 6 gives an overview of the developments in the German football market over the last decade. Like other national football leagues, the German *Bundesliga* has had to cope with tremendous financial changes. With regard to the financial situation, the media, and especially the TV market, have had a major impact on the German football market. Hence, dealing with German football from a marketing perspective requires a special focus on broadcasting rights.

Chapter 7 discusses marketing management in large and complex clubs. According to Jaime Gil-Lafuente, the stake in some games is sometimes over a million euros. However, these huge financial changes have not been reflected in the management of clubs, which is often still amateur, with presidents that do not consider the club as a business but rather as a toy that can be replaced easily when broken. Among big clubs, such as the FC Barcelona, the balance between sporting and economical results is difficult to achieve because of the significant pressure of media, and also of political and social groups. This chapter gives an overview of the management of this famous club, where 'socios' have played an important role since its creation.

Having studied the five biggest areas in Europe, Sub-part C then considers whether there is still a place for 'small' countries in the European soccer market and gives an overview of activities in football marketing in countries that are not part of the 'Big Five' – such as Portugal, Ireland and Finland. It is interesting to discover whether a relatively small market can still develop a real marketing strategy, or whether such markets are dominated by the influence of their neighbours.

Chapter 8 uses tools from economic theory and applies them to football marketing. The authors analyse the role of sponsorship in the Portuguese First Division (known since 2002 as the Superliga, or Super League) with a two-step process (DEA – Data Envelopment Analysis, a Tobit model), before making managerial recommendations.

Chapter 9 begins by underlining that the domestic game in the Republic of Ireland is played at a semi-professional level, with English clubs attracting pre-elite players aiming to pursue a professional career in football. Anne Bourke explains the role of the Football Association of Ireland (FAI) in governing and promoting the game at all levels (seniors, juniors, colleges, youths, schoolboys/girls and women). However, over the years many Irish players have achieved great success with English clubs and consequently English clubs continue to have a strong fan base in Ireland. This has implications for the status, reputation and development of the domestic game.

Chapter 10 is unusual in that it focuses more on grass-roots football than on professional football. As Finland is one of the smaller football countries, the Football Association of Finland (FAF) has a great passion to develop not only football itself but also the resources available for all kinds of quantitative and qualitative growth. This chapter underlines the importance of the production process of positive football experiences, which can ensure not only football success in the future but also (and especially) all the relevant resources – especially volunteers. At the end of the chapter, the results of five years' (1999–2004) of systematic marketing and running the All Stars Programme are presented.

Part 2: The development of dedicated football marketing in the rest of the world

Having studied the importance of European strategies in Part 1, Part 2 deals with some alternative strategies that have been developed in North America, South America and Asia. As noted earlier in the Introduction, spreading football throughout the world is seen as being key to extending its product lifecycle. However, although football is incredibly popular in poorer parts of the world, such as Africa or South America, economic structure is crucial in order to develop financially viable professional football.

Chapter 11 discusses the fact that, although Brazil is considered 'the country of football', football as a business has developed at a very slow rate compared to that in Europe since the 1990s. This is why new sports laws were created in 1993 to bring more professionalism to Brazilian sport management. This chapter analyses the evolution of Brazilian sport legislation and the reality of Brazilian football clubs by focusing on an original example, Atlético-PR, and how this club from Paraná State has developed its management, becoming the first strategic model in Brazilian football.

Chapter 12 concerns three main topics. The first is the J. League and the 2002 World Cup, which have resurrected Japanese football as a more sustainable business. The second concerns the 2002 World Cup legacy – excellent football facilities that will support the further continuous development of Japanese football. The third topic concerns the internationalization of Japanese football: Japanese footballers are going to play in Europe while European clubs come to Asia in order to develop their business and also to enhance their popularity in this emerging market.

Chapter 13 concerns the marketing of soccer in the USA. Even though the USA is the primary sport market, its consumers have never shown a big interest in the most popular sport in the world – football. This chapter is interesting because it shows that implementing a marketing strategy is not sufficient to succeed; the role of demand is fundamental. This chapter examines the past successes and failures of professional soccer in the United States, specifically focusing on Major League Soccer (MLS) and the Women's United Soccer Association (WUSA) as the most recent examples of successful and unsuccessful US professional soccer leagues. The leagues' marketing strategies and plans are then examined through the lenses of exchange theory, cause-related marketing (CRM) and strategic philanthropy.

Chapter 14 also focuses on the development of soccer in the United States. Using secondary data (websites, academic and professional publications) as well as interviews conducted with two general managers of US professional soccer teams, it presents how professional soccer is marketed in the US. The discussion shows that US professional soccer leagues have to be far more aggressive in their marketing efforts than is seen throughout much of the world of soccer.

Chapter 15 highlights the reasons for past failures and provides some guidelines regarding the long-term growth of soccer in Canada. Obviously, the lack of infrastructure (playing facilities, coaches and referees) and the absence of quality ownership are the two main reasons behind the past failure of soccer in Canada. However, overall, several intrinsic and extrinsic factors explain the problems associated with the diffusion and adoption processes of soccer in the country: the nature and rules of the game, as well as its history (intrinsic); political factors, the weak promotion of the game, the lack of local stars, the absence of financial means, geography and weather (extrinsic).

Chapter 16 illustrates the existing relationship between marketing and football in Argentina. In order to do this, it discusses theoretical questions related to marketing, such as providing elements of a sociological nature that contribute to understanding football as a social sport and a showbusiness sport, and also its actors and followers as consumer agents in Argentina.

Chapter 17 examines the relationship between sponsorship marketing and professional football in South Korea. Sponsorship marketing contributed to the success of FIFA 2002 Korea and Japan, and the chapter highlights some of the key official FIFA partners, such as KT, Hyundai and POSCO. Unofficial sponsors, also known as 'Ambush' marketers, such as SK Telecom, Nike, and Samsung, also achieved notable success. The chapter discusses the lessons to be learned for official as well as unofficial sponsors, and then goes on to look into the impact of corporate sponsorship on the Korean professional football league and teams.

References

Desbordes, M. (2004). Le cas Tony Parker à la lumière du marketing sportif, Conference on US and European Sports, National Institute of Sport (INSEP, Paris, France), 17 June.

Duchemin, R. (2003). The sport business and the Asian temptation, or the sickly smile of American and European TV. Conference of the International Association for Sports Economists, Neuchâtel, Switzerland, 23–24 May 2003.

Nys, J-F. (1999). La mondialisation du football: une réalité pour la Fédération Internationale, une nécessité pour les clubs professionnels. *Revue Française du Marketing*, **172**, 23–43.

Roger, G. (2002). La World Company. *L'Équipe*, 26 November.

Marketing football in Europe

A   The general state of football marketing in Europe

B   The 'Big Five' market

C   Is there a place for 'small' countries on the European football market?

A
The general state of football marketing in Europe

Building global sports brands: key success factors in marketing the UEFA Champions League

Simon Chadwick and
Matthew Holt

Overview

In 1992 the European Cup was transformed into the UEFA Champions League (UCL), around which a new marketing strategy and brand identity were developed and implemented by UEFA, in partnership with TEAM Marketing. This chapter begins by examining the relationship between these two organizations and then considers the context within which the new strategy and identity were developed. Thereafter, each of the components used to create the Champions League brand are examined: the emphasis on European football history and heritage, the creation of a brand identity, the composition of a UEFA Champions League anthem, the use of imagery and symbols, and the creation of a new trophy. In the concluding section, issues pertaining to brand implementation, event management identity and the presentation of a television/media identity are addressed.

Keywords

branding, Champions League, sport product, strategic sport marketing, television and new media

European football: the emergence of the UEFA Champions League

Competition between the elite clubs of Europe can be tracked back to the 1950s. Following a series of friendly matches between Wolverhampton Wanderers of England and Honved of Hungary to decide Europe's premier club, the French newspaper *L'Équipe* proposed the formation of a competition consisting of the league champions of each European nation, which was then constituted under the Union of European Football Association's (UEFA) auspices. Thus the European Champion Clubs' Cup, more commonly known as the European Cup, was born. The competition generated huge interest and popularity from the outset, and became a suitable platform for Europe's greatest talents.

The competition remained unchanged for almost forty years, with entry limited to the holders and the national champions of each country. The knock-out format consisted of two-legged ties in which each club played one game at home and one away. By the early 1990s, however, the growth of television as a key medium of football consumption and the development of satellite and pay-television digital technologies led to an exponential growth in the revenues available to clubs. The composition of the competition thus became ripe for review. The knock-out format in particular, and the risk that popular clubs could be eliminated after one tie, was unacceptable to both clubs and broadcasters, who required a greater number of guaranteed games. Proposals aimed at transforming the competition had been raised at various points, most notably by the owner of AC Milan, Silvio Berlusconi, in the 1980s. In this context, UEFA took action to reconsider both the commercial and sporting aspects of its main club competition. In 1992, the European Cup was transformed into the UEFA Champions League (UCL), a hybrid competition comprising league and knock-out. The impetus behind this was a desire amongst both clubs and broadcasters for a greater number of guaranteed games, as a means to exploit new revenues.

In the political network of European football a constant state of tension exists between the elite clubs, looking for opportunities to increase revenues and greater autonomy, and the governing bodies, which look to control the wider interests of the game. UEFA's control of the competition enables the organization to retain revenues for its own purposes, including the development of the European game. This is a source of grievance for the elite clubs. Gathered together in the G14 organization – a pressure group now consisting of eighteen of Europe's major clubs – they lobby for greater influence. Clubs such as Manchester United, Real Madrid and Juventus generate enormous leverage from the size and loyalty of their consumer bases. Thus the control, format and marketing of the competition are subject to ongoing debate.

In this complex and unstable position, UEFA has had to rely on two separate strategies as a means of retaining control of its flagship competition. First, it relies on its position within the global framework of football governance and its historical role as the organizer of European club competition to buttress its legitimacy. Secondly, the ever-increasing demands of the clubs means that UEFA has been forced to produce a competition of quality and a reward to satisfy the competing clubs. UEFA has therefore taken responsibility for developing the competition both in sporting and commercial terms in order to adapt to the transformed commercial environment, and as a means to address the demands of the economically powerful clubs. In doing so, UEFA has formed a hugely successful commercial partnership.

UEFA and TEAM

The commercial growth of football, initiated and controlled by football's governing bodies, has been facilitated by a small number of event and media management companies – most notably ISL (International Sport and Leisure) – long-term partners of both the world governing body FIFA and UEFA. The significance of these companies is such that they have been referred to as the 'cement of network football: the go-betweens who line up corporate and media sponsors and stage manage the spectacle' (Sugden, 2002: 67). In transforming European club competition, UEFA formed what has turned out to be a hugely successful alliance with two former executives of ISL. Recognizing the opportunities for growth, Klaus Hempel and Jürgen Lenz formed Television Event and Media Marketing (TEAM), based in Lucerne, Switzerland, as the vehicle through which the UEFA Champions League would be transformed. According to UEFA Chief Executive, Lars Christer Olsson (personal interview, 16 November 2004:

> 'The development of the Champions League was, in my opinion, not so much driven by wishes from the bigger clubs, as the needs of the television companies … Hempel and Lenz were early in this process and they created with Johansson and Aigner [then UEFA President and General Secretary] the concept for the Champions League, based on the needs of television which means that the major markets had to be better represented.

On instruction from UEFA, TEAM sought to apply a blueprint for sports marketing success by marrying the synergetic qualities of football, sponsorship and television, as illustrated in Figure 1.1. As Hempel explains (Ahlström, 2002: 18):

> We spent three weeks at the Villa Sassa fitness clinic in Lugano and it was there that we worked for three hours per day on a new concept of creating a 'branded' club

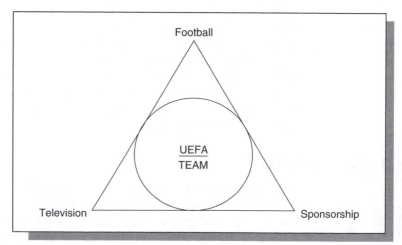

Figure 1.1
The partnership concept (Ahlström, 2002)

competition … We came up with a triangle formed by football, sponsors and broadcasters with UEFA and TEAM in the middle, harmonizing the interests and making sure that the concept was mutually beneficial for all the components.

Whilst this concept was not new, through its marketing of the UEFA Champions League (UCL) TEAM has exploited the commercial opportunities in a global marketplace and, with UEFA, has created an integrated sporting and commercial platform for Europe's elite clubs. In this chapter we focus on the key success factors in transforming the UEFA Champions League into a benchmark global sports brand.

The product: the UEFA Champions League

The fundamental factor in the successful transformation of the UCL into a benchmark global brand is the sporting product itself. This consists of a number of crucial interacting elements which blend together to produce a competition with consistently high levels of interest. These elements are illustrated in Figure 1.2.

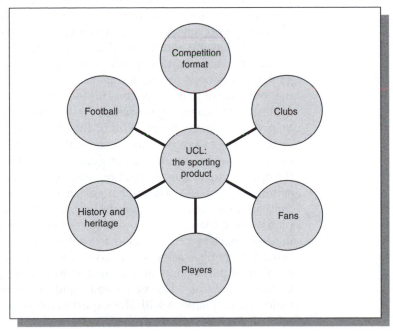

Figure 1.2
Facets of the UEFA Champions League product

It is impossible to grade the importance of the various elements of the sporting product individually, as they work together and coalesce to form an effective whole. The roots of the success of the UCL are, of course, grounded in the worldwide popularity of football. Europe is football's economic centre, and as such attracts star players from across the world. Those star players are employed by the most famous elite clubs, which in turn enjoy remarkable loyalty from their supporters. The clubs are the brands that operate within the UCL brand. As noted above, the UCL is the successor of the European Cup, first played in 1955. It is within that historical context that the UCL exists as the legitimate tournament played to decide Europe's greatest football teams.

The historical context and the heritage of the competition are at the heart of the UCL branding. As sociologist Anthony King (2004: 331) has argued, 'tradition is extremely important for the viability of the Champions League. Sports matches have meaning where there is a historical connection which fans and players recognize.' That meaning therefore exists as a vitally important aspect of the UCL product. Victory in the competition does not exist as a solitary moment of success, but rather as the latest achievement in an ongoing process. This was notable in the recent success of Liverpool in 2005. It was the club's fifth victory in the competition, the previous of which had been over twenty years previously and to which there was frequent media reference. Similarly, the importance of the players is not confined to the years in which they compete. They are part of a wider historical trajectory, in which the UCL provides the platform and recognition for the game's greatest talents.

The UCL, then, is subject to the contradictory demands of amalgamating the need for modernization whilst consistently relating the tournament to past events. This is particularly pertinent in the context of the changing format of the competition, which has also helped to facilitate the creation of the global brand. The two key developments were the introduction of a group stage in 1992–93, facilitating a greater number of guaranteed games for clubs, and the opening up of the competition to more than one club from each country in 1997–98. These changes marked a radical departure from a knock-out competition designed purely for national champions. These changes were the subject of much heated debate, and in some quarters were depicted as a betrayal of the European Cup. What the changes achieved, however, was to allow for a greater number of participants and a greater number of games between Europe's elite clubs. This generated significant extra interest in the major football nations with the largest markets, which in turn has formed the basis of the strategic commercial development of the UCL. Whilst the changes in format have created something of a virtuous circle for the top clubs (participation generates substantial revenue, enabling clubs to consolidate their success in the national leagues), another success factor is that the competition continues to be organized around important sporting and organizational principles:

> All the sporting elements, all the competition criteria, have been driven by UEFA without influence from TEAM at all. In the early days the concept was developed by TEAM. It was adapted, and adopted by UEFA to fit their needs, and I think what has happened in the last three or four years, is that it is finessing everything that we do … Both sides would take their credit for having an influence over the parts of the competition that they had the responsibility for. But it's driven by UEFA and it is supported and implemented by TEAM.
>
> *(Richard Worth, Chief Executive, TEAM, personal interview, 1 March 2005.)*

> At the end of the day we are a sporting governing body. We are not a private entity. Our duty is to the fans, to the European kids, to everybody's development of football. We've got to make sure that we develop it in a way which is appropriate, which is durable for European football … at one point sport should always prevail.
>
> *(Philippe Le Floc'h, Director, Marketing and Media Rights, UEFA, personal interview, 19 November 2004.)*

UEFA's control of the sporting format is important. It allows the organization to balance the commercial requirements of the competition with important sporting principles. These include allowing access to the tournament and its rewards to all UEFA's fifty-two national members, as opposed to just the main markets which generate the vast majority of revenue. This provides an incentive for development amongst smaller or less developed European nations, and also helps generate geographically-spread interest for the tournament. Moreover, entry to the tournament is based on merit, and no club is guaranteed entry. This enhances the legitimacy of the competition in a sporting culture based on promotion and relegation between leagues. Additionally, the format is driven by sporting as well as commercial imperatives. This means that whilst a group stage has been included (two group stages between 2000 and 2003), knock-out remains an important facet of the competition, producing games with greater excitement and unpredictability. The second group stage was removed against the wishes of the bigger clubs.

At the same time, however, the UCL is an enormous logistical operation, and UEFA has employed TEAM to implement the

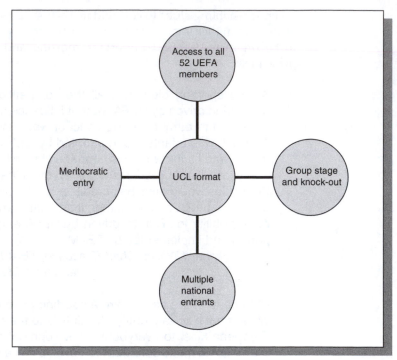

Figure 1.3
Facets of the UEFA Champions League format

competition. The breakdown of responsibilities was the cause of some disagreement early in the history of the competition, with concerns raised within UEFA regarding the large degree of control TEAM was exerting. The division of responsibility is now, however, much clearer, with UEFA retaining control over the overall strategy and the sporting elements and format of the competition. This marks an important development in that football's governing bodies, UEFA in this instance, have regained a greater degree of control over their commercial properties – namely the competitions. The overall control of UEFA and the logistical and commercial expertise of TEAM have coalesced to form an effective working partnership, adding value, as Philippe Le Floc'h explains (personal interview, 19 November 2004):

> I am a strong believer that the ISL model was gone and that it was up to the federations with real properties to take control – and when you are lucky enough to sit on two of the four biggest world properties in sport, you should control your assets … The idea is that we don't want to do everything in-house … we have an agency, which has 100

people working for us, and we have got 125 games involving 32 teams in 18 countries, and that's a lot of logistics. We're not sure we want to do it ourselves. But we want to really control the strategy of the whole thing. And as long as we're with an agency that is bringing added value, then we've got no problems to pay that price.

The format of the competition (see Figure 1.3) combined with the other crucial ingredients illustrated in Figure 1.2 are the fundamental factors in the success of the UCL. Without them, there would be no tournament to market and brand.

The strategy: central marketing

The critical commercial transition from the European Cup to the UCL was the decision to centralize commercial, marketing and branding control of the tournament. The concept of central marketing operated by TEAM and UEFA has allowed UEFA itself to both 'optimize' and control revenues generated by the competition. Previously, clubs participating in the European Cup had been responsible for selling their own television and commercial rights. These rights have now been transferred from the clubs to UEFA in return for fixed payments from a central fund generated by the central sale of television, sponsorship and other commercial rights by TEAM on behalf of UEFA. Payments to clubs are then distributed according to both sporting achievement and the market in which the clubs are based. Those clubs participating in the larger markets therefore receive higher payments on the basis that their television rights are more valuable. Whilst the market payments have been the subject of some criticism (Morrow, 2003), Umberto Gandini, Organizing Director of AC Milan, has correctly referred to them as a 'reality of the business' (personal interview, 14 February 2005). In order for the rights to be transferred by clubs to UEFA, the clubs operating in the largest markets would expect to receive a fee commensurate or greater than that which they would receive if they marketed the rights individually. By marketing the television and sponsorship rights centrally, UEFA has been able to generate greater levels of revenue than the total revenues generated by the clubs selling the rights individually.

Television

The 'sporting product' of the UCL provides the basis for the 'television spectacle'. Football is a key driver of television audiences in Europe, and television is consequently the key provider of revenues in European football – and specifically the UCL. In the 2004–05 competition, it was estimated that 320 million supporters watch the UCL every week (UEFA and TEAM, 2005: 12). In the 2003–04 season, 79 per cent of a total revenue of 883 million Swiss francs was generated through television sales (UEFA, 2005: 32). According to TEAM executives Craig Thompson and Ems Magnus, the initial intention was to create 'a UEFA Champions League Television Network' with nationally exclusive television stations, as a means to guarantee premium rates from free-to-air broadcasters (Thompson and Magnus, 2003: 50). This constituted an important aspect of the UEFA/TEAM policy to 'optimize' revenue rather than 'maximize' revenue (see www.team.ch), demonstrating the desire to ensure wider access to the tournament across Europe as a means to develop the UCL brand, and also as a means of maximizing sponsorship revenue. Whilst it could be argued that the UCL is now sufficiently entrenched in the consciousness of the European football supporter to migrate effectively to pay-TV, the decision to utilize exclusively free-to-air television until 2003 has clearly paid substantial dividends in generating maximum awareness of the competition.

The new league format provided a more enticing product for broadcasters, with a guaranteed number of fixtures consistently scheduled as part of an overall package of live games. The increase in the number of teams from the major nations further enhanced the attractiveness of the tournament in the largest markets. Following the intervention of the Competition Commission of the European Union, UEFA was forced to open the sale of TV rights to other broadcasters, but the free-to-air element remains an important aspect of the development of the UCL brand. In addition to rights fees, TV companies have also been required to provide programme sponsorship for official sponsors, and to give 'best prices and placement for commercial airtime spots' (Thompson and Magnus, 2003: 50). Central marketing therefore afforded this critical cooperation between two sides of the golden triangle.

The central marketing of the UCL has enabled UEFA to generate vast revenues for the clubs. Since 1992 UEFA has distributed a total of 5122 million Swiss francs to clubs, the vast majority of which has been generated by television income (UEFA and TEAM, 2005: 27). Of total revenues raised in 2003–04, 633 million Swiss francs were awarded to the participating clubs, and 250 million Swiss francs were retained by UEFA for running costs and distribution within European football (UEFA, 2005: 32). It has been argued, however, that UEFA fails to maximize revenue from the competition. The Media Partners proposal for a breakaway competition in 1998 exploited this view and initiated a restructuring of the competition, arguing that European revenues were artificially low.

Similarly, the decision to maintain UCL coverage on free-to-air television also means that the pay-TV market is not being fully exploited. According to the Media Partners President, Rodolfo Hecht (personal interview, 15 February 2005), 'In a €4.5 billion market, 85 per cent is generated by domestic leagues. That is a joke.' However, Richard Worth explains the rationale behind the decision to retain free-to-air broadcasting sponsors (personal interview, 1 March 2005):

> We could sell the whole of the Champions League on television to pay-TV stations around Europe and prob-ably make a lot more money than by making it available in the proportion that we do to free television and pay television ... The original concept was this should be a Wednesday night, free-to-air, European football-for-all product. Because of the volume of clubs and certain markets, that has changed a little bit now. But there is another way to look at. Okay, we go for good money, not maybe the very, very best money because the advan-tages of not taking the very best money are much more beneficial for the development of football, the competi-tion, UEFA, than going for the maximum and disregard the consequences. That's really not the way we think is the right way to work.

Rodolfo Hecht is also critical of the structure of the competition which limits the number of games elite clubs play against each other (personal interview, 15 February 2005). In reference to the UCL tie between AC Milan and Manchester United in 2005, Hecht argued:

> You should really stop and think and consider you are talk-ing probably brand number one and brand number three in world football, they played once in forty years ... that really makes you understand the magnitude of the problem.

The decision to retain free-to-air partners, and constrain the size of the league stage, means that European competition revenues are to some extent like a coiled spring waiting to be released. However, UEFA chooses not to maximize European revenues. This is due to the organization's statutory obligation to protect national as well as European football, and to help govern a com-petitive arena that is sustainable and in which there is mobility amongst clubs. This would be difficult to achieve should the top clubs gain even more revenue from European competition. Within the available framework, however, TEAM seeks to maximize revenues, as Richard Worth explains:

> We know where the value comes from. Yes, there's always going to be a little bit more you could make here and there, but can it be doubled, trebled? The market pays what the market can stand and a lot of it is driven by natural competition in those markets ... my contention is and my understanding is that the Champions League achieves what it can pretty near full value with what we have to play with inventory-wise.

Vic Wakeling, Managing Director of Sky Sports of British Sky Broadcasting, also recognizes from a first-hand position how TEAM's expertise and knowledge of the European broadcasting market has enabled UEFA to maximize the financial potential of the competition (personal interview, 23 March 2005):

> TEAM is a very good set up and the people they have recruited over the years – and there's a lot of good agencies out there, TEAM have to bid for the business every time round – what they've got is a team of people who know marketing, who know television, and they certainly know this market place [the UK] ... TEAM, when they were setting off last time around to do the rights, and everyone was saying the rights are going to drop this time around, they targeted this market. Why? Because they knew they had three people bidding, they knew that the competitive bidding would push the value up, because they had BBC, ITV and Sky. They knew they were going to get an increased price ... They were shrewd commercially.

Sponsorship

The centralization of sponsorship by UEFA/TEAM also constitutes another factor in the successful marketing of the UCL. With each club previously in control of its own stadium sponsorship, there was no coordination of sponsorship across clubs. This was changed in favour of centralized sponsorship by UEFA/TEAM. According to TEAM founder Klaus Hempel (Ahlström, 2002):

> the package was unique and the less equals more concept was very attractive to commercial partners who

> wanted greater exclusivity. The market place had become very cluttered with commercial messages ... our idea was to invite eight partners to deliver messages with a much clearer voice – and this was later reduced to four.

This concept was 'innovative and commercially adapted to changing market conditions' (Thompson and Magnus, 2003: 50), consisting of 'a select group of sponsors with an integrated communications platform' (UEFA and TEAM, 1999: 40).

Initially UEFA/TEAM opted for eight sponsors; this was reduced to four in 2000–01 (current UCL sponsors are Mastercard, since 1994; Playstation, since 1997; Heineken, since 2005; and Ford, since 1992), and will be increased to six for 2006–09. With elite football as a core driver of consistently large audiences amongst a key young, male and affluent demographic, UEFA has been able to extract maximum sponsorship value. The key to this has been offering comprehensive coverage in the areas of event and media rights, maximizing value to the sponsors through a carefully controlled synergy, as illustrated in Figure 1.4.

Sponsors receive coverage in stadiums on advertising boards, on interview backdrops, on tickets and match programmes, in hospitality areas, and with other promotional rights. The blanket event rights coverage becomes all the more valuable when connected to media rights across a global network. Sponsors receive exposure not only via the broadcast of the event, but also by receiving exclusivity for their products in commercial airtime and through broadcast sponsorship (which now includes a 'match bumper' played directly before each half and after the final whistle). This has

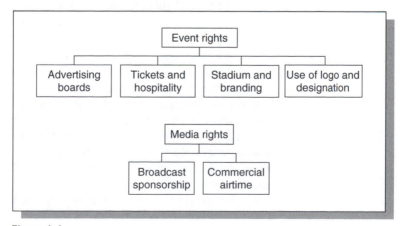

Figure 1.4
UEFA Champions League sponsorship rights (*Source*: UEFA/TEAM, 1999: 40)

made it almost impossible for rival companies to engage in 'ambush marketing' by attempting to associate with the UCL. Indeed, in the first season of the UCL, shirt sponsorship was not allowed in the competition, although this caused problems for clubs with their own sponsors and the decision was reversed. Overall, however, TEAM has created a 'multiplying media effect' that offers 'new levels of recognition' for sponsors (Thompson and Magnus, 2003: 50).

The value of the UCL is clearly recognized by sponsors, who invested a total of 177 million Swiss francs in 2003–04. Sponsors have consistently reflected on the global product that UEFA is able to deliver:

> Football is the most popular sport in Mastercard's key markets. With that in mind, our continuing partnership with UEFA is a powerful platform to build the Mastercard brand among the existing 350 million Mastercard holders in Europe, whilst also creating potential with existing customers.
>
> *(Jeremy Nichols, Commercial Director, Mastercard Europe, in 'Mastercard extends commitment with UEFA as official UEFA Champions League sponsor and UEFA Eurotop partner', UEFA Media Release 144, 7 December 2005.)*

> The significant global audience that the UEFA Champions League delivers will provide Sony Electronics with an unrivalled media platform to further build brand image and increase product awareness.
>
> *(David Patton, Senior Vice President, Sony Electronics Europe, in 'Sony Electronics to join as official partner of the UEFA Champions League', UEFA Media Release 106, 13 September 2005.)*

> This new and exclusive partnership with the UEFA Champions League, allows us to build on and consolidate our successful association with football. The UEFA Champions League offers Vodafone two new benefits: firstly it extends Vodafone's football relevance to supporters around the world and secondly it offers fans access to unique and compelling content through the Vodafone network, both of which will increase our brand awareness and drive revenue.
>
> *(Peter Bamford, Chief Marketing Officer, Vodafone, in 'Vodafone announces new football sponsorship', www.vodafone.com, 23 November 2005.)*

We are delighted to have extended our sponsorship of the UEFA Champions League. With over 4 billion viewers per season in 227 nations around the world, this premier sporting event has become truly global and fits perfectly with the Heineken brand.

(Jean Francois van Boxmeer, Heineken N.V., in 'Heineken brand to sponsor UEFA Champions League', www.heinekeninternational.com, 25 May 2005.)

Vodafone's partnership in particular points to the synergies between football as popular premium content, new technologies, and global television audiences. The success of centralized marketing for sponsors can also be positively measured in terms of the sponsorship longevity. By the twelfth season of the UCL, the average length of sponsorship tenure was ten years (UEFA and TEAM, 2004: 21). Product recall amongst consumers is high. At the end of the 2003–04 group stage, 20.75 per cent of sampled consumers were able to recall all four sponsors unprompted (UEFA and TEAM, 2004: 23). Additionally, sponsors have specifically linked the launch of new products to the UCL. For example, Ford utilized the knock-out stages of the 2004–05 tournament to launch the new Focus model. In the run-up to Christmas 2004, Playstation used all six matchdays to promote its product intensively. In addition to the sponsorship programme, UEFA also has accredited suppliers (currently adidas, Sharp and Canon) which enjoy similar privileges to sponsors, providing the goods and technology required to manage a tournament of the scale of the UCL. This integrated sponsorship platform has allowed UEFA and TEAM to maximize these revenues for the clubs.

New media and licensing

Whilst television and sponsorship revenues account for the vast majority of Champions League income, the commercial optimization of the competition is further enhanced through the sale of new media and licensing rights. The official adidas ball, for example, is the best selling licensed product. According to UEFA, this 'performs a valuable brand building function' and 'acts as a permanent reminder of the UEFA Champions League' (UEFA and TEAM, 2004: 24). Other licensed products include *Champions* (the official UCL magazine) and table football. Whilst the sums generated for UEFA by licensed goods are relatively small, such products add to the brand awareness.

New media are also providing a growing revenue stream to be exploited. In 2003–04, new media rights generated over 5 million Swiss francs (UEFA, 2005: 32). New media have become increasingly important since the intervention of the Competition Directorate of the European Commission objected to the joint selling of rights. One of the reasons for the intervention of the Commission was that 'internet and phone operators were simply denied access to the rights' and that 'by barring access to key sport content it also stifled the development of sport services on the internet and of the new generation of mobile phones' (see also 'Commission clears UEFA's new policy regarding the sale of media rights to the Champions League', Press Release OP/03/1105, Brussels, 24 July 2003). In an agreement with the Commission, UEFA opened up the sale of rights to new media outlets, sharing the rights with clubs. UCL footage is broadcast on the UEFA website (www.uefa.com) and is sold through monthly and annual subscriptions in nine languages. Footage is also available through club websites, for the clubs themselves to exploit. In order to protect the rights of broadcasters, this content is not available until after midnight on the evening of the games (UEFA and TEAM, 2005: 13). Third-generation mobile phone technology has also been exploited. Wireless content which includes video highlights, text commentary, and still pictures is available in thirty-five countries through operators such as Vodafone, Orange and T-Mobile (UEFA and TEAM, 2005: 13). Whilst new media revenues constitute just a fraction of overall revenues (6 per cent), they are likely to become increasingly important. Interestingly, new media content is one area where there is a departure from the central marketing concept, and clubs are able to deal individually, within constraints. Both the clubs and UEFA were happy with the outcome of the Commission's intervention as it allowed UEFA to continue to control the most valuable television rights but in terms of new media, according to Thomas Kurth, General Secretary of the G14 organization of clubs, 'it leaves to the individual club something valuable which can be better exploited by the clubs themselves' (personal interview, 18 January 2005). The regulatory intervention of the European Commission, alongside technological developments, made the marketing an increasingly complex task, as Richard Worth explains:

> in the early days, it was only a free-to-air Wednesday night TV product with sponsorship as well. Now it is a multilayered free-to-air, pay-TV, internet, mobile phone, sponsorship property which is a very sophisticated thing. In a sense the challenge is bringing all those components together, and making it work.

The brand

The brand theme: 'Prestige' and 'Heritage'

The sporting product and the central marketing strategy constitute the most significant factors in the successful development of the UCL. The effectiveness of the central marketing strategy is, however, enhanced and maximized through the effective branding of the competition. This constitutes one of the most fascinating elements in the development of the UCL both as a competition and as a commercial vehicle.

The transformation of the European Cup into the UCL sparked concerns amongst supporters and the media about the devaluation of the competition and the triumph of commercial interests over sporting considerations. In that context, UEFA has been acutely aware of the need to associate the UCL with the traditions and heritage of the revered European Cup. This is evident in the creation of customs with regard to the competition itself. For example, clubs which win the tournament three consecutive times, or five times in total, are entitled to keep the trophy itself. Similarly, such clubs are also entitled to wear a special badge on the sleeves of the club shirt identifying this achievement. Such customs help to entrench the longevity and legitimacy of the competition, and increase the meaning of the competition's history. In marketing terms, the result has been a concoction of contemporary, cutting-edge marketing techniques aligned with half a century of European Cup history. UEFA itself recognizes the importance of blending these two facets. Its literature on the UCL focuses heavily on the heritage of the competition, and there is an explicit recognition of the need to relate that heritage to the modernization of the competition. It is the brand that allows this to be achieved visually. For example, the UEFA publication *UEFA Champions League: Giving the Fans the Best Club Football Competition in the World* (UEFA, 2003), which is aimed at 'everyone who has a professional interest in the UEFA Champions League' and is a guide to the branding of the competition for the 2003–06 cycle, focuses immediately on the history of the competition since 1956:

The UEFA Champions League has consistently set new standards since its launch, whilst always respecting the rich heritage of the European Champion Clubs' Cup. Irrespective of whether one considers the history of the competition to have started in 1955 or 1992, the competition to establish the Champion Club of Europe has always represented the very pinnacle of club football. The likes of Alfredo di Stefano, Bobby Charlton, Johan Cruyff,

Franz Beckenbauer and Marco van Basten are among
the countless legends who have caught the imagination
over the years as well as the current stars that grace the
UEFA Champions League, including Zinedine Zidane,
David Beckham and Oliver Kahn.

(UEFA, 2003: 2)

Thus the competition is intrinsically tied to the great players and
past contests of the European Cup. The branding operation constitutes a deliberate and explicit attempt to marry the twin requirements of modernization and fostering continuity which underpin
what UEFA refers to as the brand platform. This includes the vision
('to create the ultimate stage for Europe's club championship'); the
mission ('giving fans the best competition in the world') and the
brand values ('proud, special, in touch, passionate'). According to
UEFA: 'It is the brand that helps deliver the values of the event and
provides the strategic direction for all activities connected with
the event' (UEFA, 2003: 6).

Brand identity

UEFA itself (UEFA, 2003: 8) has stated:

The UEFA Champions League, like any other global
brand, is complex in character. Whilst it is perceived in
slightly different ways by the various audiences across
Europe, *prestige* is at the heart of the UEFA Champions
League brand image.

It is through the brand that UEFA has attempted to deliver the
image of prestige to supporters and the wider European football
industry, and this brand consists of three key elements: the UEFA
Champions League anthem, the house colours and the starball
symbol. These constitute the 'long term foundations of the brand'
(UEFA, 2003: 28). To this we would add the symbolic importance
of the trophy itself.

The UEFA Champions League anthem

At 8.45 pm Central European Time on Tuesday and Wednesday
nights, the same piece of classical music can be heard at stadiums
and television screens across Europe. The choice of Handel's *Zadok
the Priest* as the theme of the UEFA Champions League epitomizes
the aim to associate the competition with very specific implications. The piece reflects a classical approach, again associating the

competition with historical and prestigious connotations. In choosing *Zadok the Priest*, not only have UEFA and TEAM sought to convey connotations of exclusivity, they have also succeeded in differentiating the competition from other club competitions. As TEAM Chief Executive Richard Worth has previously noted, sporting contests have often been brashly branded with popular music denoting youthfulness (King, 2004: 327–328). In England, music associated with the Premier League has included that by Elton John and U2. Interestingly, BBC Television has also utilized classical pieces when broadcasting the FIFA World Cup, this time reflecting the elite game in national team, as opposed to club, football.

The anthem was adapted by the English composer Tony Britten and has become synonymous with the competition. The lyrics, created and translated into a variety of languages, end with the words 'The Champions!' at the finale of a rising chorus. The consistency with which the anthem is used also consolidates its distinctiveness. This culminates in the playing of the anthem at the stadium at the moment the winning captain lifts the trophy. UEFA has clearly been pleased with the impact that the anthem has had regarding the recognition of the anthem in association with the competition. By utilizing the anthem in all UEFA Champions League television broadcasts, and at match venues prior to kick off, UEFA has succeeded in utilizing a classical piece to popularize a transformed competition. This is what UEFA has referred to as the 'ability to marry a prestige position with mass appeal' (UEFA, 2003: 8). Research has shown this to be true, as the anthem is more readily identified with the competition than the logo or even the name. The impact has been dryly noted by Rangers FC executive Campbell Ogilvie: 'the worst thing is to be out of it and hear the Champions League music on TV!' (Ahlström, 2002: 21).

Visual representations of the UEFA Champions League

The clearest visual symbols of the UEFA Champions League are again a combination of old and new. The trophy, used since 1967 following the award of the first trophy to Real Madrid after their sixth victory, is the ultimate visual emblem of European football's greatest clubs, players, and competition. The 'starball', by comparison, was created as a central aspect of the re-branding exercise following the transition from European Cup to Champions League. The starball symbol has again been created and used to drive the brand values of the competition.

A number of agencies were approached to propose a new visual identity for the competition, and the London-based agency 'Design Bridge' was charged with the brief of creating an 'identity and branding to match the very best of European football'

(Ahlström, 2002: 102). The starball was designed to reflect the eight 'star' teams that remained in the two group stages following the initial reformulation of the competition. It has been argued that the starball is invested with political meaning. Each star within the ball represents an elite club of European football, therefore entrenching the elite clubs within competition under UEFA control (King, 2004: 332–333). Whilst this overstates the importance of this single visual image, there is little doubt that the symbol has become a crucial signifier of the UEFA property. According to sports branding consultant Richard Markell:

> The UEFA Champions League logo is a modern classic that captures in its 'starball' symbol the elite world of Europe's top club competition and classic matches between top clubs. It has a subliminal aura of glamour about it.
>
> *(UEFA, 2003: 28)*

TEAM executives Craig Thompson and Ems Magnus have confirmed the impetus behind the new visual creation. Additionally, they note how the musical theme and the starball work together as part of a common theme of prestige and tradition: 'The simple yet striking new logo, combined with the classical musical theme, gave the new competition an elevated image and prestigious feel' (Thompson and Magnus, 2000: 50). Whilst more than a decade has passed since the starball emerged, to the point that it is recognized in isolation as a symbol of the Champions League, it is rare that the starball is employed without being juxtaposed to the brand of UEFA (Figure 1.5). UEFA has not sought to hide the importance or meaning of this:

> The UEFA arch in the Champions League logo is the brand behind the brand, and acknowledges within the competition logo the organization which is responsible for staging the event. The UEFA presence is measured, it does not confuse or detract from the competition logo, but provides a subtle yet very powerful endorsement.
>
> *(UEFA, 2003)*

In the context of the politics of European football, UEFA has cleverly used the opportunity to re-brand as an opportunity to consolidate its own presence as the legitimate organizer of European club competition by offering 'subtle endorsement'. TEAM Chief Executive Richard Worth also confirmed UEFA's wish that the starball and the UEFA arch should never be 'split up' (quoted in King, 2004: 325).

Figure 1.5
UEFA logo

It is within the utilization of the starball that the house colours of the UEFA Champions League brand are most evident. The house colours of black, white and silver were chosen specifically to generate connotations of history, prestige, and preciousness – according to Richard Worth: 'Let's be different. Let's go for a classical style. Let's go for simple colours. Let's go for precious silvery colours, black and white' (quoted in King, 2004: 327–328). King claims, for example, that the black and white engenders memories of the old television footage of the early days of the European Cup, again specifically relating the modernized tournament and marketing concept with the old European Cup and thus legitimizing the transformed competition. Similarly, he suggests that the silver reflects the history of a tournament under floodlights and famous European nights. More plausibly, the silver reflects the preciousness and history represented in the trophy. The use of black, white and silver has been consistently employed, and is emphasized by the deep midnight blue used as a background colour to much of UCL in particular television sequences, and various other backdrops. When the silver is superimposed onto the midnight blue, there is a clear evocation of the history and glamour of the European Cup. In the same way that other sporting competitions have used popular music, the colours employed in UCL branding also set it apart from other competitions in visual appearance.

The trophy

Whilst the starball, anthem and house colours were the audio-visual creations that emerged from the European Cup, it is the trophy that remains, predictably, the most identifiable and presti-gious symbol of the competition. Interestingly, through the bulk of the competition the trophy is conspicuous by its absence in the branding of the UCL, apart from in the opening sequences of broadcasts. Prior to the final in Munich in 1997 the image of the cup could not be used for legal reasons; however, since 1997 there has been a departure from the UCL brand concept for the final tie, and it is in this special unique branding exercise that UEFA and TEAM utilize the symbolism of the famous trophy, one of foot-ball's most iconic symbols.

By restricting the use of the trophy until the final itself, its lustre and value is enhanced. The more rarely the silverware appears, the more special and precious it becomes. Craig Thompson, an execu-tive, explains the development of his own understanding of this special symbol:

> As an American the cup hadn't meant that much to me. But when I saw how much of an icon it was to people in Europe, I felt that we should be making better use of it to promote the final and the competition. So we began the tradition of offering the trophy to the host city a month or so before the final and the Handover Ceremony has become an established part of the fixture list.
>
> *(Ahlström, 2002: 101)*

The branding of the final tie has become distinctive, and has been designed to amalgamate the image of the competition and the cup, with cultural references to the host country and city. For the Paris final in 2000 the art nouveau typeface used for the final branding mirrored that used on the Paris metro, and in Glasgow a Celtic font was employed. In Istanbul in 2005, the image and the lines of the cup were cleverly adapted and incorporated with the symbolism and colours of Turkey and the architecture of the host stadium – the moon and star, and deep scarlet reds (Figure 1.6). In the design of backdrops, a subtle and understated starball was also included. According to English and Pockett (www.english-pockett.com), the design agency responsible for the final branding:

> Our event branding combined the Champions League identity with the host country's national flag by echoing

Figure 1.6
Istanbul 2005: the image and the lines of the cup were adapted and incorporated with the symbolism and colours of Turkey and the architecture of the host stadium

> its key graphic elements – the moon and star. Traditional designs from a Turkish mosque were combined with the red of the flag to create a distinctive graphic style.

The final branding received blanket coverage in Istanbul. From the airport to city centre to stadium, lampposts were adorned with UCL final imagery, with of course ample space offered to exclusive UCL sponsors and suppliers. So whilst the overall branding of the UCL conveys history and prestige, the unique branding of the final itself develops this concept even further by integrating the trophy and heightening the sense of occasion and significance of the final tie.

Branding implementation

The UCL brand theme is encapsulated within the brand identity – the symbols of the UCL. But perhaps the most impressive of all the success factors in marketing the UCL is how the concept of centralized branding and commercial control is implemented. The successful creation of the brand is accompanied by a strategy that involves the comprehensive utilization of the brand and control of event management, both in stadiums and through the media. The comprehensive implementation of the brand identity consistently both reinforces the identity of the competition and serves to entrench the competition in the consciousness of

European football fans, and this reinforces the competition as the legitimate means by which to decide Europe's best club. This consequently reinforces UEFA's role in the organization of the contest. To complete the virtuous circle, sponsors and broadcasters accrue financial benefit from association with the competition.

Event management and identity

Implementation of the centralized marketing concept can be most strongly identified in the sporting arena. Initially, this was one of the more controversial aspects of the development of the UCL. European football clubs traditionally have a high degree of commercial and organizational autonomy. For the UCL, stadiums become the property of UEFA/TEAM and have a dedicated 'specially trained venue team' (UEFA and TEAM, 1999: 42) and each UCL venue is dressed in exactly the same fashion. Initially this caused a degree of friction with the competing clubs, as Campbell Ogilvie of Rangers FC explains: 'In the early days there were also situations where clubs resented a group of outsiders turning up at the ground and telling them how to organize a match at their own stadium. The clubs were at loggerheads with UEFA and TEAM.' However, the value of the transformation was soon recognized by the clubs as Ogilvie notes: 'Fortunately, the package was absolutely top class and the partnership concept in the UEFA Champions League has to be considered one of football's great success stories' (Ahlström, 2002: 21).

Not all analysis of the central marketing concept and the growing influence of the event managers has been complimentary. Football sociologists John Sugden and Alan Tomlinson of the University of Brighton, for example, see the transformation as evidence of a growth in commoditization and the increasing influence of the commercial deal-brokers:

> Watching UEFA's hugely influential partners ... police the commercial and company icons of the fully commodified modern football stadium, checking every detail of their constructed world like bodyguards protecting an American president, is to catch a glimpse of who controls international football's golden triangle in an expansionist phase of the people's game.
>
> *(Sugden and Tomlinson, 1998: 99)*

There is certainly some truth in this. Whilst, the centralized marketing concept has generated greater financial value, sporting arenas have become increasingly sanitized and less unique. The supporter experience, it has been argued, has become less authentic, which is alienating for some fans. This has been referred to as a process of 'McDonaldization' (Duke, 2002; Sandvoss, 2003). Similarly, the rows of empty seats at the front of some stadiums due to the requirements of sponsors and the size of hoardings identifies shifting priorities away from ordinary match-going supporters and in favour of commercial partners. However, there is little doubt that the standardization of the competition enhances its commercial value, with sponsors and broadcasters attracted to an integrated and homogenized product. Similarly, it is worth remembering that by optimizing the commercial potential of the competition UEFA is able to increase investment in the development of European football.

The stadiums are thus dressed identically, architectural differences notwithstanding. At each venue the words 'UEFA Champions League' can be seen at the halfway line facing the cameras, flanked all the way around the pitch with the advertising hoardings of sponsors and suppliers. All existing stadium advertising is removed or covered, and each tier of the stadium is wrapped by a dynamic version of the starball symbol in simple black and white colours. Before the commencement of each game, a large starball covers the whole centre circle. As the teams emerge onto the pitch, the starball is lifted and shaken to generate a simple but stirring effect. According to Keith Young of Design Bridge, the agency responsible for creating the starball, this constitutes 'a perfect way of establishing and asserting the competition's identity and we've seen this copied at other events' (Ahlström, 2002: 103). Simultaneously, the UCL anthem *Zadok the Priest* is played over the stadium sound system. Not only are these pre-match routines replicated across venues, they are also choreographed so assiduously as to be almost simultaneous. As Vic Wakeling, Managing Director of British Sky Broadcasting (BSkyB), states (personal interview, 23 March 2005):

> There is a branding there that football fans now recognize. They say 'it's Champions League; it's on Sky; it's great'. It's the detail they go into. At 7.45 on the first Tuesday, and then the first Wednesday, you are looking at our six screens on a Tuesday and eight screens on a Wednesday night and all the teams are in the tunnels, and they are all coming out in sync. And you are looking at that and you are thinking this is absolutely wonderful. Who else has made this happen? This is TEAM in liaison with UEFA officials. Just to make that happen is marvellous. For someone like ourselves, who wants to put those 8 screens up there, and you see them all coming out, you see them all lining up, they kick off … they make our life easy.

Few stones are left unturned in the venue branding exercise. Stewards sport the starball logo on jackets, the players on the arms of their shirts. All match tickets and accreditation passes are branded and include the various logos of sponsors and suppliers. Away from the immediate vicinity of play, the brand identity is also ubiquitous. A special corporate hospitality area is branded as the 'Champions' Club'. The professionalism with which implementation of the UCL marketing concept is delivered is widely recognized inside UEFA and by the competing clubs:

> At the end of the day, the players like it, they like the ambience, they like the dressing, they like the atmosphere. It's different from any league game. It's higher class. It's the best competition of the world, club-wise, by far. They are all thrilled at the big games, and the crowd, and it's much better organized with all due respect, than any domestic league. And for the clubs, which are now businesses, they are getting a lot of money … and if they were then to have to go to the hassle of organizing it themselves, and to go and get an agency, why should they do that, for the time being, as long as we deliver? Which is for us an incentive to deliver, as we know that the day that we don't deliver, somebody else may do.
>
> *(Philippe Le Floc'h, Director, Marketing and Media Rights, UEFA, personal interview, 19 November 2004.)*

> I've worked closely with them [UEFA], on Champions League games and hosting the Champions League final at Old Trafford, I think it's a very well organized body. They've got a lot of very good professionals in there, they've got a mixture of people who understand football and have been in it for a long time, and I think that to my mind it's an efficient structure as evidenced by the excellent Champions League.
>
> *(David Gill, Chief Executive, Manchester United, personal interview, 28 January 2005.)*

> UEFA, they do it well. The Champions League is perfectly well managed: the presentation, the commercialization, the dressing of the stadiums, it feels like a special competition, and it's done very, very well.
>
> *(Rick Parry, Chief Executive, Liverpool FC, personal interview, 17 February 2005.)*

> I think they are perceived by the clubs as an organization that has delivered a very high quality job; they are performing very well. They have corrected certain things the

clubs didn't like at the beginning. I think they are doing a very good job. Somebody will always have to do this job. And they, right now, are delivering it at a very high level.

(Thomas Kurth, General Secretary, G14,
personal interview, 18 January 2004.)

Television identity

Of course the impact of stadium branding is transmitted most effectively and lucratively through television, through which 99 per cent of fans access the competition (UEFA and TEAM, 2004: 16). Stadium branding, however, is only one aspect of UCL event branding. The television production itself is also a vital means through which the competition is marketed to fans and wider to consumers. This is achieved through uniformity of coverage packaged around live games.

We have already touched upon the global impact of the UCL and the worldwide television audience. Of course, it is ultimately the product that makes the UCL the global sporting success that it is, but the manner in which the competition is packaged clearly adds commercial value, through the development of a recognizable and respected brand. The television title sequence plays an important role – 'a unique and valuable promotional platform' and a 'branding tool … to differentiate the Champions League broadcasts from any other television programme' (UEFA, 2003: 30). By controlling this aspect of presentation, the UCL is removed from the control of broadcasters who might wish to portray a different image. The sequences have developed over the life of the UCL, but the key symbols of starball, colours and anthem have remained. The 2003–06 brand, developed by design company English and Pockett, is based on the theme of connection – between star players, club and fans. This is particularly effective on television, as the movement and connection of the stars in the opening sequences consist depicts the clash of clubs and players in the context of a prestigious sporting contest. Again, the silver stars housing the images appear on a midnight blue background, accentuating the distinctive night-time aura and the value of the tournament. The brand is also heavily concentrated in the overall television coverage. The on-screen graphics showing match results, group tables, fixtures, the score-line during play, the team line-ups and formations, are all branded with the starball on the midnight blue backdrop. Studios have UCL-branded furnishings, and post-match interviews are conducted in front of branded backdrops featuring the logos of sponsors and suppliers.

Perhaps the most telling indicator of how successful the branding of the UCL has been is the exemption given to UEFA by the

Competition directorate of the European Commission. Competition authorities across Europe have taken a close interest in how the rights to football competitions have been sold by the respective authorities. In Italy, for example, central selling was ruled illegal, and the European Commission has investigated central selling deals in England, Germany and France. The Commission objected to the central sale of UCL television rights due to the fact that UEFA sold to a single broadcaster on an exclusive basis in each country and the consequences of that for broadcasting markets in Europe. Although UEFA was forced to re-evaluate the manner in which rights were sold, it was allowed to continue selling the rights centrally on the basis that 'UEFA's joint selling arrangement leads to the improvement of production and distribution by creating a single branded league focused product sold via a single point of sale' (Commission decision of 23 July 2003 (COMP/C.2-37.398) – Joint selling of the commercial rights of the UEFA Champions League. See also 'Commission clears UEFA's new policy regarding the sale of media rights to the Champions League', Press Release IP/03/1105, Brussels, 24 July 2003). The Commission recognized that the central selling was important for the brand, which is:

> associated with a uniform and high quality TV coverage underpinned by homogeneous presentation which increases attractiveness for the viewer. These are also factors which attract the best football clubs who want to participate in the competition. Indeed, the quality with which the tournament is marketed is an intrinsic factor in the inclination of clubs to work within the existing framework of competition.

Conclusions

UEFA and TEAM have created a benchmark in the marketing of football's premier club competition. We have analysed the key success factors in building the UEFA Champions League into a global sports brand. At the heart of its success is the sporting product itself. The competition provides the platform for Europe's most famous and best-supported clubs and the best players, whilst offering opportunities to lesser clubs and nations. In marketing the product, the central marketing strategy allows UEFA, in association with TEAM, to control and address every aspect of the branding and organization of the competition. Only by exercising this degree of control can each important aspect of the competition be delivered to the highest possible standards, and optimize the potential of the golden triangle of football, TV and sponsorship.

Whilst the UCL constitutes a slick and effective commercial machine, UEFA's control of the competition ensures that sporting considerations remain a high priority. The removal of the second group stage, for example, has generated a greater degree of interest, excitement and unpredictability, and was achieved despite concerns from the clubs that there would be a decline in revenues. Equally, the decision to ensure that the competition remains on free-to-air television ensures that the competition is accessible, reaching the widest audience. The competition is widely consolidated in the public consciousness, whilst simultaneously delivering messages of history and continuity and thus strengthening the longevity and legitimacy of the contest. The symbolic branding of the competition has been the key means through which this has been achieved.

Whilst each individual factor plays a vital role in construction of the global brand, ultimately it is the holistic approach to the marketing of the competition that sets it apart. Each success factor is important in so far as it exists as a part of an integrated whole. By attending to every last detail in the branding and organization of the UCL, the competition, like a good football team, becomes more than the sum of its individual components. The importance and value (sporting and commercial) of the competition is therefore enhanced and magnified for all participants – clubs, spectators and commercial partners. In the complex environment of European football's political network, UEFA consolidates its own position as the legitimate controller of club competition by fostering a contest of consistently high interest and standard and by marketing that contest to the highest professional standards, and to the satisfaction of football's most influential stakeholders.

Acknowledgements

The authors would like to thank various executives of UEFA and TEAM who agreed to be interviewed in the context of a wider project on UEFA and European football, and for the information provided, which helped us to complete this chapter. These interviews were provided on the basis that the contents would remain confidential and the authors are therefore unable to accompany this chapter with any of the interview transcripts, either in part or in full.

Work enabling this chapter to be written was funded by FIFA, supported by UEFA and involved interviews with officials from organizations including UEFA, TEAM Marketing, FIFA, Manchester United, Liverpool, AC Milan, Juventus, FIFPro, BSkyB, and the Premier League.

Bibliography and references

Ahlström, F. (ed.) (2002). *Ten Years of the UEFA Champions League, 1992–2002*. UEFA.

Duke, V. (2002). Local tradition versus globalisation: resistance to the McDonaldisation and Disneyisation of professional football in England. *Football Studies*, **5(1)**, 36–42.

King, A. (2004). The new symbols of European football. *International Review for the Sociology of Sport*, **39(3)**, 323–336.

Morrow, S. (2003). *The People's Game? Football, Finance and Society*. Palgrave Macmillan.

Sandvoss, C. (2003). *A Game of Two Halves: Football Fandom, Television and Globalisation*. Routledge.

Sugden, J. (2002). Network football. In: J. Sugden and A. Tomlinson (eds), *Power Games*. Routledge.

Sugden, J. and Tomlinson, A. (1998). *FIFA and the Contest for World Football*. Polity Press.

Thompson, C. and Magnus, E. (2003). The UEFA Champions League marketing. *FIBA Assist Magazine*, **2**, 16–20.

UEFA (2003). *UEFA Champions League: Giving the Fans the Best Competition in the World, 2003–2006*. UEFA.

UEFA (2005). *Financial Report 2003/2004, Budget 2005/2006*. UEFA.

UEFA and TEAM (1999). *UEFA Champions League: Season Review 1998–1999*. UEFA/TEAM.

UEFA and TEAM (2004). *UEFA Champions League: Season Review 2003–2004*. UEFA/TEAM.

UEFA and TEAM (2005). *UEFA Champions League: Season Review 2004–2005*. UEFA/TEAM.

CHAPTER 2

Journalism – an instrument to promote TV sports rights?

Knut Helland and
Harry Arne Solberg

Overview

The nature of TV sports broadcasting has changed dramatically in recent years. Today, TV channels have to pay expensive fees to broadcast the most attractive events. Hence, sport broadcasting not only serves the function of journalism and entertainment but is also a part of an investment where achieving high rating figures, recruiting subscribers or generating pay-per-view fees is necessary to make sports rights acquisitions economically viable. The focus of this chapter is on football, and it raises the following questions: What consequences do sports media rights – and in particular football rights – have for broadcast journalism on sports? Is journalism an instrument to promote the broadcaster's own TV sports rights? The chapter is based on interviews with five leading broadcasters in Norway (see Appendices 2.1–2.5). It concludes that to a great extent journalism is used as a promotional instrument, and that this is highly problematic in relation to the important role of news and journalism in society.

Keywords

sports economy, football, TV sports, sports media rights, sports journalism

The background to TV sports broadcasting

The nature of TV sports broadcasting has changed dramatically in recent years. Today, TV channels have to pay expensive fees to broadcast the most attractive events. Hence, sports broadcasting not only serves the function of journalism and entertainment but is also a part of an investment where achieving high rating figures, recruiting subscribers or generating pay-per-view fees is necessary to make sports rights acquisitions economically viable.

In recent years fierce inter-channel competition has increased fees for the most attractive sports and tournaments significantly, and this is particularly so when applied to football rights (Kagan World Media, 1999; TV Sports Markets, 2006). In addition, new technology has introduced other ways of transmitting the programmes – for example, the Internet and mobile phones. This indicates that the number of companies involved in sports broadcasting will not decline. The competition that has paved the way for price increases seems likely to continue, even though recent history has included a number of unprofitable deals.

Negative shifts in demand from viewers and advertisers have reduced revenues significantly on several occasions – due, for example, to unforeseen incidents such as the 9/11 effect in 2001, which affected advertising on TV dramatically, or to excess supply, with too many similar programmes targeting the same viewers. Reductions in revenues can cause severe financial problems for the acquiring channel if rights fees are expensive and fixed – i.e. independent of the revenues generated by the broadcasting of the programmes (see Solberg, 2004).

The most effective instrument to promote live sport programmes is probably the attention the products (competitions, matches, tournaments) are given in the media – i.e. in ordinary journalism conducted by newspapers, radios, the Internet and TV channels. Some TV channels can produce such publicity themselves, for example by focusing on the respective sports and tournaments in their ordinary programming activities, such as sports news and ordinary news programmes. Channels that belong to multi-media companies can also benefit from their associates (e.g. other TV channels, newspapers, and radio stations) providing publicity.

The television sports genre operates in the realm encompassing journalism, drama and entertainment (Whannel, 1992; Dahlén,

1999; Reimer, 2004). However, adopting strategies where ordinary journalism is used as an instrument to generate revenues may come into conflict with the main objective of the free press, namely to conduct independent and critical journalism (Sand and Helland, 1998). This particularly applies to sports rights deals where the channels have accepted clauses guaranteeing the exposure of advertisers and sponsors. Such agreements may violate both the code of ethics and the code of advertorials, which are important ideals on which independent journalism is based.

As the commercial and 'industrial' function of the sports/media complex is becoming increasingly strong, journalism in general – and sports journalism in particular – is facing new challenges related to media rights. In the electronic media, and particularly in broadcasting, we can see that the attraction value of sports is challenging the ideals of the news institutions in new ways. We are now witnessing how the media rights to sports events are framing the news coverage of sports in what should ideally be independent sports news coverage on television. Journalists, who ideally adhere to professional ideals in their sports coverage, are fuelling the attraction value of sports in different broadcasting formats. Indeed, in this way many sports journalists seem to act as PR agents for their broadcaster's own sports-media product.

This chapter will investigate to which degree such conflicts in objectives have occurred in Norwegian sports broadcasting, paying especial attention to football. It analyses whether TV channels have altered their programme policy as a consequence of acquisitions of sports rights, by:

- showing advertisers and sponsors during ordinary programmes

- producing programmes that promote sports and tournaments for which the channel has acquired exclusive rights

- producing more journalism on activities with which the channel is financially involved, compared with other areas – in other words, operating with different news values when covering their 'own sports products' and other sports.

It also investigates whether such acquisitions influence the programming policy in associated firms that belong to the same parent company.

Methodologically, the contribution is based on semi-structured, qualitative interviews with five persons in leading positions in three different Norwegian companies. The interviews were recorded in January 2006, and lasted for 60–90 minutes. Those interviewed were Tor Aune (Head of Sports Rights) and Øyvind Lund (sports editor) of The Norwegian Broadcasting Corporation

(NRK); Bjørn Taalesen, sports editor of TV 2; and Morten Aass (Managing Director) and Hallbjørn Saunes (news editor) of TVNorge. We very much appreciate their willingness and openness. The quotations have been translated from Norwegian to English. Excerpts from the interviews can be found in Appendices 2.1–2.5.

The broadcasters were interviewed concerning the role of sports in their company, on strategies related to sports rights and sports journalism, on how the convergence of technology and business interests has consequences for sports coverage, on the pressure on the journalism from external actors, and on future trends in relations to TV sports, media and journalism.

For the purpose of our study there are limitations to this kind of approach. One aspect concerns what the broadcasters claim about relations between sports rights and sports journalism. Another aspect is what actually comes out of such relations. Ideally, the interviews would have been supplemented with content analysis focusing on the journalistic coverage of sports, and changes in the journalistic formats resulting from new or denied access to sports rights. The following statement from one of the interviewees, Bjørn Taalesen, excellently illustrates this aspect when pointing out how sports news coverage in his channel varies according to acquired media sports rights:

> I don't think it only applies to us, and I see it elsewhere. To what extent others are willing to admit to this I'm not sure. However, in my opinion we may as well face it.

Some of the interviewees were more self-critical than others, but they all seemed open-minded and pointed to crucial dynamics in the relation between media sports rights and journalistic coverage. The descriptions of these dynamics could not be approached by methodologies other than qualitative interviews.

The next section discusses the objectives of TV channels and media companies in general, with special emphasis on the conflict between commercial interests and publicist ideals. This is followed by an overview of the Norwegian TV landscape, including a description of Norwegian sports broadcasting in recent years. Special attention is paid to the recent domestic Norwegian football rights deal. Subsequently, results from interviews with five persons representing three Norwegian sports broadcasters, all of whom have publicist roles, are presented. The results from these interviews are categorized in two different sections; the first investigates whether sellers of sports rights instruct channels on how to produce sports programmes, while the second focuses on branding issues such as when TV channels and sports governing bodies are jointly involved in new products – for example, establishing a new league. The final section of this chapter discusses what lessons can be learned from these analyses.

Sport broadcasters and publicist ideals – a theoretical context

TV broadcasting – the supply side

The European market has four categories of TV channels involved in sports broadcasting:

1. *Non-commercial public service broadcasters*, which receive their entire revenues from either licence fees or public funding

2. *Commercial public service broadcasters*, which earn their revenues from advertising alone or in combination with licence fees or governmental funding

3. *Independent broadcasters*, which includes channels with publicist ideals – for example, broadcasters conducting independent journalism

4. *Entertainment channels*, which mostly covers pay-TV channels.

Further discussion of the policy and market behaviour of the these various categories can be found in Solberg (2004).

The role of public service broadcasters is different from that of independent entertainment channels. Public service broadcasters held a monopoly across almost the whole of Europe until two decades ago. This, however, is not the situation any more, following the deregulation of European broadcasting in the late 1980s, which led to a large number of commercial channels. Hence the rationale of public service broadcasters is different now when compared to two decades ago. Nowadays, it could be said that the job of public service broadcasters is to serve objectives other than the entertainment of viewers and the profitability of private broadcasting firms. According to welfare economic theory, their aim is to maximize the welfare of the society, subject to financial restrictions that are set by politicians (Brown, 1996). Such a policy places special emphasis on programmes generating externalities and merit good.

Some non-commercial public service broadcasters, however, admit that they give priority to programmes that attract large audiences, such as popular sports programmes, in order to legitimize their licence fee. This was confirmed by Tor Aune, Head of Sports Rights in the NRK and Vice President of the European Broadcasting Union's (EBU) sports group.

Profit-maximizing channels allocate inputs and organize their activities in order to ensure that marginal revenues equal marginal costs. Such a principle can also influence their programming policy – for example, producing the programmes in a manner that maximizes advertising revenues or subscription fees.

To broadcast attractive sports events, any channel will have to pay expensive rights. The majority of these are agreed on fixed terms. This means that there is a high degree of sunk costs – i.e. costs that are independent of the level of production. No matter what action the channel takes, it is impossible to dispose of sunk costs. Under such conditions, it will be extremely important for a channel to neutralize any negative shifts in demand by alternative promotion efforts. A TV channel can promote its 'own sporting events' in its other programme activities, such as news and sports news programmes, and can also promote matches, races, teams, players and competitors participating in its other programmes. Hence, journalism becomes a potential promotion instrument. If the tournament is extremely popular, then such promotion programmes can in themselves attract many viewers; in this way, the two categories of programme provide mutual promotion. Another possibility is producing such programmes in a manner that promotes sport and its events – but at the cost of conducting independent critical journalism.

In cases of extremely fierce competition, buyers may have to accept offering the sellers other services than rights fees – for example, select camera angles exposing sponsors and their products in ordinary programmes. Such exposure can be more effective than ordinary commercials. When viewers become aware that commercials are generally screened during breaks or less exciting periods, many will use these interludes to carry out other activities. Hence, rating figures can be significantly lower during commercials – which in turn will reduce advertising revenues (Solberg and Hammervold, 2004).

Recent broadcasting history has seen elements of integration on the supply side, with former rival channels merging into one company. There have been incidents where multi-channel companies have extended their ownership interests by implementing new channels – for example, pay TV platforms acquiring stakes in free-to-air channels, or the other way around. This is known as *horizontal integration*, which is when firms in the same line of business combine with one another.

Additionally, there can be *congeneric integration*, which is between producers of goods that are related but not identical. A merger between a TV channel and a newspaper is such an example.

Members of multi-firm companies can benefit from promoting one another's products (such as programmes or articles). Their main objective will be to maximize the aggregate profit of the parental company, not just the profit of the individual firm. This guarantees that any pecuniary externalities will be integrated into the company's overall policy. A *pecuniary externality* operates through price, and can be both positive and negative. This means that an activity can increase or decrease the market value of another economic variable. As an example, a newspaper can stimulate the interest in a football match by writing articles about the players and teams in the days prior to the match, which in turn can stimulate more people to watch the match on TV. Likewise, if people are aware that the match will be broadcast live on TV, this can stimulate them to buy newspapers that write about it.

Internalizing such externalities within the parental company can be extremely valuable for pay-TV channels. These have a penetration rate of around 20 per cent of TV households, and thus can be extremely vulnerable if their sports event only receives moderate attention on free-to-air channels. Therefore, any promotion support from their associates can be very useful.

There have also been incidents of *vertical integration*, with TV companies acquiring stakes in teams. In Europe, this was highlighted by BSkyB's unsuccessful takeover of Manchester United (Gerrard, 2000).

Publicist ideals, exclusive sports rights, Norwegian Broadcasting Law, and codes of ethics for journalism

Adopting profit-maximizing strategies such as those described in the former section can conflict with the traditional objective of the free press, which is to conduct independent and critical journalism. Such a conflict occurs where programmes are reviewed in a more friendly way than would otherwise be the case, and where the purpose is to promote sports and tournaments in which the channel or sponsor has invested heavily. The same applies if the aim of maximizing profit or revenues for either the channel or the sponsors/advertisers influences the editorial policy. In particular, conflict can easily be seen in journalistic magazines and news formats.

The Norwegian Broadcasting Law (para. 3.3) disallows any broadcaster from screening disguised advertising in ordinary programmes. This regulation also covers advertising of the channel's own activities (para. 1.1).

The two major directives concerning journalistic and broadcasting publicist activities are the *Code of Ethics* and the *Code of Advertorials*. The code of ethics of the Norwegian press (www.uta.fi/ethicnet/norway.html) requires, among other things, the following:

- The press must not yield to pressure from anybody who might want to prevent open debate, the flow of information, free access to sources, or debate on any matter of importance to society as a whole (para. 1.3).

- Each editorial desk and each employee must guard their own integrity and credibility in order to be free to act independently of any persons or groups who – for ideological, economic or other reasons – might want to exercise an influence over editorial matters (para. 2.2).

- The press must reject any attempt to break down the clear distinction between advertisements and editorial copy. Advertisements intended to imitate or exploit an editorial product should be turned down, as should advertisements undermining trust in the editorial integrity and the independence of the press (para. 2.6).

- The press must never promise editorial favours in return for advertisements. Material must be published as a result of editorial consideration (para. 2.7).

These are general principles guiding all forms of journalism, in national contexts as well as in specific companies. The BBC, for example, has adopted the following guidelines for its financial journalism (www.bbc.co.uk/guidelines/editorialguidelines/advice/):

- It is essential that the integrity of BBC programmes or other editorial output is not undermined by the commercial, business or financial interests of any programme-makers, journalists or presenters. There must never be any suggestion that commercial or financial interests have influenced BBC coverage or the subject matter of programmes or the choice of items.

Furthermore, regarding sponsored events, the BBC requires the following editorial principle to be followed:

- We must never enter into a contractual arrangement which guarantees a sponsor a set number of minutes of signage reflection on air.

One of the leading voices in the US on the subject of journalistic standards and ethics is the Society of Professional Journalists, which requires that journalists should be free of obligation to any interest other than the public's right to know (www.spj.org/ethics_code.asp). This includes requirements such as:

- Avoid conflicts of interest, real or perceived.

- Remain free of associations and activities that may compromise integrity or damage credibility.

The key words in all these paragraphs are *integrity*, *independence* and *influence*. From an ideal perspective, journalists (including sports journalists), editors and broadcasters should operate independently and with integrity in relation to organizations and activities they have to relate to in editorial work.

The next section will focus on TV channels involved in Norwegian sports broadcasting, and the main products.

Norwegian sports broadcasting

Table 2.1 provides an overview of Norwegian sports broadcasters and Table 2.2 lists the major TV sport programmes. Norway has two public service broadcasters, namely the Norwegian Broadcasting Corporation (NRK) and TV 2. The NRK is financed by licence fee and TV 2 by advertisements, and both are distributed by terrestrial transmission, cable, satellite and, to some degree, the Internet.

The third group of broadcasters operating nationally is the private commercial broadcasters without concession, namely TVNorge and TV3. These are more independent and hence have

Table 2.1
Norwegian sports-broadcasting channels

Parental company	Channels	Type of channel – revenue source	Penetration
Norwegian Broadcasting Corporation	NRK1 NRK2	PSB licence PSB licence	100% 84%
TV 2	TV 2 TV 2 Zebra	PSB advertising Entertainment – advertising	98% 50%*
SBS Broadcasting Group	TVNorge Canal Plus	Entertainment – advertising Entertainment – pay-TV channels	89% Unknown – ~20%
Modern Times Group	TV3 ViaSat/ TV-1000 Sport N** channels	Entertainment – advertising Entertainment – pay-TV channels Entertainment – pay-TV	63% Unknown – < 20% n.a.

*TV 2 and Canal Digital expected penetration to increase to ~80% by April 2006
**Sport N is a collaboration between Modern Times Group and the Norwegian Broadcasting Corporation, but is owned by Modern Times Group
Source: TV Sports Markets (2006).

Table 2.2
Norwegian sport broadcasting – major sport programmes

Football
Domestic elite league (Tippeligaen)
- 2002–2005: rights acquired jointly by NRK and TV 2; some matches sublicensed to Canal Digital (2002 and 2003) and Canal Plus (2004 and 2005)
- 2006–>: rights acquired by TV 2 (with support from Canal Digital, the transmission company); all matches to be broadcast by TV 2

National team home matches and domestic cup
- 2002–2005: rights acquired jointly by NRK and TV 2
- 2006–>: rights acquired by TV 2

National team away matches
- 2002–>: majority of matches acquired by Modern Times Group; broadcast on TV3

UEFA Champions League
- All matches since the early 1990s acquired by Modern Times Group; broadcast on TV3 and ViaSat pay channels

World Cup soccer finals
- Tournaments before 2002 were broadcast by NRK and TV 2
- The 2002 tournament in Korean/Japan was broadcast by Canal Digital, with the exception of the opening match, semi-finals and final, which were shared by NRK and TV 2

European Championships (national teams)
- Tournaments proper to 2004 were shared by NRK and TV 2
- The 2004 tournament in Portugal was broadcast by TV 2

Other domestic European leagues
- The English Premier League and Italian Serie A have been broadcast by Canal Plus in recent years; the Spanish Primera Liga has been on TV 2; the French Ligue 1 is currently broadcast by MTG channels; the German Bundesliga is broadcast by NRK

Cross-country skiing, ski-jumping, biathlon and skating
- In recent years, major events – including the Olympic Games, international championships, World Cup competitions and national championships – have been broadcast by NRK

Handball
- The majority of international tournaments for national teams and clubs have been broadcast by TV 2; the same applies to matches in the domestic leagues

Motor-racing
- The Formula One World Championship and the World Rally Championships have been broadcast alternately by NRK and TV 2

greater freedom to construct their programming policy than do the two public service broadcasters. TVNorge is owned by SBS Broadcasting while TV3 is a part of Modern Times Group. Since TVNorge partly is distributed by terrestrial transmission, its penetration (89 per cent) is almost of the same level as that of the two public service broadcasters. TV3 is only transmitted by cable and satellite, and thus can only be accessed by 63 per cent of the households with TV.

The fourth group of broadcasters operating nationally consists of pay-TV channels, distributed by the satellite platforms and cable. The Canal Plus channels are members of SBS Broadcasting and hence are embedded with TVNorge. The ViaSat channels belong to the Modern Times Group (MTG), which also involves TV3. As is typical for pay-TV channels, these channels offer a relatively narrow menu of programmes, mainly consisting of films and sports programmes.

The two public service broadcasters have strong publicist obligations and traditions – a pattern that particularly applies to the NRK. They both have regular news programmes as well as their own daily sports magazines. Of the two private commercial stations without public service obligations, TV3 does not carry news and sports magazines, while TVNorge does. However, both the news programme and the sports magazines of TVNorge are run on quite limited resources. The entertainment channels have very limited publicist traditions.

The Norwegian football deal

Football is the most expensive sport in Norway, as elsewhere in Europe, in terms of fees for TV rights. To date, the Norwegian TV rights for football have been sold as a single package which includes matches in the Norwegian male elite division – currently called the Tippeliga, since it is sponsored by Norsk Tipping (which is the state-regulated Norwegian betting company). The package has also included home matches for the national team and the National Cup. The Tippeliga has been the most expensive asset, accounting for 70–80 per cent of the total cost.

In June 2005, the Norwegian Football Association (NFF) sold the domestic rights for the period 2006–2008/2009 to TV 2 (the commercial public service broadcaster) and Canal Digital (a company involved in satellite and cable transmission) for a fee of NOK1 billion (€127 million). The fee does not include production costs. The Tippeliga deal is for three years, while the deal for the other products is for four years. Compared with the previous agreement, the annual value increased by 300–400 per cent. This was the result of extremely fierce competition between three bidders: NRK and MTG (which submitted a joint bid), SBS, and TV 2/Canal Digital.

A confidential document that forms the basis for the contract between TV 2/Canal Digital and the Norwegian Football Association (NFF, 2005) requires the broadcaster to:

- produce at least 270 matches per season

- produce at least twenty 'football magazine programmes' per season (there are regulations regarding the kind of matches to be covered)

- use studio design elements from the NFF

- broadcast a 10-second 'profile programme' (advertisement for the 'football product') at the beginning of each programme

- broadcast advertisements for matches – 15 seconds, five times daily – for the 3 days before a match

- cite leagues and cups by sponsor names

- interview players in front of boards advertising the sponsors of the NFF

- broadcast the live matches decided by the NFF.

Some of these requirements obviously do not correspond with the traditional publicist ideals of journalism. NRK submitted a joint bid together with MTG and, in an internal memo, NRK pointed out that the tender document raised severe problems in relation to long-established publicist ideals (NRK, 2005):

> My main impression of this tender document is that this deal will undermine our editorial freedom and threaten important principles that have been established over the years. In our opinion, there are many reasons for being critical towards many sections in this document.

It remains to be seen whether the requirements from the Norwegian Football Association will be adhered to. Morten Aass, Managing Director of TVNorge, has described the requirements and competition for football rights as follows:

> My opinion on this is that it sucks, but then again you have to put up with a few things to attain such rights. You might think you will have the opportunity to discuss these matters when the deal has been made – to attain as much freedom as possible. It's all about getting the rights, after all, and therefore your focus is on getting these rights, and

> instead you push these problems, or challenges, ahead of you. The challenge starts once you have obtained the rights, and then the question is what to do about these things that are not there in the tender document you start reading. You realize this is not good. But then you feel that if you have paid NOK1 billion, well then there must be some possibilities to influence the result.

Even if all the NFF's requirements are not followed, Aass' statement nevertheless illustrates that it is not publicist ideals which are prioritized in the competition for sports rights. Broadcasters acquiring sports rights of this kind have to accept becoming a production, exposure and public relations system for the seller and its sponsors. The fierce competition for football rights puts sellers in a position where they need to 'format' the coverage so that it corresponds with their own business strategies. This in turn exerts strong external pressure on the publicist role of the broadcasters – a role which the public service broadcaster in particular should ideally be committed to.

The obligations in the Norwegian football tender document might seem unreasonable and also non-traditional. However, there is a long tradition that sports media rights holders actively use the media to promote and develop their image and their 'product'.

There are several aspects related to the football rights deal that indicate new relations between broadcasters and media rights. First, the rights to all platforms are sold on an exclusive basis, and hence the media rights also cover *news* rights for the matches. Secondly, in a Norwegian context, the arrangement shows a new kind of alliance. TV 2, a public service broadcaster with strong publicist traditions, has, for both economic and strategic reasons, joined forces with a commercial transmission company owned by the Norwegian Telecom (Telenor) which has huge economic resources. Bjørn Taalesen, TV 2's sports editor, comments on this arrangement:

> If this collaboration turns out to be successful for both parts, it should provide us with power in the future. Alone, TV 2 is a small company [...] Canal Digital and its owners represent an economic power that is important for us.

This kind of arrangement – and a parallel arrangement between the NRK and ViaSat – will certainly have consequences for the future of sports broadcasting, but also for the Norwegian public service broadcasters and for the media landscape. To afford the extremely expensive deal, however, TV 2 is having to reduce other programming activities – including those for other sports. Since the deal was agreed, TV 2 has resold its rights for the Formula One World Championship to NRK; also, they could not afford to renew the rights for the Rally World Championship. Moreover, there have been several articles in the media indicating a significant reduction in other non-sport programmes. Taalesen states that:

> In the short run the deal will be of the utmost importance and create needs for alterations in the organization.

Such changes will influence the resource allocation regarding other programmes. While the TV rights cost NOK1 billion, the production costs have been estimated to be in the region of NOK100 million according to predictions by independent media analysts. If this is correct, then 90 per cent of the total costs are sunk costs – i.e. irretrievable regardless of the action taken by TV 2 and Canal Digital, the holders of the rights. Such a high proportion of sunk costs makes it extremely important that these specific football rights are utilized effectively and maintain the popularity of Norwegian football. Indirectly, TV 2 and Canal Digital have become production companies for Norwegian football – the deal has forced them to make the football product attractive. This, of course has consequences for TV 2's journalistic coverage of football. Bjørn Taalesen, of TV 2, states the following:

> We are producing 270 football matches. The demand of this speaks for itself. And there is a fairly high threshold for technical performance. We don't even decide the technological scale ourselves. This is regulated by contract. This entails a much larger production compared to what we have done before. We're getting much bigger. That's the biggest change at present … For journalism: Yes it entails a further shift in focus. Some will ask if this is possible. More football. The threshold is probably even lower. We have invested in becoming the football channel – so that's what we will be.

Accordingly, the Norwegian football deal has caused a paradoxical situation. On the one hand, the collaboration with Canal Digital has strengthened TV 2's market position in relation to its rivals; on the other, in order to acquire the football deal the collaboration has had to accept strict regulations that influence its editorial policy and challenge publicist ideals. To make the investment economically viable, TV 2 and Canal Digital have no choice but to promote football as their own sports product – in journalistic formats as well.

Sports rights and the pressure from external actors

NFF's tender document illustrates how a seller can place strong pressure and detailed requirements on buyers of media rights. The problem does not apply only to football broadcasting. All those interviewed have said that there is a general problem in that sellers of sports rights want to decide on aspects regarding production and presentation, and that this is one of the main problems in sports broadcasting. Both Tor Aune (NRK) and Bjørn Taalesen (TV 2) refer to Formula One motor-car racing as the most extreme example. Formula One has its own company taking care of the production in a way that exposes the sports product and the advertisements in the best possible way for itself as well as its sponsors. According to Taalesen, the Formula One organization is very concerned about how its product is promoted prior to live programmes.

Tor Aune admits to frustration regarding the limitations of working journalistically on Formula One races:

> Despite having acquired the media rights, you are, for example, not allowed to record your own images.

Aune, who is also the Vice President of EBU's sports section, comments that:

> Interference in sport broadcasting by sports governing bodies is more easily accepted outside Scandinavia.

He singles out the BBC as being a notable exception in this context; however, he says that broadcasters in other countries (for example, Germany) are more commercially oriented and there is more competition in the market:

> If a German broadcaster refuses to accept these arrangements, it knows its rivals will. They are often a bit embarrassed when we bring up these issues.

There are, however, recent examples of how such preconditions are being articulated in Norway as well, the new football deal being one of them. Another example is the Scandinavian Royal League, a Nordic football league established in 2003. TVNorge holds the media rights for this tournament, and Morten Aass underlines NFF's strategy regarding the exposing of the tournament in the media. NFF is concerned that managers and players promote themselves and their clubs positively, and in a manner that does not question the quality of the product. Royal League is a new tournament, and some of the participants have appeared not to be taking it seriously. Morten Aass says:

> Statements have indicated that Royal League is just a training tournament. This is a catastrophe for the football association. NFF continuously encourages the managers and players to be positive when being interviewed by the media.

Hence the Nordic football governing bodies not only put pressure on the broadcasters with regard to how the products are presented; there is also internal pressure within the football associations to behave strategically and avoid questioning the quality of the football product.

Similar strategies with regard to image-building are also adopted by international sports governing bodies, such as the IOC and UEFA. Broadcasters acquiring Olympic rights and the European football championship rights are obliged to screen propaganda programmes – for example, broadcasters of Euro 2004 had to broadcast twenty-six 'UEFA stories' prior to the championship. The IOC has required similar services from Olympic broadcasters. These programmes are screened as ordinary programmes, and viewers are not made aware that this exposure is actually advertising for the sports governing bodies and their sponsors. The interviewees from NRK and TV 2 were unhappy with such clauses, but admitted that the acquisition of such rights forced them to accept broadcasting such propaganda. It is clear, though, that such commitments may be in conflict with the Norwegian Broadcasting Law, the Norwegian Code of Ethics and the Norwegian Code of Advertorials.

Most of the external pressure reported in this section has been on other formats rather than journalistic formats, such as news programmes and sports magazines. However, Tor Aune admits that sports governing bodies also try to influence journalistic coverage:

> There have been incidents. Many of those we have deals with regard us as a 'PR instrument'. Examples can be found in football, cross country skiing (previously), and in ice hockey. Ice hockey is anxious not to be portrayed as a 'violent' sport.

Sports journalism as attraction-building

The previous section concentrated on sports governing bodies' attempts to influence the policy of broadcasters who acquire media rights. This section will focus on steps taken by the broadcasters themselves in order to make their own 'sports rights product' as attractive as possible.

The representatives of NRK and TVNorge were somewhat reluctant to admit to promoting their own sports rights products in their journalistic formats. The two interviewees from the NRK emphasized that sports journalism and sports broadcasting were separate activities in the organization. Aune said:

> I suppose there is more coverage of sports to which we have acquired the rights than of other sports. We have many people covering the events and use much of our air time on these events. Obviously, we will then try to maximize our TV audience. We are very concerned about distinguishing between promotion and journalism. Therefore, we distinguish organizationally between journalism and the production of sports events. Sometimes the news values for events which we have the rights to may become too low.

Øyvind Lund, sports editor of the NRK, also emphasized the clear distinction between sports broadcasting on the one hand and journalism on the other. He stated that the broadcaster would also cover sports where NRK had not any rights. However, he also claimed:

> it is obvious that the sports to which we have the rights, and where we have the commentators, are closer to us. It is easier to get news access. Hence, you are likely to produce more of what is yours. And if you have to choose between two different events, you might very well end up with reporting from your own sports.

Hence, both the NRK interviewees clearly emphasized that holding sports rights, over time, will influence the journalistic priorities in a manner that is in the interest of the broadcaster. Accordingly, they were not unfamiliar with the problem of promoting their own sports rights in journalistic formats in the NRK.

The two interviewees representing TVNorge also pointed out that the journalistic coverage of sports was not a part of a strategy to promote their own rights products. Both Morten Aass (Managing Director) and Hallbjørn Saunes (sports editor) emphasized that it was important to present a broad and attractive picture of sport in general:

> Our sports news should produce journalism, and not be a window for promotion. We also communicate that to our local stations.

To what degree broadcasters produce promotion disguised as journalism could also have been analysed by means of content analysis. NRK's coverage of the preparations prior to the 2006 Winter Olympics and TVNorge's coverage of Royal League leave no doubt that the two broadcasters actually devote more time and resources to those events they hold the rights for than to other sports.

Media coverage is good business for the governing bodies of the most attractive sports. This, however, is different for less attractive sports, where sport governing bodies or their sponsors often have to pay for the production costs to have their events broadcast. By doing this, though, the sports and their events often gain a shorter route to the journalistic formats than they would have done had they not been broadcast at all. When broadcasters have TV pictures from events, and the opportunity to use these, it may open the door to journalistic coverage.

Although the interviewees from NRK and TVNorge were careful in their replies to whether they would promote their sports in journalistic formats, the sports editor of TV 2 was very explicit. His answer to the same question did not leave any doubt:

> Yes, definitely.

He also saw problems with such a policy:

> Yes, because these reports can dominate our sports news agenda.

TV 2 has been very conscious of using its journalistic formats to promote its own media rights products, and this has characterized their broadcasting of football. They held the national rights for the English Premier League from 1997 to 1999. The sports editor, Taalesen, admits how the channel used daily sports magazine to promote their own coverage of the matches by focusing on Norwegian players in the league (Helland, 2003):

> When a television channel like ours has these kinds of sports rights, the focus will not only be on the transmission of matches, but the whole news process will, in itself, be characterized by our sports rights. When we had the rights, a Norwegian player in England could not move a finger without us doing a report on it. Since we lost them the news values have changed and our attention on English football is much weaker. Now we only report what we see as most necessary.

Taalesen describes how the promotion of a sports rights product and the economic interests of the broadcaster, as well as journalism and journalistic formats, are all integrated in TV 2's overall strategy. According to him:

> There will be a different set of news values for the sports which the channel has the rights to transmit, and another set of news values for the sports which they do not have the right to transmit. We are more present, and we want the audience's attention on our own products. The news values vary according to what sports we have the rights to.

For products, it is not only a matter of whether sports governing bodies put pressure on the broadcaster or whether the broadcaster will promote the sports among its audience; it is also a matter of symbiosis between the sports governing body and the broadcaster itself. TV 2's sports editor is very articulate on this point:

> There is no doubt that both the Norwegian Football Association and TV 2 want to succeed by investing in football … Currently, there is no better sponsor for the Norwegian Football Association than TV 2.

From a symbiotic perspective, there is also the issue of organizational and technological convergence: TV 2 has paid an enormous amount of money for the entire football product, and the problem is how to maximize the return. The sports editor gives the answer:

> We will see how we can best exploit this for all our media platforms … This has consequences regarding how to conceptualize our football coverage. I am talking about both event formats and news formats … Any other way of approaching the issue of convergence related to the football deal would be madness.

To summarize this section, TV 2's sports editor has been very explicit in stating that the broadcaster will promote its own sports rights in its journalistic formats. Although representatives of the NRK and TVNorge also admitted that such promotion could happen, they were reluctant to state this explicitly. Nevertheless, TV 2's sports editor might well have been correct when he stated that the other channels were also promoting their 'own sports' in their journalistic formats.

Conclusions

The title of this chapter also represents the main research question, namely is journalism being used as an instrument to promote TV sports rights? The Norwegian football tender document as well as the interviews leave no doubt that the answer is 'yes'. The distribution of market power between sellers and buyers is very much influenced by the level of competition on both supply and demand sides. For any seller, the ideal situation is to be a monopolist while at the same time there is fierce competition between a large number of buyers. This will maximize the price, and can also provide the seller with other advantages when negotiating agreements with buyers.

Such circumstances have characterized the markets for football rights across Europe over the last decade. Commercial TV channels have competed fiercely for the most attractive tournaments, and this competition has dealt sellers a very favourable hand of cards.

This was the situation in Norway when a new football deal was sold in June 2005. Three rival bidders were willing to offer a record amount of money to acquire the rights, which put the Norwegian Football Association (NFF) in an enviable position. Thus, it is not surprising that NFF's tender document demanded services that clearly violate basic journalistic principles, as documented in this chapter.

Journalism can be an effective instrument to promote TV sports rights. Ideally, broadcasters and sports journalists should be operating according to specific codes of ethics, publicist ideals and national broadcasting laws. These might not always be followed. Nevertheless, it is the formulation, institutionalization and social awareness of these ideals that make the journalists representatives of the journalistic institution. These principles have been developed over time, and are common across borders. Indeed, these principles are very significant, as they make the institution of news a privileged social tradition.

Of course, it is important not to be naïve when analysing journalism and its relations with commercial markets. Journalistic ideals are not necessarily the driving force of the development of the media industry, and hence there have always been discrepancies between journalistic ideals and their application by representatives of the news institution. However, this discrepancy is evident with regard to the relationship between sports rights and sports news coverage on television. This also represents a rationale for analysing the role of television sports journalism.

The Norwegian football deal contained very strong restrictions regarding how to present the 'football product', and in a way this has turned TV 2 into a production company for the Norwegian

Football Association. Although the criticism of violating journal-istic principles might be raised against TV 2, this is now a general trend. Both NRK and TVNorge, which also relate their activities to publicist ideals, made bids on the football rights. According to Øyvind Lund, NRK's sports editor, the NRK had reservations regarding some of the regulations in the tender document. How-ever, both broadcasters might easily have ended up facing the same conflict between journalistic ideals and an overall business strategy had their bids been accepted. Interviews with represen-tatives from these channels revealed that they might be willing to accept clauses that would violate the codes of ethics for Norwegian journalism – for example, offering exposure to sponsors as a part of editorial policy.

When a broadcaster acquires exclusive sports rights, it is not only the sport governing body and its sponsors that want to build the 'football product'. The broadcaster itself, and in particular its sports department, will also take strategic measures to build the attraction of the sports in order to make the acquisition econom-ically viable.

Although this chapter has focused mainly on football broad-casting, the interviews revealed that similar practices are com-mon in the broadcasting of other sports, such as Formula One motor-car racing.

TV 2's sports editor considers his channel to be the best sponsor of Norwegian football, which is probably correct, bearing in mind that the channel has a penetration level of 98 per cent of Norwegian TV households. TV 2 is the most respected Norwegian TV channel regarding news coverage, together with NRK. While TVNorge spends very moderately on news programmes, neither of MTG's Norwegian channels have news coverage.

It is also worth considering that TV 2 is embedded with other media companies, such as *Nettavisen* (the leading Norwegian Internet newspaper) and Kanal 24 (a leading Norwegian commer-cial radio station). These relationships make TV 2 an even more powerful promotional instrument for sellers of sports rights and their sponsors.

From a journalistic perspective, however, this position as the most effective sponsor also has problematic consequences. Unlike entertainment channels, TV 2 is a public service broadcaster with publicist ideals and the obligation to pursue independent and crit-ical journalism. Sporting activities should be no exception to these ideals. However, today we see an over-reliance on celebrity sources, where sports journalism does not treat sport seriously as commer-cial business (Boyle *et al.*, 2002). Sports journalists are caught in a difficult position because of the contradictory professional demands, including the promotion of sports (Rowe, 1999).

The media have a central position in the modern sports/media complex, while journalism has a central position in the media. Furthermore, acquisition of sports rights may account for a substantial proportion of the total investment by broadcasters. This chapter has revealed that the acquisition of football rights (and other sports rights) puts the media in a position where their ability to conduct critical and independent journalism can be questioned. Hence, long-established principles regarding publicist activities and publicist ideals are at stake. Broadcasters and their commercial partners prioritize making investments in sports rights economically viable, and this does not match with journalistic principles. As Hallbjørn Saunes of TVNorge says:

> Critical and investigative journalism in the sports area is pursued to a very limited degree. The reason for this is that there are few resources for this kind of journalism in the area. Sports journalism is too often about cultivating sports celebrities and promoting profiles. There is too much pack coverage, in connection with most attractive events. The journalistic resources and the journalistic format on sports are very limited.

It is indeed a paradox that in an area where heavy investments are being made, the institutions that should ideally investigate the business activities have disqualified themselves in the name of self-interest. If those who should ideally be the watchdog are unable do the job, who should then watch the watchdog?

Bibliography and references

Boyle, R., Dinan, W. and Morrow, D. S. (2002). Doing the business? Newspaper reporting of the business of football. *Journalism*, **3**, 161–181.

Brown, A. (1996). Economics, public service broadcasting, and social values. *Journal of Media Economics*, **9(1)**, 3–15.

Dahlén, P. (1999). *Från Vasaloppet til Sportsextra – Radiosportens etablering och förgrening 1925–1995*. PhD Thesis, Stockholm, Stiftelsen Etermidierna i Sverige.

Gerrard, B. (2000). Media ownership of pro sports teams: who are the winners and losers? *Sports Marketing & Sponsorship*, **2(3)**, 199–218.

Gratton, C. and Solberg, H. A. (2006). *The Economics of Sports Broadcasting*. Routledge.

Helland, K. (2003). *Sport, medier og journalistikk. Med football-landslaget til EM*. Fagbokforlaget.

Kagan World Media (1999). *European Media Sports Rights: the authoritative databook on who pays how much*. Kagan World Media Ltd.

NRK (2005). Internal memorandum about the tender document for the Norwegian football deal.

Reimer, B. (2004). Nya upplevelser, nya erfarenheter. Televizerad idrott i förändring. *Norsk medietidsskrift*, **2**, 165–182.

Rowe, D. (1999). *Sport, Culture and the Media: the unruly trinity*. Open University Press.

Sand, G. and Helland, K. (1998). *Bak TV-nyhetene. Produksjon og presentasjon i NRK og TV 2*. Fagbokforlaget.

Solberg, H. A. (2004). Sports broadcasting. In: *The Business of Sport Management* (J. Beech and S. Chadwick, eds). Prentice Hall, Pearson Education.

Solberg, H. A. and Hammervold, R. (2004). Sport broadcasting – how to maximise the rating figures. *Trends in Communication*, **12(2&3)**, 83–100.

TV Sports Markets (2006). *European TV and Sports Rights 2006*. TV Sports Markets.

Whannel, G. (1992). *Fields in Vision: television sport and cultural transformation*. Routledge.

Appendix 2.1

Interview with sports editor Bjørn Taalesen, TV 2 (Norway)

- On sports journalism and sports rights:

> The question is how to present your material. You may go by the news threshold, which I think is a criterion that is easily understood. It's probably easy to understand that we are more present at, and create more attention to, our own coverage and broadcasting rights. When we owned the rights to the English football league we spent a lot of time in England because we were broadcasting English football matches. A Norwegian footballer couldn't sneeze without us doing a story on it. The journalistic threshold is different now. It changes constantly. And I don't think it only applies to us, and I see it elsewhere. To what extent others are willing to admit to this I'm not sure. However, in my opinion we may as well face it.

- On the Norwegian football agreement:

> In the short run the deal will be of the utmost importance and create needs for alterations in the organization. We also need a lot of new people. All I do these days is discuss positions and contracts and acquiring know-how. We must rearrange the cards all over again. It's not easy to get everything into place. We are producing 270 football matches. The demand of this speaks for itself. And there is a fairly high threshold for technical performance. We don't even decide the technological scale ourselves. This is regulated by contract. This entails a much larger production compared to what we have done before. We're getting much bigger. That's the biggest change at present. ... For journalism: Yes it entails a further shift in focus. Some will ask if this is possible. More football. The threshold is probably even lower. We have invested in becoming the football channel – so that's what we will be.

- On relations between sports rights and journalism:

> The commercial value. If those who sell football, no matter what price they get – it is clearly in our common interest

to succeed with our concentration on Norwegian football. There is no doubt that both the Norwegian Football Association and TV 2 want to succeed by investing in football … Currently, there is no better sponsor for the Norwegian Football Association than TV 2.

- Can it be said that journalism has a promotional effect on the products the channel owns the rights to?

  Yes, definitely.

- Do you see any problems with this?

  Yes, because these reports can dominate the sports news agenda. I see clear tendencies towards a clearer division between those running the news and those attending to the marketing aspects. For my own part, I feel OK about not being part of the daily news wheel … Yet, when you own the rights you raise considerable attention to these topics. You become so commercial in your thinking that you find most of your contacts there, you spend most of your time there, and devote most of your attention to it. … There will be a different set of news values for the sports which the channel has the rights to transmit, and another set of news values for the sports it does not have the rights to transmit. We are more present, and we want the audience's attention on our own products. The news values vary according to what sports we have the rights to.

- On convergence:

  The way these negotiations went – we now have every-thing. When you have paid so much to have the opportu-nity to buy everything, it would be wrong not to explore the possibility of getting some of that money back. One way to get some of that money back is to look at things through convergence. We will see how we can best exploit this for all our media platforms. This has consequences regarding how to conceptualize our football coverage. I am talking about both event formats and news formats … Any other way of approaching the issue of convergence related to the football deal would be madness.

- On owners of rights who try to steer journalistic coverage:

  I feel there are examples of this, regarding one sport we no longer own the rights to. Formula One is a classic example of this. We haven't engaged in much journalism in this field, but what little we have tried has been limited by the large amount of control exerted in this sport. For instance, you are not allowed to take your own pictures, even if you own the rights.

- On collaboration with a satellite distributor:

  If this collaboration turns out to be successful for both parts, it should provide us with power in the future. Alone, TV 2 is a small company [...] Canal Digital and its owners represent an economic power that is important for us.

Appendix 2.2

Interview with sports editor Øyvind Lund, NRK (Norway)

- On the importance of sport in the NRK:

  Sport matters to the Norwegian people. We suspect Norwegians are more interested in sport than people are in other countries. As such, sport is important both as news and as live coverage in order to uphold the support for the licence fee ... Regarding the licence fee, it is important that the NRK is also engaged in areas of activity that matter to a large number of people. This is where we find sports coverage. Sport is also an issue we like to regard as something that unites the people, and is therefore important for NRK. NRK is an important institution as a mediator of big events.

- Making a sharp distinction between live coverage and news, Lund emphasizes that the NRK covers many events that the broadcaster does not have the rights to:

  At the same time it is obvious that the sports we do have the rights to, and that are covered by our commentators, are somewhat closer to us. Access to news is easier. This means that you will probably emphasize more heavily what is already the focus of your institution, and if you have equal segments and can only air one, then perhaps you end up with the segment that covers a sports event to which you have the rights rather than the other.

Appendix 2.3

Interview with Tor Aune, Head of Sports Rights, NRK (Norway)

- On the legitimacy of the licence fee in relation to sports:

Sport here at the NRK has a large and important position. Sports receive substantial attention from viewers, and without it the public's willingness to pay the licence fee could weaken. The NRK's position when it comes to the sheer volume of winter sports is exceptional in a European context.

- On pressure from external actors:

The fact that those who sell sports events would like to retain control over the terms of production – such as where in the schedule to place the events and the length of the programme – is a problem. Most extreme is Formula One. They produce the images themselves, to secure the right advertisement exposure, among other things. Despite having acquired the media rights, you are, for example, not allowed to record your own images.

- On demands for journalistic promotion from external players:

Interference in sports broadcasting by sports governing bodies is more easily accepted outside Scandinavia. Broadcasters like the BBC are particular in this regard. Other broadcasters, such as in Germany, are more commercial and are subject to more market competition. If a German broadcaster refuses to accept these arrangements, it knows its rivals will. They are often a bit embarrassed when we bring up these issues.

- On sponsors:

> If one purchases rights from the IOC, the organization decides in advance the order of sponsors. First, 'Olympic Programme', then the sponsors of the organizer, then 'Olympiatoppen', and finally other sponsors. This works according to exclusivity by branch.

- On rights and journalistic coverage:

> I suppose there is more coverage of sports to which we have acquired the rights than of other sports. We have many people covering the events and use much of our air time on these events. Obviously, we will then try to maximize our TV audience. We are very concerned about distinguishing between promotion and journalism. Therefore, we distinguish organizationally between journalism and the production of sports events. Sometimes the news values for events which we have the rights to may become too low.

- On attempts to control the news by the sellers of rights:

> There have been incidents. Many of those we have deals with regard us as a 'PR instrument'. Examples can be found in football, cross-country skiing (previously), and in ice hockey. Ice hockey is anxious not to be portrayed as a 'violent' sport.

Appendix 2.4

Interview with news editor Hallbjørn Saunes, TVNorge

- On the role of sports at TVNorge:

> We have been on and off when it comes to sports. We have previously been under the ownership of TV 2 and have shared their rights. We started our own sports coverage in September. We put sports on the programme because

we wish to be a complete broadcaster. When we decided to acquire Royal League, we saw it as important that this be an exclusive package that we could commit to completely.

Also,

Our sports news should produce journalism, and not be a window for promotion. We also communicate that to our local stations. But to what extent do we accomplish this? In 50 per cent of the cases sports coverage is merely summary and in the remaining 50 per cent of the cases work has been done to produce journalistic stories.

- On separating clearly the events on the one hand and journalistic work on the other:

  Those working daily on Royal League do not work on the journalistic aspect.

- On external pressures:

  [I] have not experienced/perceived owners of rights to have attempted to influence journalistic coverage.

- Regarding the football agreement:

  One will try to win those rights, and must grin and bear it and then try to get out afterwards. The rights to news as well as other factors put us in a bloody bind.

- On critical sports journalism:

  Critical and investigative journalism in the sports area is pursued to a very limited degree. The reason for this is that there are few resources for this kind of journalism in the area. Sports journalism is too often about cultivating sports celebrities and promoting profiles. There is too much pack coverage, in connection with most attractive events. The journalistic resources and the journalistic format on sports are very limited.

Appendix 2.5

Interview with Morten Aass, Managing Director, TVNorge

- On the dominance of football:

  When we decided to concentrate on a TV sport, football was what we believed in the most. You need only look at history, really, and you'll see what attracts viewers. The attractions are winter sports – there are a few attractive events there – and football.

- On Royal League:

  We had the chance to get in on a new tournament that we hoped would become important, namely the Scandinavian club championship, and of course we knew that it was an uphill struggle – building a new brand and a new tournament – but it is also a unique opportunity, which is what made this venture interesting.

- On sports coverage in the sports magazine/feature format:

  Our sports coverage is as our general news coverage – it should reflect today's agenda, pure and simple. It is summarizing, and gives people as complete a picture as possible in as short a time as possible, so that they feel they have received the news update they need, and don't feel the need to switch over to Kveldsnytt [the NRK's late evening news] which starts only a few minutes later.

- On 'product building':

  Statements have indicated that Royal League is just a training tournament. This is a catastrophe for the Football Association. NFF continuously encourages the managers and the players to be positive when being interviewed by the media.

- On counter-programming:

  We very often think alternatively. Our intent is to engage in counter-programming with the other channels, so that when they broadcast sports we will broadcast something completely different. This means that, for instance, a broadcaster such as ours loses few viewers to the Olympic Games and the FIFA World Cup, because our viewers are used to actively seeking our programming. We retain our viewers throughout these events by being an alternative ... it is important that it is predictable that they find an alternative.

- On problems with own programmes that promote the seller of rights:

  This type of editorial interference is a concealed process. Viewers are unaware that very often the big sponsors financing these productions do so to gain exposure, to raise awareness about the Olympics, further still. These promos run for months in advance. Their purpose is to build interest around the Olympics. But to be forced to put this in your schedule is not something you like, of course. This is not editorial freedom. But we don't have much of a choice. I haven't seen these agreements myself. There is probably a mix of choice and necessity at play here. Large amounts of money are involved here ...

- On the tender document:

  My opinion on this is that it sucks, but then again you have to put up with a few things to attain such rights. You might think you will have the opportunity to discuss these matters when the deal has been made – to attain as much freedom as possible. It's all about getting the rights, after all, and therefore your focus is on getting these rights, and instead you push these problems, or challenges, ahead of you. The challenge starts once you have obtained the rights, and then the question is what to do about these things that are not there in the tender document you start reading. You realize this is not good. But then you feel that if you have paid NOK1 billion, well then there must be some possibilities to influence the result.

- On the coverage of what the company owns the rights to broadcast:

  It is easier and less complicated to cover as news the events you have the rights to. However you can't disregard the world cup ski-jumping event just because NRK has the rights to that arrangement. News values are the same regardless of who has the rights.

- On news and competition:

  As far as we are concerned, conveying the results people expect is the main objective – or they'll just change channels. Our viewers should feel they have obtained the news they need – both in terms of news and sports – and they should feel satisfied enough by our broadcast presentation not to feel they need to turn to another station to get the full picture. It's often enough to hear that Vålerenga IF won the game, and possible see the goal.

The 'Big Five' market

The role of management control in French football's regulation – a unique model that can be exported?

Michel Desbordes

Overview

The DNCG (*Direction Nationale du Contrôle de Gestion*) or National Board for Management Control (NBMC) is an independent institution whose mission is to check French professional clubs' accounts. Its declared aim is to allow clubs that begin the championship to finish it without having to file for bankruptcy – which would distort the competition. We interviewed its President with the objective of discovering what the role, aim or utility of the DNCG is. It seems that today this consists more of coming up with a business plan than strictly controlling bankruptcy. If clubs' accounts are not in accordance with what was agreed, they are punished seriously – for example, by being relegated. This chapter leads to the issue of whether the DNCG model could be exported, considering the financial difficulties in Spain and Italy and the increasing power of the G14 (an organization of European football clubs founded in 2000, initially by fourteen members, with another four clubs added in 2002). Currently, European clubs operate in very different contexts.

Keywords

control, budget, football, France, DNCG (NBMC), balance

Introduction

France has a unique method of management control of professional sport clubs, including a system in football which is similar to those in rugby, basketball and handball. The aim is to avoid bankruptcies in the middle of the season, in order to have a true championship.

The DNCG, which acts as 'French football's policeman', is a commission internal to the FFF (*Fédération Française de Football* – the French Football Union) that is active in the clubs. A government auditor has to review the clubs' accounts, and each President (accompanied by his chosen individual) must regularly present a provisional budget to the DNCG commission. When clubs do not respect the rules of financial balance, they can be sanctioned by fines, the prohibition or control of recruitment, relegation and the prohibition of employment of professional players.

We interviewed François Ponthieu, lawyer and President of the DNCG, in order to understand this system better and to see whether it really is unique in Europe. In an interview on 25 July 2005, he commented:

> First, I want to underline my passion for football. I read the football section in *l'Équipe* every day, I love the atmosphere in the stadium, the smell of the grass … I'm 43, and have worked for about 10 years in the chambers that used to manage the legal affairs of the UCPF [Union des

Clubs de Football Professionnel – Union for Professional Football Clubs]. Inside the DNCG, we see that all the 'families of football' are represented and have to elect a representative.

I became the representative of UCFP, and I was elected President five years ago. My job focuses more on intellectual property or royalties. I did not arrive here by a happy coincidence; it is a way to combine my experience as a lawyer and my passion for football.

Following this interview, we wanted to find the answers to the following questions:

- What is the aim of this control?

- Is the control efficient and unbiased?

- Is there a similar system in any other European country?

- Does the system make French football stronger or weaker?

- Can this system be exported, and do people want this to happen?

- What other regulatory systems are available?

The DNCG and the French regulatory system

The French regulatory system cannot be analysed outside its institutional context. Indeed, the role of government and public communities is still very strong, which is not the case in England or in the US (Desbordes, 2000).

Context and principles

The organization of sport in France is of particular interest because the role of the public sector is fundamental. There are three main sectors in this system, which have various aims (Gasparini, 2000):

1. *The private sector, 'grassroots' or non-profit-oriented.* Since the 1901 law (which defined the role of non-profit associations in France), associations have been very important in France both for sport practice and also for the organization of sport events. Volunteers are the keystone of this system.

2. *The private sector, profit-oriented.* This includes private companies that produce sport equipment (for example, adidas,

Nike, Salomon, Rossignol, Decathlon) or offer services (lessons, sport events, sport tourism, etc.)

3. *The public sector*. This includes public companies, state administrations and local communities. These institutions have to control and manage physical activity. The major actor in this system since 1945 has been the Ministry of Youth and Sport. The French Olympic Committee (*CNOSF – Comité National Olympique du Sport Français*) also has a central role.

The French sport system

Professionalization and media coverage are quite recent events in the French sport system, and have led to a considerable increase in the amount of money available as well as a change in structure. Although TV exposure of professional sport is of course much greater than that of amateur sport, it is important to remember that the latter involves a huge number of people and therefore is responsible for a bigger turnover!

As in other countries, amateur sport cannot exist without the government. However, professional sport in France is also influenced by the state, although the state no longer finances it – as used to be the case. Figure 3.1 shows the organization of the French sport system.

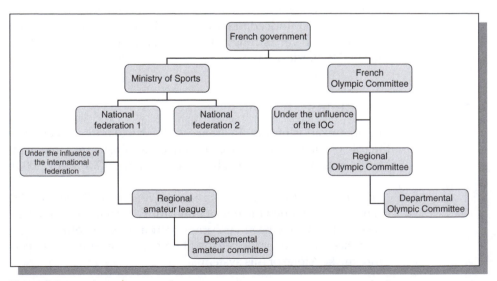

Figure 3.1
The hierarchical organization of the French sport system

The history of the regulatory system in French football

The origin of professional sport in France

Most professional sports – football, rugby, athletics and tennis – emerged from England during the nineteenth century. At this time other amateur sports did exist in France, but were far distant from the model of the professional club or championship. The English organizational model was exported along with the sports; being very hierarchical and catering solely for men, it had values comparable to those of the British public schools of the time.

In France, the system was applied with a president, a treasurer and members – most of whom were from the upper classes. Many clubs were created in France using this structure – le Havre Athletic Club in 1872, Bordeaux Athletic Club in 1877, Racing Club de France in 1881 and Stade Français in 1882. It is noticeable that these clubs were located in Paris, Normandy and Bordeaux, where upper-class populations were over-represented, and this is still the case in 2006. These clubs introduced athletics, rugby and football, and contributed both to their spread throughout the country and to the integration of French sport in the international system.

In England, football clubs became professional in 1888 (originally, six clubs in the Midlands and six clubs in Lancashire). Payment of players became acceptable from the nineteenth century onwards; in the 1920s, transfers led to monetary advantages and social security benefits. In 1931, the FFF (French Football Union) voted on the principle of professionalism. Slowly, other sports officially became professional – basketball in 1980, then ice hockey, handball and volleyball in the 1990s, along with rugby in 1993.

The need to control the professional system

The creation of the French Professional Championship in 1932 (which was won by Lille) did not change the structure of the clubs fundamentally; this did not occur until 1975. The members of parliament did not change the laws because it seemed that the French people were very involved with and concerned about the amateur system, in spite of the progressive non-adaptation of the structure.

In the 1980s and 1990s, the increased financial resources (thanks mainly to TV rights) created a new status for clubs, which was more business-oriented. At the same time, it became apparent that it was necessary to introduce a means of regulatory control for the clubs.

How the DNCG system works

The government auditor helps clubs to prepare all the documents that the DNCG needs to validate their accounts (the balance sheet, budget for the current and next seasons, appendix and treasurer's report). If the club's situation cannot be resolved within a fortnight, the DNCG can take at least two measures of the four available:

1. The fine can be doubled

2. New contracts will not be permitted for the next season

3. The club can be excluded from the French Cup (la coupe de France)

4. The club can be excluded from the League Cup.

The objectives of the government auditor are to:

- evaluate the specific financial risks of a football club (transfers, insurance, bonus, contracts for players)

- verify that certain laws are being applied properly – for example, those concerning the relationship of the association and the commercial club, or subsidies from public communities

- analyse the strategy of the club, because the situation of the major shareholder (philanthropic patron or business company) and its long-term vision for the future of the club can vary considerably

- verify the main budget items (wages, TV rights, expenses for players, agents)

- check the treasurer's report

- check the account and fiscal rules

- react in case of problems.

The sanctions are specified in Title 11 of the convention between the FFF and the LFP. If the financial situation of the club is not healthy, the DNCG can enforce the following sanctions:

- Prohibition of recruitment of new players

- Control and limitation of recruitment, taking into account the provisional budget and wage bill (this implies that all contracts have to be checked by the DNCG before a player can be bought by the club).

The club is given a set period in which to modify its budget. As a last resort, further sanctions can be imposed:

- The club may be relegated
- The club may be expelled from national championships
- The club may be prohibited from employing professional players.

Membership of the DCNG

The commission that controls professional championships includes:

- five members appointed by the FFF (French Football Union)
- five members appointed by the LFP (French Professional League)
- two members appointed by the UCFP (Union for Professional Clubs)
- two members appointed by the UNFP (Union for Professional Players)
- two members appointed by the UNECATEF (Union for Football Coaches)
- two members appointed by the SNAAF (Union for Workers in the Field of Football).

This commission therefore represents the so-called 'families of football'.

Further information can be gained by reading François Ponthieu's interview (Appendix 3.1).

Case studies

DNCG regularly sanctions French clubs when they do not respect financial criteria, and some examples are provided below.

Football

Before the 1980s, there was no law concerning the financing of professional clubs. Cities or local communities were free to subsidize clubs because they used them as a means of advertising (Auxerre and Lens, for example, achieved a very high awareness level thanks to football).

- In the 1980s, the legendary club Girondins de Bordeaux was relegated to the Second Division for misappropriation of funds.

Its President, Claude Bez, was jailed, despite being a government auditor!

- In 1994, it transpired that Bernard Tapie, President of Olympique de Marseille (1993 European Champions), had fixed matches in the run-up to the European Cup. The club was relegated to the Second Division the following season for further financial irregularities, and Tapie was subsequently jailed.

- In 2000, it was the turn of Saint-Étienne and Toulouse, both of which were relegated for financial reasons.

- On 28 May 2003, AS Monaco was officially relegated for financial mismanagement during the previous 6 months. Liabilities were officially assessed at €53 million, although other sources estimated that the figure was nearer to €80 million. There was no guarantee given in the file presented by the club to the DNCG, and the club was temporarily relegated as €25 million were missing. The club appealed the decision, and it was finally decided that it could take part in the Ligue 1 championship for the 2003–04 season although its recruitment would be controlled. Several investors belonging to Monaco Football Investissement (MFI) joined the club, bringing a capital contribution of €5 million. On 30 June 2003, Jean-Louis Campora, who had been President since 1976, resigned from the presidency. The new Director then had to limit salaries to €3 million monthly for the 2002–03 season.

Other sports

Rugby (the second biggest professional sport in France) has on many occasions been sanctioned by the DNACG (*Direction Nationale d'Aide et de Contrôle de Gestion des clubs professionnels*). This is because the structure of this sport, which became professional very recently, remains unchanged. The following factors have led to problems:

- TV rights are much weaker than in football

- Salaries have increased dangerously over the last five years

- The average fan base and audience is quite small (except for Toulouse)

- Sponsorship incomes are weak and the structure of clubs remains unchanged (often there is no marketing direction)

- Most of the time clubs are financed through patronage and depend on a single financial source.

Examples include the following:

- On 4 March 2003, Noël Mamère, Mayor of Bègles (a suburb of Bordeaux), confirmed that he was very worried about the future of the club and was afraid of it being relegated. On 26 March, DNACG asked for financial guarantees by 8 April. On 28 May, the club was relegated in spite of appealing against the decision. The club had a deficit of €1 million, compared to the global budget of €4.7 million for the next season! (*Le Monde*, 15 July 2003.) This legendary club was the only club bar Toulouse that had never previously left the First Division.

- Conversely, Bourgoin-Jallieu, a club where €1.3 million were missing and which was supposed to be relegated, was re-instated 'under conditions' in the TOP 16 because it provided an adequate guarantee for the 2003–04 season.

Conclusion

In conclusion, the transparency and the independence of the control system in football or rugby are commendable: even big clubs can be relegated. However, it seems possible that the system may contribute to making French clubs weaker in Europe compared to other countries. This is the topic for the second part of this chapter, which deals with analysis of competition among the 'Big Five'. We will focus on the eventual exportation of this system all over Europe.

Can this regulatory system be exported?

The regulatory system can not be analysed without taking into account the institutional context of clubs in their own country. Indeed, apart from the Bosman and Malaja cases, in 1993 and in 2002 respectively, which concerned the free circulation of players in the labour market in Europe (see Introduction, Box I.1), clubs do not have the same conditions regarding laws, stock exchange flotation, employer contributions, national insurance contributions or salaries.

Fundamental differences in Europe

We can see in Table 3.1 that European clubs are placed very differently in a legal context. In France, the association (since the law of 1901) is very important and clubs are not managed like private

Table 3.1
Laws regarding professional clubs in various European countries

	France	Germany	England	Spain	Italy
Legal obligation to have an association	Yes	Yes	No	No	No
Owner of the affiliation number	Association	Company	Company	Company	Company
Owner of the brand	Association	Company/ Association	Company	Company	Company
Owner of TV rights	Fédération	Société/ Ligue	Société	Société	Société
Quotation on the stock exchange	No	Yes	Yes	Yes	Yes
Multiple property	No	Under 49.9%	<9.9%	<5%	Only in different leagues

Source: (Deloitte & Touche), 2001.

Table 3.2
Quotation on the stock market

	France	Germany	England	Spain	Italy
Quotation on the stock market	No	Yes	Yes	Yes, after 2002	Yes
Number of clubs quoted	0	1	22 (UK)	0	2
Date of the first introduction	–	Borussia Dortmund, October 2000	Tottenham Hotspur, October 1983		Sté Sportiva Lazio Roma, May 1998

Source: Deloitte & Touche (2001).

companies. The phrase 'a sport exception' is used to characterize the differences between sport and 'classical' industries.

Table 3.2 indicates quotation on the stock market.

It is interesting to note that quotation was allowed in France on 31 January 2006. However, clubs have to own their stadium in order to be quoted, and there are currently only two clubs that fulfil this criterion – AJ Auxerre and AC Ajaccio! It seems that, for now, only the UK has adopted this means of financing clubs. Jean-Michel Aulas, the President of Olympique Lyonnaist, has been militating in favour of stock-market quotation for years. He has, however, had to battle the scepticism of the Minister of Sports, Jean-François Lamour, and the President of the League, Frédéric Thiriez, who have observed that, of the many clubs in Europe, since the 1990s only Manchester United has been successful on the stock market, thanks to its real commercial structure.

Table 3.3 again emphasizes the differences in football across Europe, and the need for some degree of consistency!

Autonomy of clubs regarding the League varies. In Spain or Italy the clubs own their TV rights, which gives them the opportunity to negotiate directly with networks and thus increase their revenue but does not indicate greater global efficiency. The case of Italy in 2002 is particularly interesting, because smaller clubs did not start the Calcio in September – they had no TV revenue any more, contrary to the 'big clubs' which had negotiated individually.

In France, the League negotiates and distributes the TV rights. Before 2003, TV rights were shared equally. In 2003, the system changed under the pressure of the 'big clubs', which estimated they should receive more because a club such as Olympique de Marseille would be broadcast more often – it was shown thirty times during the 2002–03 season. This system differs completely from the US, where the NBA, for example, shares the TV rights.

Table 3.4 underlines the worst handicap for French football: since the Bosman case, clubs have not been able to compete for international talent – an international player costs 42 per cent less in Italy or in England than in France!

In conclusion, France cannot compete in Europe because of the strict control of the DNCG. There are psychological aspects (see François Ponthieu's interview for examples), but above all it is economical, law or fiscal aspects that play a role. Therefore it is probably Utopian to consider applying this system all over Europe because some of the differences still exist. Moreover, some countries, such as Italy or Spain, would probably be opposed to the idea because it could threaten the success of their clubs.

'Excesses' in the financial management of clubs

Italy

In Italy, the financing of football is almost out of control. Sporting success in the Champions League in 2003 (Milan AC won and three clubs reached the semi-finals) cannot disguise the financial difficulties of clubs. Box 3.1 explains the situation in 2002.

Table 3.3

The general organization of French professional football

	France	Germany	England	Spain	Italy
Theoretical autonomy of the League regarding the Ministry of Sports	Weak	Strong	Strong	Weak	Weak
Theoretical autonomy of the League regarding the Federation	Weak	Weak	Intermediate	Strong	Weak
Legal status of the League	Association	Association + private company	Private company	Association	Association
Managerial independence of the League	Intermediate (new law?)	Strong	Strong	Intermediate	Intermediate
Board members	Clubs, individual members, players, coaches		Executive Board	Clubs	Clubs
Autonomy of League 1 clubs	Weak	Weak	Weak	Strong	Intermediate
Financial flow between the League and the Federation (difference 2001/2000)	~ €3.2 million	Almost nothing	Nil	~ €3.5 million	Almost nothing
Other financial flows	League → FNDS (National Foundation for Sport Development) = 5% of TV rights		League → Football Foundation = 5% of TV rights		

Source: Deloitte & Touche (2001).

Table 3.4
Cost of players for clubs (€)

	France	Germany	Spain	Italy	England
International player					
Annual net salary	1 800 000	1 800 000	1 800 000	1 800 000	1 800 000
Annual gross salary	4 302 184	3 675 687	3 442 621	3 354 776	2 986 487
Total cost for the club	5 728 891	3 682 519	3 453 090	3 370 741	3 341 879
Index 100	100	64.3	60.3	58.8	58.3
Average League 1 player					
Annual net salary	219 500	219 590	219 590	219 590	219 590
Annual gross salary	480 000	439 116	403 275	399 772	352 496
Total cost for the club	669 063	445 949	413 744	414 791	394 444
Index 100	100	66.7	61.8	62	59
Good League 2 player					
Annual net salary	96 513	96 513	96 513	96 513	96 513
Annual gross salary	180 000	187 100	166 588	170 899	147 367
Total cost for the club	261 733	193 933	176 719	185 545	164 904
Index 100	100	74.1	67.5	70.9	63

Source: Deloitte & Touche (2001).

Box 3.1:   Calcio declines

Benito Mussolini understood that football could reveal patriotism, had an educative and social function, and could be used in military training. The 'Squadra Azzurra', the world champion in 1934 and 1938, became the symbol of power. Today, football is still very successful in Italy: 45 per cent of the population are interested in the 'Serie A' championship, and 26 per cent regularly watch games on TV. The average audience in stadiums reaches 30 000, 75 per cent of whom are subscribers. However, Italian football has declined. First, the clubs are not winning so often. Between 1983 and 1998, Italian clubs won six Champions Leagues and were runners up five times. In 1990, they won all three European cups. Today, Spain and England have taken their place. Secondly, the Italian championship (Calcio) is ailing – violence, racism, doping and false passports have given it a bad image over the past few years. The main problem, though, is financial: for example, clubs spent €930 million during the summer of 2001, which is €150 million more than they earned after selling players. Moreover, the wage bill is uncontrolled: from 1996 to 2001 this increased by 350 per cent, and it now represents 65 per cent of the clubs' budget. This incredible escalation was, of course, due to the explosion in TV rights (50 per cent of the budgets). However, the value of TV rights may decline over the next few years: the public TV channel, RAI, has decided to pay less after 2002, and the amalgamation of satellite operators has also led to a 25 per cent decrease in costs. How can clubs compensate for this decrease in revenue? The stock market has not so far been very successful for Italian clubs. Merchandising and the shift to leisure companies (for example, Juventus and its Juvecity complex) could provide a long-term solution, but only the major clubs would be able to rely on this potential development. Smaller clubs can only expect increased revenues after good sporting performances, and these are of course uncertain. The Calcio model is threatened.

(*Source*: Michel Desbordes, *Le Monde*, 4 June 2002.)

Spain

In Spain, there have been difficulties in financing football for years. Some experts wonder how Real Madrid could afford to buy Figo in 2000, Zidane in 2002 and Beckham in 2003, for about €2000 million. The club was achieving good results at that time, but its debt was still about €250 million in 2000 and the city of Madrid bought land from the club for €750 million. This type of operation can be compared to a public subsidy, given in order to support a club that has important political influence all over Spain. Generally, Spanish football structures are strongly in debt. Box 3.2 describes the situation in 2003.

Box 3.2: Spanish football gives way under the weight of debts

Will Spanish football players go on strike next season? According to Gerardo Gonzalez, President of the Players Union, salary arrears reached €45 million for the season and 80 per cent of clubs are affected. Although some superstars earn millions of euros annually, the average salary for a regular player is quite low. This underlines the financial crisis in Spanish football, where debts have reached €1.6 billion euros, and the situation could worsen with the uncertainty concerning the next deal regarding TV rights – previously agreed in 1998 at €216 million. The professional football league (LFP) wants a €240 million deal, but Audiovisual Sport is offering half this. The situation is worrying, because big clubs (such as Real Madrid or FC Barcelona) negotiate their deals individually. In addition, Quiero TV has gone bankrupt and Sogecable (Canal+) has merged with Via Digital (Telefonica). Now Sogecable controls 80 per cent of Audiovisual Sport, which is also in debt for €300 million. Pay-per-view TV channels have been disappointed with the profitability of football. Again, clubs have asked the government for a rescue plan which consists in cancelling their fiscal debt (€240 million) and a 10–20 per cent increase in their part of the profit from the weekly betting system 'Quiniela'. However, many taxpayers do not feel that they should be financing the recruitment policy of millionaire clubs!

(*Source*: Thierry Maliniak, *La Tribune*, 22 May 2003.)

Paradoxically, big clubs are also concerned – such as FC Barcelona, Real Madrid's eternal rival (see Box 3.3).

Box 3.3: €55 million loss for Barça

Enric Reyna, the temporary President, concluded the first day of the Socios Extraordinary General Assembly with a resignation 45-minute speech, and this should start a new political process. Barcelona is out of the Champions League and only ninth in the Liga: the team has not won anything for four years. Reyna stated that the budget deficit had reached €37 million and would be even worse at the end of the 2002–03 season, at €55 million. This loss is approximately the expected budget of FC Nantes or Olympique de Marseille for the current season. According to Reyna, debts will reach the huge level of €98 million by 30 April, but could be reduced to €47 million by the end of June, if 'some plans happen'.

Reyna is planning new merchandising and sponsorship projects: apart from selling some players, he also intends to sell an area of land that the club owns in San Joan Depi, where the future training facilities are built. In spite of its terrible financial data, Barça's property has increased over recent years (to €620 million for tangible fixed assets and €240 million for the football team itself). The future President will have to destroy the Blaugrana Arena (where handball and basketball teams play), the ice-skating arena and some stands and land close to the Nou Camp Stadium, to build a new commercial and playing zone. This was dreamed up some years ago, but local authorities have never yet given their agreement.

(*Source*: Anonymous, in *L'Équipe*, 6 May 2003.)

In spite of the financial difficulties detailed in Box 3.3, Barça bought the Brazilian player Ronaldinho for €30 million in July 2003. In France, as can be imagined, the DNCG would have prohibited this signing or even relegated the club.

Towards a 'natural' regulation of the system?

According to François Ponthieu, President of DNCG, European football is at a turning point: only those clubs that are strong financially and will be able to overcome the probable decrease in value of TV rights will survive. In this context, we can imagine that the role of institutions like the DNCG will become less significant and that adjustments will be made throughout the market.

Conclusions

Is the DNCG system exportable? First, we have seen there are major differences between the football institutions in Europe, which makes it difficult to have a single regulatory system. Secondly, it appears that various interests will probably slow down the diffusion process regarding an eventual European DNCG.

If the different ministries of sport do not adopt a unanimous sport policy in Europe, a European DNCG will not be possible. Unanimity could take many years, owing to the major differences between countries and the risk of political changes.

G14 is a strong lobby that gathers together the most powerful clubs in Europe. Although it doesn't have an institutional legitimacy, it is very influential regarding subjects such as the 'salary cap', because it includes the biggest clubs (Real Madrid, Manchester United, Bayern Munich, Juventus Turin, Inter Milan, Milan AC, Ajax Amsterdam, Olympique Marseille, PSG, etc.). These clubs would prefer to keep to an unregulated system that leads to a greater economical and financial concentration. It is clear that a European DNCG is many years ahead, and thus although French clubs will be well-managed financially for years, they might also be alone!

Acknowledgements

We would like to thank François Ponthieu, President of the DNCG, who kindly agreed to be interviewed and provided very useful information regarding this chapter.

Bibliography and references

Anonymous (2003). 55 millions d'euros de pertes pour le Barça, *L'Équipe*, 6 May.

Bourg, J. F. and Gouguet, J. J. (1998). *Analyse économique du sport*. PUF.

Callede, J. P. (1987). *L'esprit sportif. Essai sur le développement associatif de la culture sportive*. PUB.

Conseil Economique et Social (2002). *Le sport de haut niveau et l'argent*. CES.

Desbordes, M. (2000). *Gestion du sport*. Vigot publisher, Paris, France.

Desbordes, M. (2002). Le déclin du calcio, *Le Monde*, 4 June.

Desbordes, M. and Bolle, G. (Eds.) (2005). *Marketing et Football: une perspective internationale*. Presses Universitaires du Sport.

Desbordes, M., Ohl, F. and Tribou, G. (2004). *Marketing du sport*, 3rd edn. Economica.

Gasparini, W. (2000). *Sociologie de l'organization sportive*. Repères – La Découverte.

Maliniak, T. (2003). Le football espagnol croule sous les dettes. *La Tribune*, 22 May.

Pociello, C. (1995). *Les cultures sportives*. PUF.

Appendix 3.1

Interview with François Ponthieu, lawyer and President of the DNCG (Direction Nationale du Contrôle de Gestion)

Q1: Why is it necessary to control the management of professional football clubs?

FP: Football is very different from profit-oriented companies, where control is connected to optimization of costs. In French football, it is more appropriate to refer to 'regulation' rather than 'control'. We want to create conditions of economic and moral equity, which, although it might appear simple, is actually quite complicated in that we have to ensure that all clubs playing in the championship can start and finish the season in good financial health.

Because the bankruptcy of a single club could cause major complications for an entire league, it is necessary to check the financial position of the clubs before and during the season, and to ask for guarantees from shareholders.

The DNCG's mission needs to be seen in the context of professional sport, where equity between participants should always be respected to ensure fair competition. Historically, this dates back to developments in French sport initiated in the early 1970s.

Q2: Can you explain exactly how the DNCG functions?

FP: First, football clubs have to satisfy the specific accounting rules. For example, a club must set out a specific expenditure and revenue plan that includes games, transfers, subsidies from communities and sponsorship, and so on. Clubs must also satisfy the usual legal obligations of private companies, particularly those concerning the control of the accounts.

The government auditor controls and certifies accounts according to Article 228 of the Law regarding Accounts Control, passed on 24 July 1966, which forms a regulatory framework. The auditor must examine the certification of accounts according to a specific accounting practice for football (set out by the Ministry of Sport) and check the information provided to DNCG by the clubs.

Q3: So the DNCG follows this procedure?

FP: Exactly. The government auditor helps the clubs to prepare documentation required by the DNCG to validate the accounts, such as financial balance sheets, budgets for the current and following season, appendices and treasurers' reports, etcetera. If a problem arises that cannot be solved in two weeks, DNCG can take at least two measures of the four available – fines may be doubled; new contracts for players will not be signed for the next season; exclusion from the French Cup; and exclusion from the League Cup.

In particular, the auditor must evaluate the specific financial risks of a football club (transfers, insurances, bonus, contracts for players); verify adherence to certain laws (for example, those concerning the relationship of the association and the commercial club, or those regarding subsidies from public communities); analyse the strategy of the club (this is important because major shareholders such as philanthropic patrons or companies could have long-term visions for the club that vary considerably); verify the main budget items (wages, TV rights income, expenses for players' agents); check the financial management; check accounting and fiscal procedures; and react in the event of problems.

Q4: Why is it that you have needed to control the clubs since the 1990s?

FP: Since the 1980s, increasing budgets in professional football have led to excesses. Clubs pay higher and higher salaries, they rarely make a profit and consequently take on too many debts (a situation common to most professional sports – notable examples are Bordeaux, when Bez was President, and Marseille, when Tapie was President). High-profile deficits led the authorities to act in the 1990s and to create this level of control. The DNCG has a legal function, and preserves its independence by carrying out various tasks.

Q5: How do you guarantee this independence?

FP: Both by the way the DNCG functions and by the way its members are nominated. The DNCG is not an appointed committee, which differs from other commissions (the disciplinary committee, arbitrage and ethics committee, competitions' organization committee, etc.) inside the League. Members of these committees are appointed by the Board of Directors of the LFP (*Ligue de Football Professionnel*). The DNCG, however, comprises distinct commissions – a control commission for professional championships and clubs that have a seat in the League; a control commission for amateur championships and clubs that have a seat on the FFF (*Fédération Française de Football* – French Football Union); and a commission of appeal for the two previous commissions, which has a seat on the FFF. These commissions are totally independent in their decision-making and there are no direct connections between them.

The independence of members is guaranteed as a result of the way they are nominated.

The commission that controls professional championships includes:

- Five members appointed by the FFF (French Football Union)
- Five members appointed by the LFP (French Professional League)
- Two members appointed by the UCFP (Union for Professional Clubs)
- Two members appointed by the UNFP (Union for Professional Players)
- Two members appointed by the UNECATEF (Union for Football Coaches)
- Two members appointed by the SNAAF (Union for Workers in the Field of Football).

The commission therefore represents the so-called 'families of football'. Members are not paid, other than reimbursement of expenses. As a result, the LFP and FFF have no power over them, and becoming a member of a commission doesn't present an opportunity to launch a career in the football industry.

The organization is not centralized, and the members come from all over France.

Control commissions have dealings with the representatives of all clubs, so it is hard to imagine they could be in favour of one particular club. On the contrary, they try to treat all clubs equally.

Neither the League nor the Federation can penalize members of DNCG, which is a 'transversal' commission, meaning that it is inside French football but not influenced by its rules.

Most members are lawyers or certified public accountants whose code of ethics is very strong; therefore there is the expectation that they will act even-handedly and confidentially.

Q6: With such a structure, what are the attributes of the DNCG?
FP: Its tasks are varied. First, it needs to check criteria and see that laws are applied: this relates to the administrative structure of the club (is the structure compatible with the club's level?) and its financial means (it has to justify its projected income). That is why we need to sanction clubs when they don't respect the rules. We now also assist and supervise clubs, and make presentations to them about the legal aspects of the rules, to ensure that clubs are aware of them.

Regarding the financial criteria, we can evoke objective ratios, but also subjective criteria founded on experience – for example, whether shareholders can honour their commitments; whether the club can enforce its budget; whether the club's expectations are realistic; whether the club's management is stable; and what the club's history and relationship with the DNCG is like.

Q7: How can the DNCG sanction clubs?
FP: These sanctions are specified in Title 11 of the convention between FFF and LFP. If the financial situation of the club is not healthy, DNCG can sanction it by preventing recruitment of new players and controlling and limiting recruitment so that it is in line with the provisional budget and wage bill. This implies that all the contracts have to be checked by the DNCG before a player is bought by the club.

The club has a period to modify its budget. As a last resort, other sanctions can be taken, including relegating the club; expelling it from national championships; or prohibiting it from employing professional players.

To conclude this 'technical' discussion, I want to underline how people who belong to the DNCG try to apply equal treatment to all clubs. This does not mean we have never failed in the past.

Q8: Considering the increasing financial resources in the world of football, should we not consider another control system employing professional magistrates?
FP: No, I do not think so. Whether you check a small amateur club or a very big professional one, you have to undertake a similar process – only the magnitude of the numbers in the accounts changes. Also, I do not believe that every club has to be policed on a daily basis: financial excess is quite uncommon, and we should not be 'obsessed' by control.

Q9: Is the DNCG model uncommon in Europe?
FP: Yes. I am not an expert on other European countries, but I think our situation is unique. Other countries seem to let clubs manage their budgets alone, which sometimes leads to disaster (for example, in Italy, Fiorentina went bankrupt).

Q10: Do you think some big European clubs might be sanctioned if they had a DNCG in their country?
FP: Usually, sport in general, and football in particular, reflects the evolution of the economic situation of a country. If English clubs dominate the rest of Europe from a financial point of view, this is connected to their strong stock exchange showing, their experience in capitalism and their professional management of clubs. On the other hand, I wonder how Italian or Spanish clubs pay their players so much money, because their economies are usually seen as being weaker than ours. Where does the money come from? How can they buy the best players in the world without having balanced budgets?

Q11: Can you tell us about the project known as the 'UEFA licence'? Is this the beginning of regulation at a European level?

FP: No, it is a national control to ensure that every club can complete its championship season and European competitions. It started in the 2004–05 season, but appeared inefficient from the outset. Can you imagine a Spanish commission forbidding Real Madrid to enter the Champions League?

Q12: What is the position of the Minister of Sport, Jean-François Lamour, regarding the DNCG and the experimental role it plays?
FP: He supports our work and has adopted a quite equilibrated and moral position towards sport business in recent months, but I do not think he believes the DNCG should be exported.

Q13: Can we consider the management of French football as being healthier than it was in the 1990s?
FP: Yes, nowadays shareholders are conscious of what they do with their money. Every year, the DNCG checks the level of their capital. Even if some French clubs are in debt, this is a far cry from the Italian or Spanish situation where clubs are heavily in debt – our clubs pay their players regularly.

Q14: Some cynics claim that these strict controls make French clubs weaker and ultimately unable to compete at the highest level in Europe. What is your view of such allegations?
FP: That is ridiculous. There are many points there that we could discuss – for example, national insurance contributions, which increase clubs' expenses. Additionally, and here I speak as a football fan, I think we are missing something in our psychological approach to the game. I do not believe that Lyon would have been eliminated from the Champions League by a small Turkish team in 2002–03 with an Italian coach focused on tactics. In 1998 France won the soccer World Cup, but would it have succeeded if the players had not become 'hardened' through playing abroad?

Q15: Is it important to discuss the implications of 'unfair competition' in Europe? For example, there are questions about the way some Spanish clubs are financed.
FP: If Barcelona and Real Madrid were being financed by public funding, and this were proved by a European Commission inquiry, I think it would stop immediately: it is very similar to the Airbus/Boeing case. I do believe that we have reached a turning point, and we will perhaps fully understand the lessons in 10 years. TV rights income created conditions of huge revenue increases for football. The TV networks have realized that sport cannot be profitable when rights are set too high, and consequently many deals have fallen in value. As a result, there is speculation about who can survive in the changing economic environment. The survivors have to be financially healthy.

Q16: Do you believe our system could be regulated in a similar way to sport in the US (NBA or NFL)?
FP: No, I am against this model. I am not an expert in the US system, but I believe this is a kind of controlled liberalism, which is supposed to lead to equity. It is opaque because, for example, clubs can go over the salary cap. I prefer a more transparent system.

Q17: The DNCG system exists in other professional sports in France. What type of links do you have with them?
FP: Yes, the system is applied to rugby, basketball and handball. In 2003 we discussed at length the idea of a DNACG (DNCG for rugby) because Bordeaux-Bègles and Bourgoin-Jallieu were relegated for financial reasons. In July 2003, Bordeaux-Bègles' budget required an extra €775000. Apart from Toulouse, it was the only club that had never previously been relegated.

We see eye-to-eye with the other DNCGs: they too believe in independence. People are experts in different sports, but there is no fundamental difference – it is all finance and budgeting as applied to sport. In conclusion, I would reiterate that independence is the key to the system, and it would be very dangerous to let institutions regulate their own sport.

Co-marketing: a new challenge for football managers

Sergio Cherubini

Overview

Football is living through a difficult period at present because of its two opposing facets – the traditional side, involving patronage, versus the innovative and professional. Co-marketing (cooperative marketing) activities in particular, which are also carried out in other industries, can be very useful in helping to overcome this problem. However, this represents a new challenge for football managers.

The concept and the applications of co-marketing, which was used initially in the retail sector, derive from two marketing practices: 'product augmentation' and 'strategic alliances'.

We can differentiate co-marketing from sponsorship because the various partners play a more active role in co-marketing than in sponsorship, where they are simply financial contributors.

The co-marketing concept has often been applied in Italy, by Italian soccer clubs of different sizes. The examples detailed in this chapter have been chosen for their originality or significance.

Keywords

B2B, B2C, co-marketing, Italian soccer clubs

Introduction

Football is living through a difficult period at present because of its two opposing facets – the traditional side, involving patronage, versus the innovative and professional.

It is a fact that football is a worldwide success, including, as it does, the more developed countries as well as the less developed ones, children and adults, men and women, rich and poor, the illiterate and the educated. In spite of this great success there is a true economic paradox in that football clubs, both big and small, are facing financial difficulties even though demand is increasing.

The reason underlying this strange phenomenon is probably the incomplete evolution towards a professional and widespread soccer management system. In the recent past, some clubs have tried to improve their financial status by making use of specific manoeuvres, such as going public or managing the capital gains in trading athletes; however, these alone cannot remedy the main issue unless a professional management system is in place. Football marketing can and must make a strong contribution in providing stability for the clubs from both a local and a global standpoint. In particular, co-marketing (cooperative marketing) activities, which are also carried out in other industries, can be very useful, although they represent a new challenge for football managers.

The virtuous circle of the football club

The co-marketing challenge must take into account the club's need to serve two markets at the same time: the business-to-consumer (B2C) and the business-to-business (B2B) markets. Even if these two markets have different characteristics, they must be synergistic in order to enable the development of a significant 'virtuous circle', as illustrated in Figure 4.1.

In fact, the achievement of significant agonistic successes can stimulate the interest of both consumers and companies, together with a general improvement of the image. This interest easily converts to an increase in the various revenue streams – for example,

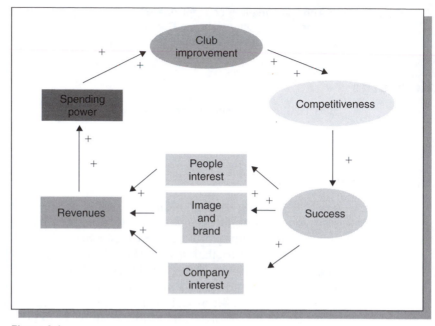

Figure 4.1
The virtuous circle of the football club

tickets, merchandising, television rights, sponsorships, stadium advertising, licensing and so on.

If properly managed, the revenue increase can encourage a company's spending power, thereby strengthening the football club on the agonistic and organizational levels, and thus resulting in stronger competitiveness on national and international scales. This virtuous circle should enable the club to improve its results and to start, if properly planned, an additional growth phase. Clearly there is the risk of failure which could, conversely, generate a downturn phase, leading to a 'vicious circle' from which it is not easy to escape because, as often happens, growth takes time but downturns tend to be sudden.

The risk of a vicious circle is particularly strong in the football industry where, as is well known, match results can depend on the consequence of hitting a post, on a defective rebound or on an arbitrary oversight. Moreover, football clubs should be more conscious of the risks during the expansive phases, when there is the danger of enthusiasm overtaking wisdom and attention. In other words, the uncertainty of results must be also managed, following the best practices used in other industries and known as 'risk management'.

To facilitate the start-up of the virtuous circle, the involvement of the various club's actors becomes crucial in what can be called 'football convergence'.

Football convergence

Sportsmen and media are becoming increasingly interested in the idea of football clubs progressively creating a 'football convergence', where different types of interested parties can be identified.

First are the football clubs and their representatives, such as the Federazione Italiana Giuoco Calcio and the Lega Italiana Calcio, which have a 'playmaker' role and should develop the initial form of co-marketing. In fact, as pointed out by numerous US sports organizations, football clubs should operate on a 'cooperation and competition' (coo-petition) base so that they can strengthen their activities at national and international levels.

Football clubs must offer their services to supporters, as part of a match or a practice, creating entertainment and emotions that can be greatly amplified by the classic media (magazines, radio, television) and more innovative high-tech media (the Internet, mobile phones, etc.). Thus, a match becomes an event to discuss seven days a week. In fact, no other sport is as attractive to the media as football.

These supporters (or football 'consumers') are actively involved in football convergence when they take on a leading role, as in all service-driven markets, as 'pro-sumers' (producers + consumers). They may have a positive influence, as when they create the atmosphere in the stadium, or a negative influence, when they cause violence, incidents and field invasions.

Technical and commercial sponsors are also playing an increasingly important role in this chain, by being able to contribute not only money but also know-how. In this sense, the technical partner base is expanding from suppliers of football/training equipment to include new partners that operate in other industries, such as ICT, insurance, finance, pharmaceuticals, travel, etc. Commercial partners are undergoing the same phenomenon, expanding from traditional consumer goods (such as food and groceries) to durable goods and services (such as cars, computers and telecommunication services). In addition to these typical profit-making organizations there is increased participation of government agencies, which have developed local marketing practices aimed at increasing tourism, both national and international, during matches and tournaments.

Figure 4.2 shows how football convergence works and how it allows the identification of new opportunities – especially in terms of cooperation – to promote the network approach.

Football stakeholders

The extraordinary development of the football world is certainly related to the fact that, for many reasons, a lot of people and

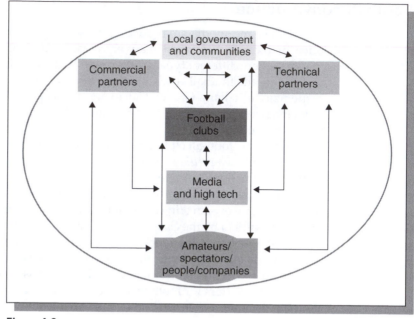

Figure 4.2
Football convergence

organizations are interested in the sport. This creates many opportunities, but also a commitment to respect the various football stakeholders. Therefore these stakeholders, both current and potential, must first be identified in order to manage them in the most appropriate way.

In this respect, football clubs – especially professional ones – need to adopt an attitude and behaviour consistent with corporate social responsibility, particularly as their success makes them a significant influence in the third millennium.

As shown in Figure 4.3, a football club is surrounded by a variety of people and organizations towards which it must show an open and positive attitude. These include local, national and international football clubs, football organizations that define rules and arrange tournaments, the organizers of football events, stadium managers, equipment manufacturers, service providers for football clubs, commercial sponsors, media companies, local and national government agencies, local communities and, last but not least, football fans. This long list of stakeholders underlines not only the vast number of people involved, but also the managerial complexity faced by football executives. Therefore, new approaches and new skills that were unnecessary some years ago have now become vital. Co-marketing is an example; it not only requires

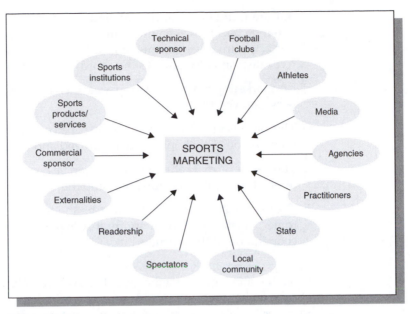

Figure 4.3
Sports marketing protagonists

current managers to widen their skill set, but also allows the creation of new managerial roles that until recently were unthinkable.

Football co-marketing

The concept and the applications of co-marketing, which was initially used in the retail sector, derive from two marketing practices: 'product augmentation' and 'strategic alliances'.

The term 'co-marketing' describes the process by which two or more subjects (public or private), one of which is at least strictly identifiable as being part of a sports organization, develop planned, organized or controlled marketing activities in order to achieve marketing objectives (which may be common or specific, but are mutually compatible) through the satisfaction of the customers.

Based on this definition, we can differentiate co-marketing from sponsorship by the fact that the various partners play a more active role in co-marketing rather than simply providing financial support, as in sponsorship.

Regarding the definition of co-marketing given above, we must emphasize a number of basic points:

1. The term 'co-marketing' can only be used when there are at least two players involved in activities that can be independent

but are mutually coordinated and reciprocally accepted. The situation becomes even more attractive when there are numerous actors involved, as this can lead to a potentially multiplicative effect and also adds to the coordination complexity.

2. Co-marketing aims to develop a partnership in which all partners gain value.

3. The various initiatives, even if only for a certain period of time, must be consciously planned, organized and controlled.

4. The partners' marketing objectives can be common or even different, but in all cases must be compatible.

5. The co-marketing objective must be the improvement of customer satisfaction ('offer more at a lower cost') through the cooperation of the partners.

Once the abovementioned elements have been clarified, we can clearly understand the significance of co-marketing today. First, in order to be successful a company must give more to the consumer, which entails higher investments – human, financial, technical and relational – which a single organization often cannot afford, especially in terms of the organizational risk involved. Secondly, co-marketing provides a great opportunity for 'cross-fertilization' among different cultures. Sports co-marketing can draw big advantages from these cooperative experiences, in that it stimulates a sharing of experiences and culture. This in turn can accelerate the innovation process, which is necessary in order to compete – especially at an international level.

A further interesting aspect of co-marketing concerns the multitude of marketing areas in which it can be applied – from analytical marketing to strategic and operational marketing. Typical examples include events organizations, trade agreements, promo-advertising campaigns, technical collaborations, market research, overseas market penetration, programmes for mass media, etc.

Some points in particular should be analysed in more detail, and these are discussed below.

1. *Which are the possible leading actors in football co-marketing?*
   The main actor(s) will comprise not only one or more football clubs (either single team or professional league), federations, organizing committees and individual athletes, but also equipment and clothing producers, sponsors, partners, specialized agencies, mass media, etc. Players involved in the organizational context can also be included, such as companies involved with insurance, finance, transportation, food, tourism, assistance, etc.

2. *Which models of cooperation can be adopted for football co-marketing?*
   In effect, as in many other sectors, collaboration is first of all a state of mind rather than a juridical form – although the emotional aspect can be either a help or a hindrance to the cooperative process. There is a vast array of models of cooperation, ranging from a strong formal relationship in which equity is swapped, to occasional agreements with no structure at all.
   The collaboration can be implemented, from an organizational standpoint, in various ways:
   - formally or informally
   - horizontally or vertically
   - for the short term or an indefinite length of time
   - as an occasional or continual process
   - equitably or inequitably
   - with specific or separate brands;
   - for profit or not for profit.

   Obviously, a formalized relationship can help to consolidate the cooperation and therefore be viewed in a positive way; nevertheless, the legal and administrative aspects can become a burden and prevail over the marketing purposes, thereby contradicting the very nature of football co-marketing.

3. *Which are the critical success factors?*
   The success of a collaboration becomes critical after the agreement (formal or informal) has been signed. In many cases, a great deal of effort and energy is spent in defining the terms and making the agreement official via press conferences, releases, etc. In reality, the critical path to success starts when the agreement is actually enacted – when the two or more partners must begin to cooperate on a day-by-day basis, in a coordinated and loyal way. Generally, major issues in a collaboration arise after the agreement has started rather than before; this is also true in the football industry. Moreover, successful cooperation is not guaranteed by legal agreements but, as is often said, by the 'spark in the eyes of the partners' that allows the partners to understand, sometimes instinctively and irrationally, that they are speaking the same language, share the same objectives and have a common will to achieve a successful collaboration.
   The risks related to collaboration are increased when the partners come from different industries or cultural backgrounds; however, the results from such a partnership can be much better than those achieved by companies that have similar profiles. This is why it is often worth taking such a risk.
   Finally, in this context, the central role of the human factor in successful cooperations and also in football co-marketing must be emphasized. Consequently, organizations such as universities,

other educational organizations and research agencies become crucial players that must somehow stimulate enrichment and cultural learning in an innovative way.

Football co-marketing experiences in Italy

The abovementioned concepts have been applied in many Italian football clubs, of different sizes. The examples detailed below have been chosen for their originality or significance.

Juventus FC[1]

Juventus, as it is commonly known, is the 'squadra' that has won the greatest number of Italian football championships (twenty-seven). It can be considered as the Italian football benchmark, also known as 'the Juventus style'. Among the numerous experiences of co-marketing some are particularly memorable, and these are described in Boxes 4.1–4.3.

Box 4.1:   Juventus FC–Fastweb

Objectives
- To increase the awareness of Fastweb services via an itinerant promotion to support the Fastweb sponsorship of Juventus FC
- To create brand awareness
- To sell Fastweb subscriptions.

Targets
Supporters of Juventus FC and residents of the visiting towns. The itinerant promotion followed Juventus FC to its football matches outside Turin.

Initiatives
- An itinerant tour to promote Fastweb services followed a number of matches: Torino–Juventus, Juventus–Bologna, Inter–Juventus, Juventus–Lazio, Juventus–Milan and Juventus–Udinese. The dates were: Turin, 21–24 February; Bologna, 1–3 March; Milan, 7–10 March; Rome, 28–30 March; Genoa, 11–14 April; and Naples, on 2–5 May.
- At each town visited, a balloon was present in the main square; inside this it was possible to try the Fastweb services. The balloon was equipped with PC, Fastweb TV, videocommunication stations and game posts.

---

[1]In spite of being a marketing example, the club was relegated in 2006 for being involved in corruption scandals.

- The theme of the tour was 'Challenge Juventus', and an *ad hoc* video game was developed in which it was possible to challenge (and perhaps win) against Juventus. Winners received a small football. This campaign allowed the promotion to reach non-Juventus supporters.
- There was a 'Home cinema' incentive – those people who subscribed to Fastweb in the balloon were entered into a draw to win one of three Sony home cinemas.

Box 4.2:   Juventus FC–Ospedale Gaslini

(This co-marketing activity won the Italian Football Marketing Award in 2003.)

This project was born in June 2000 and themed 'A dream for the Gaslini' ONLUS (i.e. a non-profit organization dedicated to social aims). It was established by the players of the Juventus Football Club and by the Area Marketing Atleti of the Club.

Objectives

- To renovate the Abbey of San Gerolamo di Quarto, adjacent to the Gaslini Hospital in Genova, and dedicate it to non-medical activities – classrooms for the children who are missing school because of illness, a gymnasium for physical rehabilitation, an area for games and entertainment, and guestrooms for parents so they can afford to stay near their hospitalized children
- To use the funds raised to renovate the Abbey and also to help with the patients' convalescence and their transition back to the outside world.

First phase

The commitment to make this dream come true began in September 2000, with the publication of a photographic book, *A Dream in Black and White* (black and white are the colours of Juventus), containing all the players of Juventus. Big companies (such as L'Oréal Professionnel, Giochi Preziosi Sport, Kodak, Weber & Broutin, Lotto, Ciaoweb, Banca Sella and TNT) contributed to the making of this book. In the following months, a T-shirt with the inscription 'A dream in black and white' and the signatures of the players was released, together with a videocassette of the backstage areas and the visits of the players to the children in the hospital. The money collected from sales and the contribution of the companies amounted to a net total of €619 748 at Christmas 2001, plus €1 032 914 from an inheritance of the founders of the hospital.

Second phase

The objective of the second phase was to collect additional funds. In the second year of the project, called 'the dream goes on', new merchandise with the image of the players was released and new pro-motional activities were being carried out in order to reach a wider audi-ence, differentiating the offer according to the spending power of the target segment. Calendars (13 719), T-shirts (7 399) and phone cards of the Tiscali collection (5 000) were sold at €15.50, €20.60 and €5 each, respectively. To make the general public aware of the project, during the Juventus–Perugia match the players of the team wore a jersey with the inscription 'the dream goes on' and a helmet from Weber&Broutin; this symbolized their commitment. The jerseys were then sold on the eBay site, in synergy with the Tiscali site.

The Dream Goes On *and the presentation to the media of the restructuring project of the Abbey.*

On Monday 6 May 2002, some Juventus players, on behalf of the whole the team, celebrated the victory of the twenty-sixth *scudetto* with the children of the Gaslini Hospital. During that event, the book *The Dream Goes On* was presented to the media – a crane delivered a sack containing the first volumes of the book into the garden of the abbey, and this was opened by the players, who were wearing hard hats. As well as releasing the contents of the book, the restructuring project for the Abbey of San Gerolamo was presented during a press conference. The day continued with a visit to the Abbey, during which the project's technical staff illustrated the phases of the restructuring project. The day ended with the players visiting the children in the hospital.

eBay sales of the materials used to create the calendar and the book

From 25 June to 24 October 2002, each Tuesday more than 220 exclusive personal articles belonging to the players and to Juventus' management, together with the materials used to create the book *The Dream Goes On* and the 2002 calendar were sold on eBay. The technical material used by the players (including the hard hats) was sold.

Later, during preparation for the new tournament, the players added personalized autographs to the fifty-six articles sold during the first four days of the online auction. On Tuesday 24 October 2002, in the Stadio Comunale of Turin, the players delivered the last of their articles to be sold on eBay.

Additional activities in 2003

At the beginning of 2003 a television programme on RAI UNO was organized, in which the Juventus team, together with its VIP sup-porters, helped to raise the funds necessary to restructure the Abbey of San Gerolamo di Quarto. Some players also participated in the Sanremo Festival, supporting the initiative by singing and asking the audience for donations to the hospital.

Box 4.3: Juventus FC–Caffè Mauro

Objectives
- To create and market a line of coffee devoted to a specific target
- To launch the Juventus brand in the coffee market.

Targets
Juventus FC supporters and their parents and friends, characterized by young age, medium/low economic segment and with an above-average female presence.

Opportunities
- The distribution of the supporters of the Juventus FC in Italy is in line with the distribution of the selling outlets of Caffè Mauro; in particular, the companies of the GDO (Grande Distribuzione Organizzata) are prominent in the regions with high levels of Juventus supporters
- The typical consumer of Caffè Mauro has similar characteristics to those of Juventus supporters, in terms of income, age, sex and geographic distribution
- Both the companies have a strong penetration of their market (60 per cent for Juventus, 90 per cent for Caffè Mauro)
- The two partners have similar values (energy, passion, popularity, tradition, Italian spirit).

Positioning
An exclusive product, of quality, palatable for general occasions, and not aimed for seasonal consumption; positioned in the high segment of the market.

Product
- Name: Juvespresso
- Packaging: tin, from 250 g, black in colour
- Mixture of high quality (70 per cent Arabic/30 per cent robust) beans, grinding by express.

Pricing
- Premium price
- Price to the dealer.

Distribution
- Traditional channels – sold using the distribution channel used by Caffè Mauro (modern distribution, specialized retail, public exercises, overseas market)
- Other channels – innovative distribution channels, such as the merchandising catalogue of the Juventus FC, and the Juvestore.

Communication

The launch of the Juvespresso product was implemented by the following initiatives:

- Presentation mailing to the retailer
- Promotion on the point of sale, with tasting opportunities in an *ad hoc* stand with the Juventus FC and Caffè Mauro brand
- An advertising campaign on Hurrà Juventus (started in August 2001) characterized by a friendly message, simple and immediate, and structured according a 'tease and reveal' approach (double page)
- Promotional activity during the house matches of Juventus
- Consumer promotion (started in October 2002) with access to exclusive premiums and with loyalty cards.

Internazionale FC

The Internazionale FC has developed numerous co-marketing initiatives, some of which are linked with the financial industry (see Boxes 4.4 and 4.5).

Box 4.4: Internazionale FC–Winterthur Assicurazioni

In 2002 Inter presented to its supporters, in collaboration with one of its 'more faithful' partners, Winterthur Assicurazioni, a co-marketing initiative: the insurance service 'Intersicura'. This consisted of three policies characterized by strong services and exclusive benefits:

1. A vehicle policy named 'Drive&go', with benefits of reserved parking and a taxi to the stadium in case of a breakdown or accident
2. A policy dedicated to the practice of every amateur sport, named 'AllSport'
3. A '100Stadi' policy, including travel insurance and all risks cover, allowing the holder to follow the team without anxiety or stress.

Technically, this is a form of direct insurance, with customer/company interaction by telephone or the Internet. Presented on the occasion of the Inter–Juventus match, the initiative was promoted by a live event on the website Inter.it and on InterChannel.

The launch made great use of the Inter site, with many banners and rotors in the stadium, and a specialised sound system and rigging for two thirty-minute radio spots. Mural billposting was also important, with a teaser phase and one at the launch. There were postings in the dailies *La Gazzetta dello Sport*, *La Repubblica* and *Corriere della Sera*, and in the magazines *Sportweek* and *Inter FC*. There was also a promotional initiative (a discount of 20 per cent on the season ticket price for subscribers to the Drive&go policy), where dynamic billposting was used on the underground.

> **Box 4.5: Internazionale FC–Banca Popolare di Milano**
>
> From the collaboration between Banca Popolare di Milano (the financial partner of Internazionale FC) and CartaSì; was born a new opportunity for the *neroazzurri* supporters: InterCard, the Inter credit card. To differentiate it from similar products issued by other clubs, InterCard presents specific advantages, tuned to the world of football, in the Classic, Gold and Platinum versions. InterCard was promoted by advertising in *La Gazzetta dello Sport*, by dynamic promotions in the subway, by posters and rotors in the stadium, and by radio announcements. Events and premiums were promoted on the Inter website, and with postcards of the Promocard network.

AC Milan

AC Milan has developed many co-marketing initiatives during recent years, starting with one with its main sponsor, GM-Opel. However, here we describe a less well-known example, activated in the ambit of the Progetto Giovani (see Box 4.6).

> **Box 4.6: AC Milan (Progetto Giovani)–Azienda Promozione Turistica Dolomiti di Brenta and Altopiano della Paganella**
>
> In 2001 an agreement was made between AC Milan, the Azienda di Promozione Turistica (APT) Dolomiti di Brenta, and the Altopiano of Paganella. This was aimed at families and children throughout the year. Having evaluated the positive results of the collaboration in the previous season, the APT decided to renew the agreement with the Milan Progetto Giovani for the season 2002/03.
>
> **Objectives**
>
> The Milan Progetto Giovani was chosen as a qualified vehicle for the promotion of the Trentino area within the ambit of marketing aimed at the implementation of a tourist strategy directed at families and children. Over the whole year, Andalo and the other two resorts of the Altopiano of Paganella (Molveno and Fai) organized many initiatives and activities scheduled by AC Milan, becoming the official tourist resort of the Progetto Giovani. The territory that includes Andalo, Molveno and Fai of Paganella is to a large extent within the natural park Adamello Brenta. The Dolomites, the splendid waters of the Molveno Lake and the natural park are very popular destinations for

excursionists and nature-lovers. The sports facilities and the natural beauty of the district are only some of the reasons why the Progetto Giovani chose this area as the official tourist resort of the project.

The points of the agreement

- Special discounts for the *rossoneri* supporters – all AC Milan supporters could take advantage of exclusive discounts of 10 per cent on skiing facilities in the Trentino district in the winter months
- The 'Week-Rossonero' Event in Andalo was held on 8–10 March 2002. AC Milan scheduled a weekend trip to Andalo, appearing on the snow with the *rossoneri* colours. This was a weekend holiday of 3 days, with sport, amusement and culture, and attracted more than 300 persons. On Friday 8 March 2002, there was a celebration of the 'Festa delle donne' (Women's Celebration) in the local ice palace, presented by the DJ of Radio Dimensione Suono. On Saturday 9 March 2002, in the morning there was the first round of the skiing Mgeneration Cup. All day on Saturday, in Andalo town square, there was the Mgeneration Park – the theme park of AC Milan – for young people. In the afternoon there was a Broomball Tournament – a game similar to hockey, where the traditional stick and puck are replaced by street-sweeper and ball, and where in place of classic skates the players wear shoes with suction cups on the sole so they can remain on their feet. The evening was open-ended, with a typical *trentino* dinner in the hotels. Later, all the participants went to the big Pala Congressi for the Mgeneration Party, a big final event presented by Ugo Conti and Roberto Ceriotti. Among the hosts were Claudio Amendola and Jury Chechi.
- The Milan Junior Camp. Molveno was chosen as the centre for the summer sports activities for the Milan Junior Camp, and the retreat of the 'Primavera' team. Milan Junior Camp is a sports holiday that is safe, entertaining and informative for football fans. All the young footballers, aged between eight and fifteen years, were coached by the trainers of the Milan juvenile sector. Molveno was one of the centres of the MJC that had some weeks dedicated exclusively to girls.
- Retreat pre-championship of the 'Primavera' team. The retreat was unrolled in Molveno from 1–12 August 2002. During the retreat different activities were scheduled, including a friendly match against a local team and a public meeting with the trainer Mauro Tassotti.

Smaller Italian clubs

Clubs much smaller than Juventus, Internazionale and Milan can develop co-marketing activities in a coherent way. Among the various experiences, three cases have been chosen (see Boxes 4.7–4.9).

Box 4.7: Reggina Calcio–Caffè Mauro

Objectives
- To create a concrete social value in the partnership between Reggina Calcio and Caffè Mauro
- To stimulate the ability of young people regarding the project
- To involve young people in the economic theme, thanks to enthusiasm for the local club.

Target
Students of middle schools in Reggio Calabria.

School project
This was entitled 'The values of sports and companies'. The driving idea was to promote the values of the enterprise (economic and social).

Project content
Concorso asked that students form teams to collaborate in elaborating on the theme 'The values of sports and companies'. The students were asked to understand and explain the values of productiveness and personal challenge that the two types of organizations represented. There was complete freedom regarding the choice of the presentation format (pictorial, model, multimedia, etc.). There was the opportunity for participants to examine the Mauro facilities (to investigate the production process of the coffee) and to watch a Reggina training session, so that they could interact with representatives of Caffè Mauro and Reggina in order to study the theme in depth.

Prize
The prize was €5165 to be used for improvement of the school structure of the winning team. Presentation of the prize would be at the last home match of the season (Reggina–Milan).

Box 4.8: Vicenza Calcio–Centrale del Latte di Vicenza

Vicenza objectives
- To create a stadium safety area suitable for families and young people
- To encourage families to go to the stadium
- To construct a programme to encourage young people to become supporters
- To create a positive image of football, the club and players.

Centrale del Latte objectives

- To target families and young people from six to sixteen years of age
- To regain market share after two years of downturn
- To join the brand to the town and the province
- To create more visibility for the brand in the province
- To allow young people in the province to sample the products.

Activities

- Modernizing stand in the Menti stadium and naming it 'Tribuna Famiglia Centrale del Latte'
- Scheduling an initiative called 'school and sport' in the middle and high schools of the province
- Scheduling 'shoot-out' for boys during the interval of matches.

The family stand Centrale del Latte

The family stand in the Menti stadium was to consist of 1200 seats, exclusively for families and children under the age of sixteen years. The sponsored stand was to be named 'Centrale del Latte', with company branding inside the stadium.

Vicenza Calcio invested €7500 to renew the ex lateral stand and make it more attractive and comfortable for families. Prices in the stand were also lowered – for example, a season ticket cost only €15 for children aged eight to sixteen years.

The school and sport initiative

The initiative, implemented with the collaboration of the players, consisted of visiting the middle and high schools in the province, speaking about sport values (for example, 'say no to drugs', 'say no to racism', 'say yes to a healthy diet for well-balanced physical growth'.

The project, sponsored by Centrale del Latte, included the distribution of products in visits to the students. The visits were scheduled weekly; one player attended each visit, accompanied by some managers of the Vicenza Calcio and of the Centrale del Latte. The students were able to ask questions of the player for about an hour. In every visit, Vicenza Calcio gave two official balls to the school and a gadget to every student. The player also donated his jersey to the school. During the meeting, Vicenza Calcio had a cloth on the table with the logos of the club and of Centrale del Latte, with the inscription: 'Together to win tomorrow'. Photographs were taken and published in the local press.

The project was supported by the coordinator for physical education of the provincial office of Vicenza.

The shoot-out

Vicenza Calcio, together with Centrale del Latte, invited 50–100 students from each visited school to a tournament match, seating them in the family stand. Ten students were invited onto the field in the interval to take part in a shoot-out. The students wore jerseys sponsored by Centrale del Latte, there was a stadium commentary on the penalties, and the spectators were involved.

Results

1. *The family stand Centrale del Latte.* The stand has been full for every home match. To communicate the sponsorship to the stadium, many media have been used:
   - advertising in the stand
   - aural messages, during and after matches
   - printed advertising on the back of every admission ticket to the stadium in the season 2002/03 (about 200 000 tickets)
   - printed advertising on the posters giving the prices of the game for the season 2002/03 (500)
   - advertising to the stadium (about 200 000 spectators in the audience in a season)
   - advertising in the Vicenza magazine (3000 copies monthly)
   - advertising in the match programme (5000 copies per game).
2. *School and sport.* By the end of the season, Vicenza Calcio and Centrale del Latte had visited about 35 schools in the province and seen 6000 students. The project created high visibility for Vicenza Calcio and Centrale del Latte in the *Giornale di Vicenza*, TV di Vicenza, TV 68, TV Serena, and Rivista Vicenza Biancorossa. After just 3 months, the company was able to see results of the project in which it had invested.
3. *The shoot-out.* Every school accepted the invitation to the stadium. The event created visibility on the field in the interval of every game. Vicenza Calcio used the sound engineer to communicate the project to the fans when the children took part in the shoot-out. By the end of the season, nearly 200 boys had had the opportunity of taking part, and Centrale del Latte gave every boy a numbered coat.

Box 4.9: Treviso FC–Benetton Basket–Sisley Volley–Benetton Rugby Club–Verde Sport Club–Treviso Provincial Council

Objectives
- To create a 'School for Fair and Creative Supporters'
- To teach pupils of Treviso Provincial Council civil relationships, fair support and enthusiasm, coming from a true sporting spirit, through meeting the most significant sportsmen of local teams
- To create positive group relationships among children inside stadiums and the Palaverde in order to promote interest, active participation and enthusiasm regarding Treviso FC, Sisley Volley, Benetton Basket and Benetton Rugby Club

- To encourage children's creativity by teaching simple figurative and expressive techniques to support their favourite teams
- To train children to discover how important it is to be enthusiastic in all life activities
- To arouse interest in a team in order to show children that their support may be of crucial importance in winning a match.

Activities

During the domestic matches, in Treviso many children, wearing colourful scarves, have started supporting their champions with the help of three adult educators of the Comunica Association. Before the beginning of the matches, a workshop is open where the young supporters can use their imagination to make each match a creative occasion and use different figurative and expressive techniques to support their champions.

Thanks to the contribution of Treviso Football Club, Treviso Provincial Council and the Sport Councillor, since 2004–05 the 'School for Supporters' has had the chance to develop two more ideas: organizing meetings on fair support between primary–secondary school students and basketball players, and supporting Treviso FC matches. Since the end of the last season, some referees of different sports have also taken part in the meetings together with the children.

Thanks to the help of the Treviso Sport Councillor, during the school year several meetings are organized in primary and second-ary schools. These are important occasions for the students to talk to basketball, football and volleyball players, as well as to referees, jour-nalists, policemen and other people who have an active role during the matches. These meetings are planned in advance together with the teachers. The main aim is to let students ask questions and get involved in discussion with players and referees.

During the matches of Treviso FC, Sisley Volley and Benetton Basket, joining the 'School for Supporters' is free of charge. The 'School for Supporters' is located in a reserved area where children can hang up their banners, rehearse their animated settings, sing their songs and play the simple musical instruments given by Treviso Provincial Council. The children are always guided by a group of educators from the Comunica Association – there are at least three adults, and the maximum ratio of children to adults is 25 : 1. In order better to involve the children and to make them feel proud of being members of the Dragons, they are allowed to take part in special activities – for exam-ple, to go into the venue before a match together with the players, get-ting their autographs and visiting the locker rooms.

In 2005–06 the project should increase again, and involve the Benetton Rugby Club – especially during the European Cup matches. All the meetings taking place during next school year among players, referees and students have the aim of creating a short magazine on fair support, collecting together all the ideas and contributions. It will be distributed at Palaverde, at Tenni Stadium and in Monigo Stadium during the last matches of the season, as well as being sent to the main sporting clubs and press agencies. Students will have the task of writing a list of rules to be followed by fair supporters, some articles on sport, some interviews, and their opinions on the experience of going to the stadium. This magazine will become an important part of the White Book on fair support that is going to be written on the occasion of the European programme 'Tifiamo insieme' ('Let's support together').

Conclusions

Football is living through a very complex period, but this also represents an opportunity to build a more professional and transparent management system within the football industry. In this respect, marketing can contribute significantly to improve the service and product performance offered to consumers, and thereby increase their satisfaction. However, this offer enhancement requires investments and know-how that are not easily available in the short term, and therefore alliances are a necessary step in the context of football convergence, enabling companies to access a diverse and skilled pool of people.

In this managerial growth context, co-marketing (or cooperative marketing) represents a specific challenge whereby we can offer more at a lower cost. Clearly this challenge can be addressed only if the players, irrespective of their industry, are able to develop a 'win–win' partnership.

Co-marketing examples are becoming more numerous, but there are still opportunities to grow remarkably in both quantity and quality. In this sense, football marketing can be at the forefront not only of the sports industry but also of other businesses, and become a frontier of the new marketing applications rather than a tailgate, as it has been considered for many years.

These cooperation models can involve not only players operating in the same sports sector, but also technical or commercial partners, local and governmental agencies and non-profit organizations. In such sense, creativity and rationality are fundamental skills that have to be properly blended in the project management – an increasingly important reference for the football manager.

Bibliography and references

Ballarin, A. (1988). *Il calcio da Franchi a Berlusconi*. SugarCo.
Bottelli, P. (1996). E il pallone sgonfio finisce in rete. *Mondo Economico*, 16 September.

Cafferata, R. (1998). Tendenze strutturali della crescita dello sport come business. *Economia e Diritto del Terziario*, **1**.

Censis Servizi (1996). *Struttura organizzativa e orientamento al marketing nelle società calcistiche*. Censis Servizi.

Cherubini, S. (1996). *Il marketing dei servizi*. Franco Angeli.

Cherubini, S. (1998). Principali tendenze del marketing sportivo. *Economia e Diritto del Terziario*, **1**.

Cherubini, S. (2000). *Il Marketing sportivo*. Franco Angeli.

Cherubini, S. and Canigiani, M. (eds) (1997). *Il marketing delle società sportive*. Guerini&Associati.

Cherubini, S. and Canigiani, M. (eds) (1998). *Esperienze internazionali nel marketing sportivo*. Giappichelli.

Cherubini, S. and Canigiani, M. (eds) (1999). *Il Co-marketing sportivo. Strategie di cooperazione nel mercato sportive*. Franco Angeli.

Cherubini, S. and Canigiani, M. (eds) (2000). *Media e co-marketing sportivo. Strategie di convergenza nel mercato sportivo*. Franco Angeli.

Cherubini, S. and Canigiani, M. (eds) (2001). *Campioni e co-marketing sportivo*. Franco Angeli.

Cherubini, S. and Canigiani, M. (eds) (2002). *Internet Sport Co-Marketing*. Franco Angeli.

Cherubini, S., Canigiani, M. and Santini, A. (eds) (2003). *Il co-marketing degli impianti sportivi*. Franco Angeli.

Cherubini, S., Canigiani, M. and Santini, A. (eds) (2005). *Marketing, comunicazione, eventi. L'esperienza dello sport*. Franco Angeli.

dell'Osso, F. and Szymansky, S. (1991). Who are the champions? (An analysis of football and architecture). *Business Strategy Review*, Summer.

Echikson, W., Dawley, H., Larner, M. and Robinson, A. (1996). Football's big score. *Business Week*, 16 September.

Ferrero, G. and Cherubini, S. (1999). *Dalle transazioni alle relazioni, ai network: il caso dello sport*. Convegno AIDEA, McGraw-Hill.

Mullin, B.J., Hardy, S. and Sutton, W.A. (1993). *Sport Marketing*. Human Kinetics Publishers.

Nys, J. F. (1999). La mondialisation du football: une realité pour la fédération internationale, une necessité pour les clubs professionnels. *Revue Française du Marketing*, **172**.

Polizzi, D. (1996). Il calcio? E' nel pallone. *Il Mondo*, **36**.

Schapira, L. (1999). Le sponsoring de la coupe du monde de football 1998. *Revue Française du Marketing*, **172**.

Szymanski, S. (1993). The economics of footballing success. *Economic Review*, April.

Szymanski, S. and Smith, R. (1996). The English football industry: profit, performance and industrial structure. *International Review of Applied Economics*, Winter.

Szymanski, S. and Kuypers, L. (1999). *Winners & Losers. The business strategy of football*. Viking.

Tropea, S. (1996). Business e spettacolo, la mia Juventus è nel futuro. La Coppa di Umberto Agnelli. *La Repubblica*, 24 May.

Venables, T. (1996). *Venables' England. The making of the team.* Boxtree Ltd.

Welling, B., Baker, S., Templeman, J. and Ryser, J. (1986). The biggest game on earth. *Business Week*, 2 June.

Sport marketing and facility management: from stadiums to customer-based multipurpose leisure centres

Paolo Guenzi

Overview

This chapter discusses a market research technique managers may use to support decision-making processes concerning the transformation of football stadiums into multipurpose recreational facilities. First, we briefly introduce the more peculiar aspects of sport marketing and elaborate an interpretative model of brand equity for a sports club. We then analyse strategies and processes of marketing management aimed at achieving and increasing customer equity, and in doing this point out some trends in the football business and their consequences for clubs, especially in terms of the implications for marketing strategies and activities. More specifically, we analyse the prospects of transforming stadiums into multipurpose leisure centres which provide a wide range of services. To do this, we assess the preferences of prospective users of such centres, in comparison with alternatives and other offers, by empirical research based on conjoint analysis.

Finally, we present an interview with Giuseppe Rizzello of FC Internazionale (see Appendix 5.1) regarding stadium management today.

Keywords

professional football teams, stadium, marketing strategy, conjoint analysis, market research

Introduction

Sport management is a field traditionally overlooked in academic managerial literature, despite the growing economic significance and management complexity that characterize it.

This work aims at defining some interpretative models of marketing management which can be employed for professional sports club, as well as studying one of the most relevant topics regarding such a context – that is, the reshaping of the facilities provided for sporting events in multipurpose leisure spaces. To that end, we will focus on professional football clubs and will present the output of exploratory empirical research.

In more detail, the aims of this study are:

- to introduce the more peculiar aspects of sport marketing

- to elaborate an interpretative model of brand equity for a sports club

- to analyse strategies and processes of marketing management aimed at achieving and increasing customer equity of professional sports clubs

- to indicate some trends in the football business and their consequences for clubs, especially in terms of implications for marketing strategies and activities

- to analyse the prospects of transforming stadiums into multipurpose leisure centres which provide a wide range of services
  within the same area

- to assess the preferences of prospective users of such centres, in
  comparison with alternatives and other offers, by performing
  empirical research based on conjoint analysis.

These points are dealt with below.

Sport marketing: preliminary observations

Sport represents a relevant and constantly growing business.
According to some figures, sport accounts for 2.5 per cent of international trade (Meeneghan and Sullivan, 1999). Parallel to the economic development of this market, sport marketing – which can be
defined as all activities designed to meet the needs and wants of
sport consumers through exchange processes – has also expanded.
Sport marketing has developed two major thrusts: the marketing
of sport products and services directly to consumers of sport, and
the marketing of other consumer and industrial products or services through the use of sport promotions (Mullin *et al.*, 1993: 9).

Such definition emphasizes the importance of first distinguishing
between marketing *of* sport and marketing *through* sport: in fact, the
former refers to the activities performed by actors who take part
directly in the production of sport phenomena, while the latter is
meant to stress the presence of a number of subjects who employ
sport as a communicative means or tool to promote the awareness
or image of their own brand or goods. Mass media – which perform
a fundamental role between producers and consumers of sport
entertainment, that is between supply and demand – are positioned
between these two classes of actors.

Naturally, the abovementioned actors are closely interconnected,
and thus there are potentially virtuous circles between managing
processes related to the marketing of sport and marketing through
sport which can allow the subjects involved in sport marketing to
benefit from one another (Cherubini, 1997).

We do not, however, mean to analyse sport marketing as a
whole here; that is beyond the scope of our study. We simply wish
to stress the variety of the subjects which are to be found – with
different 'products' – within the complex sport business, as well
as the wide range of meanings and practical applications of the

marketing concept in this sector (Brooks, 1996). It is difficult to circumscribe sport marketing in general terms, as it is problematic to present an ultimate and commonly shared definition of sport as a product and also of the customer to whom it can be offered (Meenaghan and O'Sullivan, 1999).

An interpretative model of brand equity of professional sports clubs

Our aim here is to analyse the role that can be performed by marketing activities in managing professional sports clubs, as well as the nature of the resources which such activities should try to produce and increase. With regard to this, Irwin *et al.* (1999) have developed a multidimensional performance indicator for sports clubs, called the Team Marketing Index (TMI). This simultaneously takes into consideration four different indicators: the number of spectators, the percentage of season-ticket holders, the rate of those who renew their tickets, and the rate of both sponsor and advertiser retention. Authors have investigated the correlation between such measures of marketing performance and a number of indicators of management excellence, on the one hand, and the percentage of victories achieved by teams in agonistic competitions on the other. This research, which involved 100 employees of the marketing function of 15 US professional clubs of various disciplines (baseball, basketball, ice hockey and football), winning records and prospective catchment areas, has shown that TMI is correlated not only with the team's winning record – which evidently does not depend on the marketing function – but also with other factors at least partially controlled by it, in particular the club's capability to be close to customers. Such closeness (expressed in terms of being able to listen to the customer, to offer post-sales service and personalized customer care) has been found also to be correlated with specific performance indicators of the TMI, such as the number of spectators and the rate of renewal of season tickets. On the contrary, the indicator of performance expressed as 'rate of sponsor and advertiser retention' does not seem to be correlated with the team's winning percentage, but rather with other factors expressing the management excellence of the professional sports club. Based on the results of this research, the capability (either actual or prospective) of winning in agonistic competitions represents the fundamental driver to the acquisition of both mass and business customers. However, the retention of the latter seemingly depends, for the most part, on management factors that the company can have more control of, such as customer orientation and the creation of a dedicated staff who specialize in managing the relationship with a specific target (namely sponsors, corporate customers, season-ticket holders, etc.). Although, as previously stated, success in sporting events considerably contributes to a team's commercial performance, it can also be inferred that marketing processes may make a significant contribution to it.

It is necessary to emphasize in particular the role that market orientation and marketing processes may perform as far as the aim to increase a club's brand equity is concerned. To this end, we intend to propose a conceptual model that stresses how such a purpose can be achieved mostly through a club's ability to attract spectators, media and sponsors alike, thanks to mechanisms of reciprocal fuelling (see Figure 5.1).

To sum up, the team's success in competitions allows an increase in customer equity in many ways – in particular, by virtue of the acquisition of new supporters, which leads to expansion of the customer base, and by an increase in the involvement and loyalty of pre-existing supporters. The latter typically shows in the increase in the number of spectators and season-ticket holders, as far as both competitions and recognition by the media are concerned, but it also expresses itself through a stronger propensity to purchase the club's branded goods, and it therefore enhances the pursuit of brand extension strategies.

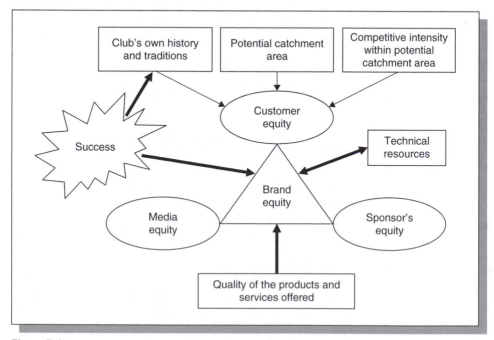

Figure 5.1
Competitive success and brand equity in sports clubs

Of course, the availability of considerable customer equity favours the acquisition of media equity, which basically means increased coverage and attention for the club. In fact, the presence of a hard core of attentive, loyal and involved supporters ensures that the media can count on a wide and stable audience. For the club, there is no doubt this has great potential – for example, the club will appear more frequently in the media and in a positive light, which means greater exposure for the brand and continuous confirmation of brand awareness; moreover, valuable contracts can be made with the media for the broadcasting rights of competitions. In turn, media equity enables an increase in the number of opportunities to make contact with prospective customers (who, in the case of TV broadcasting of matches, are often supporters of other clubs as well) and thus increase the potential buyers of the club's products, leading to increased profits for the club.

Such a process of mutual benefit between customer and media equity is closely connected with the team's capability to attract and involve other companies in sponsorships (or rather, more generally, partnerships) of various kinds, as well as to establish and develop profitable relationships with them. In fact, the availability of a wide and dedicated customer base (ranging from supporters to occasional television viewers) along with the powerful chamber provided by the media coverage of the team and its activities represents the key factor that makes the club attractive to companies eager to optimize the communicative and promotional potentialities connected with matching their own brand with the team.

Although this aspect is beyond the specific scope of this study, it is proper to point out that the team's brand equity also manifests itself in the club's ability to attract the best talents and the most qualified human resources. The image of a successful club and, above all, the prospect of future success represent a powerful attractive force for first-class athletes and coaches, provided that the necessary financial resources are available (Gilson, 2000). Furthermore, athletes and coaches can in turn contribute in fuelling the team's brand equity, since the presence of crowd-pulling champions and trainers may help to attract the attention of spectators, media and prospective sponsors to the club.

This last observation allows us to point out that sport success is actually no more than one (and not necessarily the most important) of the decisive factors in brand equity for a professional sports club; equity can be also bolstered by choices made within sport management (which in turn contribute to determining the team's success rate) and, most of all, by decisions made within the context of extra-sport management, and marketing in a specialized way. Such marketing can contribute to creating and increasing the resources referable to both brand awareness and brand image, with regard to the abovementioned classes of targets (i.e. mass customers, the media and business partners), which represent the key consumers of sports clubs' marketing activities.

The importance of some context factors (such as the dimension and quality of the prospective catchment area, as well as the competitive intensity which characterizes both the direct and enlarged competitive field within the geographic area concerned), and also the relevance of the team's own history and traditions, as well as the decisions made by the technical staff (which often considerably influence its capability to be winning in competitions), must be pointed out. Yet we should also acknowledge the decisive role performed by marketing activities in fuelling the club's brand equity through the offering of a broad range of products and services consistent with the needs and preferences of the abovementioned classes of stakeholders. Among the broad range of products and services offered by a sports team there is also the package of services offered at the stadium, and this will be analysed later in this study.

Marketing management and customer equity in professional sports teams

Sport marketing is meant to achieve and develop a mix of both tangible and intangible resources, as well as maximize the economic and competitive appreciation of the potentialities connected with such resources through a number of processes of an analytic, strategic and operational nature and also through the constant monitoring of the attainment of appointed goals (Graham, 1994). The main aim is to create and continuously reinforce the relationships with all stakeholders – most importantly, customers. Professional sports clubs simultaneously interact with several categories of subjects who require different approaches, and with regard to this it is important to distinguish between mass customers (that is, supporters) and business customers (such as sponsors). With reference to mass customers, it is possible to identify a variety of sub-groups that are characterized by a different degree of intensity regarding their relation with the team, and therefore a different degree of both emotional and economic involvement with the club. Naturally, different sub-groups of supporters lead to different customer segments, which may stimulate a number of marketing strategies and activities.

Starting from a wide base of basic sympathizers, it is possible to identify more and more limited customer segments that show attitudes of growing empathy with the club, and this leads (from a behavioural viewpoint) to a wider number and range of purchasing acts with regard to the goods and services than can potentially be marketed by the club.

The core objective of marketing with reference to mass customers (in the sense of a generic class of supporters) therefore clearly consists of regular attempts to enlarge the base of such customers on the one hand, and to increase their degree of involvement, the opportunities for them to interact with the club and its economic value on the other (Mullin *et al.*, 1993). To achieve the creation of positive, stable and mutually favourable relationships with mass-market customers, sports clubs' marketing can employ a variety of strategies aimed at enlarging the supporter base or, rather, increasing the degree of their emotional and economic involvement.

In general terms, marketing strategies can be schematically summarized as in Figure 5.2, which shows the major feasible alternatives used to optimize the quantity and quality of the relationships that a professional sports club can maintain with its own mass customers.

Market penetration consists of trying to increase customers' loyalty and also the frequency and intensity of their consumption of the products and services already provided. In this respect, we can mention by way of example all the activities of Customer Relationship Management regarding the customer base, such as Fan Club coordination and campaigns to promote season tickets. Such initiatives usually imply the creation, constant updating and use of a specific database for decision-making purposes, which is essential in implementing one-to-one marketing policies (Milne and McDonald, 1998). On this point, Ferrand and Pages (1999) have found that a team's image can influence the supporters' propensity to increase

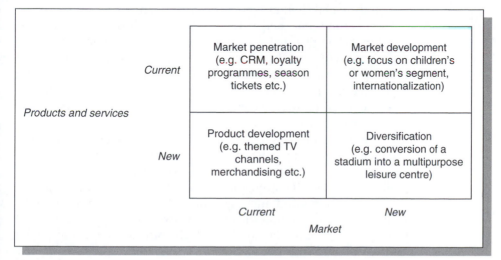

Figure 5.2
Marketing strategies of a professional sports club with regard to mass customers

the degree of their involvement with the team, in particular stimulating the purchase of season tickets instead of occasional ones for single competitions. They showed that, with reference to the specific case of Olympique Lyonnais, some aspects associated with the team's image (such as the sense of community, distinction/privilege and the capacity to entertain) affect the decision to buy season tickets and may be therefore used as communicative keys in advertising campaigns, so as to stimulate supporters to purchase season-ticket packages.

For a professional sports club, corporate identity is also crucial as far as the adoption of *product development* strategies is concerned – in particular brand-extension policies, typically implemented through the licensing and marketing of merchandising. This can also lead to multiple interactions with mass customers, in particular by creating the club's own magazine, themed TV channel and website. Optimizing brand-extension opportunities allow sports clubs to increase their revenues through the introduction and marketing of new goods and services.

Another typical strategy, *market development*, consists of enlarging the customer base at which the established services are aimed. With regard to this, in addition to the traditional option of looking for new customers/supporters at an international level, sports clubs may try to attract new customers by focusing their efforts on, for example, the children's segment. Since individual preferences form at a 'sensitive' age connected with childhood and adolescence, 'supportership' of a team usually begins at an early stage, when it is influenced by past successes (which may originally have determined the parents' own affiliation, which tends to be passed on from parents to children) as well as by current and expected successes. These supporters then usually stay loyal throughout their life, without changing their preference regarding the 'brand', although perhaps with a different degree of intensity and involvement. Marketing can perform a crucial role in such a process, together with the acquisition of new customers in general (such as the female segment, for instance, which is traditionally less interested in sport than the male).

The final strategy, *diversification*, consists of offering new products and services to new types of prospective customers. The scope of this study – that is, the reshaping of stadiums as multipurpose leisure centres – is within such an ambit, along with other options. In fact, stadiums and, more generally, the other structures used by clubs (such as training grounds, for example) represent a major resource which can be employed by sports clubs to expand their offer and improve the quality of the experience provided to customers (Davis, 1994). From this viewpoint, marketing managers have the responsibility to contribute to making the best use of such resources by defining the optimal mix of services to be proposed to customers according to their needs and preferences, and also by spotting the targets to which the new services could be offered with the best chances of success.

This strategic option evidently represents the choice with the biggest margin of uncertainty and error, and is therefore a field particularly worthy of analytical study from the marketing management viewpoint. As a consequence, it is precisely on this aspect that the present study will be focused hereafter.

Incidentally, observations for the most part similar to those hitherto developed regarding mass customers apply also to business customers, since there are different types and degrees of intensity in the relationships with business partners. These range from 'mere' sponsorship to the establishment of long-term strategic partnerships, as well as the planning and carrying out of co-marketing activities with sponsors (Cherubini and Canigiani, 2001), and various forms of partnerships with the media (Cherubini and Canigiani, 2000) or even with other workers in the entertainment business.

The football business: evolution and implications regarding professional club management

Numerous environmental and competitive changes are rapidly and significantly transforming the European football scene, giving increasing relevance to professional clubs' economic management in parallel to sports management. Among the major environmental changes that have recently influenced football clubs' management, we should mention the rise of sport professionalism, the Bosman ruling and the liberalization of the sale of rights for the TV broadcasting of competitions in a special way.

In Italy, over the past ten years there has been a massive increase in the revenues of Serie A clubs, which have risen from €399 million in the 1992–93 season to €1078 million in 2001–02. Over the same period labour costs have also skyrocketed, from €252 million to €954 million. As a consequence, the labour cost–turnover ratio reached the alarming figure of 88 per cent. Recently, the Italian Serie A had a total deficit – including all other cost items – of about €500 million, which exposed the state of crisis of the so-called 'football system' (Malagutti, 2002).

A comparison between the 1987–88 season and that of 2000–01 reveals that during this period there was a true reversal in the composition and the relative significance of revenues. In particular, the TV rights increased from 17 per cent to 56 per cent of the total turnover, whereas revenues from competitions (ticket-office takings) decreased from 59 per cent to 19 per cent of the total. Figure 5.3

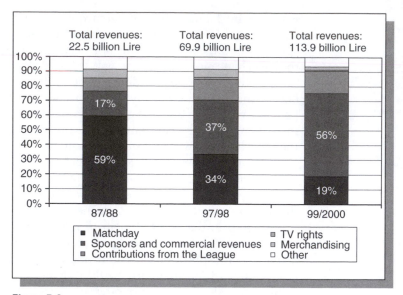

Figure 5.3
The change in composition of the revenues of Serie A clubs
(*Source*: Lega Calcio)

shows such evolution. It should be noted that this reversal of revenue components concerned all the football clubs in the Italian Serie A and B (Premier League and First Division), although the effect varied depending on the level of the team concerned and the competitions in which it participated.

It is also necessary to point out that the breakdown of football clubs' revenues is very different in the main European countries (Westerbeek and Smith, 2003). In this respect, see Figure 5.4, which shows the relevance of commercial revenues (mainly from corporate hospitality and sponsorship) in Holland and, to a slightly lesser extent, Germany.

In short, in recent years the Italian football market has taken on considerable economic relevance. Parallel to this development, the urgent and serious need to turn professional clubs into corporate businesses has emerged. The results achieved, in this sense, seem to be definitely unsatisfactory.

According to many observers, the need to curb costs can no longer be delayed. However, recourse to this policy is hampered by the current lack of initiatives (such as a salary cap) commonly shared and agreed upon by clubs in order to peg players' fees. It follows that there is a need to maximize possible sources of income.

With reference to this aspect, within the Italian context merchandising continues to have a marginal role (accounting for just 2 per cent of the team's total turnover); also, it is difficult to increase

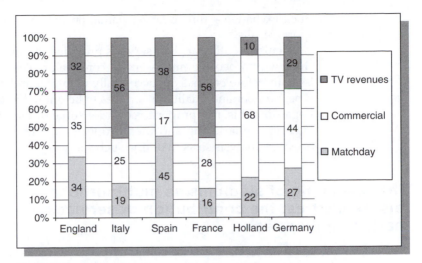

Figure 5.4
Breakdown of clubs' revenues in the major European countries
(*Source*: Westerbeek and Smith, 2003)

certain revenues – such as those from the cession of TV rights and from sponsorship, which have already reached saturation level (rising, on average, by 256 per cent and 30 per cent respectively over the past four years). It therefore appears advisable that professional football clubs should dedicate special attention to the range of goods and services with the best business development opportunities. Among these, stadiums hold a major position.

The optimization of this resource started with business customers, giving rise to initiatives such as the creation of exclusive corporate hospitality boxes for companies (where competitions can be seen from a privileged viewpoint) and the supply of services specifically conceived for this target.

As for mass customers, clubs may develop some services enabling them to offer more alternatives to their target spectators, so as to encourage them to go to the stadium more often and to use the related facilities as well. At the same time such reshaping may attract new customers, making the club's sources of income more varied and stable, transforming the stadium into a place where spectators can enjoy the event and feel safe while also benefiting from a wide range of facilities which may free the centre, at least partially, from the single weekly event. To this end, the main aim of many Italian clubs is to be able manage the facilities directly, so as to plan the necessary investments in the best possible way and enjoy the freedom necessary to carry them out. Furthermore, having a stadium of its own implies that a club has the stability necessary to reduce the volatility of stock prices – if it is quoted on the stock exchange – thus binding valuation not only to the team's sports results.

By enlarging the range of services provided within the stadium, clubs would become multi-service companies. The management issue therefore consists of successfully planning and choosing the type, number and quality of services to be offered at the stadium. Regarding this, it is proper to consider some of the contributions of services marketing and then propose a method of customer-oriented analysis so as to define such services.

The reshaping of stadiums as multipurpose leisure centres: the contribution of services marketing theories

In broad terms, a service company may offer core and peripheral services. The former satisfy the customers' main needs, while the latter are of lesser importance in that they complete, integrate and widen the core service (Eiglier and Langeard, 1987). While some peripheral services are necessary or even compulsory in order to gain access to the core service, some others are discretional – they may either be used or not be used by the customer – and therefore represent an 'extra' to the core service, the quality of which they can further improve. Each elementary service, both core and peripheral, is the output of a relative 'servuction' (i.e. service production) system, the main traits of which are as follows:

- The elements of the system consist of single elementary services and the respective production systems and processes

- Each element is connected with the others, and such connections are put into effect by a single element common to all services supplies – that is, the customer.

In every services offer there is no less than one peripheral service, which represents, at least for some customers, the main reason for their choice, thus becoming a core service. Such new core service, usually referred to as 'derived', together with some other peripheral services, can become a different global service with regard to another customer segment. We can thus distinguish between a 'main' core service and one or more 'derived' ones. For instance, as far as a stadium is concerned, the food and beverages outlets may pass from being a peripheral service to a derived core one if customers go to the facility exclusively to have lunch or dinner. There can therefore be customers who choose a peripheral service as a core one. The food and beverages area, though, is usually conceived as being a peripheral service in addition to the core service.

Empirical analysis

The empirical research was conducted through a series of phases, described hereafter, which can be summarized as follows:

1. Design of research guidelines

2. Operational planning

3. Data collection

4. Data processing

5. Analysis and interpretation of results.

Design of research guidelines

During the design phase we outlined the targets pursued in our empirical research, which were aimed at understanding the combinations of services favoured by customers (i.e. supporters who see the match) if the stadium were to be reshaped as a multipurpose leisure centre, and also at detecting, quantifying and describing customer clusters characterized by such ideal combinations of services.

Operational planning

During the operational planning phase, a questionnaire was developed. It was designed with a view to the technique usually preferred to pursue the abovementioned aims – that is, conjoint analysis, which is based on global judgements expressed by consumers about a set of complex alternatives. It consists of splitting the original assessments into utility values – referring to every single trait of the good – through which global assessments can be tracked down. In more detail, conjoint analysis presupposes the carrying out of the following activities:

1. Identifying the salient attributes consumers use to evaluate and discriminate between product or service class offerings. It should be noted that the number of attributes to be included in the research design is limited due to the fact that respondents are not capable of processing large amounts of comparative information (Ross *et al.*, 2003).

2. Organizing the attributes into levels, according to the different ways in which each attribute may manifest itself concretely.

3. Defining a set of alternative profiles by selecting some of the possible combinations that can be obtained when intersecting the levels of each attribute.

4. Collecting, by means of personal interviews, each customer's assessment of the selected profiles, using evaluation scales. Respondents rated each hypothetical profile in terms of preference, measured by a Likert-type scale anchored by 'Definitely don't prefer' (1) to 'Definitely prefer' (9) (see sample profiles in Appendices 5.1 and 5.2).

The main characteristic of such a method is that respondents are asked to make choices similar to those they make when deciding what to purchase – namely, comparing all the different features simultaneously and resolving what they are willing to give up in one attribute in order to have a certain amount of another. A study based on the conjoint analysis technique therefore allows not only the 'creation' of a combination of services in line with the desires and expectations of prospective consumers, but also the 'modification' of the existing offering, directing investments towards the most highly-valued attributes. In fact, empirical analysis conducted through conjoint analysis, by spotting the choice factors and the levels that they may assume, allows definition of single utility values that are associated with each level as well as with relative importance of the product's various attributes.

The choice of the attributes submitted to the consumer was made according to an assessment of the main categories of services that can go together with sport entertainment. To this end, some of the services already tested in countries where the stadium as a multipurpose and multi-service centre is already a fact have been inserted. The 'attributes' identified were entertainment services, food and beverages services, and commercial services. Such classes of services were subsequently organized into more analytical 'levels' (meant as elementary services within each class), as follows:

1. Entertainment services – club museum, children's playground, multiplex cinema, fitness centre

2. Food and beverages services – pizzeria, fast food, themed restaurant

3. Commercial services – sport store; club megastore; other shops.

In short, the consideration of peripheral elementary services (both necessary and discretional) provided to complete the core one (that is the game) in US stadiums and in some European venues has enabled identification of some typical derived core services ascribable to three main classes of entertainment, food and beverages, and commercial services (see Table 5.1).

As already mentioned, derived core services may perform various functions for sports clubs. For one thing, they can attract new

Table 5.1
Possible services at the stadium

Main core service
  Match

Peripheral services
  Reception
  Tickets
  Parking

Derived core services
1. Entertainment services
   – club museum
   – multiplex cinema
   – children's playground
   – fitness centre
2. Food and beverages services
   – fast food
   – pizzeria
   – themed restaurant
3. Commercial services
   – sport stores
   – club megastore
   – other shops

customers and involve them in taking part in the original core service (for instance, stimulating women and children to watch the matches). Secondly, derived core services may boost the use of facilities at other times and with aims different from those of the core service, thus attracting new customers who are not interested in competitions. This aspect is particularly significant for stadiums, as they have high operating costs but have traditionally been used no more than once a week, and only for a single purpose.

Data collection

The next phase, data collecting, was conducted as follows. Empirical research was carried out through individual interviews with a random sample of 150 supporters who were at Delle Alpi Stadium in Turin on the occasion of two different matches played by the same team (Juventus FC). The selection of the sample was totally random. A visual association with the alternatives proposed was the method of presentation chosen, so as to make it easier for consumers to identify the services being assessed.

In keeping with the exploratory aim of our research, the analysed sample was not representative of the overall population. However, the interviewed sample followed the demographic of both residents and supporters in many ways, with some exceptions – for instance, the age bracket eighteen to twenty-five years is overrepresented, while under-eighteens and over-sixties are underrepresented. Also, the male segment is overrepresented. However, this is hardly surprising, as women who go to the stadium in Italy are still in the minority compared to men.

Data processing

The next stage was data processing, where we employed Excel software for data entry operations and an SPSS statistics package for conjoint analysis and cluster analysis processing.

Analysis and interpretation

The final step, namely analysis and interpretation of results, enabled us to develop the various observations described here.

The overall outputs are presented in Figure 5.5, which shows the relative importance (as a percentage) of the three classes of peripheral services examined. Clearly, entertainment services have a rating higher than that of commercial services, while food and beverages services get an almost marginal assessment.

The survey conducted through conjoint analysis also represents a point of departure to try and define clusters of consumers who

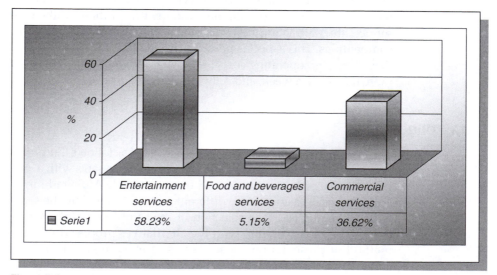

Figure 5.5
The relative importance of services

share common preferences – in fact, by means of cluster analysis it is possible to spot customer segments marked by different uses associated with the abovementioned characteristics (see Appendix 5.3). The analysis carried out enabled us to identify four clusters; the main traits of these customer segments are described in Table 5.2.

The clusters identified were subsequently described individually in terms of class of preferred peripheral services, favourite specific service ('attribute'), percentage of total sample examined, and typical socio-demographic and behavioural traits.

Table 5.2
Dimensions and socio-demographic composition of clusters

	Cluster 1 (%)	Cluster 2 (%)	Cluster 3 (%)	Cluster 4 (%)
Proportion of total %	49	15	13	23
Gender				
Male	67.6	82.6	73.7	64.7
Female	32.4	17.4	26.3	35.3
Age (years)				
<18	8.1	8.7	5.3	2.9
18–25	18.9	39.1	36.8	17.6
26–35	33.8	26.1	21.1	26.5
36–45	18.9	4.3	10.5	26.5
46–60	13.5	13.0	21.1	20.6
>60	6.8	8.7	5.3	5.9
Family unit				
Single	14.9	8.7	21.1	11.8
Couple with one child at home	31.1	52.2	47.4	20.6
Childless couple	16.2	4.3	0	11.8
Couple with children aged <18 years	23.0	30.4	10.5	23.5
Couple with adult children	12.2	4.3	21.1	32.4
Other	2.7	0	0	0
Travel time from stadium (minutes)				
<30	23.0	0	26.3	16.0
30–60	32.4	21.7	36.8	33.3
60–120	17.6	39.1	15.8	24.7
>120	27.0	39.1	21.1	26.0
Season ticket holder %	47.3	43.5	73.7	32.4

*On average, a non-season-ticket holder saw the following number of matches: Cluster 1, 5.46; Cluster 2, 4.69; Cluster 3, 3.80; Cluster 4, 5.13.

Table 5.3
Cluster 1 (Sport shoppers)

Relative importance of peripheral services	Entertainment, 56.66%; food and beverages, 6.14%; commercial, 37.20%
Favourite attribute	Fitness centre
Cluster size	49% of interviewees
Interviewees	Childless couples, living close to the stadium, non-season-ticket holders, see more matches than average

Table 5.4
Cluster 2 (Excursionists)

Relative importance of peripheral services	Entertainment, 65.28%; food and beverages, 6.03%; commercial, 28.29%
Favourite attribute	Club museum
Cluster size	15% of interviewees
Interviewees	Child at home, living far from the stadium

In the first group, the most important category of complementary services was entertainment, followed by commercial services and then food and beverages (see Table 5.3). Of entertainment services, the most highly valued was the fitness centre, followed by the club museum. Of commercial services, the club megastore met with the widest approval. Finally, regarding food and beverages, a pizzeria was the most highly valued service, although the significance of food and beverages was minimal in this segment.

Unlike the previous cluster, among excursionists (Cluster 2) commercial services received less approval, while food and beverages remained stable and were little appreciated (see Table 5.4). Of entertainment services, the favourite was the club museum which, within this cluster, seemed to attract a lot of interest. Of food and beverages services, fast food was the most highly valued; of commercial services, the club megastore was again the most appreciated. The most remarkable descriptive trait regarding this segment was the number of subjects who lived far from the stadium – thus explaining the cluster's name.

Cluster 3 (Table 5.5) showed a remarkable propensity for entertainment services: of these, the most highly valued was the multiplex cinema, followed by the fitness centre. The main difference from the other segments was in the rating of food and beverages services, which was preferred by 18.88% of interviewees (namely more than commercial services; this happened only in this cluster,

Table 5.5
Cluster 3 (Hungry faithful followers)

Relative importance of peripheral services	Entertainment, 65.06%; food and beverages, 18.88%; commercial, 16.06%
Favourite attribute	Multiplex cinema
Cluster size	13% of interviewees
Interviewees	Single, child at home, season-ticket holders, living close to the stadium, ideal stadium seen as a mall (cinema and shops)

Table 5.6
Cluster 4 (Playful families)

Relative importance of peripheral services	Entertainment, 85.71%; food and beverages, 6%; commercial, 8.29%
Favourite attribute	Multiplex cinema
Cluster size	23% of interviewees
Interviewees	Couples with children (both over and under 18 years of age), interested in the children's playground, living a maximum of an hour's distance from the stadium

hence the name given to it). Of food and beverages services, the themed restaurant met with the highest approval; of commercial services, shops of various types are the most appreciated.

Cluster 4 had a more noticeable predominance for entertainment services (85.71%) compared to all the others (see Table 5.6), while interest in both commercial and food and beverages services was minimal. Once again, of all entertainment services the most highly valued was the multiplex cinema, immediately followed by the children's playground. Of food and beverages services, the pizzeria was the favourite, while the club megastore was the most appreciated commercial service. A high level of family units was found in this segment.

 ## Conclusions

The research conducted here was obviously of an exploratory nature, and therefore lays no claims to being exhaustive or generalizable in its results. With this work we simply mean to give an example of the potentialities connected with the use of research regarding customers, so as to define an offer package consistent with their major needs. A study of the heterogeneous characters to be found in customers, as well as the detection of the various clusters, makes it easy to plan a service offering that is as close as possible to that desired by the various segments of consumers.

By way of an example, the sample examined in our research, although not representative, showed a clear preference for recreational and entertainment services as compared to the commercial and food and beverages ones. To sum up, such a finding may usefully orient the management's decision-making, at least with regard to the overriding areas where money should be invested in order to minimize risks.

In more detail, the analysis of the benefits sought by mass customers, and then the identification of segments according to their ideal preferences, allows sports clubs' managers to identify customer clusters characterized by different combinations of peripheral services. Such an analysis, which can be fruitfully conducted with the conjoint analysis technique, therefore supports a process of 'customer-based' definition of the set of services that can be marketed with specific reference to the planning of multi-purpose entertainment centres.

Naturally, different 'services packages' should ideally correspond with different clusters. Since customer profiles detected are heterogeneous, it is up to sports club management teams to use a method of accurate targeting in order to detect and select customer segments that represent the club's main target; as such, they must be then privileged in terms of services to be marketed and marketing initiatives in general. Such selection can be made according to several criteria, such as the segments' current and potential dimensions, compatibility with company policies, feasibility for the club, and prospective profitability.

Market research can strongly contribute to better understanding of customers' expectations and needs. While gaining a firm understanding of the needs of the market is critical to the success of new products and services, many sport organizations do not carry out this part of the new product development process. Skipping this information-gathering stage, or conducting it poorly, is often the main reason for the failure of innovations. This is particularly risky when such innovations require high investment, as in the case of the redesign of sport facilities. As shown in the present study, by means of an illustrative example, the conjoint analysis method provides an effective way to concentrate limited resources on aspects that will provide the highest return on investments.

Bibliography and references

Brooks, C. (1996). *Sports Marketing: competitive business strategies for sports*. Prentice Hall.

Cherubini, S. (1997). *Il Marketing sportivo*. Franco Angeli.

Cherubini, S. and Canigiani, M. (eds) (2000). *Media e co-marketing sportivo*. Franco Angeli.

Cherubini, S. and Canigiani, M. (eds) (2001). *Campioni e co-marketing sportivo*. Franco Angeli.

Davis, K. A. (1994). *Sport Management: successful private sector business strategies*. Brown and Benchmark.

Eiglier, P. and Langeard, E. (1987). *Il marketing strategico nei servizi*. McGraw-Hill.

Ferrand, A. and Pages, M. (1999). Image management in sport organisations: the creation of value. *European Journal of Marketing*, **33(3/4)**, 387–401.

Gilson, C. H. J. (2000). *Peak performance: business lessons from the world's top sports organizations*. Harper Collins Business.

Graham, P. J. (1994). *Sport Business – Operational and Theoretical Aspects*. Brown and Benchmark.

Irwin, R. L., Zwick, D. and Sutton, W. A. (1999). Assessing organizational attributes contributing to marketing excellence in American professional sport franchises. *European Journal of Marketing*, **33(3/4)**, 314–327.

Malagutti, V. (2002). *I conti truccati del calcio*. Carocci.

Meenaghan, T. and O'Sullivan, P. (1999). Playpower – sports meets marketing. *European Journal of Marketing*, **33(3/4)**, 241–249.

Milne, G. R. and McDonald, M. A. (1998). *Sport Marketing – Managing the Exchange Process*. Jones and Bartlett.

Mullin, B. J., Hardy, S. and Sutton, W. A. (1993). *Sport Marketing*. Human Kinetics.

Ross, S. D., Norman, W. C. and Dorsch, M. J. (2003). The use of conjoint analysis in the development of a new recreational facility. *Managing Leisure*, **8**, 227–244.

Westerbeek, H. and Smith, A. (2003). *Sport Business in the Global Marketplace*. Palgrave Macmillan.

Appendix 5.1

Help us identify the complementary services for stadiums to come

Which services do you prefer?

ENTERTAINMENT

| Club's museum | Children's playground | Multiplex cinema | Fitness centre |

FOOD AND BEVERAGES

| Pizzeria | Fast food | Themed restaurants |

COMMERCIAL

| Sport shop | Club's megastore | Other shops |

Mark from 1 to 9 each of the 16 following combinations of services

Figure A5.1
Presentation of cards

A visual association with the several alternatives proposed was the method chosen to assess opinions, so as to make it easier for consumers to identify the services. In Appendices 5.2 and 5.3, some of the sixteen combinations proposed in the questionnaire are presented.

Appendix 5.2

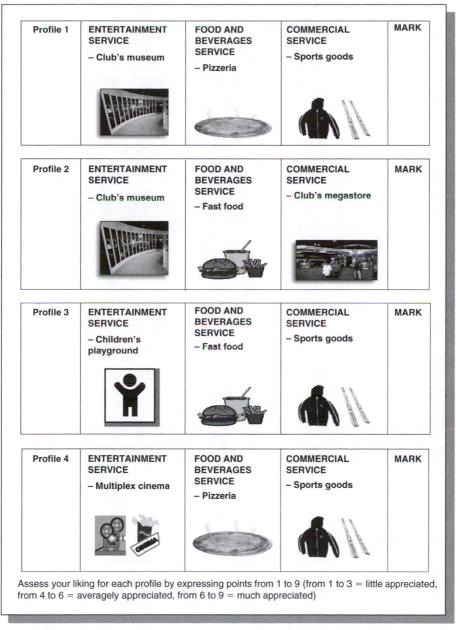

Figure A5.2
Examples of evaluation cards

Appendix 5.3

Output from the conjoint analysis carried out on all interviews

```
Averaged
Importance    Utility      Factor
                           ENTER.      ENTERTAINMENT SERVICES
58.23%        -.3146       ----|       Fitness centre
               .2604          |--      Club's museum
               .1537          |--      Multiplex cinema
              -.0996         -|        Children's playground

                           REFRE.      FOOD AND BEVERAGES SERVICES
 5.15%         .0328          |         Fast food
              -.0181          |         Pizzeria
              -.0147          |         Themed restaurant

                           COMM.       COMMERCIAL SERVICES
36.62%        -.0572         -|         Sports goods
               .2094          |---      Club's megastore
              -.1522         --|        Other types of shops

              6.1657       CONSTANT

Pearson's R    = .949                  Significance = .0000
Kendall's tau  = .833                  Significance = .0000
```

Output concerning cluster 1

```
QCL_1:              1
Case cluster number =        1

Averaged
Importance    Utility      Factor
```

```
                        ENTER.      ENTERTAINMENT SERVICES
56.66%         .2804    |----       Fitness centre
               .1757    |---        Club's museum
              -.1757    ---|        Multiplex cinema
              -.2804    ----|       Children's playground

                        REFRE.      FOOD AND BEVERAGES SERVICES
6.14%          .0180    |           Fast food
               .0214    |           Pizzeria
              -.0394    -|          Themed restaurant

                        COMM.       COMMERCIAL SERVICES
37.20%         .0203    |           Sports goods
               .1740    |--         Club's megastore
              -.1943    ---|        Other types of shops

              6.6019    CONSTANT

Pearson's R   = .942                Significance = .0000
Kendall's tau = .867                Significance = .0000
```

Output concerning cluster 2

```
QCL_1:                 2
Case cluster number =          2
Averaged
Importance      Utility      Factor
                             ENTER.      ENTERTAINMENT SERVICES
65.68%         -1.1060       --|         Fitness centre
                1.7962       |----       Club's museum
               -.5951        -|          Multiplex cinema
               -.0951        |           Children's playground

                             REFRE.      FOOD AND BEVERAGES SERVICES
 6.03%          .1558        |           Fast food
```

```
              −.0453              |        Pizzeria

              −.1105              |        Themed restaurant

                         COMM.            COMMERCIAL SERVICES
28.29%        −.3152             -|        Sports goods

               .7826             |-        Club's megastore

              −.4674             -|        Other types of shops

             −4.9719     CONSTANT

Pearson's R   = .986                      Significance = .0000
Kendall's tau = .874                      Significance = .0000
```

Output concerning cluster 3

```
QCL_1:              3
Case cluster number =          3
Averaged

Importance      Utility      Factor
                             ENTER.     ENTERTAINMENT SERVICES
65.06%           .2632        |-        Fitness centre

                −.9605       ---|       Club's museum

                1.1711       |----      Multiplex cinema

                −.4737       --|        Children's playground

                             REFRE.     FOOD AND BEVERAGES SERVICES
18.88%           .0614        |         Fast food

                −.3399       -|         Pizzeria

                 .2785       |-         Themed restaurant

                             COMM.      COMMERCIAL SERVICES
16.06%          −.1930       -|         Sports goods

                −.1404        |         Club's megastore

                 .3333       |-         Other types of shops
```

```
              6.0461      CONSTANT

Pearson's R   = .961              Significance = .0000
Kendall's tau = .879              Significance = .0000
```

Output concerning cluster 4

```
QCL_1:              4

Case cluster number =        4

Averaged

Importance   Utility     Factor
                         ENTER.     ENTERTAINMENT SERVICES
85.71%       -1.3971     ----|      Fitness centre
              .0882          |      Club's museum
              .8088          |--    Multiplex cinema
              .5000          |-     Children's playground

                         REFRE.     FOOD AND BEVERAGES SERVICES
6.00%        -.0343          |      Fast food
              .0944          |      Pizzeria
             -.0600          |      Themed restaurant

                         COMM.      COMMERCIAL SERVICES
8.29%         .0245          |      Sports goods
              .0944          |      Club's megastore
             -.1189          |      Other types of shops

              6.0907      CONSTANT

Pearson's R   = .978              Significance = .0000
Kendall's tau = .778              Significance = .0000
```

Figure A5.3
Output from the conjoint analysis

Appendix 5.4

An interview with Giuseppe Rizzello – FC Internazionale

Q1: What are the main traits regarding stadium management in Italy today?

GR: In my view, stadium management in Italy is still somewhat at the embryo stage; almost all facilities are not owned by clubs and this considerably hampers decision-making. A lot of stadiums are old and therefore lack the infrastructure necessary to guarantee adequate security standards or good business opportunities. Since they have been built and updated at different times, they also have many structural inefficiencies; suffice it to mention that at San Siro–Meazza (Milan), more than 600 people are needed just to watch entrances to the stadium.

Furthermore, bureaucracy is a very heavy weight and causes a great deal of delay; in fact, the building and modifying of sports facilities is severely restricted. Also the rise of pay-per-view TVs has worked against stadium attendance – in fact, the league match calendar is no longer definitively fixed at the beginning of each season, and this may have discouraged the purchase of season tickets. For instance, those who work on Saturdays certainly do not wish to risk buying a season ticket and paying for matches they may not be able to see at all.

The Italian context is also peculiar as far as supporters are concerned, as they have an almost religious approach to the match. Such an attitude makes it hard to carry out initiatives before, during and after games, limiting the possibilities for supplying other forms of entertainment and enriching the spectators' experience at the stadium.

Finally, ticket touting is a widespread phenomenon in Italy, and our regulations do not help us to fight it, or to struggle effectively against violence at the stadium either – which keeps interesting targets such as families with children away from us.

In addition to such problems, there is also a certain obtuseness on the clubs' part, as they have concentrated on TV rights over recent years while neglecting facility management. As a consequence, the contribution of stadium revenues to clubs' total turnover has dramatically lowered.

Q2: Which development policies should be followed for Italian stadiums?

GR: In general terms, we should improve the exploitation of stadiums, which have high fixed costs (both maintenance and running), by acting in many ways – for example by:

- increasing the chances of success by no longer limiting the use of a stadium to a match every 2 weeks
- boosting profits from matchday events
- increasing the average time that people spend at the facility.

Q3: What is different about San Siro–Meazza as compared to the other Italian stadiums?
GR: Unlike in other cities, two teams play in this stadium, and they are both renowned throughout the world. This increases the chances of its success, but also makes decision-making processes harder, since every decision must be approved by both clubs – which often have clashing opinions and aims. Also, operations management is complex – for example, because the two teams have different sponsors, it is necessary to change the set-up every matchday.

Q4: Which major interventions have been carried out at San Siro–Meazza in recent years?
GR: We have implemented interventions specifically meant for business targets in a different way. In particular, the following initiatives have been carried out:

- Fifteen suites have been created in the red ring and as many in the orange one. All of them can accommodate some ten people; they are provided with couches, monitors, kitchenette and toilets. Besides this, there is an attendant attached to each suite for the customers' own disposal. These suites are used by companies mostly for public relations, guest hospitality and incentive activities. They are each sold for €100 000 a season. They are used by the Inter and Milan club by turn.

- Twenty-six boxes with either four or six seats have been provided. These are purchased for the whole season at the price of €30 000–45 000, by companies and families, and are provided with some collateral services (catering, parking, monitor, etc.).

- Seats have been added to the VIP box, increasing the number from 297 to 820. These were each sold at €3000 for a year, and were snapped up; they include some collateral services such as catering. This intervention required moving the Press Gallery to the upper ring; the journalists complained, but it allowed us to increase the revenues from tickets and season tickets by 33 per cent in a single year, the total number of seats being equal. Another 1300 such seats were then created in the orange ring too.

In addition to such initiatives, we have worked to improve the quality of the services supplied (for instance, all seats are now numbered), security (there are 75 active cameras today) and some services – such as the museum, which has been visited by some 45 000 people a year so far, with tickets costing €18, and with practically no commercial or promotional investment. Furthermore, the megastore selling both Inter and Milan merchandise has been totally refurbished.

Moreover, we have launched a virtual tour of the stadium, complete with a set of services which involve the visitors: in fact, they can have a picture taken with the virtual team, see a lot of footage on screen and so on.

Q5: Which are the main achievements, both economic and otherwise, that have been fulfilled thanks to such interventions?
GR: For one thing, the improvement of facilities and services has contributed to the increase in the occupation rate of seats, which is now about 75 per cent over the national average. This is also thanks to some pricing policies, such as the sale of mini-season tickets for a few matches.

In addition to the abovementioned considerable revenues, I would say that the supporters' perception of the safety guaranteed and, more generally, of the image of innovation and modernity we are offering them by reshaping all stadium services have both increased.

Q6: Which are the main interventions either underway or scheduled in the future for the stadium, with reference to corporate customers, supporters and other prospective targets?
GR: We have certainly set ourselves the goal of managing relations with the organized supportership much better: as a matter of fact, these are special supporters who deserve *ad hoc* management policies and preferential treatment. There are some 80 000 people, who are members of 800 clubs. We wish to foster their loyalty and bind them to the world of Inter, also independently of sports results. Moreover, they may also be a very interesting target for our sponsors. We intend to give such supporters incentives to club membership and to create events exclusively conceived for them, as well as to enable them to meet and share moments other than the game itself (in particular during periods before and after the match). The stadium, together with the supply of special, personalized services, can offer a big contribution to such an end. In order to define targeted supply packages, though, we ought to analyse and understand better what their needs, wishes and preferences are.

Q7: What is your organizational structure like, and how is it placed within the club's organizational structure as a whole?
GR: First of all, the stadium belongs to the Town Council, which rents it to both Inter and Milan for some €7.5 million a year, equally shared between the two clubs, which have created a pool for the management of the stadium. Such a rent is very hard to accommodate, but luckily every single expense for the improvement of the stadium's structure can be deducted from the rent itself. In practice, this stimulates us to invest in the continuous adjustment and development of the services supplied. As far as Inter is concerned, the stadium management falls between the activities whose responsibility rests with InterActive, a company completely owned by Inter club and aimed at coordinating and optimizing the integration between the various profit-generating initiatives (such as management of TV rights, sponsorships, partnerships – i.e. licensing, merchandising), and the stadium itself, of course.

Q8: Which services do you manage and which have you outsourced, and why?
GR: We manage central services, which are particularly critical, internally. We know, by experience, how best to deal with them, and we also wish to exert more control over them. These are the reception services, the ticket office on match days, security controls, and entertainment services specifically planned for and supplied on the occasion of games. On the contrary, we outsource security services, first aid, catering, food and beverages, and all audio and video services, as well as all entertainment attractions not specifically connected with the match – like the museum, for instance.

Q9: Which are the main skills and expertise a good facility manager needs?
GR: I like to see myself as some sort of a conductor, who has to coordinate and integrate the work of numerous and heterogeneous specialized skills. You need to be able to see the whole picture, and to have some basic competence in all sectors concerned. The most relevant characteristics about my job are a mix of know-how (regarding regulations about security, for instance, of the structure itself, and contracts as well) and some personal endowment. You need to be patient, ruthless, sympathetic, and capable of negotiating and managing relationships with a very high number of interlocutors – both internal and external to the organization. In a sense, being the manager of a stadium like San Siro–Meazza is like being the mayor of an average city (with about 85 000 inhabitants) for 4 hours every 2 weeks.

Q10: Looking ahead, which are the major issues and opportunities regarding the evolution of stadiums within the Italian context?

GR: The most remarkable issue, at least in comparison with other European countries, is the lack of specific football stadium regulations in Italy. Laws are not precise, there are many vague areas, and frequently they are not applied in a rigorous way. Sometimes it is not even clear what you have to do, or what consequences some events might have. Besides, the culture and behaviour of Italian supporters are probably quite different from those of other countries – for example, flags and banners should be forbidden, as elsewhere, as they are highly inflammable and therefore quite dangerous. Yet in Italy it is inconceivable to prohibit supporters from bringing them to the stadium. Anyway, all Italian teams will have to conform to both UEFA standards and European rules very soon.

As to prospects, I am resolutely convinced that Italian clubs will have to increase revenues considerably by better use of stadiums, although the current situation is rather backward when compared to other markets. Personally, I am very doubtful as to plans for a total reshaping of stadiums into highly commercial structures. I think that, except cities with no malls at all, potential synergies between the latter – or multiplex cinemas – and stadiums are quite limited: at most the big parking lots available might be exploited. In other words, I find it quite unlikely that stadiums may serve as a centre of attraction for extra-sports services – that is, services completely separated from football and from clubs which play at the facility. On the contrary, I think that there are many opportunities to widen the services bundle connected with matches, sports in general or supportership. At any rate, I think that analysing and understanding what prospective customers would like to have may significantly help with making successful decisions.

A new paradigm for sport management in the German football market

Herbert Woratschek, Guido Schafmeister and Tim Ströbel

Overview

This chapter gives an overview of developments in the German football market during the last decade. Like other national football leagues, the German *Bundesliga* has had to cope with tremendous financial changes. The media – and especially TV rights – have a major impact on the financial situation of the German football market, and hence when dealing with German football from a marketing perspective there is a need for a special focus on broadcasting rights. As a consequence, the chapter explains how values are created in football markets in general, and TV markets in particular. In order to discuss issues like these, an insight into the German football market is given first.

Second, value creation models are discussed as a theoretical framework. Third, interviews with managers of various sports-associated organizations (leagues, teams, consultancies, agencies and TV stations), that reflect the issue of value creation, are quoted. Finally, arguments regarding the added value of German TV football markets are derived.

Keywords

German football market, German TV market, broadcasting rights, value creation, added value

Introduction

In the last decade, the German football market has developed in a similar way to other national football markets. Stadium attendance, which has the same determinants in Germany as elsewhere in the world, has followed similar trends (Czarnitzki and Stadtmann, 1999, 2002), and the player market is no longer solely national but has become global. Accordingly, as elsewhere, player salaries have increased. This could be explained by Akerlof's 'rat race', which has an analogy to sport competitions (Akerlof, 1976). The rats compete for a piece of cheese, and the one that runs the fastest gets to eat the cheese. However, each rat does not know how its performance relates to the performance of the other rats and, as a consequence, makes the maximum effort to win the race – the rats all run as fast as they can to win the cheese. The same principle applies in football clubs. Here, putting maximum effort into competition means hiring the best players, and thus paying higher and higher salaries – but this is possible only as long as sufficient financial funding is available. Financial funding depends on value creation, and hence the question is asked: does value creation take place in football, and how? It is to answer this question that we indicate the value creation logic of football markets in general.

The German TV market, however, is different in some aspects from many other European TV markets. First, there is only one pay-TV provider; secondly, the broadcasting rights of the German Football League are sold collectively; and thirdly, an extraordinary occurrence took place in 2002 – the Kirch crisis. Kirch's media company went bankrupt while it owned the TV broadcasting rights for the German *Bundesliga*, and revenue shortfalls for the clubs and the league resulted from this bankruptcy. Subsequently, German football clubs and the league administration got into financial difficulties because most of their income is derived from selling the broadcasting rights. The fact that the broadcasting rights are sold collectively made the problem even greater; the revenue shortfall did not only impact on a single club, but on the whole league.

The media, and especially the TV market, have a major impact on the German football market – in one or the other way, the German football market depends on the TV market. Hence, dealing with German football from a marketing perspective requires a special focus on broadcasting rights. As a consequence, in this chapter we first explain how values are created in football markets in general; subsequently, we argue just what the added values of German TV football markets are.

To discuss issues like these, insights into the German football market are given first. Value creation models are then discussed as a theoretical framework to show how value creation in the German Football League actually takes place. Value creation is necessary for survival and for success in the market. The next part reflects interviews with managers of sports-associated organizations on the issue of value creation. Finally, by analysing the reported value creation activities and processes we derive some arguments regarding the added value of German TV football markets.

Football in Germany

Football on the screen

The rating figures for football matches on TV are far ahead of those for other sport events. Only Formula One racing, with 7.62 million spectators at Spa – a famous Formula One circuit in Belgium (Sponsors, 2005) – and winter sports, with 6.76 million watching the ski-jumping on 1 January (Sponsors, 2006), have similar rating figures. This preference for football on the screen leads to highly profitable sales of broadcasting rights for the sport.

Figure 6.1 illustrates the growth in broadcasting fees from 1965 to 2005. Prior to 1965, the German Football League had to pay in order to be broadcast.

As shown in Figure 6.1, the broadcasting fees rose continuously apart from those in 2002 (as a consequence of the Kirch crisis), reaching an all-time high for the upcoming seasons 2006/07–2008/09 with total sales of €420 million. For most clubs of the Premier and Secondary Leagues, the revenues derived from selling broadcasting rights are the largest source of income; however, broadcasting fees for the German Football League are lower than for other European football markets.

The lower income level is a particular problem for those clubs that take part in international competitions, such as the Champions League or the UEFA Cup. The participating clubs from Germany lack the financial resources to acquire the most promising players

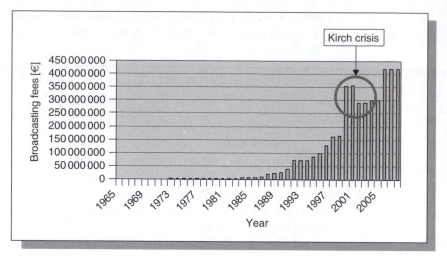

Figure 6.1
Broadcasting fees 1984–2005

in order to be successful. Clubs from other countries with higher revenues from selling broadcasting fees have a much better financial background from which to appoint the best players.

The collective sale of the broadcasting rights in Germany therefore causes major discussion regarding how the fees should be shared among the clubs. Internationally established clubs, such as FC Bayern Munich, demand a higher proportion of the fees. They use the abovementioned argument of higher revenues in other countries to claim a bigger slice of the cake – and, beginning with the 2006/07 season, they are getting a bigger piece than before. Until then, the maximum income from the broadcasting fees was €15.8 million; the new allocation allows €27.3 million for the top club in the National Football League (FAZ, 2006).

Giving this higher proportion to the more successful clubs also ensures their support of the collective sale of broadcasting rights. Successful clubs, such as FC Bayern Munich, frequently threaten the league and the other clubs with initiatives to quit the collective sale. However, the league administration obviously wants such clubs to stay part of the collective sale because it believes that the whole is more than the parts. The question is, can this argument be supported by theoretical or empirical evidence?

Organization of the German football market

Before going further, a brief introduction to the German football market structure is necessary.

At the centre of the German football market is the German Football Association (DFB). The DFB is responsible for nominating the German football champion, for promoting or relegating teams, and for naming the participants in international competitions. Furthermore, the DFB is responsible for men's and women's leagues, regional leagues, junior leagues and administrative tasks (DFB, §4). However, all duties connected to the professional men's football leagues are passed on to another organization called the German League Federation (DFB, §16).

The German League Federation constitutes the football clubs of the First and Second Divisions. Hence, the professional football clubs in Germany are responsible for running their own competition. In return, the German League Federation has to provide financial funding for the DFB.

In order to run the business of the First and Second Divisions, the German League Federation founded a private company, the German Football League GmbH (DFL). In essence, the DFL is responsible for:

- managing the First and Second Divisions
- organizing the tournaments
- marketing the First and Second Divisions exclusively.

A requirement of football clubs participating in one of the professional leagues is that they pass their own broadcasting rights to the German League Federation – and hence to the DFL. The DFL then markets all rights connected to TV, radio and internet transmission exclusively and collectively. Thus, at the moment the clubs are not allowed to sell their broadcasting rights individually if they want to take part in the German championship series. These regulations, though, hold true only for national tournaments. Once a club takes part in international competitions, that club can sell the broadcasting rights individually, as long as FIFA and UEFA allow it to do so.

Hence the DFL, which runs the professional leagues, is influenced by the DFB as well as by the thirty-six football clubs that belong to the First and Second Divisions. However, apart from the 'official football organizations' – such as the DFL, the clubs and the German League Federation – there are also other significant groups. One such group is the TV stations. TV stations usually buy the broadcasting rights. They are the customers of the DFL, although their demand in turn derives from the TV spectators' demand – if spectators did not demand a broadcast, TV stations would not buy the broadcasting rights.

TV stations, though, are not homogenous:

- Free-to-air stations offer their broadcasts free of charge to the TV viewers. They earn money by advertising, which means that advertising companies are their customers as well. As a consequence, they have to meet the expectations of both advertisers and spectators.

- With pay-TV, TV viewers have to pay for their usage. At the moment, there is only one pay-TV provider in Germany. This is also a peculiarity of the German TV market. Some argue that the lack of additional pay-TV stations might be the reason for lower broadcasting fees in comparison with those in other nations (Solberg, 2002). From a marketing point of view, it would be interesting to observe the establishment of a second pay-TV provider.

- Strong public TV stations are another German particularity. They are financed by a compulsory public fee, and owners of a TV set are charged regardless of whether they want to watch public television (Woratschek and Schafmeister, 2005). Besides the public fee, public television also earns money from selling slots for commercials, although advertising on public TV channels is restricted. The issue of public television is important in understanding the German football market, because several sport broadcasts are shown on public television and the most prominent football-highlights programmes are public ones. Hence, the public TV sector is essential to German football.

Of course, there are many other organizations and individuals that have an impact on the German football market, but these involved parties are neglected here because focus is on German football on TV.

The national championship title

Looking both at football on screen and at organizations in the football market, the DFL has always been involved and played an important role. The DFL is responsible for the collective sale of broadcasting rights and for the mediation between different organizations on the market – in fact, it is responsible for whatever comes to mind. However, there is something else that is very important.

National sport leagues such as the DFL manage a national championship series with competitions between different clubs or athletes. The DFL decides year by year who is allowed to participate in this competition, arranges the schedule for the tournaments and organizes the competition and cooperation between the clubs. The German football championship is a well-established title.

The national championship title goes to the team that is the best in the country – but the title is valuable only as long as the organizers (in this case the DFL) are able to ensure that their championship series is the only one in the country. It has to be a monopoly to be highly attractive. Imagine a country with two or three competing championship series for the same type of sports – which team would be the best? Maybe the champion of one of the series would not be as good as, for instance, the team coming fifth in one of the other competitions. Hence, the organization of a national sport series is successful only if the organizers achieve the required monopoly in the market for nominating the champion and for mediating between the participants.

Being successful in organizing a championship series does not, though, mean that the league is allowed to sell the national championship title – namely the league competition – on its own. Often, the collective sale is not accepted by German researchers (see, for example, Parlasca, 1999; Schellhaaß, 2000; Kruse and Quitzau, 2002). However, although there is a variety of arguments for forbidding the collective sale, an argument from the sport-marketing perspective is missing completely in this context. From a sport-marketing perspective, national sport organizations are a brand in themselves. They offer a highly valued product, namely the competition for a national championship title. Spectators do not appreciate the same two football teams playing against each other in the context of a friendly game as much as they do if the teams are fighting for a national championship title. Hence, the league administration offers added value. Real Madrid, Manchester United and FC Bayern Munich are favourites with spectators because of their participation in national and international competitions. Success in these series is often seen as a driving force for demand (Becker and Suls, 1983; Schofield, 1983; Janssens and Késenne, 1987; Dobson and Goddard, 1992, 1996; Czarnitzki and Stadtmann, 2002), so why should the leagues then not sell this added value by themselves? And why else should they add the value?

Value creation models

Value creation

At this point, the value creation of the DFL is more or less diffuse. On the one hand, the DFL mediates between clubs and organizes a championship series; on the other, it sells broadcasting rights. A theoretical basis for the underlying value creation is still missing.

Value creation in general takes place when the output is more valuable than all inputs put together. In this sense, value can be interpreted as the consumers' willingness to pay. Therefore, an enterprise can be profitable if the generated value exceeds the costs of manufacturing (Porter, 1985: 38).

In business literature, value creation models are used to analyse and illustrate all value-creating activities of an organization. Value creation models help to identify the strength and weaknesses of an organization in terms of how the business is run. However, before a value creation model can be used for the analysis of an organization, it has to be proved that the particular value creation model fits the organization's value creation. In this particular case, it has to be proved whether existing value creation models fit to organizations of the sport market, and particularly the football market.

Our own research shows that the ongoing presented value creation models do represent the value creation of diverse sport organizations. To prove these models, expert interviews were conducted with managers from different sport organizations, among them managers of professional sport clubs. These managers explained the value creation of their organizations from their own perspective. Afterwards, the research team compared the managers' descriptions with three different value creation models – the value chain, the value shop and the value network (Stabell and Fjeldstad, 1998). These comparisons gave a strong indication for the appropriateness of the value creation models to describe the value creation of sport organizations. Some of the results will be discussed later in the chapter. The value chain and value network models will be introduced as a theoretical foundation; the value shop is neglected here because it did not occur in sport league administrations and it is also unnecessary to show the differences between a traditional and a new paradigm.

The value chain

The most prominent and traditional value creation model seems to be Porter's value chain (Porter, 1985). This model is often used for analysing organizations, and is frequently modified (Hergert and Morris, 1989; Armistead and Clark, 1993; Norman and Ramírez, 1994; Preece *et al.*, 1995; Brooks and Reast, 1996; Dess and Picken, 1999; Lawton and Michaels, 2001; Walters and Jones, 2001; Eustace, 2003).

The value chain model was specifically developed for manufacturing organizations, such as car manufacturers, and is based on a sequential order of activities. Input factors have to be carried to the production facility before the production process can start. The input factors are then transformed into products or services according to a fixed and sequential set of activities. Finished products or services can either be stored or shipped to dealers before they are actually sold. To ensure that customers are satisfied with the products, after sales services are installed. An activity can start only if the preceding activity is completed. This characteristic puts the value chain model in direct connection to the long-linked technology of Thompson (Thompson, 1967). However, services are often sold before they are produced, and in this case, marketing activities take place before inbound logistics. Thus, for specific companies the primary activities can have a slightly different order. By using the value chain, the model is also applicable to service production (Fantapié Altobelli and Bouncken, 1998) and hence to sport service organizations as well.

Within the value chain model, Porter distinguishes two kinds of activities: primary and support. Figure 6.2 shows the common value chain diagram.

Primary activities have a direct impact on value creation for the customers. Primary activities include inbound logistics, operations, outbound logistics, marketing and sales, and service (Porter, 1985: 39–40). Each of these activities can provide an opportunity to gain competitive advantage by executing the activity either as simply and cheaply as possible or in as differentiated and individual a manner as possible. In the former case, an organization aims at providing services or products more cheaply than its competitors; cost advantages might, for example, be derived from many repetitions of the same production process, as repetition enables increasing returns to scale (Varian, 2003). Superior economic results are expected because of the cheaper execution of activities. Differentiation means

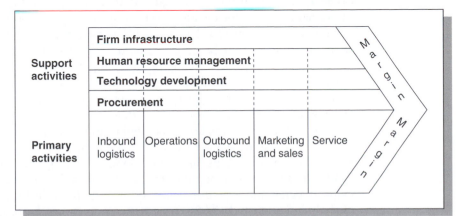

Figure 6.2
The value chain
(*Source*: Porter, 1985: 37)

that an organization provides products or services in as individual a manner as possible to the customer. Customers are therefore expected to pay a premium price for the offer, leading to superior economic results for the organization. Porter sees these two strategic options – cost advantage or differentiation – as the most promising options to be economically successful (Porter, 1985: 11).

Support activities assist the primary activities. They do not have a direct impact on value creation for customers. Support activities include a firm infrastructure, human resource management, technology development and procurement.

Last but not least, the value chain model has a margin. The margin describes the amount of money by which the revenues exceed the production costs. For a more detailed introduction to the value chain model, see Porter (1985).

Now, the value chain model could be used to analyse and explain the value creation of sport organizations. However, out of twenty-five interviewed sport managers – the interviews being conducted in another context – not one described value creation using the value chain. Accordingly, sport managers appear not to assume a kind of sport production. This calls the idea of 'team production' into question (Neale, 1964). Of course, the sample is not representative; nevertheless, it provides a first impression that the value creation of sport organizations does not primarily seem to be the production of some kind of tournament or match.

At this point, it is worth mentioning that the interviews were conducted with managers of sport leagues, clubs, TV stations, racing teams, sport consultancies and sport marketing agencies. Managers of manufacturers of sport equipment, such as adidas, were not interviewed. Hence, the sample is biased towards 'sport service organizations.' However, although biased, the sample gives a good impression of the value creation in sport service organizations.

However, Norman and Ramírez (1993) considered that the value chain model should not be the only instrument for analysing strategic activities in a quickly changing and competitive environment. They considered globalization, constantly changing markets and new technologies as driving forces for new possibilities of value creation. Also in 1993, Armistead and Clark found that the value chain is not suitable for organizations belonging to the service industry because many of these organizations do not fit to the value creation logic of this model (Armistead and Clark, 1993: 224). Stabell and Fjeldstad used the evident criticisms and developed two additional value creation models: the value shop and the value network (Stabell and Fjeldstad, 1998). They took Thompson's typology of technologies (Thompson, 1967) as a starting point to develop the value shop model for problem-solving organizations and the value network model for intermediating organizations (Stabell and

Fjeldstad, 1998: 420, 427). Thus, sport organizations should be differentiated into production, problem-solving and coordinating (intermediating) organizations, which indicate the use of the value chain, value shop and value network models respectively.

Value network

A value network creates value as it mediates and coordinates relationships between network participants. Thereto, a network facilitates, promotes and maintains a platform for the interaction of network participants. According to Stabell and Fjeldstad (1998: 427), 'Linking, and thus value creation, in value networks is the organization and facilitation of exchange between customers'. Network participants do not actually have to use the network services to derive utility from the network; sometimes the contact opportunity offered by the network represents a value of its own, as the network participants have access to it whenever they want. They do not actually have to use the network services; sometimes, saying 'I am a fan of FC Bayern Munich' is a value in itself. Belonging to the first national league is an added value for the clubs. Nevertheless, the value of the network increases or declines with each additional member, and hence depends on positive network externalities (Katz and Shapiro, 1985). Thus, value is created by the rules that include or exclude members of the network. A national league with 100 teams could lead to a lower value, as could a league with just 3 teams, compared to 18 league members.

Besides the number of participants, the composition of the customer base is also of interest. Customers of a network are not interested in interacting with anybody but the right person. This might be true for a golf club, for example, where business people want to meet each other. The networking services for the interaction between network participants can occur in different forms. Three dominant ones are contact initiation, mediating contracts, and distribution (Woratschek *et al.*, 2002).

Contact initiation includes offering a platform where one group can reach another. An example of such a value network is a sports event. If sports clubs organize a tournament, the advertisers can use the tournament as a platform to reach spectators with their advertising message. The tournament is then a platform for interaction. The value network of the German football league is not only created for the interaction between sponsors, advertisers and spectators; the fans can also interact with group members or other spectators. Furthermore, journalists and TV companies spread information and advertisements throughout the nation. The tournament is thus a platform for different interactions, some of which are business-connected. Hence, it seems that the football league is a network for a wide variety of different stakeholders with diverse interests. Among these stakeholders are several customer stakeholder groups.

Network operators do not differentiate between suppliers and customers. Both groups are customers for the network operator, even if there is a customer–supplier relationship between the customers. Furthermore, each value network itself usually belongs to a group of networks with layered and interconnected network services. One network can extend its services to the customers of other networks, or network services can be sourced out to other networks. Value networks show the coordination is productive by itself, as coordinating the connection between customers adds value to their relationship (Stabell and Fjeldstad, 1998: 427–429).

Figure 6.3 shows the value network diagram as introduced by Stabell and Fjeldstad (1998: 430). The margin has also been added (Woratschek *et al.*, 2002):

Again, the primary and support activities are disaggregated. The support activities are similar to those of the value chain and the value shop. The primary activities are: network promotion and contract management, service provisioning, and infrastructure operation. Network promotion and contract management consists of activities such as inviting potential customers to join the network, signing up new members and terminating memberships. Service provisioning has to do with establishing, maintaining and terminating the connection between customers. Service provisioning is oriented towards the management of individual contacts between customers, while network promotion and contract

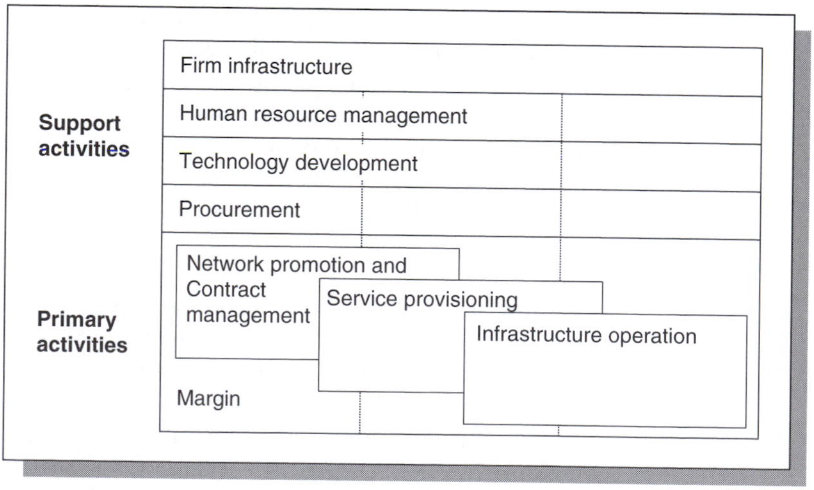

Figure 6.3
Value network
(*Source*: Stabell and Fjeldstad, 1998: 430)

management focuses on the network membership. Infrastructure operation is maintaining and running the physical and information infrastructure of the network, the platform for interaction, and communication (Stabell and Fjeldstad, 1998: 429).

The value configuration analysis of networks differs from the analysis of value chains because various items can be drivers of both costs and values. The scale and composition of the network are examples of such an item. A value network can be more attractive the more members it has – in, for example, a fan club. However, at the same time the network must also offer an access opportunity and a capacity for all the members. New members require additional capacity and access opportunities, and hence increase the operating costs of the network. Capacity utilization is thus a cost and value driver at the same time. On the one hand, higher capacity-utilization leads to a lower unit cost, as it is the case in the value chain model; on the other, it increases the risk of members having to wait for the network service until sufficient capacity is vacant (for example, if tennis courts are fully booked). In this case, the value of the network is reduced by high capacity-utilization (Stabell and Fjeldstad, 1998: 431–432).

The strategy options of a value network can be seen as cost advantage versus differentiation, too. Here, the question of strategy is whether or not to integrate vertically or horizontally. Vertical integration describes the degree to which a network controls the preceding and succeeding activities that are required to fulfil the coordination task of the network. Hence, vertical integration describes the level of control over the co-producing activities of other networks. Horizontal integration describes the customer-base scope – the broader the customer base, the more horizontally integrated a network is. A network with a higher degree of horizontal integration provides network services for a variety of customer segments (Stabell and Fjeldstad, 1998: 432). A low degree of horizontal integration will only be successful if the niche is large enough and has sufficient purchasing power to pay for the network services. If certain niches are too small or lack purchasing power, a higher degree of horizontal integration becomes necessary. Returning to cost advantage and differentiation, a cost advantage strategy would require a few members, limited access opportunities, and low capacity or low degree of integration. A differentiation strategy would mean offering easy access and various contact opportunities for different customer groups.

DFL and clubs – a value network

From a theoretical perspective, the value network model is suitable for the DFL and the clubs on the German football market.

Playing football would be possible without the league organizing a championship series, but the championship series adds value to the games, as the best team is rewarded with the championship title. A championship series is more attractive for the spectators than a single friendly game, because of the chance of winning the championship title and also the relegation threat (see, for example, Borland and Lye, 1992; Dobson and Goddard, 1992; Wilson and Sim, 1995). Hence, the DFL provides value by organizing the football league network, as this gives meaning to the matches. The league network puts the matches into perspective.

A primary activity of the DFL is the selection of the participants in the championship series. The network promotion of the DFL means the identification of teams which are able to fulfil the requirements of the championship series. The attractiveness of the league depends on the performance of the participating teams and on the number of top teams.

As mentioned above, 100 teams are too many for an interesting championship series, and 3 teams are too few. Therefore, another way of determining value creation is to decide how many teams should compete in a league. As well as signing up members for the championship series, terminating membership is also a key value activity. The league has to make sure that, for example, clubs with financial problems do not harm the league if they have to resign during the season due to lack of funds. Hence, the league must check the finances of each participating club. Furthermore, it has to exclude teams that do not meet the performance requirements (relegations) that ensure high-level matches. Thus, if the league terminates the membership of a club, it is protecting the value of the championship series as a whole.

An example of service provisioning is the organization of the games and the settlement of the entrance and broadcasting fees. The DFL fixes the schedule for the championship series – fixtures, as well as dates and times. The infrastructure operations of a football league mainly deal with rules and regulations for the championship series. In some countries, transfer payments are supposed to guarantee the competitive balance between the teams (see, for example, Knowles *et al.*, 1992; Schmidt and Berri, 2001). In other countries, salary caps and draft systems are installed for similar reasons (see, for example, Késenne, 2000). Furthermore, to make the football competition more attractive in relation to other sports, the points system for football tournaments was changed some years ago. Three points are now awarded for a win, instead of two, to motivate the teams to play more offensively. Developing the rules for the games, organizing relegation, and penalizing athletes and teams for violating the rules are other examples of infrastructure operations. All these activities are aimed at maintaining or increasing the value of the network 'championship series'.

The strategic options of the DFL are horizontal, vertical or lateral integration. An alternative to integration is cooperation. An example of horizontal cooperation is the international link between different national football series via FIFA. The DFL and most other national football leagues cooperate in this manner and are embedded in different sorts of cooperation. In this way, FIFA is a value network and the national series are network participants. An example of vertical cooperation on the national market is the link between the DFL and the TV markets.

Furthermore, from a theoretical perspective, football clubs seem to work as value networks, too. This impression is derived from a case study involving interviews with sport managers regarding value creation. We interviewed sport managers, using a theory-based interview guideline, on value creation. Here, the statements of two football club managers are reflected. One manager works for a Premier League club (M1; see Appendix 6.1) while the other works for a club of the second league (M2; see Appendix 6.2).

The following expressions are taken from the interviews and show what the managers actually think about their value creation. First of all, the managers see the matches as a platform which is characteristic of a value network – they 'offer a location for fans to meet each other' (M2), and 'Fans feel some kind of affiliation' (M2). However, the idea of providing a platform is not limited to the fan level. A platform is also installed for sponsors – 'The same is true for sponsors; the match is a means to an end' (M2). Sponsors are very keen on interacting with fans, and 'We link fans and sponsors together' (M2). Linking different customer stakeholders means that the core business is coordinating network members. At the same time, though, not all sponsors and fans are welcome. The sponsors have to fit with the club to ensure that sponsorship is a value creation activity of a value network – 'We do not accept every sponsor; they have to support our values' (M2). This is also true for the fans. For example, fans have to ensure peaceful behaviour – 'We work against right-wing radicalism' (M1), and 'Fan clubs have to sign an agreement' (M1). However, the managers do not know whether the group of spectators or of sponsors is more important; they assume that both customer stakeholder groups are of the same importance – 'We would make a big mistake if we were to focus either on sponsors or spectators' (M1).

Thinking of cooperation with media, the managers see the media as a very important partner – 'The media form a very important partner because they communicate our messages' (M1). All in all, good partners are necessary – 'We have good partners' – and the partners have to work together – 'All parts have to work together'

(M1). Obviously, working together with partners and installing a platform is the core business of football clubs. However, working together with and for diverse partners requires certain skills from the managers. Being at the top of a club organization makes it necessary to have a broad knowledge base: 'It is necessary to know everything' (M1).

Looking at the league, the football club managers describe the value creation as follows: 'The league loses its attractiveness if there is only one good playing club' (M2). They recognize the importance of highly qualified athletes and teams in remaining attractive, both nationally and internationally. This is part of the sector 'infrastructure' as a primary activity in a value network. Competitive balance on a high level seems to be their approach to ensure attractiveness. Belonging to the league is a value itself for the clubs, too: 'We want to belong to the league because it is the top of the top' (M2).

All these statements reflect characteristics of the value network as it is described by Stabell and Fjeldstad (1998).

Conclusions

Generally speaking, coordination is a value-creating activity because the coordination itself provides value for different interest groups. Value creation by coordination is best described by the value network. The German football league DFL creates a value in itself because of the national championship title. Hence, DFL is a brand which should probably be marketed as a whole because the whole is worth more than the sum of the parts.

Furthermore, the income ratios of the German football league have shown that vertical cooperation with the media adds value to the national sport series. In particular, cooperation with the TV market is fruitful. For most German football clubs, the biggest part of their income is derived from the sale of broadcasting rights.

Added value mainly exists because the DFL and the clubs offer a platform for sponsors and advertisers to get in contact with spectators, both in the stadium and in front of the TV set. However, media coverage – and particularly TV coverage – ensures a much bigger audience. In Germany, the DFL organizes the cooperation with the TV market. The DFL coordinates the cooperation and creates value by doing so. At the moment, this cooperation is worth €420 million.

Finally, German football clubs can only take part in the international football rat race because a link between the league and the TV market exists. This link ensures financial funding which allows for paying higher salaries and hence appointing better players. Hence, the DFL ensures a competitive German football league by organizing the link to the TV market. Furthermore, selling the broadcasting rights collectively seems advantageous as long as the whole series is of higher value than would be the fees for individual games.

We have found empirical and theoretical evidence that the value creation of football leagues in general and the DFL in particular is not characterized by some kind of 'production' process, but instead by coordinating customer stakeholder groups with diverse interests.

Bibliography and references

Akerlof, G. (1976). The economics of caste and of the rat race and other woeful tales. *Quarterly Journal of Economics*, **90**, 599–617.

Armistead, C. G. and Clark, G. (1993). Resource activity mapping: the value chain in service operations strategy. *Service Industries Journal*, **13(4)**, 221–239.

Becker, M. A. and Suls, J. (1983). Take me out to the ballgame: the effects of objective, social, and temporal performance information on the attendance at major league baseball games. *Journal of Sport Psychology*, **5(3)**, 302–313.

Borland, J. and Lye, J. (1992). Attendance at Australian Rules football: a panel study. *Applied Economics*, **24(9)**, 1053–1058.

Brooks, I. and Reast, J. (1996). Re-designing the value chain at Scania Trucks. *Long Range Planning*, **29(4)**, 514–525.

Czarnitzki, D. and Stadtmann, G. (1999). Uncertainty of outcome versus reputation: empirical evidence for the first German football division. *ZEW Discussion Paper* (99/46).

Czarnitzki, D. and Stadtmann, G. (2002). Uncertainty of outcome versus reputation: empirical evidence for the first German football division. *Empirical Economics*, **27(1)**, 101–112.

Dess, G. G. and Picken, J. C. (1999). Creating competitive (dis)advantage: learning from Food Lion's freefall. *The Academy of Management Executive*, **13(3)**, 97–111.

DFB. Satzung des Deutschen Fußball Bundes (http://www.dfb.de/dfb-info/interna/index.html).

Dobson, S. M. and Goddard, J. A. (1992). The demand for standing and seated viewing accommodation in the English Football League. *Applied Economics*, **24(10)**, 1155–1163.

Dobson, S. M. and Goddard, J. A. (1996). The demand for football in the regions of England and Wales. Regional Studies, **30(5)**, 443–453.

Eustace, C. (2003). A new perspective on the knowledge value chain. *Journal of Intellectual Capital*, **4(4)**, 588–596.

Fantapié Altobelli, C. and Bouncken, R. B. (1998). Wertkettenanalyse von Dienstleistungs-Anbietern. In: A. Meyer (ed.), *Handbuch Dienstleistungs-Marketing*, pp. 282–296. Schäffer-Poeschel.

FAZ (2006). '27,7 Millionen Euro für die Bayern', *Frankfurter Allgemeine Zeitung*, 3 February 2006, p. 31.

Hergert, M. and Morris, D. (1989). Accounting data for value chain analysis. *Strategic Management Journal*, **10(2)**, 175–188.

Janssens, P. and Késenne, S. (1987). Belgian football attendances. *Tijdschrift voor Economie en Management*, **32(3)**, 305–315.

Katz, M. and Shapiro, C. (1985). Network externalities, competition, and compatibility. *American Economic Review*, **75**, 424–440.

Késenne, S. (2000). The impact of salary caps in professional team sports. *Scottish Journal of Political Economy*, **47(4)**, 422.

Knowles, G., Sherony, K. and Haupert, M. (1992). The demand for major league baseball: a test of the uncertainty of outcome hypothesis. *American Economist*, **36(2)**, 72–80.

Kruse, J. and Quitzau, J. (2002). Zentralvermarktung der Fernsehrechte an der Fußballbundesliga. *ZFB Ergänzungsheft*, 63–82.

Lawton, T. C. and Michaels, K. P. (2001). Advancing to the virtual value chain: learning from the Dell model. *Irish Journal of Management*, **22(1)**, 91–112.

Neale, W. C. (1964). The peculiar economics of professional sports. *Quarterly Journal of Economics*, **78(1)**, 1–14.

Norman, R. and Ramírez, R. (1993). From value chain to value constellation: designing interactive strategy. *Harvard Business Review*, **71(4)**, 65–77.

Norman, R. and Ramírez, R. (1994). *Designing Interactive Strategy – From Value Chain to Value Constellation*. John Wiley & Sons.

Parlasca, S. (1999). Wirkungen von Sportkartellen: Das Beispiel zentraler Vermarktung von TV-Rechten. In: G. Trosien and M. Dinkel (eds), *Verkaufen Medien die Sportwirklichkeit*, pp. 83–118. Meyer and Meyer.

Porter, M. E. (1985). *Competitive Advantage: Creating and Sustaining Superior Performance*. Free Press.

Preece, S., Fleisher, C. and Toccacelli, J. (1995). Building a reputation along the value chain at Levi Strauss. *Long Range Planning*, **28(6)**, 88–98.

Schellhaaß, H. M. (2000). Die zentrale Vermarktung von Europapokalspielen – Ausbeutung von Marktmacht oder Sicherung des sportlichen Wettbewerbs? In: M.-P. Büch (ed.), *Märkte und Organizationsformen im Sport: Institutionenökonomische Ansätze*, pp. 27–41. Karl Hofmann.

Schmidt, M. B. and Berri, D. J. (2001). Competitive balance and attendance – the case of major league baseball. *Journal of Sports Economics*, **2(2)**, 145–167.

Schofield, J. A. (1983). The demand for cricket: the case of the John Player League. *Applied Economics*, **15(3)**, 283–296.

Solberg, H. A. (2002). The economics of television sports rights: Europe and the US – a comparative analysis. *Norsk Medietidsskrift*, **9(2)**, 57–80.

Sponsors (2005). Sport im TV: Hits und Flops im Aug./Sept. *Sponsor News*, **10**, 11.

Sponsors (2006). Sport im TV: Hits und Flops im Januar. *Sponsor News*, **2**, 6.

Stabell, C. B. and Fjeldstad, Ø. D. (1998). Configuring value for competitive advantage: on chains, shops, and networks. *Strategic Management Journal*, **19(5)**, 413–437.

Thompson, J. D. (1967). *Organizations in Action*. McGraw-Hill.

Varian, H. R. (2003). *Intermediate Microeconomics*, 6th edn. W. W. Norton & Co.

Walters, D. and Jones, P. (2001). Value and value chains in healthcare: a quality management perspective. *The TQM Magazine*, **13(5)**, 319–333.

Wilson, P. and Sim, B. (1995). The demand for semi-pro league football in Malaysia 1989–1991: a panel data approach. *Applied Economics*, **27(1)**, 131–138.

Woratschek, H. and Schafmeister, G. (2005). Assessing the determinants of broadcasting fees – theoretical foundations and empirical evidence for the German football league. *Wirtschaftswissenschaftliche Diskussionspapiere Universität Bayreuth [Economical Discussion Papers University of Bayreuth]* (11-05).

Woratschek, H., Roth, S. and Pastowski, S. (2002). Geschäftsmodelle und Wertschöpfungskonfigurationen im Internet. *Marketing ZFP*, **24** (Spezialausgabe 'E-Marketing'), 57–72.

Appendix 6.1

Interview with practitioner M1 (sport manager of a *Bundesliga* club)

Q1: Would you please give us an overview of the central tasks of your business unit?

M1: I take care of the sports-related interests of the club and coordinate the public relations. I also have to deal with customized sponsorships. Furthermore, I am directly responsible for fan issues.

Q2: What kind of stakeholders would you identify? How important are these groups?

M1: There are the club itself, fans, journalists, sponsors, and our hometown, for example. We would make a big mistake if we were to focus either on sponsors or spectators. That also means that we have very different stakeholders, varying from the single fan to the chairman of the board of management of a multinational company.

We have good partners. All parts have to work together.

Fans are also an economically interesting group, but they are no longer the biggest budget item. Therefore, we also receive a lot of benefit from our hometown. Sponsors are, of course, very important economic supporters because the receipts from sponsorships make up about 35–40 per cent of the whole revenue. Above that, sponsors can have a positive influence on the image of the club.

The media are an important partner because they communicate our messages.

Q3: What are the stakeholders expecting from your work? What kind of values do you generate?

M1: The print media mainly increase their circulation by reporting on our club. Hence, the media are focused on the sport.

The media would like to have a headline and special stories about the club every day.

On the one hand, we concentrate on increasing our recognition, but on the other hand, image and customer care for our sponsors are very important issues, too.

We know that the club and its football players are responsible for the image. That is why the football club and the corporate entity have to form a union to establish the image.

We are also responsible for marketing and merchandising and we have a social mandate that we take very serious. We serve as a model for the youth and we are able to fulfil their dreams, too.

Fans want to feel safe and comfortable, but they also want to see attractive football matches with little commerce.

Club and sponsors benefit mutually from their image. Sponsors want to reach a high media perception. Therefore, they need personalities or testimonials that represent their company.

Q4: What kind of activities are you performing for your customers?
M1: We are responsible for the decisions that affect the club and we participate in strategic questions. For that matter, we are cooperating with fan clubs and schools and try to involve our hometown. Hence, we must carry on negotiations with the authorities.

We work against right-wing radicalism. Therefore, fan clubs have to sign an agreement.

We work very closely with the media.

The core business can be seen in the progression of the sportive success and the external presentation of our athletes.

All together, the fans must feel comfortable. That is why it is necessary to know everything. I have to be kept informed about the tasks and developments of every department.

Appendix 6.2

Interview with practitioner M2 (sport manager of a second league club)

Q1: Would you please give us an overview of the central tasks of your business unit?
M2: I am responsible for two areas: first of all, for the professional football department of the club, and also for youth development programmes. Especially, I am responsible for the human resources management, the controlling department, public relations, and the whole organization.

Q2: What kind of stakeholders would you identify? How important are these groups?
M2: All things considered, there are fans, sponsors, the media, employees, our hometown and schools.

Fans benefit from a successful team. Our hometown profits from a major transfer. The media report on our football club.

Although fans are becoming less important on an economical level, they should not be neglected because football is the most popular sport in Germany. This becomes evident if one takes a look at the referee affair in 2005 and its impact on society.

If there were not any fans visiting the football matches, the whole match would be senseless. We are also very dependent on our sponsors. Therefore, we must ensure that there are as many fans as possible because then the sportive rating of the matches increases.

We must concentrate our work on the sportive success of our professional teams. This is our primary task.

Q3: What are the stakeholders expecting from your work? What kind of values do you generate?

M2: There is a great potential of identification between our hometown and our football club. But first of all, we try to build up a strong identification between the youth and our football club.

Fans feel some kind of affiliation. They expect a certain kind of entertainment. Hence, we organize football matches and offer merchandising articles in order to fulfil the expectations of our fans, but also to guarantee economical success.

Football matches offer a location for fans to meet each other.

The same is true for sponsors. The match is a means to an end.

The media benefit from our image in order to achieve economical success.

Schools use our image for acquiring new pupils. We provide them with free tickets and give lectures.

Young athletes benefit from our training by getting a special reputation.

The league loses its attractiveness if there is only one good playing club.

Q4: What kind of activities are you performing for your customers?

M2: I have to manage conflicts between stakeholders.

Furthermore, I must react if somebody does not work according to the principles of the club.

We search for young talents in schools. Therefore, our logo must be represented upon the platform school.

We support our sponsors in getting in contact with fans. We link fans and sponsors together.

We care about the press in a very special way – for example, we try to fulfil every interview request.

Concerning the youth development programmes, we try to improve the skills of our young athletes by training within the whole team as well as by training individual exercises.

We do not accept every sponsor. They have to support our values. This is very important for us.

We want to establish the best youth development program in Germany. Hence, quality and reputation of our trainers are essential for the attractiveness of our training schools.

We want to belong to the league because it is the top of the top. Winning the championship would create a lot of benefit to our fans and sponsors.

Marketing management in a socially complex club: Barcelona FC

Jaime Gil-Lafuente

Overview

Professional sport has changed since the beginning of the 1990s, and this is particularly the case for football. The stake in some games is now sometimes millions of euros. However, these changes have not modified the management system of clubs, which is often still amateur, with presidents that consider clubs not to be real companies but rather toys that can be replaced easily when broken.

Among big clubs such as Barcelona, the balance between sporting and economical results is difficult not only because of significant pressure from the media but also because of that from various political and social groups. Until now, only one president has been successful in managing these different variables –Josep Lluís Núñez.

Keywords

FC Barcelona, social complexity, socios, marketing

Introduction

Applying the criteria of a business to sports clubs is (and must be) a basic element for their successful sporting, economic and social operation. Nevertheless, the success of the brand of a football team depends to a huge degree on their sporting results – which is, of course, perfectly logical, since the potential consumer is motivated by impulses that are mainly emotional. In the space of a very few days, it is possible to go from absolute defeatism to total triumphalism. This causes continuous and extreme fluctuations, which are not the norm in non-sporting businesses.

This is why the most important clubs in the world increasingly require a solid marketing department which is prepared to cope with the large degree of uncertainty that is the cause of these fluctuations. Barcelona FC is no exception, and for the past few years has been able to count on a very good professional in the person of Esteve Calzada, who heads the marketing department of the Catalan club.

It is not the intention to fill the pages of this chapter with statistics that, in the majority of cases, are of little use and are always highly involved. We do not intend to copy data or analyses included in other books, newspapers or magazines. Our objective is to offer an overall vision of some of the aspects that we consider to be of interest, without delving deeper in terms of a merely technical nature. Barcelona FC is, as will be explained, more than a club; it is the union of certain views that are a very good reflection of Catalan society. For this reason, the chapter will concentrate on the causes and consequences of the very strong and permanently influential aspects that exist in the sphere of this magnificent club.

Personal comments on the interview with Esteve Calzada

Following an interesting conversation with Esteve Calzada, Marketing Director of Barcelona FC (see Appendix 7.1), the following comments of a technical nature are made without wishing in any way whatsoever to criticize the way in which a very difficult task is carried out by professionals working in a much admired sporting club.

The truth is that, prior to becoming occupied professionally in research and teaching in the sphere of marketing, I had always wondered what the specific commercial tasks that could be carried out in a football club might be, where, *a priori*, the only product that can be sold is the spectacle and a main objective is the signing on of new members. On the other hand, just a few years ago this statement could have been considered to be strange, since at that time Barcelona FC had a membership that was totally disproportionate relative to any other club in the world – and consequently, seeking more members appeared to be a little incongruous.

The constantly increasing number of fans was the impulse behind the club building and extending 'Camp Nou', the stadium where the first football team plays. This is still today the most prestigious among the large stadiums of Europe, and is placed second worldwide after the gigantic (although rather worn and elderly) Maracana. However, the goals, star players and spectacle that gathered there seemed to leave a very requirement for the development of marketing techniques for signing on new members or fans. The people, by family tradition or by identification with certain colours (and not with any political ideology), had enough reason to be proud of being members of a club which had not only a prestigious football team but also supported several other sports – both professional (basketball, handball and roller hockey) and non-professional (ice hockey, athletics, ice dance, rugby, baseball, etc.).

However, times have changed. The membership has been divided up, in what is rumoured to have been a very unjust manner, by external institutions which saw in the economically healthiest club in Europe a showcase that any businessman or possibly ambitious politician could count on for attaining their objectives. This surely must have been the point that led the club – which found itself, in full economic and sporting splendour, seeking a renewal of its image, which had been terribly worn down – to opt for working with professionals who could contribute to making decision-taking easier and more decisive: those in marketing. Improving the agreements with sponsors and seeking new income – such as by the sale of products under licence (often referred to as 'merchandising'), exploiting the facilities of the club and the difficult task of encouraging people to return to the club stadium after increasing the cost of season tickets by 40 per cent – were some of the great challenges they had to face.

The choice of Mr Calzada as Director of Marketing was significant in an attempt to resolve certain problems that may well appear to have been non-existent in the past. His pleasant agreement to an interview has allowed us to analyse some of the aspects raised.

It is of vital importance to structure a marketing department correctly and conveniently to allow for maximum coordination of each and every one of its functions. The department is divided basically into four specific areas:

1. Barcelona FC's brand image

2. Sponsorship and other commercial activities

3. Recruiting and loyalty

4. Contents and media.

Managing Barcelona FC's brand image

The great advantage for the club is that, through nearly 105 years of existence, it is the only football club that has:

- always, year after year, participated in European competitions, whether the European Cup (now the Champions League), the 'Copa de Ferias' (now the UEFA Cup) or the already extinct Recopa de Europa
- along with Real Madrid, never been relegated to the National Second Division
- won, at least on some occasions, all the competitions except for the Intercontinental Cup
- until this year, had the lowest membership fees and stadium season tickets of all the top-flight clubs in the whole of Europe.

For several reasons, it is considered to be 'more than just a club':

1. It has a very large number of members (at one time greater than 108 000 – a figure that will doubtless be surpassed in the future), in conjunction with a stadium that is the envy of every club in the world.

2. The very strong emotional tie among Catalans maintains a rivalry, much more than just sporting, with the main club in the Spanish capital.

3. The need of the inhabitants of a magnificent but very stressful city has led to them seeking distraction, identification and/or an escape valve. Any person, rich or poor, of any political leaning or social tendency, can identify with the club – to the point that in any café, office, shop or work place it is normal to discuss the latest 'Barça' match, or of the internal or external conflicts existing within the club.

It is important to point out here that the Catalan people are characterized by being both Latin and Mediterranean, which differentiates them from other sporting fans – they are hugely demanding, 'spoilt', impatient and not particularly understanding as far as the players are concerned. On many occasions they have been the involuntary cause of a decline in the football team. For this reason, it seems that it could be a very serious error to take any action with this fan base using strategies that may have been particularly successful in the United States or in the Scandinavian countries. In Catalonia alone, there are at least three daily sporting papers that are 80 per cent full of articles about Barcelona FC. This means reading, on innumerable occasions, news that has not always been verified and that may question – many times unjustly – the efforts of the different people responsible for the club. If to all this we add the immense although paradoxical unconditional following of the different segments of the public, which have as their sole source of information the aforementioned media, it is clear that a large portion of the image of 'Barça' is in outside hands. It is at these times that the public relations department of the club should act, attempting to seek a balance between cordiality with all kinds of communications media and a firm hand that prevents excessive interference – and avoiding, at all cost, any favouritism.

Tools arising from commercial research, such as the very well-known objective techniques (surveys, panels, etc.) or new techniques derived from multivalent logic, allow us to know, on a continuous and evolutionary basis, of the opinion of fans: What do they want? What are they looking for? Will they agree with a certain type of decision? It is fundamental to be informed at all times on their points of view, but above all else on the opinions of the members who attend the stadium to watch the matches and who, in short (at least in theory), are the people who will have the last word. However, we must never confuse being informed with blindly listening to and acting on all that is said by the public, who (although this is not a particularly political point of view) are influenced all too easily. It is important not to forget that members, as well as many other fans, who talk quite outspokenly and sometimes harshly about football, are not experts – and however numerous any group is, its members will always know far less than a professional expert. The conclusion seems to be that we need to be informed of the opinion of the general public, and above all of the members, but must not allow this conditioning to affect excessively any decision-making. Obviously there will be cases where, oriented by true professionals from both the world of football and the economic and legal worlds, decisions will, *a priori*, be unpopular, but will in the medium or long term be rewarding for club fans – and all parties are looking for a common end: that the team is successful on the sports field as well as economically and socially.

Another of the matters handled by this unit, although directly related with others, is to complement the commercial communication directed at the members of the entity. For example, after a complicated season recently the first team was only able to qualify for the UEFA Cup. This minor award, independently of the decrease in income that this would have meant if it had not been for the previous president, Josep Lluís Núñez, who set up and signed agreements in order to compensate for any losses if the team did not reach the top level of continental competition, has provoked generalized bad feeling in the public who normally attend the stadium. To see the top rival competing in Europe every Tuesday and Wednesday with the best clubs on the continent has deeply injured the pride of the fans, and this has become very evident at times in the attendance at dull UEFA matches. In order to counteract this effect, the marketing department has sought (perhaps basing itself excessively on North American formulae) ways of motivating members to fill the stadium, even during less attractive games. 'The Way to Goteborg' is the result of this effort, which started in August 2004 when the new Board of Directors (in accordance with one of its election promises) attempted to revive the enthusiasm of the members, encouraging them to fill the near-100 000 seats at the stadium. At the date of writing, in 2004, it seems that the friendly tournament that starts the football season at Barcelona FC, the Joan Gamper Trophy, is expected to be a pilot test of great interest – even more so taking into account the fact that spectators have to pay for a ticket, independently of any season ticket held. The cartoon character 'Barça Toons', which characterizes and caricatures the players and team manager, has taken part in a number of television advertisements which have finished by encouraging fans to see the 'new Barça' of the new Board of Directors, headed up by the brand new player Ronaldinho, and the success of this campaign was clearly shown by a practically full Camp Nou.

At this point it might be worth considering whether the economic result of the Joan Gamper Trophy will be positive, after so much investment. If the answer is in the affirmative, we can be sure that the work that has been done was excellent – independently of the fact that the fans may have filled the stadium attracted either by these new actions or by the expectation of seeing the new 2003–2004 Barça headed by Ronaldinho, who had already given such pleasure in the friendly matches played in preparation for the season. However, if this is not the case, the marketing department of Barcelona FC may consider this to have been an investment in public relations which, by definition, is assumed to be a long-term investment. In this case there may be the need for an in-depth study to analyse the repercussions of this investment on the image of the club. Only time will tell if this investment was profitable.

The formula for success should have been taken advantage of – and at what better moment than at the first league match, which was played at home? Also, a curious coincidence was that for this match (Barcelona FC–Sevilla FC) the new Board of Directors, for the first time ever, decided to play the match at 0005 h on a Tuesday so as not to lose any of the international players, who had to leave with their respective national teams. Again, what better excuse was there to make the investment in such a spectacle? Offering gazpacho (a typical cold soup from Sevilla, based on vegetables) to the public, which was considered one of the most singular images of the day, has today become engraved on the retina yet still leaves us ambivalent. For some, this was a novelty that refreshed the spectator before a match held on a hot summer evening; for many others, it was a sorry spectacle that was reflected in long queues, crowding and at times heated discussions between fans disputing this much appreciated 'trophy', turning the noble image of the club and its fans upside down. It is not my intention, and neither would it be justified, to judge this action, which was qualified by many as a great success; however, as specialists in marketing it would be nice to think that those who were commercially responsible did the corresponding market research in order to understand the degree of acceptance of this novelty.

From here forwards, it would be a considerable error to think that the corporate image, which has been laboured over with greater or lesser skill over so many years, will maintain itself alone. It is the fruit of many circumstances united with the efforts of managers and employees, who have always sought what is best for the club. For this reason it is necessary to continue working in order for this image not to be weakened at any time, acting with great coherence and respecting the identity of a public or fans who are very particular, but deeply love 'Barça'.

Sponsorship and other commercial activities

The most attractive word in the eyes of a person interested in economic sporting matters is, without any doubt whatsoever, 'sponsorship'. Normally, modest sports entities that are not particularly well known have great difficulty in finding one or more companies willing to offer large sums of money in exchange for appearing with the players or becoming corporately joined to the club. One of the solutions to this problem has always been taking advantage of any personal relationships that club directors may have with an executive of a possible sponsoring entity. On many occasions it has been normal to get by by means of the accumulation of several perhaps modest contributions, which in the end resulted in great utility to the club.

From a different angle, it can be stated that the spectacular importance of Barcelona FC grants it the greatest of opportunities for gaining sponsors. Proof of this popularity can be seen by the fact that if we were to ask any person, in any part of the world, who the President of Barcelona FC is, we could be sure that the percentage of correct answers would be far higher than if the question had been, who is the president of the Generalitat of Catalonia (Catalan Autonomous Government), where is Catalonia, or even who is the President of the Spanish government?

A club that is known throughout the world and loved by millions of Catalans is very desirable for any business. Nevertheless, Barcelona FC needs sponsors that have a certain attraction and, as commented by Mr Calzada, 'add and not subtract'. Imagine, for example, that a company producing condoms (with all the respect warranted by such a noble and useful product) was the one making the best economic offer to appear alongside the club, and was accepted as a sponsor. It would be logical to assume that Barcelona FC would then become the constant victim of innumerable jokes, apart from finding itself mired in mockery.

The club must be respected and never subject to any political ideology. Perhaps for this very reason, in the past, it was considered as a refuge for these.

Some particularly interesting examples are those of At. Madrid and Deportivo de la Coruña. The first of these Spanish First Division clubs opted for the sponsorship of an American cinema distributor. Thanks to this, when films are shown they frequently appear alongside the team, and very often actors such as Will Smith or Harrison Ford will appear wearing the colours of the first team – which increases further the friendly image that is proof against all frontiers; any television viewers who see a favourite actor wearing the At. Madrid colours during the midday newscast will, without a doubt, have increased positive feelings towards this particular team. If they are potential football fans, they will have been provided with an added reason for becoming a follower.

No less striking was the interesting campaign by Deportivo de la Coruña. The player Naybet, who is of Moroccan origin, played in this team from Galicia, and involuntarily had a great deal to do with the selection of the name of the company that is shown on the blue and white shirts: 'Fadesa'. This real estate company was considering constructing a hotel in Casablanca at a time when the relationship between Spain and Morocco was particularly tense and difficult. The sponsorship bid therefore profited from the country of his birth, thanks to the popularity of this player.

When discussing sponsorship, it is impossible to ignore sponsors' bids to appear on the first team's shirts. After more than a century in existence, Barcelona FC has never carried advertising on its first team's shirts. The reasons for this have changed over the years. Up to thirty years ago this possibility could not be contemplated, since the marketing departments of the potentially interested large companies (at that time, Spanish) did not work with this type of sponsorship and the football teams did not appear on television or in other communications media with the frequency that they do at present. They were therefore far less attractive a proposition. Latterly, during the twenty-two years under the presidency of Josep Lluís Núñez, this aspect was considered as an option that should only be adopted if the economic deficiencies of the club required this imperatively. To be the only team in the whole world to enjoy this 'virginity' was another significant factor, in this case rather romantic but of a great impact, which differentiated Barcelona FC, 'more than a club', from any other team. Unfortunately, in the last three years financial management has led the economically healthiest club in Europe (with the added value of not being a Limited Company and of therefore belonging to all its members) to become an entity with financial difficulties. Has the time come to break away from the policy that has always differentiated the club from any other in the world? As for nearly all questions, the possible replies must all be weighed up. This drastic step should only be taken in the event that the financial incentive offered is really worthwhile. To 'stain' the team shirt is to lose this differentiation, and although not the most important, it is still that 'something else'. Today, Barcelona FC is not the most competitive team in Europe with regard to football, and this can only lead to top-flight brand names offering lesser amounts in comparison with what they were offering five or ten years ago. If this is not the case, then brand names of little interest will be those that are offering slightly higher amounts, and the prestige of the club requires, as Esteve Calzada so rightly put it, brand names that add and do not subtract.

Another function carried out in this area, directly related to image and sponsoring, is the organization of friendly matches and tours on other continents. The objective? Apart from certain economic payments or compensations for some contracted players, the objective is to attempt to relate with fans from other countries in order to gain their following and consequent interest in licensed products. However, is this really worthwhile? Relative to the institutional image of the club, certainly; but economically? Well, this would have to be analysed, although there are very few countries that potentially have sufficient buyers. One of these, which today is surely the most attractive not only for sporting entities but also for any business, is China. Its more than 1 300 000 000 inhabitants make managing directors and presidents dream of purchases which, even if only limited to 1 per cent, would be extraordinarily profitable. Reality is, though, at times misleading, and to reach satisfactory agreements with other countries, especially if they have very different cultures or ways of interpreting the economy, can be difficult. In any event, we can state that Barcelona FC is working on trying to tie up certain agreements with this interesting and heavily populated country.

The Barcelona FC Foundation saw the light of day in 1994, on a trip to Paris made by the then President of the club and a professor in financial economy, later President of the Economical-Statutory Committee of the Club, Professor Dr Jaime Gil-Aluja. The latter suggested to the president that the entity could set up a foundation that would be capable of attracting new financial resources that could support a sport company that is not currently lucrative. This brilliant idea was put in motion immediately, with interesting results. Nevertheless, insufficient commercial work meant that the club did not take advantage of this option to its maximum degree. Members, fans and others were informed of the possibilities of obtaining shares in the club and of being of great use. In fact, this was the road to travel – although in my modest opinion it was not sufficient; the existence of some desks close to the club offices and a telephone number that allowed the interested party to gather information appear to have been less than adequate. Without a doubt, many people left the Foundation because they were not called or visited at their offices for signing up and collecting payment of dues; they themselves had to do this on their own initiative and this, as we well know, invites the potential 'client' not always to be bothered in taking the initiative. In any event, it seems certain that this subject is not still pending in this area of the marketing department of Barcelona FC. Finally, this second unit handles part of the management of licensing (incorrectly termed 'merchandising', as was clarified at the 1st World Congress on Sports Management that took place in Barcelona on 14–16 May 2003). Licensing has always been the eternal false goose that lays the golden eggs. When just a few years ago Real Madrid signed Luis Figo for exorbitant fees, and also Zinedine Zidane, Ronaldo and, more recently, David Beckham, its president commented that with these contracts, the club would gain such large amounts from the sale of their shirts that investment in them would be well and truly paid off. After a few simple studies, it seems that this is seriously in doubt. Let us take, for example, one of the less costly of these contracts – that of Beckham. If luck were on the side of Real Madrid, it could sell up to 20 000 shirts with the number of this player; if each shirt costs €60 and all 20 000 buyers buy the most expensive shirt, the income would reach the figure of €1 200 000. If we consider (being generous) that the net profit made on each shirt is 50 per cent, that gives a total profit of just €600 000 – enough for Mr Beckham to go for a short shopping trip with his wife Victoria. However, this is not all. Would the fathers and sons who have bought the Beckham shirt also buy those of Raul, Roberto Carlos, Figo, Zidane and Ronaldo? You be the judge.

Returning to the club with which we are occupied, as a consequence of its difficult economic situation Barcelona FC decided, a short time ago, to sell 50 per cent of its licensing rights to Nike – which, to be sure, took advantage of this wonderful occasion to obtain the same at a relatively low price. As mentioned by Mr Calzada, FCB Merchandising then saw the light of day – a company totally occupied with managing the sale of all the products with the Barcelona FC brand name. Its highly professional employees will surely guarantee an interesting source of income, although, we suspect very small relative to the rest. Nevertheless, its exploitation is necessary and important, although in this case, as always, the best strategic commercial tool will always be that which we all expect – winners and trophies.

Recruiting and loyalty

Attention to members must always be one of the services that a club the size of Barcelona FC takes care of. The members are the 'owners' of an entity which, as already mentioned, is one of just four clubs in Spanish football that was not obliged, following Law 10/1990 on Sports, to become a Limited Sports Company. They have the power to decide who will be the president, and of vetoing him, if necessary, by means of a vote of no confidence. How, though, can football fans in general and fans of Barcelona FC in particular be persuaded to pay large sums of money in order to be able to vote, and on rare occasions visit the stadium to watch a team match?. Naturally, the answer to this is difficult. Now, in 2004, the 'Blaugrana' Club (blue and maroon, the club colours) is launching a campaign for recruiting members, under the name of 'The great challenge for Barcelona FC'.

This, without any doubt, is a very large economic investment. Commercial communications should allow for recruiting a previously determined number of members, which will not only compensate the financial means invested but also allow for a certain amount of net income in the future. This is a difficult task, taking into account that the theoretical attractions are:

- receiving, every two months, a free copy of the club magazine

- free access to the club museum

- the possibility of attending three matches, with a waiting list, and paying for an additional season ticket

- the option of acquiring a ball with the team colours

- paying only €3 more if the members are under fifteen years old

- elimination of the entry quota

- the possibility of voting at new elections for president or votes of confidence

- discounts to other public facilities at the club.

Making an objective and technical analysis of this latest campaign, we confirm its commercial aim: a written presentation in good taste, its dark-yellow colouring stands out, giving it light and warmth. It is made from high-quality paper along with careful wording, written in the majority in blue and maroon ink (the team colours), and perfectly complemented with images that make the ideas that it is intended to transmit stand out well.

The main point that is taken into account is the feeling that unites all Barcelona FC fans. On opening the brochure, in the upper right-hand corner there is the most incisive and convincing message – 'Together we will make Barcelona FC the best and largest club in the world' – accompanied by a message written by the Board of Directors of the Club.

It should be stated that this campaign was launched with great skill just a few days prior to the ever-important match between Barça and Real Madrid at Camp Nou. This match always guarantees a full stadium, and the fans, among whom are members without season tickets and non-members, fight for the few seats that will allow them to attend such an important event. However, in this case, 3 days before the great match Barça was sadly beaten 5–1 by the modest Malaga team – and this, without a doubt, was a serious setback for the recruiting plan for new members.

Lastly, as a promotion, the brochure emphasizes the fact that 'now it costs less and gives greater advantages'. In this respect, it might be worth asking if potential members who do not aspire to attending any matches will pay an amount nearing €132. Will they take the decision to become a member just so as not to pay the entry fee? Will this flexibility exist regarding the price? The explanation may be found in the manner in which those responsible for the campaign have sought to differentiate the same from those carried out before.

Is it sufficiently clear in the message that new members are not guaranteed attendance at the matches they may want to see at Camp Nou, even when paying the full entrance price? It is true to say that in the small print there is the addendum: 'Available for 2004/2005, according to waiting list'. Even so, could new members feel misled? The possibility exists that, having recruited a pre-determined number of members and exceeded objectives at the end of one or two seasons, these members could then resign as they were unable to get a seat at the Barcelona coliseum. And we all know that what is important is a service such as that which is offered by Barcelona FC to its 'clients' – that is, not just to recruit them but also to maintain them year after year. If members were to leave, would it have served any purpose to set the €396 of the initial quota for an adult member against the tremendous economic output made? The future, without any doubt whatsoever, will provide the answer.

Having said this, At. Madrid again provides an interesting example of recruitment of members and fans. A few seasons ago, this team dropped down to the Second Division. To the logical sporting depression was added a double economic problem:

- the foreseeable decline in the number of members who would stop paying their season tickets and not go to the stadium, disappointed at having to watch only second-rate teams
- the economic decrease that meant receiving much lower amounts for television rights than those received by First Division clubs.

However, the model handling of marketing carried out by At. Madrid not only managed not to lose members whilst the team was in the Second Division, but also managed to increase the number of members – exceeding even the most optimistic estimates. The club's excellent campaign, 'A year in hell', as well as all those carried out later, makes this club a model to follow.

Contents and media

A step that could be of great interest for Barcelona FC is that already taken by the marketing department in repurchasing assets that had previously been sold, in order to manage both static advertising as well as the rights of the web, magazine, etc. If this step (i.e. investment in a team to handle them and be responsible for their success or failures) is economically profitable, it will allow avoidance of misunderstandings such as the sale of adjacent advertising boards to two competing multinational companies, and management of all these spaces coherently. If the professionals operating here are successful, Barcelona FC will benefit in spite of having assumed a great risk.

Neither should we forget that new technologies have opened up new opportunities, which should be taken advantage of. The birth of digital platforms just a few years ago has opened an interesting door to all the clubs in the Spanish League. In this sphere, however, the best decision (and perhaps the least known by the communications media) was the negotiation carried out by the ex-president, Josep Lluís Núñez, when he signed a long-term agreement with one of them that has avoided the merger of said platforms and the subsequent monopoly effect that exists today. If these negotiations had not taken place, Barcelona FC would have been affected in the same way as the remaining clubs in the First Division.

The growing development of new technologies, and specifically the Internet, has allowed us today to communicate with any part of the world almost instantaneously. This, then, provides a great opportunity, which is being worked on by the marketing department. Using the 'Barça' web page, a member of fan, wherever located, may access club information on a day-to-day basis. The opportunity of purchasing any Barcelona FC licensed product whenever desired and without moving from home is another objective to be aimed at. For this it is absolutely essential to increase as far as possible the number of fans, members and followers all over the world, without limiting these to those spectators who go to the stadium.

New technologies, licensed products, recruiting members and followers, organizing teams tours to different continents and, above all, goals and trophies are some of the multiple parts that comprise the puzzle which can only be perfectly put together if coordinated by prepared professionals who are perfectly trained – such as those headed by Mr Calzada. In this way it will be possible to arrive at the maximum yield of the extensive, although complex and uncertain, possibilities available to this magnificent club.

Bibliography and references

Cruz Roche, I. (1990). *Fundamentos de Marketing*. Ariel.

Desbordes, M. (2000). *Gestion du sport*. Vigot.

Desbordes, M. and Falgoux, J. (2004). *Organiser un évènement sportif*, 2nd edn. Editions d'Organisations.

Desbordes, M., Ohl, F. and Tribou, G. (2004). *Marketing du sport*, 3rd edn. *Economica*.

Gil-Lafuente, J. (1997). *Marketing para el Nuevo Milenio. Nuevas técnicas para la gestión comercial en incertidumbre*. Pirámide.

Gil-Lafuente, J. (2002). *Algoritmos de la Excelencia. Claves para el Éxito en la Gestión Deportiva*. Milladoiro, Publicaciones del FC Barcelona.

Gil-Lafuente, J. (2004). La gestion marketing dans un club très complexe socialement: le FC Barcelone. In: G. Bolle and M. Desbordes (eds), *Marketing et Football: une Perspective Internationale*. Presses Universitaires du Sport.

Gil-Lafuente, J. *et al.* (1999). *Les Universitats en el Centenari del Futbol Club Barcelona. Estudis en l'àmbit de l'esport*. Malladoiro, Edicions FC Barcelona.

Gil-Lafuente, J. *et al.* (2004). *Economics, Management and Optimisation in Sport*. Springer-Verlag.

Kotler, P. (2000). *Dirección de Marketing*, 10th edn. Prentice Hall.

Lambin, J. J. (1995). *Marketing estratégico*, 3rd edn. McGraw-Hill.

Martin Armario, E. (1993). *Marketing*. Ariel.

Munuera Alemán, J. L. and Rodríguez Escudero, A. I. (2002). *Estrategias de Marketing. Teoría y casos*. Pirámide (Grupo Anaya).

Santesmases, M. (1996). *Términos de Marketing*. Pirámide.

Santesmases, M. (2001). *Marketing. Conceptos y Estrategias*, 3rd edn. Pirámide.

Stanton, W. (1992). *Fundamentos de Marketing*, 9th edn. McGraw-Hill.

Stanton, W. J., Etzel, M. J. and Walker, B. J. (2000). *Fundamentos de Marketing*, 11th edn. McGraw-Hill.

Appendix 7.1

Interview with Esteve Calzada, Marketing Director of Barcelona FC

Q1: What are the tasks that are carried out in a marketing department such as that of Barcelona FC?

EC: In the first place, it should be clarified that the marketing department of Barcelona FC is different from that of other conventional businesses in that we do not have a marketing department that is independent of the commercial department, insofar as the tasks are performed jointly. It has as its final objective that of generating income through the exploitation of the different assets held by the club (team, players, the 'Barcelona FC' brand name and its facilities). This seeking for income includes different lines of business: sponsorship, media content (Internet, mobile phones, television, etc.), merchandising (in cooperation with 'Nike'), and club members and fans. Contrary to other times in which the teams were only working on their area of influence in order for more spectators to fill up the stadiums, at present we as a top-flight club look for their fans on a worldwide scale, in an attempt to get people from every corner of the globe to visit our website, buy our products through the Internet, or watch our matches on television. Apart from this, we are working with the typical activities of a marketing department of a large conventional company, such as setting up communications campaigns (generation, strategy and execution), market research and all other things relative to control of the brand (corporate image) and finally all that which has to do with promotional campaigns. With regard to the latter, we would like to highlight, just as an example, those campaigns carried out for the matches of the first team in the UEFA Cup – 'The Way to Goteborg'; we are attempting to create a certain complicity between the fans and the team in a second-level competition relative to that to which the team has been accustomed to playing in over the last few years: the 'Champions League'.

Q2: How is the marketing department of Barcelona FC structured?

EC: At present our department is divided into four units:

1. Brand management, or marketing as such. This is where communications campaigns are carried out, as are work on the corporate image, market research and promotions. It is precisely in this unit that the humorous and delightful idea of the 'Barça Toons' for the 'Joan Gamper Trophy' arose. From this we became aware of the fact that this manner of communicating had great potential, and

not only through television, as these figures could be sold to strengthen our merchandising.

2. Sponsorship or commercial. Here the search for new sponsors begins, where the star media figure is the search for publicity on the team shirts. The task for sponsors is also done at other levels (cooperators or official suppliers) – the selling of friendly matches for the club and tours such as those recently made in the United States and Mexico. Just at present we are negotiating the possibility of travelling to Asia next year. Selling the Foundation is another of the tasks of this unit. We feel that it is important that the person selling sponsorship should also do it with the Foundation in order to avoid any competition. Also controlled from this unit is 'FCB Merchandising', the company responsible for our merchandising. The income obtained is shared fifty/fifty with Nike. In spite of the fact that FCB Merchandising has its own work team, our area intervenes in a follow-up and control capacity. The selling of campaigns for the image rights of players is another of the tasks carried out from this area. If a company wants to film an advertising spot with any of our players, because the personal image rights of many of them are the property (partially or totally) of the club then that company must of necessity contact our unit.

3. Recruiting and loyalty. This includes everything related to the members (including attention). Just at present we are working very hard at recruiting new members and fans. Last year the work was directed at searching for new fans 'Gent del Barça' (People of Barça'), whilst this year we are concentrating on recruiting new members independently of whether these buy season tickets for the football matches played by the first team in the club stadium or not.

4. Contents and media. Here, we handle television contracts (with the autonomous channel TV and Sogecable), the selling of television rights for friendly matches, relationships with the thematic channel 'Canal Barça' (which very recently has its own team occupied with the exploitation of its contents), and the subject of the Internet and mobile telephones. In this latter case we have been seeking a partner, just as we did with sales under licence with Nike, in order to assist us in exploiting the different services. On this subject we are working with 'Movistar' of Telefónica.

We are assuming that the Barcelona FC brand name means certain complexities at the time of selling. For one thing, its image is subject to a high degree of instability due to the uncertainty of results, whilst on the other hand, working with a club that symbolizes so much and that is known by everyone and all over the world must open a lot of doors.

Today, it is not an easy task to sell sponsorship. We must make it clear that the idea that because Barcelona FC is a great club, everybody is fighting to buy our products, does not respond to reality: we must go out to try and sell. At the moment, when all the companies are reducing their budgets, a job such as this is no easy task, although it is also true that, because it is 'the Barça', many doors are open to us and we have many more opportunities than other clubs. Therefore, we must know how to modulate the situations at different moments. There are certain times when selling is more difficult exclusively due to the results obtained by the first football club. When we win 8–0, the offers multiply; following one or two defeats, these offers are reduced considerably. But, in spite of all this, we are fortunate because our club, which differs from others, does not obtain success sporadically, as was the case with 'Bayer Leverkusen' – where after a historical year in which they made all the finals they almost dropped down to the Second Division the following season. This sports instability is clearly shown in the variability of their income. I would not be surprised to find that in one year they invoiced half that of the previous year. In spite of the fact that recently we have not won any title, we have much more relative fluctuations and, independently of the fact of whether we win or not, Barcelona FC is still considered a first-class team.

Another important matter to be taken into account, and one that means a change in respect of preceding years in the commercial sense, is that previously Barcelona FC supporters and enthusiasts stopped buying certain brands on the mere fact that these brands sponsored our oldest rival, Real Madrid, and *vice versa*. In this respect it is paradigmatic to see what happened with the Zanussi, Parmalat, etc., brand names, the sale of which decreased dramatically in Barcelona. But today, when we work with global projects (that is, they take in the whole world), we have become aware of the fact that the consumer has become more sophisticated and objective and that this minimizes the impact. All of which, added to the fact that the market is worldwide, attenuates the problem. We have seen that the brand name 'Siemens' (the current sponsor of the team from the Spanish capital) has reacted by thinking in terms of generating an image over the entire world, and not worrying too much that their sales have decreased in Catalonia. Even so, Siemens in Catalonia has not suffered the same effect that at the time prejudiced Zanussi or Parmalat. Fans of Barcelona do not now think: 'What is the brand name of our eternal rival, so that I do not buy a mobile phone with the Siemens brand name?'.

Q4: Could you highlight some of the successes attained by your marketing department?

EC: Since I arrived at Barcelona FC, in January 2002, we have attempted to change the manner of marketing since, prior to then, the system carried out by the club was very much more static, reactive instead of proactive, closing agreements with fixed amounts and later not participating in the income, etc. My entry into the club had as its basic objective that of generating income, coinciding with a very complicated time: the club was not enjoying much success in the sporting world, there was not any institutional stability and, in spite of the fact of working for the object of attaining successes, with a platform adequately prepared with more illusion, such as we have at present, there is a greater potential for income and it is easier to work. Among the more outstanding events we have recently carried out, for example, was the re-launching of our web page and the launching of the fan's credential *Gent de Barça*. The latter event, as it is a particularly emotional product, very much depends on results. In spite of this, we have managed to work on something about which much has been said for a long time, without ever anything being achieved. We have some 120 000 fan credentials which, in spite of the fact that many of these were given away to members of fan clubs, have allowed us to obtain an important database of addresses that are of great interest to the club.

On the other hand, we have done a lot of work on the recuperation of assets. Barcelona FC has an enormous amount of sales made in advance, such as static advertising, the rights on the Web, sponsorship rights, the rights from the magazines, etc., and if we are wanting to generate income from sponsorship and we have all the assets sold to third parties, it will be very difficult to present an interesting offer to a sponsor – such as two bill boards in our football stadium, a presence on the pages of our magazine or on our web page. This means going around one by one to repurchase the spaces where we have sold our assets, without being able to guarantee the most elemental conditions of exclusivity in each commercial area – a vital condition for a sponsor (the case could occur of selling a space to one brand alongside that of a competitor, which is totally unacceptable). Fortunately, since I arrived at the club we have been able to recuperate the nine most important assets that had been granted elsewhere. Now we are able to manage these directly, we are generating more profitability by incorporating them into packs.

Another project of which we are particularly proud is the tour we made last summer to the United States. It is the first time that the team has done a tour with the object of selling, passing later through Mexico. Up to now this had been particularly complicated, since the team managers were never very keen to do it – which seems quite logical, taking into account that the latter always defend their own terrain and look for the best options for training in order for the players to be in optimum physical condition. In spite of this fact, it was a great success; being able to fill the North American stadiums has given Barcelona FC a projection that was becoming urgent.

We have closed deals for important sponsorship, such as those arrived at with Coca-Cola and Damm (beer), which have allowed us to increase income considerably. During this season, one of the events of which we are also particularly proud is that carried out during our summer trophy competition, the 'Joan Gamper trophy'. Our work was fundamental in getting 93 000 spectators to fill the stadium. A great party was set up along with a campaign to get people to see the match. There were certain factors that contributed to this success, such as the search for other contents, so that people went to the stadium long before the match, but of course all this is reinforced if the team plays well and the results match this. Today the work we are doing is highly valued, whilst only 6 months ago we were severely criticized; there is no need to add to this comment that before we were neither so incapable nor now so brilliant; the marketing team is the same. What's the difference? Currently, sponsorship is working better because within the club there is now a great deal of enthusiasm, which before there was not, and this has a very strong positive influence, which allows us to sell our products better.

Q5: What are the general steps taken by the club for finding sponsors?
EC: The first consists of identifying the sectors of activity traditionally associated with the world of football. As everyone is aware, we have other professional and non-professional sports sections, but of course football, logically, is the one that stands out from the remainder and also the most important relative to income. If we take it from here, we have to decide which categories have been identified as interesting for companies in this sector that can be associated with the world of football, and whether they are categories in which we already have a sponsor or not. For example, in the drinks sector we are not going to look any further, as we already have agreements with Coca-Cola and in beers with Damm; also with financial entities in La Caixa. If we take a look at the automobile sector, which is particularly active, we have to negotiate with several companies in order to see which will be the Barcelona FC car. The same occurs in the electronic sector, where each team normally carries one brand. The search, then, is aimed at identification of the hot sectors and companies that wish to grow and have an interest in increasing

their image and knowledge of their brand name, or those where Barcelona FC can offer a good return. For an entity that everyone knows about it will be difficult to improve their image, as opposed to when we are dealing with another that is just commencing sales in our country.

Q6: And Ronaldinho? Has he been a big influence in the Barcelona FC marketing department?
EC: Obviously. His influence has been fundamental. He has given us total and absolutely necessary projection, which was very necessary. We are very optimistic, because he has proved far better than our most optimistic estimates. He is totally confirmed as a great player. Just yesterday, on the CNN channel they showed a great Ronaldinho goal. This is fundamental, not only for the sale of the shirts with his number and name, but also for what it does for the image of the club. If someone is going to buy the shirt with this player's name, it is quite possible that another product sold in our shop will be bought. Also, he has a great media pull – just the place where we had lost ground – in Japan and also Brazil.

We should not forget, though, other players with media interest, such as the Mexican player Márquez, who has introduced us to a market which up to now had always been for Real Madrid owing to the effect of Hugo Sánchez. Proof of this is that that country received us during our last tour as the most important team.

Q7: What can you say about the innovative advertising on the first-team shirt?
EC: This is also an important project for the club. Just now, we are working very hard on this subject. There is a series of companies with which we are negotiating and others which have made us important offers but to which we have said no. The reason for this is that not just any kind of product can be placed on the Barcelona FC first-team shirt; it must be a brand that adds to us and doesn't subtract, that is dynamic, with worldwide projection, with the need to grow and that does not seem strange in its association with our 'Barça'. The work has to be very intense but extremely discreet, without forgetting the fact that a decision of this magnitude (it will be the first time in history that the first football team has had advertising on the shirts) requires time. We must not sell badly. We are speaking, normally, of an agreement for three years, and the right moment has to be found for closing the contract at a good price – above all, taking into account that it is the first time that this event has taken place in the history of our club. We did not receive formal approval from the Board until the end of August and, in spite of having commenced negotiations before this, we could not make any firm offers, because this had first to be approved by the Board.

This is therefore something that is difficult, that has to ripen; the fact is that Real Madrid has had many years in which it could not close any deal with a sponsor and remained without any: the agreement reached with Siemens was not closed in 2 days. Surrounding us there is much speculation, but we can make no further comment; when the time comes, everyone will become aware of the fortunate brand name.

Q8: To end, would you like to comment on some future project?
EC: We have many things in hand. One of these is the exploitation of our facilities, which have great potential. We should not forget that the Barcelona FC Museum is the most visited in the whole of Catalonia, with more than 1 000 000 visitors per annum. For this reason we have taken on a person responsible for 'Port Aventura', Laurent Colette, who has a vast experience in development in the commercial world. He will be the new director of facilities. What we are looking for is that as well as the visit to the museum, people gain other experiences from our club. When the time comes for the first team to train in the new sport facilities, we will have some spectacular opportunities relative to their exploitation. Here we will have the necessary platform for further income, which is sorely needed in order for us to comply with the objective promised by the new Board of Directors – that is, deficit zero.

C

Is there a place for 'small' countries on the European football market?

Efficiency and sponsorship in Portuguese Premier League football

Carlos Pestana Barros, Catarina de Barros and Abel Santos

Overview

All Portuguese football league clubs are limited liability companies, and a small number of them are listed companies quoted on the stock market. Concentrating on their traditional core business, they are supposed to pursue sporting success to improve their financial performance. However, it is worth considering how a football club can improve its financial performance, given first its *raison d'être* of achieving success on the football field, and secondly the fact that, if the 'game is about winning', there are only limited opportunities each season to emerge as champions, major cup-winners, or with a move upwards on the promotional ladder. We analyse the role of sponsorship in the Portuguese First Division (known since 2002 as the Superliga, or Super League) with a two-step procedure. In the first step a DEA (Data Envelopment Analysis) is performed, taking into account sporting as well as financial and marketing variables. In the second stage, a Tobit model identifies the drivers of sponsorship in the league. Managerial implications are derived.

Keywords

Portuguese First Division football clubs, performance, DEA, Tobit regression, sponsorship

Introduction

Professional football clubs compete in a league with the goal of winning, supposing that sport success enhances financial wealth. The link between sporting and financial activities is therefore of paramount importance for the competitiveness of football clubs (Szymanski and Kuypers, 2000: 22). Among the accounting variables displayed in the balance sheet, sponsorship is the most significant (Desbordes *et al.*, 2001).

In this chapter we analyse the efficiency of the Portuguese football clubs, using a DEA (Data Envelopment Analysis) combining sports, financial and marketing variables.

Regarding a football club's performance, its efficiency is usually measured by its performance on the pitch, neglecting financial and marketing performance – which should also be deemed of importance. DEA has been applied in sport economics and management to analyse the performance of sports institutions (see Fizel and D'Itri, 1997; Barros, 2003; Barros and Santos, 2003; Haas, 2003).

DEA was first developed by Farrell (1957) and consolidated by Charnes *et al.* (1978) as a non-parametric procedure that compares a decision unit with an efficient frontier using performance indicators. DEA is particularly appropriate in cases where the researcher is interested in investigating the efficiency of converting multiple inputs into multiple outputs and has only a small number of observations, which prevents a parametric analysis.

DEA is a linear programming technique that enables management to benchmark the best-practice decision unit (DMU), i.e. the football clubs. Furthermore, DEA provides estimates of potential improvement for inefficient DMUs. DEA has emerged as a particularly useful service management technique. It is theory-based, transparent, and a reproducible computational procedure. Gollany

(1988) points out that DEA is emerging as a leading method for efficiency evaluation, in terms of both the number of research papers published and the number of applications to real problems, namely in the area of management. We shall assume throughout this chapter some knowledge of DEA on the reader's part. Readers not familiar with DEA are referred to Charnes *et al.* (1995), Coelli (1996), Coelli *et al.* (1998), Cooper *et al.* (2000), Thanassoulis (2001) and Zhu (2002).

In this chapter, we present an application of DEA to the analysis of two disparate success measures – sporting success, and financial success and marketing performance – extending the efficiency research to football clubs, using data on Portuguese First Division clubs obtained from the Deloitte & Touche Annual Report on Professional Football Finance.

The chapter is organized as follows: in the next section we describe the institutional setting before going on to survey the literature on the topic. Subsequently, we present the theoretical framework, followed by the data and results; next, the DEA results are presented. We then go on to identify the determinants of sponsorship and present the managerial implication of the analysis. There is also an interview with a reputed football club commercial executive, Esteve Calzada, Marketing Director of Barcelona FC, focusing on aspects of our findings, as well as other related issues (see Appendix 8.1). Finally, we compare the subjective opinions of the business executive referred to with the DEA and Tobit model results before providing a conclusion. Appendix 8.2 presents the DEA model used.

Market structure

It is fair to say that Portuguese professional football lags far behind the European powerhouse Premier Leagues of England, Spain and Italy, in terms of spectacle, consumer satisfaction, attendances and financial power – in fact, when measured by most indicators. The market is small, GDP (measured by purchasing power) is lower than in most European countries and the population of a little over 10 million is concentrated on the Atlantic coast, principally in the country's two largest urban conurbations, Lisbon in the centre and Oporto in the north. This explains the fact that three clubs – Benfica and Sporting in Lisbon, and FC Porto – dominate the domestic game to such an extent that they are universally known as the 'Big Three'. The Superliga presently has eighteen clubs. It is rare indeed for any usurper from among the lesser clubs to challenge for the league championship, and even less common for one actually to win it. As evidence, when the second, smaller team in Oporto, Boavista, won the title in 2001, it was the first time that one of the

Big Three had not taken the championship since 1946. Outside of these two cities, the fan base is small and financial weakness allows little scope to buy the quality or number of players necessary to mount a serious championship assault, or to keep any players of sufficient talent from playing on a more glamorous stage.

With reference to the financial dimension of the sport in Portugal, and as an indication of how far behind giants such as Real Madrid, Manchester United or Juventus the Big Three are in organizational and commercial terms, comparative figures published for the 2000/01 season show that the total income receipts generated by the Portuguese First Division fell a little short of 13 per cent of those in the English Premiership and 15 per cent of Italy's Serie A. At club level, the total income of FC Porto was approximately €25 million, while Manchester United received almost €180 million in the same season (Deloitte & Touche, 2001). Clubs in financial deficit are in abundance, with total First Division costs having risen by 38 per cent in 2000/01 (to €246 million) from those in 1997/98. Regarding financial deficits, Benfica was the champion in 2001, registering net losses of more than €37 million – which was more than 40 per cent of the total for the entire First Division. Costs for the season were double the club's income. This provides a vivid illustration of the financial difficulties and weak economic performance and management which the sport must confront in Portugal. Furthermore, Benfica has not won the First Division title since 1993/94, and its last major trophy was the Portuguese Cup in 1996. However, it should also be emphasized that examples of financial equilibrium in football clubs around the world are few.

Clubs have tended to have squads of players which are much too large for the club's requirements and too expensive, given that players' salaries represent the largest single item of expenditure on the balance sheet. The biggest clubs must pay salaries in line with those in England or Spain to their star players, if they are to persuade them not to move elsewhere in Europe. This is a severe managerial weakness, as was revealed by the example of Boavista, which became champions in 2001 with a total monthly salary bill of only €20 000. Thanks to the sound, wise financial management of Boavista PLC, the club is a rare case of financial equilibrium.

It is therefore naturally understandable that Portugal is not a destination for the best-known, most talented players in their prime in Europe or Latin America. On the contrary, it is economically obliged to be an exporter of talent. This appears to be a rising trend, with young Portuguese players of outstanding ability – but still unfinished products – increasingly being sold on to rich and hungry giants to the east and north of their home country. Between

Table 8.1
Structure of Portuguese club costs in the 2001/02 season

Football clubs	Wages/total cost (%)	Amortization/ total cost	Supplies/ total cost	Total cost/ points won in the season
FC Porto	51.8	29.0	10.1	775 842.40
Sporting	46.7	35.3	10.9	728 421.40
Benfica	33.8	36.9	12.6	1 028 544.00
Boavista	44.8	25.8	10.0	218 704.10
Alverca	31.2	48.6	16.6	232 435.60
Victoria Guimarães	53.2	9.4	9.5	177 939.00
Salgueiros	64.7	1.8	17.4	147 427.90
Leiria	81.5	0.2	15.9	70 216.33
Sporting Braga	65.3	12.1	12.4	154 939.90
Maritimo	33.0	16.9	46.4	117 576.50
Belenenses	57.3	24.4	12.2	95 928.89
Farense	62.8	5.5	16.5	123 305.00
Gil Vicente	75.8	5.2	9.2	59 845.61
Mean	53.9	19.3	15.3	302 394.40

June 2002 and August 2003, Sporting sold three teenagers (Viana to Newcastle, Quaresma to Barcelona and Cristiano Ronaldo to Manchester United) for a combined total of approximately €28 million, while FC Porto sold the twenty-year-old Postiga to Tottenham Hotspur for €8.75 million in June 2003. Whilst this may constitute astute business for the selling clubs, it is a footballing loss to the Portuguese League. It remains to be seen whether such a lucrative form of income can become a staple of the sport's sustainability, whether the game's popularity and fan loyalty suffer as a result, or whether this is only a temporary phase. Whatever the outcome, this strategy raises searching questions relating to football success and the clubs' financial management and performance. Viana, Quaresma and Postiga have meanwhile returned home.

In Table 8.1, we present the structure of costs of the clubs used in the analysis, which are those that maintained their presence in the First Division throughout the three consecutive years analysed.

We verify that the cost per point varies, with the Big Three presenting a very high value compared with the rest of the division, confirming the dominant role of these three clubs. The average cost is €302 389 per point; the leading clubs attain this value, with the other clubs depicting lower than average values. The ratio wages/total cost shows that the salaries make up on average 53.9 per cent of costs, a value smaller than the average value in the economy, which amounts to 60 per cent. We also verify that

Table 8.2
Structure of Portuguese club receipts in the 2001/02 season

	Tickets/ total receipts (%)	Member subscrip- tions/ total receipts (%)	Sponsor- ship/total receipts (%)	TV/total receipts (%)	Gains – players sold/total receipts (%)	Finance income/ total receipts (%)
FC Porto	31.8	5.5	14.9	12.0	26.4	3.6
Sporting	21.6	9.4	5.0	18.5	35.1	3.2
Benfica	20.9	10.3	6.7	22.2	20.7	0.4
Boavista	46.8	0.0	4.3	22.7	21.9	2.4
Alverca	5.1	0.0	8.1	28.7	54.1	1.6
Victoria Guimarães	14.5	10.0	3.0	34.8	21.0	2.2
Salgueiros	10.0	4.1	9.8	20.8	13.1	0.0
Leiria	9.4	1.9	33.2	48.0	0.0	0.0
Sporting Braga	7.4	7.8	6.1	28.9	47.0	0.3
Maritimo	8.1	5.4	14.0	20.4	0.0	0.4
Belenenses	42.2	0.0	6.5	22.0	28.1	0.03
Farense	10.5	7.3	8.2	38.5	11.6	1.1
Gil Vicente	5.8	4.6	14.0	47.8	0.0	0.04
Mean	18.0	5.0	10.3	28.1	21.5	1.2

amortization is on average 19.3 per cent, but this small value includes some clubs which play in municipally-owned stadiums, and therefore have a low amortization cost. The supplies and services costs are on average 15 per cent.

In Table 8.2, we present the structure of receipts by club.

We verify that the mean match ticket receipts amount to 18 per cent of receipts, club membership subscriptions are worth only an average of 5 per cent (three clubs do not have a membership scheme), sponsorship 10.3 per cent, TV receipts 28.1 per cent and gains from the transfer of players 21.5 per cent. Financial income has a residual value of 1.2 per cent. This table shows that there are different management strategies among the clubs. Some do not ask their supporters to pay a membership fee, while others appear to make no profit from players' added value in the trans- fer market.

Overall, it can be observed that the Big Three clubs, which have a scale dimension much higher than the average, dominate Portuguese football, in financial as well as sporting terms.

Literature review

Analysis of sports efficiency is scarce, due to the lack of adequate data for this purpose (Slack, 1997). There are two contemporary approaches to measuring efficiency: the econometric or parametric approach, and the non-parametric. Besides these two approaches, we observe other works that rely on ratio analysis and which address the same issue.

Among the research that has taken the non-parametric approach, and that is thus of particular interest for the present chapter, we mention that of Fizel and D'Itri (1996, 1997), who applied DEA analysis to measure the managerial efficiency of college basketball teams to assess the conflicting theses concerning the impact of managerial succession on organizational performance, and Porter and Scully (1982), who analysed the managerial efficiency of baseball managers with a non-parametric approach. Barros (2003) analysed the incentive regulation on sports organizational training activities, disentangling technical and allocative efficiency with DEA. Haas (2003) analysed the efficiency of the USA Major Soccer League with plain DEA, and Barros and Santos (2003) estimated a Malmquist index for Portuguese sports organizational training activities.

Among the research that has used the econometric frontier, Zak et al. (1979) analysed production efficiency in the basketball market with a Cobb–Douglas deterministic frontier. Scully (1994) analysed measures of managerial efficiency for professional baseball, basketball and American football coaches, with a deterministic and a stochastic econometric frontier. A survival analysis was used to measure the coaching tenure probability in these sports. Extending the analysis of efficiency in sports, Hoeffler and Payne (1997) analysed the stochastic frontier of American basketball with cross-sectional data. Audas et al. (2000) analysed involuntary and voluntary managerial job termination, with hazard functions for English professional football. Hadley et al. (2000) analysed the performance of the American NFL, using a Poisson regression model. Dawson et al. (2000) analysed the managerial efficiency of English soccer managers with an econometric stochastic frontier, and Carmichael et al. (2001) analysed the efficiency of the English Premiership clubs with residuals. Gerrard (2001) analysed the production function of coaches working in the English Premier League with win-ratios for the period 1992–1998. Barros and Leach (2006a, 2006b, 2006c) analysed the sport and financial efficiency of the UK Football League.

The non-parametric approach research mentioned above is clearly insufficient for such an important management technique as DEA, which is being increasingly used elsewhere in management and economic fields, and should be a focus of sport management research. DEA is particularly useful when the data set is small and prevents an econometric frontier being established, as is the case in the present chapter.

Theoretical framework

Following Farrell (1957), Charnes *et al.* (1978) first introduced the term DEA (Data Envelopment Analysis) to describe a mathematical programming approach to the construction of production frontiers and the efficiency measurement of the constructed frontiers. The latter authors proposed a model that had an input orientation and assumed constant returns-to-scale (CRS). This model is known in the literature as the CCR model. Later studies have considered alternative sets of assumptions. Banker *et al.* (1984) first introduced the assumption of variable returns-to-scale (VRS), and this model is known in the literature as the BCC model. There are four other basic DEA models, used less frequently in the literature: the additive model of Charnes *et al.* (1985), the multiplicative model of Charnes *et al.* (1982), the Cone-Ratio DEA model of Charnes *et al.* (1990) and the Assurance-Region DEA model of Thompson *et al.* (1986, 1990). The latter two models include *a priori* information (expert opinion, opportunity costs, rate of transformation or rate of substitution) to restrict the results to just one best DMU (Assurance-Region DEA model) or to link DEA with multi-criteria analysis (Cone-Ratio DEA model).

Extensions of the DEA model are the DEA-Malmquist model, which disentangles total productivity change into technical efficiency change and technological efficiency change (Malmquist, 1953) and the DEA-Allocative model, which disentangles technical and allocative efficiency.

In the programming method, DEA 'floats' a piece-wise linear surface to rest on the top of the observation (Seiford and Thrall, 1990). The facets of the hyperplane define the efficiency frontiers, and the degree of inefficiency is quantified and partitioned by a series of metrics that measure various distance from the hyperplane and its facets.

In order to solve the linear-programming problem, the user must specify three characteristics of the model: the input–output orientation system, the returns-to-scale, and the relative weights of the evaluation system. In relation to the first of these, the choice of input-oriented or output-oriented DEA is based on the market conditions of the DMU. As a general rule of thumb, in competitive markets DMU_i are output-oriented, since we assume that inputs are under the control of the DMU, which aims to maximize its output, subject to market demand – something that is outside the control of the DMU. With exogenous inputs, the production function is the natural choice (Kumbhakar, 1987). In monopolist markets, the units analysed (DMU) are input-oriented, because the output is endogenous in this market while the input is exogenous, and therefore the cost function is the natural choice. The input-orientation system searches for a linear combination of DMU_i that maximizes the excess input usage of DMU_j, subject to the inequality constraints presented below. With regard to the returns-to-scale, these may be either constant or variable. We calculate both forms (the CCR and the BCC model) for comparative purposes. As far as the relative weights that may be placed on inputs and outputs in the objective function are concerned, these are subject to the inequality constraints mentioned. Weights are endogenously defined by the algorithm and measure the distance between the DMU and the frontier.

The DEA-CCR and DEA-BCC models are strong in identifying the inefficient units, but are weak in discriminating between the efficient units (Seiford and Zhu, 1999). The DEA-CCR and DEA-BCC models often rate too many units as efficient. To overcome this problem, we use the Cross-efficiency DEA model (Sexton, 1986; Doyle and Green, 1994) and the Super-efficiency DEA model (Andersen and Petersen, 1993).

Data

To estimate the production frontier, we used balanced panel data on Portuguese football clubs in the seasons 1999/00 to 2001/02 (3 years × 13 clubs = 39 observations), published by Deloitte & Touche. The clubs considered in the analysis are listed in Table 8.1, being those that maintained their presence in the First Division in the consecutive years under analysis. This small data set precludes the use of econometrics, but is suitable for DEA.

Frontier models require the identification of inputs (resources) and outputs (transformation of resources). It is important for the applicability of the model results and the Football Federation's 'buy in' to the process that the measures of inputs and outputs be relevant and adequately measurable, that appropriate archival data is available and that 'more is better' in the case of outputs.

Several criteria can be applied to the selection of inputs and outputs. Usually, the available archival data criterion is used. The literature survey is a way to ensure the validity of the research and, therefore, another criterion to take into account. The research referred to in the literature review above uses, for the most part, only sports variables, except for that of Haas (2003), who used sports and financial variables, as is the case in the present chapter. The last criterion for measurement selection is the professional

Table 8.3
Descriptive statistics of the variables used, 1999/2000 to 2001/02

Items	Observations	Minimum	Maximum	Mean	SD
Outputs					
Match receipts	39	119 661	17 968 755	3 136 389	4 597 677
Membership receipts	39	0	5 999 216	1 029 559	1 636 988
TV receipts	39	7521	10 516 320	25 093 46	2 390 294
Gains on players	39	0	13 413 000	2 471 316	3 226 143
Financial receipts	39	0	2 617 252	297 623	583 142
Points won	39	27	77	50	14
Tickets sold	39	11 685	477 741	106 935	122 210
Inputs					
Supplies & services	39	180 025	21 548 305	3 429 015	4 250 786
Wage expenditure	39	491 096	31 996 437	8 428 136	9 543 537
Amortization expenditure	39	3187	29 463 468	5 047 051	7 905 890
Other costs	39	87 998	10 750 059	2 068 742	2 736 888

opinion of managers in the area concerned. In this chapter, we follow all three of these criteria.

We measured output by seven indicators: first, financial indicators (namely, the match ticket receipts, annual membership fees paid by supporters, TV receipts, gains on players sold and financial receipts), then sports indicators (i.e. championship points won and the total number of attendances measured by the total number of tickets sold).

We measured inputs by four financial indicators and one sports indicator: supplies and services, wage costs, amortizations and other costs, and the number of players.

All the monetary variables are expressed in euros, and were deflated by the GDP deflator and denoted at constant 2001 prices. We ensured the DEA convention that the minimum number of DMUs be greater than three times the number of inputs plus output ($38 \geqslant 3(7 + 5)$).

Table 8.3 summarizes the descriptive statistics of the variables used.

DEA results

The DEA index can be calculated in several ways. In this study, we estimated an output-oriented, technically efficient (TE) DEA

Table 8.4

DEA technical efficiency scores for Portuguese football clubs, with CRS and VRS, 1999/2000 to 2001/02

Club	Technically efficient, constant return-to-scale CCR model	Technically efficient, variable return-to-scale BCC model	Technically efficient scale	Position of the club in frontier
FC Porto	1.000	1.000	1.000	–
Sporting	0.707	1.000	0.707	DRS
Benfica	0.824	1.000	0.824	DRS
Boavista	1.000	1.000	1.000	–
Alverca	0.603	1.000	0.603	DRS
Victoria Guimarães	1.000	1.000	1.000	–
Salgueiros	0.842	1.000	0.842	DRS
Leiria	1.000	1.000	1.000	–
Sporting Braga	0.986	1.000	0.986	DRS
Maritimo	1.000	1.000	1.000	–
Belenenses	1.000	1.000	1.000	–
Farense	0.399	1.000	0.399	DRS
Gil Vicente	1.000	1.000	1.000	–
Mean	0.874	1.000	0.874	–

DRS, decreasing return-to-scale.

index, assuming that outputs are endogenous and inputs are exogenous because of the competitive nature of professional football clubs (Kumbhakar, 1987). Moreover, as far as sports are concerned, production control seems to be the natural choice due to their competitive position in the leisure market.

The variable return-to-scale (VRS) hypothesis was chosen because scale size is paramount in football clubs management. The VRS scores measure pure technical efficiency only. However, for comparative purposes we also present the constant return-to-scale (CRS) index, which is composed of a non-additive combination of pure technical and scale efficiencies. A ratio of the overall efficiency scores to pure technical efficiency scores provides a scale efficiency measurement.

The relative efficiency of the clubs is presented in Table 8.4.

The rankings are ordered according to the Deloitte & Touche report. We verify that the DEA index is lower than 1 for some clubs when the overall level of efficiency is assumed (CRS scores), but becomes efficient when VRS is assumed, signifying that the dominant source of inefficiency is scale economies. This conclusion is consistent with the fact that three clubs dominate, both on and off the pitch. The average efficiency score under CRS is equal to 0.874. Including all sources of inefficiency, clubs observed in this chapter could, on average, operate at 87.4 per cent of their current output level and maintain the input value. However, efficiency scores under VRS are equal to 1.000, signifying that the clubs are in the efficient frontier. Given the scale of operation, some clubs are inefficient in managing their resources, with a magnitude of waste (on average 13.6 per cent), due to inappropriate income, measured here by sales and operational results.

The output-oriented efficiency index, which is used in this chapter, measures by how much output quantities can be proportionally increased without changing the input quantities used.

The last column of Table 8.4 shows the position of the clubs in the VRS frontier. Since the frontier is convex, we verify that some clubs are positioned in the last part of the frontier where the decreasing return-to-scale (DRS) appears. The other clubs are in the constant return-to-scale part of the frontier. Since there are many efficient clubs with the BCC model, we re-estimate the model with cross-efficiency scores and super-efficiency scores.

Table 8.5 presents the results of the Cross-efficiency DEA model (Sexton, 1986) and the Super-efficiency DEA model (Andersen and

Table 8.5
Cross-efficiency DEA model and Super-efficiency DEA model, technical efficiency scores for Portuguese football clubs, 1999/2000 to 2001/02

No.	Name	Technical efficiency, cross-efficiency scores	Technical efficiency, super-efficiency scores
1	FC Porto	1.250	1.230
2	Sporting	1.120	1.120
3	Benfica	1.110	1.118
4	Boavista	1.012	1.115
5	Alverca	1.003	1.110
6	Victoria Guimarães	1.000	1.108
7	Salgueiros	0.987	1.103
8	Leiria	0.945	1.000
9	Sporting Braga	0.918	0.975
10	Marítimo	0.911	0.941
11	Belenenses	0.863	0.835
12	Farense	0.834	0.812
13	Gil Vicente	1.068	1.038
	Mean	1.068	1.038
	Median	0.993	1.105
	SD	0.309	0.126

Petersen, 1993), which were applied to the Portuguese football clubs with two objectives: first, to cross-validate the DEA-CCR and DEA-BCC models; and second, to restrict the number of DMU$_i$ in the frontier of best practices.

It can be verified that these two DEA models rank the football clubs in a clear way.

Determinants of sponsorship

To identify the drivers of football sponsorship, we estimated a Tobit model regressing the sponsorship receipts on the technical efficient variable return-to-scale index and in contextual variables. We follow the two-step approach, as suggested by Coelli *et al.* (1998), estimating the Tobit regression. It is recognized in the DEA literature that the efficient scores obtained in the first stage are correlated with the explanatory variables used in the second term, and then the second stage estimates will be inconsistent and biased. A bootstrap procedure is needed to overcome this problem (Simar, 1992). In order to overcome these problems the DEA models have been selected from the balance sheets, but the variables in the Tobit model are independent from the balance sheet, establishing the separation between efficiency drivers and balance sheet variables which characterize the management practices of the football clubs:

$$Sponsorship_{i,t} = \alpha_{i,t} + \beta_1.T + \beta_2.EffScores_{i,t} + \beta_3.Location_{i,t} +$$
$$\beta_4 Agglomeration_{i,t} + \beta_5 European_{i,t} + \beta_6 Share + \varepsilon_{i,t}$$

where *Sponsorship* is the sponsorship receipts of football clubs obtained in the balance sheet; *T* is the time trend variable, which pretends to capture time dynamic effects active in the period; *EffScores* are the CCR efficiency scores estimated in by the DEA model in the first stage; *Location* is a dummy variable, which captures the location position of the football clubs, with 1 being used for football clubs in the main cities of Lisbon and Oporto and 0 elsewhere; *Agglom* is a variable that is intended to capture the effects of agglomeration on sponsorship, being measured by the population living in the municipality of the football club; *European* is a dummy variable, which is 1 for football clubs entering the European cups and 0 elsewhere; and *Share* is the market share of football clubs measured by the Herfindhal index on the estimated number of supporters. The results are presented in Table 8.6.

The model appears to fit the data well, with a statistically positive sigma coefficient. A likelihood-ratio test (chi-square = 12.52) rejects the joint hypothesis that the coefficients on all variables are not significantly different from zero at the 1 per cent level (Green, 2000).

Table 8.6
Censored Tobit model (dependent variable: sponsoring receipts)

Variable	Parameters
Constant	−0.968
	(−10.511)*
T	0.215
	(0.011)
EffScores	0.667
	(2.315)**
Location	0.284
	(2.646)**
Agglom	0.535
	(4.325)**
European	0.286
	(3.702)
Share	0.415
	(14.832)*
Sigma	0.238
	(11.325)*
Number total of observations	39
Loglikelihood	−68.97

*significant at 1 per cent level; **significant at 5 per cent level.

The estimations generally conform to *a priori* expectations. The sponsorship receipts are positively related and statistically significant with all variables with the exception of the constant. This result signifies that efficiency scores, location, agglomeration, European cup participation and sound market share contribute to the sponsorship receipts.

The conclusion that emerges from this research is that sponsorship receipts for football clubs depend, first, on the dynamics of the market, displayed by the trend. The present result signifies that this market is in a growing mood that may prevail in the near future. Attention must be paid to any changes in this trend in the future. Secondly, sponsorship receipts depend on management, with some clubs displaying efficiency in the period, independent of their dimension attracting more sponsorship than non-efficient clubs. Thirdly, the sponsorship receipts of football clubs are higher for clubs with strategically location and economies of agglomeration. Fourthly, participation in European cups is beneficial for sponsorship receipts. Finally, the market share is also beneficial to sponsorship receipts.

Managerial implications of the study

A number of points emerge from the present study. First, the best-practice calculations indicate that almost all clubs operated at a high level of pure technical efficiency over the period. Secondly, all technically efficient CRS clubs are also technically efficient in VRS, signifying that the dominant source of efficiency is scale. Thirdly, on the basis of the scale efficiency, some clubs are efficient while others are not. It is noteworthy that the two dominating clubs which performed worst in the period under analysis, Benfica and Sporting, displayed scale inefficiency. Fourthly, although DEA identifies inefficient football clubs in the sample, it does not identify the cause of the inefficiency. DEA identifies the slack for the inefficient club and gives to each a reference set (peer group) which allows for specific recommendations to improve efficiency. Adjustments for the inefficient clubs can be identified for outputs and inputs in order for them to join the efficient frontier. We also verify that sporting success is not equal to financial success, since there are clubs that won the championship in the period but which did not simultaneously achieve sporting and financial efficiency with scale efficiency.

Despite not being the focus of the present analysis, we can suggest the main causes of the waste depicted by CRS. Among these causes, which are attributable to the management, we identify the following:

1. Rigidities that are associated with the pattern of ownership and may induce the principal–agent relationship (Jensen and Meckling, 1976). The principal–agent relationship relates to the difficulty of controlling those empowered as managers to act on behalf of the stockholders (the owners), preventing a club from developing an adequate scale.

2. Structural rigidities associated with the labour market, which give rise to the collective action problem (Olson, 1965) where players can 'free-ride' on the management's own efforts to improve sporting performance, prevent a club from achieving scale efficiency.

3. There is unequal access to information on activities among different clubs, with some of them enjoying more privileged access to information than others, which is inherent in the lack of transparency (Williamson, 1998). Contextual examples of this include the actual physical condition of players bought, and the knowledge of schoolboys with potential talent around the country.

4. There are time lags in acquiring new technology and the necessary commensurate skills upgrades due to inertia effects.

225

5. Organizational factors associated with cross-efficiency (Leibenstein, 1966) are a factor. Inefficiencies associated with incomplete markets exist everywhere, but are prevalent in public markets. In this situation, the management may be unable to adopt the correct strategy since they do not know what it is.

6. Organizational factors associated with human capital, such as a lack of incentive for the improvement of organizational efficiency, are an issue.

7. Size factors are associated with scale and scope economies.

Owing to some or all of these factors, inefficient clubs may produce at a level below their potential, which is the maximum possible output.

Regarding sponsorship receipts, it is recognized that the main drivers are efficiency scores, location, agglomeration, participation in European cups, and a sound market share. What is the rationale for such a result? First, efficient clubs are those that combine sports and financial performance, therefore displaying a sound managerial position that gives confidence to the sponsors. Second, location and agglomeration are strategic positions that leverage the sponsorship. Participation in European cups also gives greater visibility to the clubs and to the sponsors, which is an attribute the sponsors aim for. Finally, market share is the cradle where all managerial decisions start, and is therefore a main driver of sponsorship. Therefore, clubs aiming to increase sponsorship should adopt a sound managerial strategy that combines sports and financial decisions. This will ensure an efficient benchmark that translates into sponsorship. Other sponsorship drivers should be adopted, such as location, agglomeration, participation in European cups and the building of a sound market share. It should be recognized that some of the identified drivers (location, agglomeration and market share) are contextual and impossible to change in the short term. However, these can be changed in the long term. Moreover, participation in European cups is a short-term decision.

Comparing the results with the interview

The interview (see Appendix 8.2) addresses the questions analysed in the DEA model, confirming the link between a club's football competitiveness and its financial performance. These two criteria are necessary for the realistic evaluation of a quoted club.

The competitive balance issue, as treated in the interview, yields inconclusive results. This question is a battle-horse of sport economics (Anderson and Siegfried, 2003), but despite the consensus observed in research, the interview presented here and the long-term imbalance of the Portuguese Superliga do not confirm the theoretical results (Barros, 2006).

Labour market issues are also touched upon and management matters emphasized.

Finally, the responses suggest a strategy to minimize inefficiency and to raise the standard of competition in Portuguese football, if the gap between this league and the powerhouse leagues in Spain, Italy and England is to be narrowed at all.

Conclusions

This chapter proposes a simple framework for the evaluation of football clubs and the rationalization of their financial and sporting activities. The analysis is based on a two-step procedure. In the first step, a DEA model allows for the incorporation of multiple inputs and outputs, combining financial and sporting activities, in determining relative efficiencies. Benchmarks are provided for improving the efficiency of less well-performing football clubs. Several interesting and useful managerial insights and implications from the study are discussed. In the second stage, a Tobit model analyses the determinants of sponsorship. Finally, an interview tests the findings of the model against the professional opinions of a financial executive who is a football 'insider'. The general conclusion is that there is much room for improvement in the financial and sporting activities of the Portuguese Superliga clubs. Therefore, club management teams should take into account the benchmarking of the clubs which compete in the league, because on the pitch they only compare sporting issues, not financial issues. The latter are equally important, if not more so, for the overall long-term health and survival of the sport and, by extension, the clubs. The identified drivers of football sponsorship should be the basis of a sound managerial strategy.

Bibliography and references

Andersen, P. and Petersen, N. C. (1993). A procedure for ranking efficiency units in data envelopment analysis. *Management Science*, **39(10)**, 1261–1264.

Anderson, A. R. and Siegfried, J. J. (2003). Thinking about competitive balance. *Journal of Sport Economics*, **4(4)**, 255–279.

Audas, R., Dobson, S. and Goddard, J. (2000). Organizational performance and managerial turnover. *Managerial and Decision Economics*, **20(6)**, 305–318.

Banker, R. D., Charnes, A. and Cooper, W. W. (1984). Some models for estimating technical and scale inefficiencies in Data Envelopment Analysis. *Management Science*, **30(9)**, 1078–1092.

Barros, C. P. (2003). Incentive regulation and efficiency in sports organizational training activities. *Sport Management Review*, **6(1)**, 33–52.

Barros, C. P. (2006). Portuguese football. *Journal of Sport Economics*, **7(1)**, 96–104.

Barros, C. P. and Santos, A. (2003). Productivity in sport organizational training activities. *European Sport Management Quarterly*, **1**, 46–65.

Barros, C. P. and Leach, S. (2006a). Analysing the performance of the English football league with an econometric frontier model. *Journal of Sport Economics* (forthcoming).

Barros, C. P. and Leach, S. (2006b). Performance evaluation of the English Premier League with Data Envelopment Analysis. *Applied Economics* (forthcoming).

Barros, C. P. and Leach, S. (2006c). Technical efficiency in the English Football Association Premier League with a stochastic cost frontier. *Applied Economic Letters* (forthcoming).

Carmichael, F., Thomas, D. and Ward, R. (2001). Production and efficiency in Association Football. *Journal of Sports Economics*, **2(3)**, 228–243.

Charnes, A., Cooper, W. W. and Rhodes, E. (1978). Measuring the efficiency of decision-making units. *European Journal of Operations Research*, **2**, 429–444.

Charnes, A., Cooper, W. W., Seiford, L. and Stutz, J. (1982). A multiplicative model of efficiency analysis. *Socio-Economic Planning Sciences*, **16(5)**, 223–224.

Charnes, A., Cooper, W. W., Golany, B. *et al.* (1985). Foundations of Data Envelopment Analysis for Pareto–Koopmans efficient empirical production functions. *Journal of Econometrics*, **30(1/2)**, 91–107.

Charnes, A., Cooper, W. W. and Huang, Z. M. (1990). Polyhedral cone-ratio DEA with an illustrative application to large commercial banks. *Journal of Econometrics*, **46**, 73–91.

Charnes, A., Cooper, W. W., Lewin, A. Y. and Seiford, L. M. (1995). *Data Envelopment Analysis: theory, methodology and applications*. Kluwer Academic Press.

Coelli, T. J. (1996). *A Guide to DEAP version 2.1: A Data Envelopment Analysis (Computer) Program*. Working Paper No. 8/96, Centre for Efficiency and Productivity Analysis. University of New England, Armidale, Australia.

Coelli, T. J., Prasada, R. and Battese, G. E. (1998). *An Introduction to Efficiency and Productivity Analysis*. Kluwer Academic Press.

Cooper, W. W., Seiford, L. M. and Tone, K. (2000). *Data Envelopment Analysis*. Kluwer Academic Press.

Dawson, P., Dobson, S. and Gerrard, B. (2000). Stochastic frontier and the temporal structure of managerial efficiency in English soccer. *Journal of Sports Economics*, **1(4)**, 341–362.

Deloitte & Touche (several years) *As Finanças do Futebol Profissional. Anuário Portugal*. Joint edition, A Bola and Deloitte & Touche.

Desbordes, M., Ohl, F. and Tribou, G. (2001). *Marketing du Sport*, 2nd edn. Editions Economica.

Doyle, J. and Green, R. (1994). Efficiency and cross-efficiency in DEA: derivations, meanings and uses. *Journal of the Operational Research Society*, **45(5)**, 567–578.

Farrell, M. J. (1957). The measurement of productive efficiency. *Journal of the Royal Statistical Society, Series A*, **120(3)**, 253–290.

Fizel, J. L. and D'Itri, M. P. (1996). Estimating managerial efficiency: the case of college basketball coaches. *Journal of Sport Management*, **10(4)**, 435–445.

Fizel, J. L. and D'Itri, M. P. (1997). Managerial efficiency, managerial succession and organizational performance. *Managerial and Decision Economics*, **18(4)**, 295–308.

Gerrard, B. (2001). *Football, Fans and Finance: understanding the business of football*. Mainstream Publishers.

Gollany, B. (1988). An interactive MOLP procedure for the extension of DEA to effectiveness analysis. *Journal of the Operational Research Society*, **39(8)**, 725–734.

Greene, W. (2000). *Econometric Analysis*, 4th edn. Prentice Hall.

Haas, D. J. (2003). Technical efficiency in major league soccer. *Journal of Sport Economics*, **4(3)**, 203–215.

Hadley, L., Poitras, M., Ruggiero, J. and Knowles, S. (2000). Performance evaluation of national football league teams. *Managerial and Decision Economics*, **21(2)**, 63–70.

Hoeffler, R. A. and Payne, J. E. (1997). Measuring efficiency in the National Basketball Association. *Economic Letters*, **55**, 293–299.

Jensen, M. C. and Meckling, W. (1976). Theory of the firm: managerial behaviour, agency costs and capital structure. *Journal of Financial Economics*, **3**, 305–360.

Khumabhakar, S. C. (1987). Production frontiers and panel data: an application to US class 1 railroads. *Journal of Business & Economic Statistics*, **5(2)**, 249–255.

Leibenstein, H. (1966). Allocative efficiency vs. 'X-efficiency'. *American Economic Review*, **56(3)**, 392–415.

Malmquist, S. (1953). Index numbers and indifference surfaces. *Trabajos de Estadistica*, **4**, 209–242.

Olson, M. (1965). *The Logic of Collective Action: public goods and the theory of groups*. Harvard University Press.

Porter, P. and Scully, G. W. (1982). Measuring managerial efficiency: the case of baseball. *Southern Economic Journal*, **48**, 642–650.

Scully, G. W. (1994). Managerial efficiency and survivability in professional team sports. *Managerial and Decision Economics*, **15**, 403–411.

Seiford, L. and Thrall, R. (1990). Recent developments in DEA: the mathematical programming approach to frontier analysis. *Journal of Econometrics*, **46**, 7–38.

Seiford, L. M. and Zhu, J. (1999). Infeasibility of Super-efficiency Data Envelopment Analysis models. *INFOR*, **37(3)**, 174–187.

Sexton, T. R. (1986). The methodology of DEA. In: R. H. Silkman (ed.), *Measuring Efficiency: an assessment* of DEA, pp. 7–29. Jossey-Bass.

Simar, L. and Wilson, P. W. (2000). Statistical inference in non-parametric frontier models: the state of the art. *Journal of Productivity Analysis*, **13**, 49–78.

Slack, T. (1997). *Understanding Sport Organizations – The Application of Organizational Theory*. Human Kinetics.

Szymanski, S. and Kuypers, T. (2000). *Winners & Losers: the business strategy of football*. Penguin Books.

Thanassoulis, E. (2001). *Introduction to the Theory and Application of Data Envelopment Analysis: a foundation text with integrated software*. Kluwer Academic Press.

Thompson, R. G., Singleton, F. D., Thrall, R. M. and Smith, B. A. (1986). Comparative site evaluation for locating a high-energy physics lab in Texas. *Interfaces*, **16(6)**, 35–49.

Thompson, R. G., Langemeier, L. N., Lee, C. and Thrall, R. M. (1990). The role of multiplier bounds in efficiency analysis with application to Kansas farming. *Journal of Econometrics*, **46**, 93–108.

Williamson, O. E. (1998). The institutions of governance. *American Economic Review*, **88(2)**, 75–97.

Zak, T. A., Huang, C. J. and Siegfried, J. J. (1979). Production efficiency: the case of professional basketball. *Journal of Business*, **52**, 379–392.

Zhu, J. (2002). *Quantitative Models for Performance Evaluation and Benchmarking: Data Envelopment Analysis with spreadsheets*. Kluwer Academic Press.

Appendix 8.1

Some comments about the DEA method

DEA optimizes at each observation for the purpose of constructing the cost frontier, which consists of a discrete curve formed solely by efficient DMU_i – i.e. those that minimize cost. The inefficient DMU_i are above the cost frontier, since they do not minimize total cost for the production level.

We define a Pareto-efficient or DEA-efficient DMU in those cases in which we have n football clubs with s outputs, denoted by y_{rk} ($r = 1,...,s$) and m inputs denoted by x_{ik} ($i = 1,...,m$). The efficiency measure for football club k is:

$$h_k = Max \frac{\sum_{r=1}^{s} u_r y_{rk} + u_0}{\sum_{i=1}^{m} v_i x_{ik}} \qquad (1)$$

where u_r are the output weights, v_i are the input weights and u_0 is a slack. An additional set of constraints requires that the same weights, when applied to all football clubs, do not allow any football club to have an efficiency score of more than one. This is displayed in the following set of constraints:

$$\frac{\sum_{r=1}^{s} u_r y_{rj} + u_0}{\sum_{i=1}^{m} v_i x_{ij}} \leq 1 \qquad \text{for } j = 1,...,n. \qquad (2)$$

The system of equations in (1) and (2) is a fractional programming model of computing technical efficiency, and can be solved with non-linear programming techniques. To simplify computation, a transformation of the fractional programming model allows for the system of equations in (1) and (2) to be formulated as a linear programming problem. For the BCC model with variable returns-to-scale and strong input disposability, the following linear primal programming is solved to ascertain whether DMUi, which is output oriented, is DEA-efficient.

$$h_k = Max \sum_{r=1}^{s} u_r y_{rk} + u_0$$

subject to

$$\sum_{i=1}^{m} v_i x_{ij} - \sum_{r=1}^{S} u_r y_{rj} + u_0 \geq 0 \qquad \text{for } j = 1,\ldots,n, \qquad (3)$$

$$\sum_{i}^{m} v_i x_{ik} = 1$$

$$u_r \geq 0 \qquad \text{for } r = 1,\ldots,s,$$

$$v_i \geq 0 \qquad \text{for } i = 1,\ldots,m.$$

For the CCR model with constant returns-to-scale and strong disposability, the following linear programming is solved to ascertain whether DMUi is DEA-efficient:

$$h_k = Max \sum_{r=1}^{s} u_r y_{rk} + u_0$$

subject to

$$\sum_{i=1}^{m} v_i x_{ik} - \sum_{r=1}^{S} u_r y_{rk} + u_0 \geq 0 \qquad \text{for } k = 1,\ldots,n, \qquad (4)$$

$$\sum_{i}^{m} v_i x_{ik} = 1$$

$$u_r \geq \varepsilon \qquad \text{for } r = 1,\ldots,s,$$

$$v_i \geq \varepsilon \qquad \text{for } i = 1,\ldots,m.$$

where ε is an infinitesimal amount.

The model assesses efficiency in a production context, and its counterpart assesses efficiency in a value context. By virtue of duality, the primal and dual models yield the same efficiency ratings with respect to DMUk$_0$ (see Charnes et al., 1978, for details).

The Cross-efficiency DEA model was first seen in Sexton (1986) and later in Doyle and Green (1994). It establishes the ranking procedure and computes the efficiency score of each football clubs n times, using optimal weights obtained with the DEA-CCR model. A cross-evaluation matrix consists of rows and columns ($j \times k$), each equal to the number of football clubs in the analysis. The efficiency of football clubs j is computed with the optimal weights for clubs k. The higher the values in column k, the more likely it is that football clubs k is an efficient club using superior operating techniques. Therefore, calculating the mean of each column will provide the peer appraisal score of each football clubs funds. In other words, the peer score is calculated for each football club, but the cross-efficiency score is the average of all of a club's peer scores. The cross-evaluation model used here is represented by:

$$h_{kj} = \frac{\sum_{r=1}^{s} u_{rk} y_{rj}}{\sum_{i=1}^{m} v_{ik} x_{ij}}, \qquad k = 1, \ldots n, \quad j = 1, \ldots, n, \qquad (5)$$

where h_{kj} is the score of the football clubs j cross-evaluated by the weight of the football clubs k. In the cross-evaluation matrix, all football clubs are bounded by $0 \leq h_{kj} \leq 1$, and the football clubs in the diagonal h_{kk} depict the DEA efficiency score as $h_{kk} = 1$ for efficient football clubs and $h_{kk} < 1$ for inefficient football clubs. The equation shows that the problem is generated n times in trying to distinguish the relative efficiency scores of all football clubs.

The Super-efficiency DEA scores (Andersen and Petersen, 1993) are obtained from the regular DEA model by excluding the football clubs under evaluation from the reference set. Because of the infeasibility of doing this (Seiford and Zhu, 1999), we adopt the CCR Super-efficiency model as follows:

$$h_k = Max \sum_{r=1}^{s} u_r y_{rk}$$

subject to

$$\sum_{i=1}^{m} v_i x_{ij} - \sum_{r=1}^{s} u_r y_{rj} \geq 0 \qquad \text{for } j = 1, \ldots, n, \quad j \neq k, \qquad (6)$$

$$\sum_{i}^{m} v_i x_{ik} = 1$$

$$u_r \geq \varepsilon \qquad \text{for } r = 1, \ldots, s,$$

$$v_i \geq \varepsilon \qquad \text{for } i = 1, \ldots, m.$$

The model assesses efficiency (see Zhu, 2002, for details).

Appendix 8.2

Interview with Fernando Gomes, Chief Executive of FC Porto

This interview was conducted with a reputed football club Chief Executive, Fernando Gomes, of FC Porto, and addresses questions related to the DEA study. FC Porto is currently the most successful club in Portugal. In the 2002/03 season, it made history by winning all four of the competitions in which it participated. Besides conquering the domestic 'treble', the greatest success for the club and for the country was in winning the UEFA Cup, thereby enhancing its prestige, image and credibility among a much wider audience. Mr Gomes is responsible for overseeing the club's affairs and interests in the stock market.

Q1: What are the main positive and negative characteristics of the Portuguese Superliga (i.e. First Division)?
FG: The most positive aspect is the professional structure that centrally manages the league now, which will allow us to analyse in depth all of the problems related to football. The negative aspect is the excessive dependency of the league management on income derived from the clubs, as well as the insufficient work done on safety and comfort in stadiums.

Q2: Is a league division with 70 per cent of its income allocated to three teams (FC Porto, Benfica and Sporting) sustainable in the medium/long term?
FG: Yes, it is sustainable, but it will be difficult to reach the competitive and qualitative levels of the Spanish, Italian and English leagues. Probably, we will stay at a lower level, on a par with such leagues as the Dutch and Belgians.

The imbalance in terms of receipts triggers an imbalance in competitive capacity in the domestic league, which in turn creates difficulties for Portuguese teams approaching big matches in the European competitions. These demand a change of rhythm. A way to overcome this imbalance would be to improve the management, the infrastructures and the training methods of the smaller clubs.

Q3: What is the income structure of FC Porto?
FG: In an average year, 30 per cent comes from profits on transfers, 25 per cent from ticket sales, 15 per cent from television, 15 per cent from marketing and 15 per cent from European games.

Q4: Which is the source of income that has the greatest future growth potential?
FG: The income related to the new stadium, now almost ready for Euro 2004, in particular, from marketing and sponsorship. The

new stadium offers excellent, state-of-the-art suite facilities in the area of VIP hospitality, for corporate leasing. In addition, match ticket receipts are forecast to double, compared to the recent past.

Q5: How can the club combine success on the field with the desired financial objectives?

FG: We feel that it is closely related to sound investment and strong commercialization. We are trying to invest less and to stay competitive at the same time.

Q6: What are the financial conditions necessary for a team to take part every season in the European Champions League?

FG: It is the domestic competition and results in the European club competitions that determine the access to these competitions. FC Porto's achievements in Europe have earned Portugal a second qualification place in the Champions League.

Q7: Will extraordinary income from selling players continue to be an earnings strategy for clubs, or will the rise of youth academies lead to a devaluation of the transfer market?

FG: In my opinion, the income from transfers is an operational rather than an extraordinary gain, since it is a regular source of income inherent to a football club's core business activity. It will continue to be so, but it would be healthier if the accounts' dependency on these earnings were reduced. More players may come from the academies to the clubs and so transfer market activity will decrease, but I think that if transfer earnings go down, then investment in academies will also be reduced.

Q8: Can a club listed on the stock market create financial and sporting value for its shareholders, or should it concentrate solely on its players and management?

FG: A quoted club such as FC Porto can create value for its shareholders through sporting success, financial equilibrium and the subsequent rising price of its shares. FC Porto PLC's share value is not as high as at the time the shares first went on the market for trading. Still, with the recent market volatility and liquidity, it's clear that many investors have made money.

Q9: Are the shareholders of FC Porto investors or football fans?

FG: They are a mixture of both, therefore, whenever the one wants to sell his shares, the other wants to buy. Fortunately, their behaviour is not symmetrical.

Q10: What are the main criteria for evaluating a quoted football club?

FG: The value of the shares in the market and the club's sporting success.

Q11: How can the financial performance of the Portuguese Superliga be improved?

FG: By reducing the number of clubs, treating the supporters as clients and regulating the match kick-off times to suit the clients' preferences, as far as possible.

Q12: How can Euro 2004 contribute to football's development in Portugal?

FG: Most clearly, by providing better conditions and comfort for the fans. We must capitalize on the excitement generated by Euro 2004, attracting and keeping a new fan base for our domestic league. We must also take full advantage of the new high standards of infrastructure and comfort in the new stadiums. They will naturally be the concrete legacy to Portuguese football of Euro 2004.

Marketing football in the Republic of Ireland

Anne Bourke

Overview

This chapter briefly describes the main sports which are popular in the Republic of Ireland and the characteristics of the market for sporting goods and services. The sports infrastructure (playing and training facilities, coach education, elite player development) is poorly developed. While football is a popular sport among young people (in and outside school), the domestic game is played at a semi-professional level, with English clubs being an attraction for pre elite players aiming to pursue a professional career in football. The role of the Football Association of Ireland (FAI) in governing and promoting the game at all levels (senior, junior, colleges, youths, schoolboys/girls and women's) is explained. In addition, the contribution by the media, the ownership of clubs and the extent to which funding is available for sponsorship is considered. Reference is also made to the intense competition among sports bodies for key resources (physical and human) and the role of government in their allocation. Over the years, many Irish players have achieved much success with English clubs; consequently English clubs continue to have a strong fan base in

Ireland, which has implications for the status, reputation and development of the domestic game.

Keywords

Irish sports industry, marketing football, governance in sport, football infrastructure, media and football

Introduction

Sport in Ireland is popular and widespread. Levels of participation and attendance are high, but, as in other Western regions, participation has been dropping due to the increasing popularity of other activities such as watching television and playing computer games. A wide variety of sports is played in Ireland, the more popular being Gaelic football, hurling, rugby union, football and field hockey. By attendance figures, Gaelic football is by far the most popular sport in Ireland. Some sports are organized on an all-Ireland basis (rugby, Gaelic football and hurling), with a single team representing Ireland in international competition. Football has separate governing bodies in Northern Ireland (the Irish Football Association, IFA) and in the Republic of Ireland (the Football Association of Ireland, FAI).

This chapter provides insights on the sports industry in Ireland and an update on football, focusing on the marketing strategies used by various parties (governing body, clubs and sponsors) to promote participation and further interest in the sport. It comprises six sections. Following this general introduction, the next section details the characteristics of the Irish sports industry. The third section provides a brief overview of football in Ireland, while the focus in section four is on the domestic game, describing governance arrangements, the competition structure and the football infrastructure. The fifth section discusses the key marketing strategies and techniques utilized by the various stakeholders associated (directly and indirectly) with football in Ireland, drawing on two personal interviews (Appendix 9.3) and various secondary source materials (journal articles, newspapers, websites, annual reports). In the final section, concluding comments and pointers for further research are provided.

The Irish sports industry

The sports market comprises individuals, firms, organizations and institutions associated directly and indirectly with sport participation on a competitive or non-competitive basis. According to Shank (2005), the sports industry consists of three major elements:

1. Consumers of sport

2. The sports products they consume

3. The suppliers of the sports products.

The consumers of sport include spectators, participants and sponsors. The sports product is a good, a service or any combination of the two that is designed to provide benefits to a sports spectator, participant or sponsor. Sports products include events, goods, training and information. To satisfy the needs of sports consumers, producers and intermediaries design, develop, produce and deliver goods and services. Such parties include team-owners, governing bodies, agents, corporate sponsors, media and sports goods producers.

   Mason (1999) identifies the unique characteristics of professional sport and the nature of the professional team sport product. He details the factors which have contributed to the growth of the professional sport industry, and the role of television, corporate ownership, sponsorship and patronage. Few sports in Ireland are fully professional (rugby at the elite level is the exception, and the professional leagues and cup competitions are international), and the industry is less developed than is the case in certain countries such as the United States, the United Kingdom and Australia. The global sports apparel and equipment market is worth $145 billion, and while many leading multinationals (Nike, adidas, Slazenger, NTL; BSkyB; Eurosport) supply goods, services and equipment to the Irish market, for these organizations the Irish market is tiny and yields a small fraction of total sales. A few firms in Ireland (O'Neills, Azurri and Gaelic Gear) manufacture sports goods and equipment, but in general the market is serviced by international suppliers. Direct employment in the sports sector arises from service provision (media, consulting, financial, legal, event management, psychology, hospitality, coaching and education) and the production of goods (infrastructure, apparel and equipment) for sports bodies, clubs, leisure centres/clubs, commercial enterprises or governing bodies.

   A large number of sports organizations/clubs in Ireland are still organized and managed on a voluntary basis, and few have full-time administrators and/or commercial personnel. The three leading sport governing bodies (the Gaelic Athletic Association, GAA; the Irish Rugby Football Union, IRFU; and the FAI) do employ personnel (managerial and administrative) on a full-time basis either at the central or head office or at provincial level (Regional Development Officers). An interesting example of the combined efforts of sporting and commercial interests arises in golf – new golf courses have been designed and developed, and many clubs are now operating and managed as commercial for profit entities. For the past ten years the Irish government has actively promoted Ireland as a golfing destination (competitive and leisure), using various agencies (governmental and non-governmental), and it would contend that hosting the Ryder Cup at the K Club in September 2006 is evidence of the success of the campaign.

There are several major events in the Irish sporting calendar which attract large attendances (both local and international), providing business management and marketing opportunities. Such events include the Budweiser Irish Derby (July), the Gaelic Football and Hurling All Ireland Finals (September), the Six Nations Rugby Union Internationals (February, March), and competitive and friendly International Football matches (various dates). The associated sports governing body personnel are usually actively engaged in the planning and staging of each event; however, certain aspects (hospitality, media, transport) are more often than not subcontracted to external suppliers (local and international).

According to the 2002 census, the population of the Republic of Ireland is just under 4 million (www.cso.ie) and is predicted to rise to 4.2 million in the CENSUS 2006. Given the small size of the market and the variety of sports played, there are few opportunities in Ireland to pursue a professional sporting career (rugby union and boxing are exceptions); consequently, a large number of aspiring professional sports people (jockeys, golfers, tennis players, football) relocate to another country at an early age to advance their career prospects. Aspiring elite track and field athletes frequently avail of sports scholarships at tertiary-level institutions, usually in the United States (Bale, 1991). Traditionally, many pre-elite football players have left Ireland to pursue a professional career with an English club at an early age. McGovern (1999) asserts that this has had a major impact on the development (or lack thereof) of the domestic game, leading to an attachment to English clubs by many Irish fans. Many English clubs – for example, Liverpool, Manchester United, Arsenal and Newcastle United – have fan clubs in Ireland whose officers arrange for members' match and travel tickets for league and cup home games. The extent of the connectivity between fans in Ireland and clubs (local, English and Scottish) can be gauged by the list of fan-club notices posted each week in the *Evening Herald* (the only daily evening newspaper in Dublin). Details in relation to fan-club season tickets, club match tickets, travel packages to club home games and official merchandise are provided. The information included in these notices also covers contact names for the fan-club branch, addresses for each fan club (email or web page), procedures for joining the fan club, and the membership status (open or closed). It is interesting to note that fan-club notices pertaining to thirteen Irish clubs were published in the 2 February 2006 edition of the newspaper. In addition, Irish-based fan clubs for thirty-two of the ninety-two English clubs are listed, along with three Scottish clubs (Scottish Premier League) – Celtic, Hibernian and Rangers – see Appendix 9.1 for the complete list of fan clubs for Irish, English and Scottish clubs. While the domestic game in Ireland has been drained of many young, talented players (McGovern, 1999; Bourke, 2003), some commentators might argue that by playing with leading English clubs, the fortunes of the Irish national team in international competition (European and World Cups) have been considerably improved.

In summary, the sports market in Ireland is characterized by the popularity of Gaelic games (football, hurling, camogie and ladies football), particularly from the spectator standpoint, by a lack of professional competitive sport and by its small size.

Football in Ireland – a brief overview

While football is the national sport in England, in Ireland for many years it was considered by various people to be anti-Irish and was commonly referred to as 'the garrison game' (Hannigan, 1998). The game in Ireland is not fully professional, as the majority of personnel (players, mentors, coaches, medical and administration, etc.) attached to clubs are employed on a part-time or voluntary basis; few are employed on a full-time basis.

As noted earlier, the opportunity to play football in Ireland on a full-time basis is limited; consequently, many aspiring players (and their families) accept the fact that it is essential to go overseas, usually to England. Coakley (1998) noted that football has higher rates of talent migration than other sports, although hockey, track and field and basketball have high rates too. Over the years many Irish youngsters have joined English clubs at an early age (fourteen years) and achieved successful playing careers – for example, John Giles, Liam Brady and Frank Stapleton. Focusing on the fifteen-year period from 1984 to 1999, Bourke (2003) examined the reasons why many Irish youngsters choose football as a professional career and do so with an English club. While the potential to earn money was clearly a motivating factor, the three main reasons cited by study participants (individuals who had signed at least one professional contract with an English club – $n = 90$) for their career choice were first, the love of the game; second, the dream of playing for Ireland; and third, the possibility of winning trophies. With the Irish national team's success in the late 1980s and early 1990s in international competitions (European and World Cup), the young players' outward mobility gained momentum; however, it trailed off towards the end of the last decade. Currently, many Irish youngsters are still invited over to England for trials (particularly during the school Easter holidays), but the number invited to join club academies is quite low.

The completion of transactions (transfers) between Irish and English clubs has led to close personal and interdependency ties developing between many individuals and personnel associated with the game in Ireland and England. These ties have been further cemented by way of international alliances which allow clubs to get information on emerging talent. In recent years, several English clubs have engaged in backward integration by forming international alliances with clubs (usually schoolboy) in various countries, most notably in Ireland, Belgium, Australia and South Africa. Such alliances benefit Irish clubs as, in addition to the finance invested by the English club, better quality coaching and training facilities and equipment are made available for Irish boys and girls at an early age. Despite the benefits to the Irish clubs, there are those who would argue that the growth in the number of these alliances is further evidence to support McGovern's (1999) contention that the English football industry dominates the Irish version. One interviewee contributing to this chapter disagreed with such a viewpoint, as more recently a small number of players (Kevin Doyle, Wes Hoolahan) have established themselves in the domestic game (Eircom League) before joining a UK club.

Maguire and Stead (1998) maintain that the flow of football players between Ireland and the UK can be explained by geographical closeness and historical links, a shared cultural and linguistic heritage, and a long record of migration between Ireland and the UK. They also assert that Ireland has been seen as a fertile and relatively cheap source of raw talent by personnel associated with various leading English clubs. To raise the profile (and attractiveness) of these clubs among Irish youngsters, over the years English providers (The Bobby Charlton Football School; Manchester United Football Club) have organized football schools during the summer holidays at destinations throughout Ireland. While these providers are no longer involved, it is interesting to note that this exercise is now to be replicated by Glasgow Celtic during the summer of 2006, with a view to strengthening the Irish Celtic connection and recruiting young talent.

The domestic game

According to the FAI Chief Executive Officer (FAI Annual Report, 2004/05: 2), football is the highest participation team sport in

Ireland. In this section, governance arrangements for football in Ireland are outlined. Details in relation to the competition structure in the men's and women's game are set out, and insights into the football infrastructure provided.

Governance arrangements

The Football Association in Ireland (FAI) has overall responsibility for the coordination, promotion and management of football in the Republic of Ireland. To this end, it oversees the activities of the national teams at all levels (senior to underage) and the various domestic leagues and competitions. The FAI was formed in 1921 following the partitioning of Ireland into the Republic of Ireland and Northern Ireland. At its foundation, the FAI formed a league championship and cup competition along the lines of the Football Association (FA) Cup and Scottish Cup competitions. The activities and operations of Irish National Governing Bodies (NGBs) are given partial funding by the Irish Sports Council (ISC) (www.irishsportscouncil.ie). During 2004, the FAI was given €2 million (FAI Annual Report 2004/05), which was used to partly fund non-senior international matches, development squads, women's football, Eircom U21 National League, schoolboy football, Buntus (the primary school programme) and Futsal, career guidance and code of ethics, plus programmes run by the FAI's technical department.

In organizing its activities today, the FAI operates through its affiliates – the Junior Council, the Schoolboys FAI (SFAI), the FAI Schools (FAIS), the Women's Football Association of Ireland (WFAI), the Irish Football Referees Society (ISRS), the Irish Universities Football Union (IUFU), the Colleges Football Association of Ireland (CFAI) and the Defence Forces Athletic Association. These affiliates receive funding from the FAI each year, but also seek and get sponsorship from independent sources to support playing and non-playing activities.

The Women's Football Association (formerly the Ladies FAI (LFAI)) was established in 1973 to coordinate the women's game. At the outset, the association functioned independently of the FAI. During the 1990s, due largely to the efforts of the late Dr Tony O'Neill (former General Secretary of the FAI), closer ties between the two associations developed, and the FAI now oversees the development of the women's game. There are approximately 12 500 registered players in the women's game in Ireland (FAI Annual Report, 2004/05) who compete in league competitions (national and regional). The FAI recently published a development plan for the women's game covering the four-year period from 2005 to 2009. One of the major initiatives announced was the appointment of a full-time manager for the National Senior team. Apart from focus on the national squads and elite player development, the plan is designed to increase participation in the underage game, encourage women to become involved in the administration of the game, develop coaches and referees, and provide a formal structure for the development of elite players. The WFAI (as an affiliate of the FAI, with its day-to-day affairs been taken care of by a council) is funded by the FAI, and uses the major part of its funding received to support the activities of the national teams (senior, U19 and U17). During 2004, the WFAI spent €750 000 on the women's game, whereas ten years previously the amount spent was €50 000 (FAI Press Release, 5 July 2005). As with the men's game, the 'brawn' drain also exists in women's football, as many senior national team squad members have gained sports scholarships with US universities and colleges or joined an English club (normally on a part-time basis).

Payne (1996), cited by Ferrand and Pages (1999), notes that there are four keys to the successful management of sport organizations:

1. Total control

2. Mutual integration of all different programmes

3. A positive relationship with the community environment

4. Professionalism.

Sports organizations have to take account of the pressures and barriers (internal and external) as sports organizations operate in a complex environment. They have common goals: to create loyalty among members, to increase the number of spectators and to manage their sponsorship arrangements.

Major concerns about the FAI's capability in the area of logistics management emerged following the 2002 World Cup. Roy Keane (the national team captain at the time) questioned the quality of the team's travel arrangements to Japan and training facilities available post-arrival. This episode led the FAI to undertake a root-and-branch review of its organizational structure, using the services of a UK consulting firm, Genesis Consulting. The consultants commented on the weaknesses with respect to the Republic of Ireland team travel and accommodation arrangements for the World Cup 2002, and also made many recommendations regarding the structure of the Association, which were noted (and later adopted) by senior executives. Such recommendations included a reduction in the number of board members (from twenty-three to ten) and the formation of subcommittees to reflect the organization's activities (Domestic, Underage, Legal/corporate Affairs, International, Development and Finance). Stipulations regarding membership of such committees have also been put in place and the duration of individuals' term of office has been specified. The current Chief Executive Officer (CEO) now asserts that a 'robust organizational structure has been developed to serve the organization and its members' (www.fai.ie).

In recent years, the FAI has made progress in relation to the provision of coaching (under the Technical Director of the Association and in conjunction with Regional Development Officers, RDOs) and the development of young players. The implementation of the FAI's Technical Development Plan 2004 received support funding from the Irish government, with emphasis on the participation initiative at the underage level. Formerly, football was not popular among students attending secondary schools; however, this has changed in recent years. The Football Association of Ireland Schools (FAIS) represents the schools (boys and girls) sector and was established in 1968 with five schools. Since then, school membership has grown considerably and now stands at 1200 (www.fais.ie). The association oversees interschool competitions at primary and secondary level (league and cup) using an interprovincial structure. For youths (boys and girls) who play football outside school with a community-based club or with junior teams attached to leading senior clubs (Cork City, Shamrock Rovers, Bohemians and Waterford United), the leagues are administered and managed by the Schoolboys Football Association of Ireland (SFAI – an affiliate of the FAI).

Competition structure

During the 1998/99 season, there were 187 000 players registered to play football in the Republic of Ireland with just over 4000 clubs (FAI, 1999). The greater proportion of these players and clubs are located in the Leinster (which includes Dublin) and Munster (which includes Cork) regions. There are ninety-six leagues organized in the Republic, with ladies' football leagues comprising just over one-fifth of the total. Many leagues are organized on a regional rather than county level – for example, the South Dublin League comprises teams from Dublin and Wicklow. There are twenty-one women's football leagues in Ireland, and probably the most developed and extensive (in terms of the area covered) is the Dublin Women's Football League (DWSL), which was founded in 1993 (Bourke, 2004). Some women's football clubs have emerged from men's clubs, but there are some that were established independently (such as Castle Rovers, in Dublin; Benfica, in Waterford;

and Lifford, in Donegal). Certain Eircom League clubs (Shamrock Rovers, Bray Wanderers) have women's teams, but this fact is rarely revealed on the club's home web page. League and Cup competitions at national level exist for women, and the winning teams now participate in European competition.

There is a range of National Cup competitions organized by the FAI for all levels of the men's game. These include the FAI Carlsberg Cup, the FAI Carlsberg Intermediate Cup, the FAI Statoil Junior Cup, the FAI Youth Cup, the FAI Inter League Cup, the FAI U17 Cup and the Setanta Sports Cup (a north/south inter-league competition, which was reintroduced in 2005). The Setanta Sports Cup is considered a very successful competition in terms of cross-border interest and attendance, and is also televised live by the dedicated sports TV provider, Setanta Sports. In 2006, four teams from each jurisdiction will compete for the trophy.

The national league (Eircom National League) comprises two divisions (the Premier and First Divisions) involving twenty-two clubs. As at February 2006, there are twelve clubs in the Premier Division and ten in the First Division (see Appendix 9.2 for club listing and league division details). While the national league until now has been a separate entity from the FAI, plans are going ahead to merge it with the FAI. The authors of the Genesis White Paper (www.fai.ie) on the Eircom League recommend radical change to the League format. This stems from the fact that the annual losses incurred by the League were €3 million on a turnover €14 million. According to the consultants, attention needs to be paid to such matters as the league management structure, league structures in general, facilities development, marketing, club administration, player wage controls, development structures and community links. While representatives from the twenty-two Eircom League clubs ratified the FAI plan (on Saturday 28 January 2006) to hand control of the league over to the FAI, there are individuals (club personnel and fans) who are not happy with the proposals and argue that such improvements should have been achieved within the UEFA club licensing rules. Decisions regarding membership of the Premier League have yet to be made – most likely it will be based on marketability and attendance. As negotiations progress, these latter points are likely to get much attention.

For many years, the annual football season in Ireland ran from August to May. In 2003 it was decided to change to 'summer' football, and the Eircom League season now runs between March and October. This, according to the FAI, has contributed to increased attendance figures – almost half a million (www.fai.ie) during the 2005 season. The arrangements vary in women's football – the senior national league and cup competitions are scheduled during the 'summer' season, but other leagues operate under the old system, as is the case for the men's and boys' – the Leinster Senior League, Universities and Colleges League and Schoolboys'.

There are many schoolboy/girl leagues throughout the country – the Dublin District and Schoolboys' League (DDSL) is the largest in terms of the number of teams participating. While youngsters tend to play with the local community-based club, in recent years some players have joined clubs outside the community which, in their view (and that of their parents), have a better coaching and playing infrastructure, and perhaps will provide a clearer pathway to a club in England. As noted previously, several Irish football clubs have close ties with English clubs, and being on the books of a particular club – such as Cherry Orchard, Belvedere, Home Farm, Stella Maris, St Joseph's Boys, Crumlin United and the like – from an early age is often considered by youngsters (and their parents) to be an ideal springboard to a career in professional football. Many of these clubs are based in the Dublin area and attract young players from distant parts (Kerry and Mayo), as there is no restriction (FAI rules/regulations) on travel time to and from coaching sessions (as is the case in the UK with respect to centres of excellence and youth academies).

A competition that gets attention at schoolboy level is the Kennedy Cup – an interleague competition played each year. In 2006 it was played at the University of Limerick, in mid-June, with thirty-two league teams participating. According to the Schoolboys FAI, it is the only competition in any European country where all leagues come together and compete in a national competition on an annual basis (www.sfai.ie). The competition is notable in that it is attended each year by club personnel (scouts, coaches, youth academy directors) representing English and Scottish clubs. Another reason why this competition gets attention is that it has marked the starting point of many international players' careers – for example, Roy Keane captained the Cork team to success in 1984. Other well-known international players who have participated in this competition include Damien Duff, Ian Harte and John O'Shea.

To attract participants to any sport it is essential to provide a modern infrastructure (playing fields, training facilities, social amenities, etc.). The Irish sports infrastructure is relatively underdeveloped, as detailed in the following paragraphs.

The football infrastructure

According to Malone (2006), two leading Dublin football clubs (Bohemians and Shelbourne) are to engage in ground-sharing arrangements. Shelbourne Football Club is reported to be planning to sell its home ground (Tolka Park) for development, while Bohemians FC will develop its stadium (Dalymount Park) into an all-seater stadium at a cost of around €15 million. At present, some national league clubs (Derry City, Waterford United and Cork City) are upgrading their venues, while others (Finn Harps and Athlone Town) have plans to move to new stadiums. The Department of Arts, Sports and Tourism operates two grant programmes each year – the Sports Capital Programme and the Local Authority Swimming Pool Programme. The National Lottery-funded Sports Capital Programme is advertised on an annual basis and allocates funding to projects that are directly related to the provision of sports facilities and are of a capital nature (www.arts-sports-tourism. gov.ie). Advertisements are placed in the National Press each year inviting applications for capital project funding. In July 2005, the Sports Capital programme grants awarded to Eircom League football clubs amounted to €5.27 million. The sum allocated to each of the sixteen clubs differed depending on the type and detail of the project plan submitted to the FAI. At the top end of the scale, €1.25 m was awarded to Athlone Town towards the construction of the new stadium, while in the middle range €500 000 was given to Waterford United in support of the development of a new stand. Smaller amounts for safety work were allocated to three clubs – €40 000 to UCD, €30 000 to Drogheda United and €14 000 to Bohemians. The most recent Eircom League funding (2005) was in doubt for some time, as questions were raised in relation to previous (2004) spending. It is probably fair to say that the main driver of these capital project initiatives for football stems from the necessity to meet UEFA licensing demands, rather than any strategic planning or focus on the main sports consumer – the fan.

Ownership details of Irish national league clubs are difficult to establish. The majority of the clubs are private companies (there are no PLCs), with investment being made by business people. In recent years, two clubs (Dundalk and Sligo Rovers) have adopted a cooperative structure. Drawing on information available on each of the twenty-one clubs' 'official' websites (Limerick FC had no official website as at February 2006), the table in Appendix 9.2 provides basic insights regarding each club's management structure. It is unsurprising that the two clubs which have the cooperative structure provide greater detail with respect to the management arrangements (board, etc.). In general, the information pertaining to clubs' Board of Management, the Directors and other key managerial (non-football) positions are scant. There is quite a variation in the level of detail provided, and no indication of how individuals were appointed to the position/role or whether they function on a part-time, full-time or voluntary basis.

While Ireland has the fourth largest stadium (Croke Park, Dublin) in Europe, there is no national stadium for football. Croke Park was redeveloped by the GAA (drawing on its own and government resources) and has been solely used to host Gaelic games (men's, ladies' and youths'). The ban on hosting other sports fixtures (rugby, football) at this ultra-modern stadium was removed with the revision of the Association's Rule 42 at the GAA's Annual Congress (Annual Meeting) in 2004. Until now, all senior football international fixtures have been played at Lansdowne Road (the home of Irish rugby). Due to the redevelopment of Lansdowne Road (a joint initiative by the Irish government, the Irish Rugby Football Union and the FAI), from 2007 all international football and rugby matches will be played in Croke Park, which seats 87 000. The redevelopment of Lansdowne Road stadium is expected to begin in 2007, and on completion its capacity will be 50 000 (all seated). Prior attempts to develop a national football stadium (Eircom Park) came to nothing for various reasons; however, plans for a sports campus have been announced by the Minister for Arts, Sport and Tourism. This will allow the FAI to put in place a head-quarters and academy that provides training, education, competition and advisory facilities, which are an integral part of the Association's Technical Development Plan.

The youth development infrastructure (academies, coaching schools) in Ireland is relatively poorly endowed when compared with that in other countries such as England, France, Spain and Australia. The main focus is on skills development and coaching; however, in certain instances attention is also given to a young-ster's education and to diet and medical issues. Certain clubs (Shelbourne, St Joseph's Boys) and leagues (Wexford and District Schoolboys' League Academy of Football, WDSLAS; the North Dublin Schoolboys' League; The Oscar Traynor Coaching and Development Centre) have established youth academies to facili-tate the development of young players. As noted previously, quite a few clubs in England – for example, West Bromwich Albion with St Kevin's Boys – and Scotland have close ties with Irish clubs and have provided support for the development of youth academies, giving them first call on emerging talent.

A close relationship has existed between Foras Aiseanna Saothar (FAS, the Irish Training and Employment Authority), the FAI and the Eircom League for many years. This link continues by way of four FAS/FAI training programmes for aspiring young players aged between sixteen and eighteen being offered in Dublin (two schemes), Mayo and Cork. The FAI coaching courses are now part of this programme, and participants must complete stages 1 and 2. Furthermore, where a participant is aged less than eighteen years and has not completed secondary studies, he must get written con-sent from a school to attend such a programme. The development of elite football players is also made possible via sports scholar-ships at Irish tertiary educational institutions – universities, colleges and institutes of technology. University College Dublin (UCD) was the first Irish higher-education institution to set up such a scheme, in 1979, whereby students are given some support – financial or in kind – and also have the opportunity to play football at the highest level (UCD participates in the Eircom National League and is currently in the Premier Division) and pursue their studies at the same time.

Marketing football in Ireland – strategic issues

According to Gray and McEvoy (2005), sport marketing has unique characteristics and considerations not found in most areas of product marketing. Intangibility, subjectivity, inconsistence, unpredictability, perishability, emotional attachment and identification, social facilitation, public consumption, and focus and locus of control are factors that interact to form a series of challenges for the sport marketer. The notion of service for consumers of sport has been widely acknowledged in many countries. Shank (2005) takes the view that sport marketing is the specific application of marketing principles and processes to sport products, and to the marketing of non-sports products through association with sport. Whannel (1992) notes that there are three interrelated drivers for corporate–sport relationships:

1. Sports' ability to attract media coverage

2. The link between sponsor and sponsored

3. The demographic profiles of participants and spectators.

According to Shank (2005), for many organizations, sports are quickly becoming the most effective and efficient way to communicate with current and potential markets. Organizations are keen to inform, persuade and remind target audiences of their product/service offerings and ultimately induce action (purchasing a product/service, attending an event, volunteering to assist in administration).

So what are the strategic marketing options for the major 'players' in the football market in Ireland? The following paragraphs outline and discuss the main marketing efforts by the FAI, leagues, clubs and commercial enterprises.

Sponsorship

Sports marketers will communicate with their publics using a variety of techniques – advertising, personal selling, sales promotion, public or community relations and sponsorship. The more common strategies used by Irish sports bodies are advertising, public or community relations, and sponsorship. Sponsorship has been defined as 'investing in a sports entity (athlete, league, team, event and so on) to support overall organizational objectives, marketing goals and more specific promotional objectives' (Shank, 2005). According to McCarville and Copeland (1994), sponsorship involves an exchange of resources with an independent partner in the hope of gaining a corresponding return for the sponsor. Stotlar (2004) notes the variety of corporate objectives that may be pursued through sports sponsorship, including hospitality, trade relations, enhanced corporate image, increased market share, client acquisition, product awareness and on-site sales. Due to limited revenue-earning potential, many Irish sports bodies (the FAI, IRFU, GAA, Irish Golfing Union, Tennis Ireland) clubs, organizations and leagues (senior, intermediate, schoolboys/girls) actively seek sponsorship deals.

Amis and Slack (1999) stress the importance of treating sponsorship as an investment which, when used as a key resource either singly or in combination with other resources, can be developed into an area of distinct competence and form the basis of the firm's (or organization's) competitive advantage. To that end, the GAA has recently undertaken a review of the Association's marketing strategies used to promote its sports offerings. One of the outcomes of this exercise, according to the Ard Stiurthoir (Chief Executive) of the Association in his annual review for 2005 (www.gaa.ie), is the danger of having too many brands based around GAA games and confusing marketing partners with advertisers. While research evidence points to a clear association and brand recall between major sponsors (Guinness, Bank of Ireland, Allianz) and Association events (All-Ireland Hurling Championship, All-Ireland Football Championship and the National Football League respectively), at the local level there can be confusion in relation to the identity of sponsors as opposed to advertisers.

Eircom is the FAI's primary sponsor providing support for the international teams and the domestic game. A survey completed by Onside Sponsorship (www.onside.ie) revealed that Eircom's sponsorship of Irish football teams (national: men's and women's) was second in the Top Sponsorships of 2005 in terms of totally spontaneous national appeal (15 per cent of those surveyed identified Guinness and the All-Ireland Hurling Championship as the top sponsorship of 2005 – www.onside.ie). The specific arrangements (amount, duration, outcomes, objectives, evaluation methods) of the FAI sponsorship deals are difficult to establish, and few of the main enterprises engaged in supporting Irish football via the FAI (the exceptions being Pepsi, Lucozade; see Table 9.1)

Table 9.1

FAI commercial partners

Sponsors	Sponsored activities
Eircom	Primary sponsor of the FAI; national teams and Eircom League
Umbro	Official kit sponsor and official sportswear of the Irish Team
Fiat	Official car sponsor to the FAI
Pepsi	Official sport drink of the FAI and title sponsor of the FAI Pepsi Summer Football Schools and SFAI National Cups
Paddy Power	Official betting partner of the FAI
Carlsberg	Official beer of the FAI and title sponsor of the FAI Carlsberg Cups
Lucozade	Official sports drink sponsor of the FAI and Eircom League
Statoil	Official sponsor of the FAI Junior Cup Competition
Nivea for Men	Official skincare supplier to the FAI
HP	Official technology partner of the FAI
Ballygowan	Official mineral water supplier to the FAI
DHL	Official worldwide couriers to the FAI
Waterford Crystal	Official crystal supplier to the FAI

Source: FAI Annual Report, 2004/05.

have direct links to the FAI on their company home web page, or even mention the Irish football connection.

The FIAT motor company is the car sponsor for the FAI, and as such contributes marketing support and vehicles for key personnel. Under the terms of the agreement, the cars are to be renewed each year for a five-year period (2004–2009) and include Alfa Romeos for senior management and specialist vehicles for the Association's Regional Development Officers.

The FAI Annual Report (2004–2005) provides details of what is referred to as a 'unique multi-broadcaster TV deal' negotiated with three broadcasters in March 2005 – Radio Telefis Eireann (a public service broadcaster with three stations, RTE1, RTE2 and Telefis na Gaeilge), TG4 (which produces Irish-speaking programmes) and Setanta Sports (an independently-owned broadcaster which provides sports programmes only). This deal was completed in addition to the existing deal with TV3 (again, a privately owned company). Under this new agreement, more than thirty domestic games will be broadcast live each year for a four-year period. Information in relation to sponsorship deals is patchy – it is stated that the RTE deal is worth €5 million to the FAI. Other recently concluded commercial agreements are set out in the winter edition of the FAI newsletter (www.fai.ie). These include a €10 million, long-term deal with Umbro and €2 million sponsorship by

Lucozade. It should be noted that Lucozade has sponsorship agreements with all three major governing bodies – the Gaelic Athletic Association (GAA); the Irish Rugby Football Union (IRFU) and the FAI.

The primary sponsors for the women's national football team are Eircom and Umbro. Other parties involved in sponsoring the women's game include Ballygowan, Master Foods, Ray Treacy and Sports World. Women's football according to an interviewee (directly associated with the WFAI), is the poor relation when compared with Ladies' Gaelic Football. She noted that the Ladies' Gaelic Football Association (LGFA) currently has 82 000 regis-tered players and sizeable sponsorship deals for its inter-county National Football League (Suzuki) and All-Ireland Championships (TG4). Due to its close relationship with the GAA, the LGFA has access to good-quality playing facilities for its league and cup competitions. At provincial, county and club levels a certain level of cooperation exists between officials from the men's and ladies' games. A bonus for players (who, while not paid to play, receive expenses) is the opportunity to play at Croke Park at the finals of the major competition (the All-Ireland Championship finals, Senior and Junior, are played in Croke Park on the first Sunday in October each year. For the first time ever, in 2005 the WFAI Cup Final was played in Dublin's Lansdowne Road Stadium on the same day as the men's final (FAI Cup), and the attendance at the game was around 25 000 spectators.

Other major sponsored initiatives include the summer football schools organized by the FAI (sponsored by Pepsi) in many loca-tions throughout the country. These are designed to target young-sters who during the school year may or may not have been involved in football. In 2004, more than 400 coaches encouraged 17 000 boys and girls aged between seven and fifteen years to enjoy the special atmosphere of the FAI/Pepsi summer school (FAI Annual Report, 2004/05).

In the FAI Annual Report 2004/05, details in relation to the average number of employees are provided. For the financial year under review (2004), this numbered fifty-nine (nine manage-ment and fifty administration and operations). Association staff costs for the year amounted to €4.12 million. The names of the members of the Board of Management (nine) and the National Council Members of the Association are provided; however, no information is given in relation to executive roles, apart from John Delaney being the Chief Executive Officer (CEO). It is left to the reader to conclude that the FAI does not employ a market-ing manager. There is an individual assigned to media relations (full time), and in December 2005 the position of corporate sales manager with the FAI was advertised. The job specification for that position seems to focus more on the sale of corporate boxes and ten-year tickets for the redeveloped Lansdowne Road Stadium. The lack of attention to marketing may possibly stem from the fact that the Association was obliged by government in late 2004 to undertake organizational restructuring in order to retain Irish Sports Council funding. At present, association executives appear to pay little attention to marketing – as is evident from the most recent FAI Annual Report (2004/05). A paragraph (with the subheading 'Commercial and Sponsorship Agreements') informs the reader that the revenue received from the most recent sponsorship agreements is primarily reinvested in funding the development of the game, and that the prize money within the Eircom League has now been increased by 300 per cent to €400 000.

Technology – the role of the Internet

The benefits of the Internet to business have been pointed out by Strauss and Frost (1999) – it is cheap for both businesses and consumers, extremely convenient for anyone with PC access, global in nature and unbounded by time constraints. It also acts as a distribution channel, and can reduce the costs of establishing physical distribution channels for businesses. Certain service enterprises (banks, retailers) have realized that the Internet enables transaction marketing (the 4Ps) and relationship marketing. Many sports organizations have sophisticated web pages, particularly those in the United States. From the point of view of sports clubs, the Internet facilitates communication between the club personnel and its consumers – supporters and fans. In their study pertaining to English football clubs, Beech et al. (2000) discovered links between clubs' marketing orientation, departmental structure and subsequent website management.

Gillentine (2003) asserts that the successful use of the Internet as a marketing tool will be limited if technology is not acknowledged as being a tool for sports marketing and not the marketer. He maintains that it is necessary to develop an Internet philosophy which can be used as a basis or starting point for effective use of Internet technology. The key question a sport marketer must ask is, 'Why am I using the technology'? In answering this question, the following queries should be considered:

- Will the use of technology augment the visibility of the sport product?
- Will it enhance consumer awareness?
- Will it increase consumer demand?

So apart from focusing on the 'why' question, the sport marketer will also address the 'who', 'what', 'where' and 'how' questions.

While there are many websites (official and unofficial) associated with national league clubs and leagues, for the purpose of this exercise the comments regarding web-page design, content, etc. refer to the 'official' club and organization pages only. For this exercise, the author has reviewed all 'official' national league club websites and that of the FAI, and it is apparent that the main focus is on the provision of information pertaining to the organization/club. The home-page menu in most cases consists of the following options: news, results and fixtures, matchzone, squad, video library, league tables, chat, sponsorship, shop and club information. In certain cases, details of links to the supporters' club are provided on the 'official' web page. As noted earlier, information about the club ownership, mission statement, governance, annual report, operations and management personnel is non-existent. Some of the sites are attractively designed and well laid out, while others are poorly organized (the FAI web page) and the information on them often quite dated. For example, the new season (National League) began on the weekend of 10 March 2006, yet in February 2006 much club information/news had not been revised since the end of the previous season. It is obvious that some clubs employ the services of professionals for the web design while others rely on the efforts of personnel (voluntary and professional) associated with the club. Many web pages consist mainly of web advertisements which no doubt are designed to provide better brand awareness and image enhancement for the advertisers, but at times suffer from information overload.

League marketing efforts

An organization's marketing strategy describes how the firm will fulfil the needs and wants of its customers (Ferrell and Hartline, 2005). According to Ashill *et al.* (2003), strategic marketing refers to the decisions taken to develop long-term strategies for survival and growth. Some years ago, individuals at the helm of the Eircom League managed to put together a plan to develop awareness of the league, its fixtures, services offered and the like by placing advertisements in the national and local press for the weekend games. This concerted effort drawing on the skills/competencies of a marketing person and endorsed by the league management and club personnel was designed to raise the profile of the National League. Care was also given to the existence of a match-day programme, its content and quality. After some time the efforts faded, and currently personnel from each club strive to market their enterprise drawing on resources available.

In general, there is little evidence to suggest that Irish football administrators or clubs' management engage in strategic marketing. Based on details posted on the 'official' club websites, just one National League club, Longford Town, has a marketing manager (although one of the interviewees contributing to this chapter questioned the existence of such a position and person, adding that this club has, to his knowledge, no full-time employees); other clubs tend to have a public/media relations person and/or a commercial manager. For most National League clubs marketing activities are pretty fragmented, and in the main include advertising (ground/outdoor) and sponsoring match-day packages.

The majority of Eircom National League clubs encourage match-day advertising by way of programmes and around the ground advertising. Recruiting corporate advertisers is pursued actively by club personnel; much of this is achieved by way of personal contacts. Many established clubs (Shelbourne, Bohemians, Cork City) produce high-quality match-day programmes, whereas other clubs pay less attention to this owing to lack of resources – both human and financial. As television coverage is now the norm for many games, ground-board advertising is very popular and is encouraged. The price for such advertising will vary, depending on whether it is undertaken as part of a package or for specific games only and on the location of the boards. It is common practice by many clubs to give key personnel from advertising firms complimentary match-day tickets for the club's home fixtures. Another benefit from participating in ground advertising is the opportunity to watch the game from the club's corporate facility. While many stadiums now have bar and catering facilities, in certain cases these are not well organized and the service offered is limited. Few advertising hoardings at club stadiums are electronic, so they are usually positioned bearing in mind the location of television cameras for either a live or a deferred transmission.

As noted in Appendix 9.2, almost all National League clubs have a sponsor for their team, ground and kit. In general, the firms/organizations associated with clubs tend to be located locally – such as Toher's Chemist, Carroll's Gift Shops and Century Homes. There are exceptions, such as Nissan (Cork City), Budweiser (UCD), the Radisson SAS (Galway United) and Goodyear (Cobh Ramblers). However, in some cases there is a subsidiary or branch of the multinational enterprise located near the club, or it does business with it. According to an interviewee for this chapter, one Eircom League club invites businesses/individuals at the end of each year to sponsor the club for the following season. In this instance (and perhaps many others), it seems little attention is paid to matching the sponsorship objectives of the sponsor with those of the sponsored club. The more common kit sponsors are Umbro and

O'Neills. Details of match (home and away) sponsorship packages are provided by many clubs, along with player and match-ball sponsorship opportunities. Eircom clubs encourage businesses and fans to sponsor a player for the season. By so doing, the sponsor's name will be contained in the match programme for the season, alongside the photograph of the player.

The role of the media in Ireland

Football in Ireland gets less attention in the national media (television, radio, and press) compared with the English/Scottish Premier Leagues. It is common practice on many radio and television (national and local) stations for sports news bulletins to commence on the latest/final scores from the English and Scottish Premier Leagues. This can be partly explained by the connectivity between many Irish fans and English/Scottish clubs, but it begs the question as to the level of media exposure sought for the game by officials, clubs and leagues. The role of the television networks was referred to earlier in this chapter: during 2005 there was live and deferred coverage of many Eircom League games, with Radio Telefis Eireann (RTE) showing fourteen, TG4 broadcasting ten and Setanta Sports delivering twenty (with three deferred). It is reported by the FAI (www.fai.ie) that an average viewing figure of 179 000 for the FAI Cup Final (broadcast live on RTE 2) was recorded. In addition to the coverage of games, TV3 broadcast a programme entitled *Eircom League Weekly*, which further enhanced the profile of the league.

Much interest exists among media personnel regarding the fortunes of the Senior International team. The recent departure of Brian Kerr from the position of Irish National Team manager drew much discussion. Similarly, the appointment of Stephen Staunton (along with his backroom team) and the Euro 2008 draw occupied much space in the press and on the airwaves. However, the promotion of the Women's Senior International team to elite level and the improved fortunes of the U19 Women's National Team gained less media attention.

The three Irish national daily broadsheets (*Irish Times*, *Irish Independent*, *Irish Examiner*) all have designated football writers who generally report on the Eircom Premier League developments (results and reports), but the main focus of attention is on England, Scotland (Celtic and Rangers) and Europe (Spain and Italy). Many English papers (especially the tabloids) have an Irish edition specifically designed to meet the needs of Irish readers. The *Irish Sun* and the *Irish Daily Star* offer comprehensive coverage of sports (football, Gaelic football, rugby and racing) during the week. They employ columnists (Pat Dolan and Eamonn Dunphy) who contribute weekly comment on football in Ireland, but needless to say these commentators also devote time, space and energy to the English game. In line with all other newspapers on Mondays, much attention is given to the English Premiership during the season, with detailed analysis, player ratings and attendances.

The *Evening Herald* (Dublin's only daily evening newspaper) focuses on junior and schoolboy's football each Monday. While much of the information centres on Dublin and the surrounds, reports are included pertaining to football in rural areas – Carlow, Meath, Kildare and Wexford. This feature (approximately twenty tabloid pages) provides results and reports on junior, amateur and schoolboy games at the weekend. It also details the fixtures for the following weekend for many leagues (the Dublin District and Schoolboys' League, the EBS Leinster Senior League, the Wexford District League, the Guinness Amateur Football League and the Carlow District League).

Public relations

Public relations (PR) has been defined as the element of the promotional mix that identifies, establishes and maintains mutually beneficial relationships between sports organizations and various publics on which its success or failure depends (Shank, 2005). The author distinguishes between the internal and external publics with which sports bodies interact, and details the tools that can be used to communicate with the targeted audience. Among the Eircom League clubs, five indicate on their website that they employ a PR person, but do not state on what basis (full-time, part-time or voluntary).

As in the UK, press conferences are a common tool used by the FAI and the leading clubs when communicating with external audiences. For instance, the FAI organized a formal launch of the Eircom League season for 2005. The event was sponsored by Eircom, and took place in Dublin Castle. The *Irish Daily Star* published the *Official Eircom League Season Guide*, which was distributed to over 130 000 *Star* readers. A national radio campaign was undertaken too, to raise the awareness of the league and its fixtures. Other forms of PR include participating in community events, producing written materials (annual reports and press guides) and lobbying (personal selling necessary for stadium development/ location decisions). Following a lengthy delay and protracted discussions, on 13 February 2006 South Dublin County Council announced that the development of Shamrock Rovers' ground in Tallaght, Co. Dublin can now proceed. Shamrock Rovers FC's Chairman (Jonathan Roche) issued a press statement welcoming the news. Apart from stadium development, this club (Shamrock Rovers) also has plans that will involve players and coaches visiting schools and community groups throughout the South Dublin Region, in order to encourage participation in sport among young children (www.shamrockrovers.ie/press_release).

Publicity is also a widely-used form of public relations. It is the generation of news in the broadcast and print media about a sports product via news releases and press conferences. In many instances, publicity can come from external sources (unlike PR) and is not controlled by the organization or sports body; hence it is often considered to be more reliable, as it has come from 'unbiased' sources. However, publicity may not always enhance the reputation and image of the sports organization. The FAI may possibly face further legal proceedings due to what Brian Kerr alleges was a breach in confidentiality with respect to the termination of his employment by the Association. Many sports bodies get bad publicity (about on- and off-the-field matters); however, some are better at managing this and in many instances use it to their advantage.

Conclusions

This chapter provides an update on sport and the sporting infrastructure in the Republic of Ireland with particular reference to football. Issues pertaining to the management and marketing of the sport are set out and some weaknesses/gaps identified. The chapter is based on secondary-source material and two personal interviews; nevertheless, the author contends that pertinent insights into the strengths and weaknesses of Irish football from the marketing and management perspectives emerge.

While great strides have been made by FAI senior personnel to improve its organizational structure, the practice of not publishing complete information pertaining to certain aspects of the Association needs to be addressed. For instance, details in relation to its governance arrangements (FAI Annual Report, 2004/05) are incomplete, as are those for the full-time management executives and their roles. Several Eircom League clubs do not disclose their mission, operating policies, marketing plans, etc., and there is little evidence (based on the 'official' web page audit) that they publish an annual review of activities and events.

Sport marketing gets much attention in the literature, and there are now numerous sports journals and research publications dealing with various strategic issues. From this brief review, it still seems that, from the FAI perspective, the notion of marketing is not taken seriously – the Association has no marketing manager – and is equated with sponsorship. According to the Eircom League Acting Chairman, the league marketing activities for 2005 were built on three promotional pillars: Eircom League/FAI Promotional

Activity, Eircom Promotional Activity and TV. Many marketing initiatives and efforts outlined in this chapter have yielded 'success' for the league/club/sports body, but in general there is no long-term strategic marketing policy for the game.

The introduction of the UEFA Club Licensing/facilities development scheme in October 2002 is a positive development. It should be used to inform Eircom League club personnel (and other clubs) about the club infrastructure standards required for the future, covering various dimensions. The reality seems to be that rather than focusing on improving the quality of Irish football management, club status and image, etc., it is stated that this scheme will be used to maximize 'the Sports Capital Grants allocations for future infrastructural developments for Eircom League clubs' (FAI Annual Report, 2004/05: 10). Other sports bodies in Ireland (the GAA and IRFU) have developed their infrastructure nationwide, drawing on their own funds in addition to some local authority and government funding. An ethos appears to exist among FAI personnel that, as football has the most participants (in terms of playing personnel at all levels) in Ireland, it should automatically be funded externally – particularly by government. Should such an organizational culture exist, it would be interesting to research the reasons for this being the case and establish the extent to which it would restrict efficient and effective marketing and management of Irish football.

Acknowledgements

The author would like to acknowledge the contributions made by three individuals to this chapter who wish to remain anonymous.

Bibliography and references

Amis, J., Slack, T. and Berrett, T. (1999). Sport Sponsorship as distinctive competence. *European Journal of Marketing*, **33(3/4)**, 250–272.

Ashill, N., Frederujsibm, N. and Davies, J. (2003). Strategic marketing planning: a grounded investigation. *European Journal of Marketing*, **37(3/4)**, 430–460.

Bale, J. (1991). *The Brawn Drain*. University of Illinois Press.

Beech, J., Chadwick, S. and Tapp, A. (2000). Emerging trends in the use of the Internet – lessons from the football sector. *Qualitative Market Research: An International Journal*, **3(1)**, 38–46.

Bourke, A. (2003). The dream of being a professional football player. *Journal of Sport and Social Issues*, **27(4)**, 399–419.

Bourke, A. (2004). Women's football in the Republic of Ireland: past events and future prospects. *Football and Society*, **4(2/3)**, 162–181.

Coakley, J. (1998). *Sport in Society*. McGraw-Hill.

FAI (2004/05). *Football Association of Ireland Annual Report – 2004*. FAI.

Ferrand, A. and Pages, M. (1999). Image management in sport organizations: the creation of value. *European Journal of Marketing*, **33(3/4)**, 387–401.

Ferrell, O. C. and Hartline, M. (2005). *Marketing Strategy*. Thompson South Western.

Gillentine, A. (2003). Developing an Internet philosophy. *Sport Marketing Quarterly*, **12(1)**, 63–64.

Gray, D. P. and McEvoy, C. D. (2005). Sport marketing: strategies and tactics. In: B. L. Parkhouse (ed.), *The Management of Sport: Its foundation and application*, Ch. 14. McGraw-Hill.

Hannigan, D. (1998). *The Garrison Game*. Mainstream Publishing.

Maguire, J. and Stead, D. (1998). Border crossings. *International Review for the Sociology of Sport*, **33(1)**, 59–73.

Malone, E. (2006). Clubs set to ratify FAI control of the League. *Irish Times*, 30 January (sports supplement: 2).

Mason, D. (1999). What is the sports product and who buys it? The marketing of professional sports leagues. *European Journal of Marketing*, **33(3/4)**, 402–414.

McCarville, R. and Copeland, B. (1994). Understanding sport sponsorship through exchange theory. *Journal of Sport Management*, **8(2)**, 102–114.

McGovern, P. (1999). The Irish brawn drain: English League clubs and Irish footballers. *British Journal of Sociology*, **51(3)**, 401–418.

Shank, M. (2005). *Sport Marketing: A Strategic Perspective*. Pearson.

Stotlar, D. (2004). Sponsorship evaluation: moving from theory to practice. *Sport Marketing Quarterly*, **13**, 61–64.

Strauss, J. and Frost, R. (1999). *Marketing on the Internet*. Prentice Hall.

Whannel, G. (1992). *Fields in Vision: Television Sport and Cultural Transformation*. Routledge.

Appendix 9.1

Fan club notices

Irish clubs	English clubs	English clubs	English clubs
Bohemians	Arsenal (2)	Gillingham	Tottenham Hotspur
Bray Wanderers	Aston Villa (2)	Huddersfield Town	Watford
Derry City	Birmingham	Ipswich Town	West Bromwich
Dublin City	City	Leeds United (5)	Albion
Finn Harps	Blackburn	Liverpool (5)	West Ham United
Galway United	Rovers	Luton	Wigan
Kildare County	Blackpool	Manchester City (4)	Yeovil Town
Limerick F.C	Burnley	Manchester United (3)	
Longford Town	Bury	Nottingham Forest	Scottish clubs
Shamrock Rovers (4)*	Cardiff City	Peterborough United	Celtic (13)
Shelbourne	Chelsea (2)	Queens Park Rangers	Hibernian
St Patrick's Athletic	Coventry	Scunthorpe	Rangers
UCD	Everton	Stockport County	
	Fulham	Southampton	

* Number in brackets refers to the number of fan club branches which posted a notice on that date.
Source: Fan Club Notices, *Evening Herald*, 2 February 2006, p. 80.

Appendix 9.2

National League clubs – management details

Club	Division	Sponsors	Governance	Marketing/PR/media personnel
Athlone Town	First	Ganley's of Athlone	President, Chair and other positions	None cited
Bohemians	Premier	Des Kelly; O'Neills	President, Secretary and other positions	Marketing, PRO, Commercial manager
Bray Wanderers	Premier	Slevin; adidas	Chair, Vice Chair, Committee	No information
Cobh Ramblers	First	Goodyear	Chair, Vice Chair, Committee	No information
Cork City	Premier	Nissan (team); O'Neills (kit)	Chair, Management Committee, Director of Operations	Commercial manager
Derry City	Premier	Smithwicks	No information	No information
Drogheda United	Premier	Sponsorship packages	Presidents, Club Directors, General Manager	Media and PRO
Dublin City	Premier	Carrolls Gift Shops	No information	No information
Dundalk	First	A–Z of Business Partners and Sponsors	Chair, CEO, General Manager (co-op)	None cited
Finn Harps	First	Blaney	Board of Directors, members, General Manager	Press Officer
Galway United	First	Radission SAS Hotel; Umbro	Chair, Secretary, Directors	Press Officer

(continued)

National League clubs – management details (*continued*)

Club	Division	Sponsors	Governance	Marketing/PR/ media personnel
Kildare County	First	Celbridge Football Park; Errea	Chair, Secretary, three Directors	No information
Kilkenny City	First	Site not available	No information	No information
Limerick	First	No official website	No information	No information
Longford Town	Premier	Flancare	Chair, President, Executive Committee	Marketing Manager, PRO
Monaghan United	First	The Steering Wheel Pub; Century Home	Chair; key positions	PRO
Shamrock Rovers	First	Woodies DIY; Umbro	Board of Directors	PRO
Shelbourne	Premier	JW Hire; Umbro	No information	No information
Sligo Rovers	Premier	Toher's Chemist; Jako Team Sports	Management Committee members	PRO
St Patrick's Athletic	Premier	Smart Telecom	Chair, President CEO, Operations Manager	Commercial Manager
UCD	Premier	Budweiser; O'Neills	No information	No information
Waterford United	Premier	TBA	Two Directors, President, Club Administrator, Finance Officer	Media Officer

Source: Club 'official' web pages, February 2006.

Appendix 9.3

Primary data collection – interviews

Two interviewees participated in this exercise. Interviewee A is a media and communications expert, and is closely associated with the organization of football in the Republic of Ireland. Interviewee B has formerly held an executive position with the Eircom League, and is currently involved at a senior level in management of one of the Premier League clubs. Both interviewees contributed generously to the exercise and provided direction in relation to useful source material in some instances. They emphasized the fact that their views are personal, based on experience gained from their roles in organizational administration, marketing and management. While much of this chapter relies on secondary-source material, the interviewees' responses have been incorporated into the text to give it a practice-driven focus. The interviewees were contacted in early January 2006, and arrangements were made to complete the interviews by early February 2006. The interviews were semi-structured and lasted approximately one hour each. They were completed at a neutral venue which was convenient to the author and the interviewees.

Interviewee A

Q1: Could you provide an update on the governance arrangements for football within the Football Association of Ireland?
A: Considerable changes have occurred in governance arrangements within the FAI. These changes have mostly stemmed from the Genesis Consulting Review, which was completed post-Saipan 2002, following comments by the Irish team captain, Roy Keane in relation to travel and post-arrival arrangements for the team participating in the World Cup. The number of people on the main Board has been reduced and the subcommittee structure streamlined.

Q2: Do the seven subcommittees which exist in the Association have clear mandates and operational arrangements?
A: The committees with which I am familiar include the following: International, Domestic, Legal and Corporate Affairs, and Underage. I am not sure how clear the mandate for each would be.

Q3: The role of sponsorship is critical for football in Ireland – who are the main sponsors?
A: Sponsorship deals are critical for football at all levels in Ireland. However, the sponsorship deals in most cases are not as large as those secured by certain other sports organizations. Information

pertaining to the main sponsors is provided in the Annual Report and on the Association web page – Eircom and Umbro are two of the leading sponsors.

Q4: How are sponsors recruited and selected?
A: Sponsors tend to self-select or get involved because representatives from a company or organization like the game, or would like to be associated with a particular event and/or team. For example, there has usually been little difficulty in attracting sponsors for the Irish National Senior Team since the success achieved in the late 1980s and early 1990s. But, as indicated earlier, there can be sponsor deficits in other areas of the game – junior, schools and community levels. There are many other sports organizations that seek sponsors – for football, the main competitors are the Gaelic Athletic Association (GAA) and the Irish Rugby Football Union (IRFU).

Q5: Are sponsorship deals with the FAI evaluated on a regular basis?
A: While there are several models/frameworks for evaluating sponsorship deals in the literature, there is little evidence to suggest that great attention is given by organizational personnel to evaluating such deals. When representatives of a sponsor indicate that it is no longer interested, then another party is sought by the FAI.

Q6: What mechanisms are in place for such appraisals?
A: Appraisals of sponsorship deals tend to be completed by parties independent of the arrangements. For instances, many consulting firms will engage in research designed to inform on the connectivity between the sponsor and sponsored and the extent of consumer recall of such deals.

Q7: The FAI has thirteen leading sponsors (www.fai.ie); is there a difference in the status of each?
A: Yes, there is a difference in status as detailed in the Annual Report – some are main sponsors, while others are sponsors of particular activities/events.

Q8: It is noted that Fiat has a sponsorship deal with the FAI – is this deal still current?
A: This deal was negotiated a few years ago, and is current, with a few modifications.

Q9: Is there much evidence of 'fit' between the FAI main sponsors and their business?
A: Based on research completed by online marketing, many people would suggest there is 'fit' between Eircom (main sponsor) and the FAI.

Q10: What is the connection between the Women's Football Association (WFAI) and the FAI?
A: The Women's Football Association (WFAI) is now affiliated to the FAI, whereas formerly both bodies were very separate. Currently, the FAI has funded the activities of the WFAI and has appointed a Regional Development Officer to promote the women's game who works in conjunction with personnel from the WFAI.

Q11: Does the FAI produce an Annual Report? If so, why is this report not available on the website?
A: The FAI produces an annual report for its Annual General Meeting (AGM) in July. At present it is not available on the association web page, as it is being redesigned.

Q12: Could you describe the ownership arrangements for National League football clubs in Ireland?
A: It is difficult to get information on the ownership arrangements for National League clubs as most are private companies. There are no Public Limited Companies (PLCs), and two clubs have recently assumed cooperative status.

Q13: What are the main hindrances for club development in Ireland?
A: The lack of finance and financial management is possibly the main hindrance to club development in Ireland. The Irish football industry is less developed than in other countries, and this may stem from strong ties over the years with English clubs and the small size of the Irish market.

Q14: Do National League clubs avail of Sports Capital grants from the Irish government? If so, please give examples of more recent grants and usage.
A: Yes, National League clubs avail of Sports Capital grants from the Irish government, many of which are used for stadium/ground improvements.

Q15: What marketing strategy has the Eircom League got to promote the game at local level?
A: The FAI does not focus particularly on marketing – there is a section in the Annual Report devoted to Financial/Commercial Affairs (see Annual Report). The FAI does not need (at present) to advertise national team fixtures, and a minimal amount of advertising is used for Cup (FAI and Setanta) League Competitions.

Q16: The technical development programme has advanced various initiatives: what are the main ones? How 'successful' have these initiatives been?
A: The publication of the FAI Technical Development Plan is designed to promote the development of young Irish players. The

appointment of Regional Development Officers (RDOs) has been crucial in establishing the game in many parts of the country where traditionally the GAA games or rugby were more popular team sports.

Q17: What are the main barriers to young player development?
A: One of the major barriers to young player development is the poor sporting infrastructure in Ireland, specifically with respect to football. Another barrier is the lack of attention given to elite sport development during compulsory schooling.

Q18: At provincial level, how do clubs organize and market their own competitions?
A: Promotion/marketing at provincial level occurs at a local level. Evidence for this being the case can be gauged by reviewing the list of sponsors associated with clubs at all levels.

Q19: The Kennedy Cup (which takes place in June in 2006) is the main showpiece for Irish young talent. Is this 'appropriate' practice, as many attendees are scouts from English clubs and the participants are aged under thirteen years?
A: This has been the practice for years, and it is unlikely to cease at this stage.

Q20: As the interest in football among the Irish population is closely linked to the success of the national teams, in your view, do the international games get too much attention (media and otherwise) at the expense of the local game?
A: The local media try to get the balance right during the domestic season. Most media (TV and print) carry results and reports following games, especially following weekend games.

Q21: Is the Irish-based fans' association with English (Scottish, Italian and Spanish) clubs fostered by media developments (Sky), or due to club history, culture and ties with former Irish players? Does this concern you?
A: It is due to all of these. It is drawing resources (fans) away from the game in Ireland, but there is little that can be done to stop that occurring.

Q22: What in your view are the major factors that will increase the number of players participating in football in Ireland?
A: Better infrastructure (training and playing) for the game, with player support. Also, if the league were fully professional, this would retain players in the Irish game.

Interviewee B

Q1: What are the main issues facing football administrators in the Republic of Ireland today?
B: The main issues facing football administrators in the Republic of Ireland is complying with UEFA club licensing arrangements and getting adequate funding for club activities and events.

Q2: Is the provision of a national football stadium in Dublin critical for the future development of the game? Give reasons for your view.
B: It would be nice to have a national stadium for football; however, given the size of the market, it is debatable as to whether we in Dublin have the need for three ultra-modern stadia. Redeveloping Lansdowne Road is probably a sensible compromise.

Q3: What are the positive and negative aspects of being associated with managing a club in the Premier Division (Eircom League)?
B: The positive aspect in recent years has been the change in the calendar for the National League – it is now between March and November. Needless to say, the negative feature is the lack of resources, particularly capital.

Q4: What effect has the UEFA licensing arrangements had on the management and control of Irish clubs?
B: UEFA licensing is a welcome development. While some club personnel are very slow to embrace change, it has forced senior executives in clubs to pay attention to critical aspects of club management.

Q5: Are there difficulties implementing such arrangements in clubs? If so, what type of difficulty has emerged?
B: The main difficulty would stem from lack of investment for infrastructure development and getting informed personnel to complete and submit the documentation in the required format.

Q6: The FAI (Genesis) has published a 'White Paper' on the future of Irish football. Do you support the view that the Eircom League needs to be merged with the FAI? Give reasons for your opinion.
B: It remains to be seen as to what happens in relation to the structure of the National League. While it has been accepted in principle, further information on what exactly it entails, and discussions, will be necessary.

Q7: It is expected that the Premier Division will be reduced once again to ten teams. What is your view of the proposed restructuring of the league?

B: If it sees my club being designated to Division 1, I will not be too supportive of the restructuring – much will depend on the final details.

Q8: What are the main ownership arrangements for National League football clubs?

B: All National League clubs are private companies, although two are organized and managed as a cooperative with dispersed ownership arrangements.

Q9: Football has the highest level of participation, yet the Gaelic Athletic Association (GAA) Games have the greater number of attendees. How do you account for such a variation?

B: The history and culture of the GAA (nationalist aspirations) are two factors which account for its popularity. In recent years, the association has adopted a more corporate ethos (yet maintaining original values) and managed to extend its activities by drawing on resources – government and non-government.

Q10: Could the Football Association of Ireland personnel learn lessons from the GAA or the Irish Rugby Football Union (IRFU)? Please specify key areas for learning.

B: Both organizations have built up a tremendous volunteer network, with individuals engaged in many areas of their activities. This network includes many professionals who supply various services out of their love for the games rather than personal advancement. The parish network is the essence of the GAA – every parish will have a team(s), and playing fields. The quality or lack of playing facilities throughout the country needs to be addressed.

Q11: The Norwegian model for young player development is regularly mentioned as the ideal. What are the difficulties with adopting such a model in the Republic of Ireland?

B: Over the years, close personal ties have developed between representatives from Irish and English clubs, so it would be difficult for Irish clubs to put a rule in place prohibiting the outward mobility of young players until they reached twenty-one years.

Q12: Are English clubs still the main option for Irish youngsters who wish to pursue a career in professional football?

B: In a small number of Irish clubs, players are full-time professionals – but the professional career opportunities here are very limited. Due to geographic and cultural closeness, English clubs are still an attractive prospect for young players. Many young players also opt for Scottish, Welsh and Northern Irish clubs.

Q13: Many universities and tertiary-level colleges in Ireland offer football scholarships. What is your opinion of this method of developing elite sports personnel?
B: This development, now popular in many Irish universities, has allowed aspiring elite players to complete higher education while playing sport. I believe that education (secondary and tertiary level) is important for all sports people, and would recommend this route for talented youngsters.

Q14: Is market size (smallness in terms of population and business operations) a major inhibiting factor for the development of football?
B: There are many barriers to progressing football in Ireland – yes, the market size is a factor, but also competition from other sports and sports bodies.

Q15: What changes (if any) would you make to the administrative structure for football in Ireland?
B: In recent years the role of the provincial bodies has been established, and this assists the development of the game. Some leagues draw on teams across many boundaries, and it might be more appropriate to have a more organized structure. The Association and clubs could benefit from assistance from individuals with management (organizational) expertise.

Q16: In your view, could the Irish government do more to advance/promote football among youngsters in Ireland?
B: Obviously, the Sports Capital Grants could be increased and more attention paid to education policy in respect of the role of sport during compulsory schooling.

Q17: As Irish football (at most levels) relies greatly on volunteers, are these individuals appropriately trained for their assignments, and are their efforts appreciated by the 'powers that be'?
B: In most cases they would be briefed for the occasion, but more training is needed – particularly to handle large-scale events.

Q18: What is your view of the Kennedy Cup (U13 inter-league competition) being the showcase for young Irish talent, and attended by scouts/representatives from English and other clubs? Do Irish club personnel attend in large numbers?
B: Many budding internationals have made their name at the Kennedy Cup, and it is held in high esteem by many players (current and past). While representatives from clubs in England (at all levels) do attend the competition, there will be personnel from Irish clubs on the sidelines too.

Q19: Have Regional Development Officers (RDOs) added value to Irish Football since they were appointed?
B: One of the more evident contributions of RDOs is the growth of football within schools. Through the FAI Schools, both boys and girls are now playing the game while at school in addition to being with the local community-based club.

Q20: From your club's perspective, what are the main challenges – marketing, management, financial, etc. – that you face in the next five years? How do you and your club personnel propose to meet such challenges?
B: The main challenge at present is the restructuring of the league. The lack of a modern infrastructure is also a challenge, but the development of a Sports Academy by the government should provide opportunities for young player development and retention.

Marketing and football: the case of Finland and the All Stars Programme

Kari Puronaho and
Timo Huttunen

Overview

Finland is one of the smaller football countries, and the Football Association of Finland (FAF) has a great passion to develop not only the football itself but also the resources available, for both quantitative and qualitative growth. According mainly with the general principles of strategic marketing for non-profit organizations, the FAF started the All Stars Programme in 1999 in order to develop the game to become the most popular in the country, to bring the spirit of fair play to all levels of the game, to lift the standard of the game permanently to the top international level, and to strengthen the position of the FAF nationally and internationally.

This chapter focuses on the importance of understanding the production process of positive football experiences in order to be able to ensure not only football success in the future, but also (and especially) the development of all kinds of relevant resources – particularly volunteers. Furthermore, it discusses the separation of marketing through football in order to guarantee resources, from football marketing in order to ensure there will be the demand for football. At the end of the chapter, some results are presented following five years (1999–2004) of systematic marketing and running the All Stars Programme.

Keywords

All Stars Programme, Finland, non-profit organizations

Introduction

Finland is a sports-loving country with one of the most physically active populations in the world. It is also one of the most successful countries in Olympic history, when comparing the number of Olympic medals with the number of inhabitants. The special features of Finnish sport culture, as well as Finnish football, are active volunteers, non-profit sports clubs and higher sport demand than supply in sports clubs. The biggest problems of Finnish football have been continuous lack of resources, youngsters' drop-out and the lack of football facilities. Finnish football also has a very powerful competitor – ice-hockey, in which the team won the 2006 Olympic silver medal, and which has the highest number of spectators. On a world scale Finland is a small football country (forty-sixth in the world ranking), but Finnish football wants to grow and develop.

Finnish football achieved a historical mark at the end of year 2001, when licensed players exceeded 100 000 for the first time. More and more players are professionals in the bigger European football clubs, and the Finnish women's national team, together with that of Sweden, came third in the Euro 2005 tournament. Fine work is being done daily in about a thousand football clubs, and this work has also brought more and more enthusiasts into the sport. The goal of Finnish football is to be the number one sport in the country, no matter how measured. Achieving this requires common vision and principles of all the people associated with football. During the last ten years the Football Association of Finland (FAF) has paid special attention to the values of club action, and versatile, logical marketing activities, with the All Stars Programme.

Facts and figures regarding Finnish football

Two children out of three participate in sports club activity during their lives, and more than 260 000 children (defined as under eighteen years of age) play football weekly as a hobby. About 0.01 per cent of them reach the international level of their chosen sport. At the end of 2001, Finland had just over 100 000 licensed football players of which the main group, roughly 97 000 players, participated as a 'hobby' on many different levels and in many different age groups. Out of those 100 000-odd players, about 3000 (3 per cent) belong in the sphere of top-level or competitive football.

According to the official FIFA website (accessed March 2006), Finland is forty-sixth in the men's ranking and sixteenth in the women's. The Premier League, First Division and Women's National League are considered to be national top-level football in Finland, and have approximately 800 players. The Second Division, Women's First Division, the National League of A-juniors and the National League of B-juniors (both men and women) are considered to be competitive football, and have approximately 2200 players. Roughly 50 Finnish football players play abroad on a professional status. More than 10 national teams play annually in about 100 international matches.

There are over 100 000 official national matches played in a year. The Football Association of Finland (FAF) is responsible, with the assistance of the District organizations, for the organization and development of the national- and regional football activities. The twelve Districts of the FAF organize multiple options regarding playing, match and competitive events on a local basis, and they also arrange 'nets' for talented players, as well as competitions for District selections and education for different football functionaries. Educational football events, organized by the FAF and the Districts, have approximately 15 000 participants annually.

The Football Association of Finland

The Football Association of Finland (FAF) is a sport federation that is responsible for all the football-affiliated action in the country, as a member of FIFA. FAF's function is to develop the game at both the top and recreational levels. The latter includes the goal of educating the young. To achieve the goals, benevolent and client-centred marketing methods are to be used. The values of the Finnish football were reinforced in the General Assembly of FAF in 1991, and are fair play, a solid football family, internationality, responsibility for the people and environment, interaction, joyfulness and tolerance. The FAF Activity Plan, which is based on the above-mentioned values, aimed from the very beginning at everyday

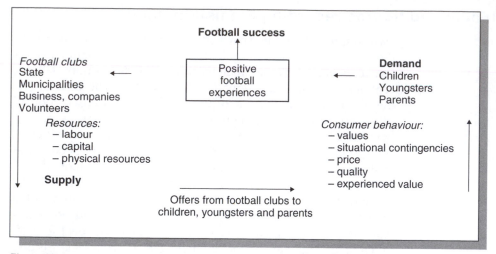

Figure 10.1
Production process of positive football experiences and success

practice, and led to the birth of the All Stars Programme in 1999 (see Appendix 10.1). The goals of the Football Association of Finland are developing the game to become the most popular sport in the country, bringing the spirit of fair play to all levels of the game, lifting the standard of the game permanently to the top international level and strengthening the position of the FAF.

The production process

Finnish football clubs are normally registered organizations and members of the Football Association of Finland (FAF) in order to participate in national playing, match and competitive events. Club activities are guided by the Finnish organizational law and run by volunteers. Almost all football clubs in Finland are non-profit organizations. One of the key things in developing market-ing has been the understanding of the production process of all the positive elements and effects of football by stakeholders and positive football experiences by players. We do not talk of football services or products, because the key element in this process is the experience. Figure 10.1 illustrates the production process of positive football experience and success.

The difficult task for football clubs is to create a 'positive circle' (Figure 10.2). Football activities and experiences must be based on values that are appreciated in the society – especially health and security. Appreciation brings resources from the stakeholders. With the resources you can develop facilities, clubs and, finally, the offers to children and youngsters (and their parents) of cooperation

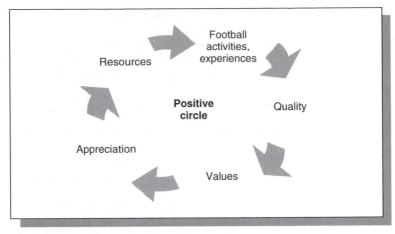

Figure 10.2
The positive circle

with the club. Personal involvement of players creates positive football effects and experiences, and so on.

Football, security and health

According to the All Stars Programme, each child has a right to practise football safely in a supportive atmosphere, according to his or her own wishes. Securing youngsters' safety is the responsibility of every adult in a club, no matter what that adult's main function is. As a part of quality enhancement and improving the feeling of safety, FAF developed an entirely new system for helping children to try football as a hobby. This system offers the opportunity, at no cost, to play under adult guidance for one month as a new member of the football family. An insurance company has also approved insurance coverage during this time.

The main principles regarding the protection of youngsters in the All Stars Programme are as follows:

- The children's wellbeing is to be ensured at all levels of action
- Each child has a right to equal treatment, regardless of age, gender, level of physical development/readiness, cultural background, colour, religion, sexuality, etc.
- Any inappropriate behaviour, or suspicion of it, must be investigated and dealt with immediately. In more serious cases, the help of experts is advised.

Child protection is paramount and any offences must be investigated immediately. Taking care of children's wellbeing is an overall responsibility, and cooperation among those involved in youth activities is very important. The goal of the All Stars Football Programme is to give youngsters in all parts of the country a fair chance to play football. It takes care of those who want to play football once a week with their friends, as well as those aiming to play as professionals one day. The programme is based on two main elements:

1. An atmosphere of appreciation and support (values, health)

2. Playing under positive adult supervision (security).

Studies have shown that, according to children, a good guide, coach and referee has the following qualities:

- The ability to maintain order (security)
- Know-how in teaching new skills (development)
- The ability to make players feel good during a match/practice (joy)
- Patience (licence to succeed/fail).

High-quality work, in accordance with the existing values, leads to appreciation and success – we hope.

The principles of the All Stars Programme

The All Stars Programme is a brand and, as such, it is important that it is visible and stands out from others. If a programme is not recognized as a part of an organization's portfolio of programmes, that organization can lose valuable stakeholders and public support; moreover, youngsters and their parents may be less likely to participate in a programme if they are not aware of the organization's name or its link to the Football Association of Finland. The FAF's programme portfolio consists of the following: Seal Clubs, Football Schools for the National Team, Green Card, Football Tournaments for Children, Football for Schools, All-Involved Football Events in Schools, Football Skills, the FUN project for girls and women, Operation Rules and the All Stars Programme. The lifespan of these programmes is normally about five years. The All Stars Programme is probably the best-known throughout the country, but the brand mindshare has not yet been measured.

The All Stars Programme is based on the following programme principles:

1. *Playfulness*, which means the attitude and the atmosphere while working with youngsters. Drills and matches can be simultaneously both challenging and enjoyable. Quality drills – which also advance learning – are fun.

2. *Equality*, which is present when all the participating children are recognized, supported and given the chance to succeed. Each and every young person has a right to participate in the best moment of football – playing together with friends.

3. *An individual approach*, which means that personal development is far more important than the team's competitive success. Personal development must be compared not with the other members of the team, but also according to each youngster's previous achievements.

4. *Individualism*, so difference and personality are strengths, not threats. Skill is the foundation of football, and developing the skill means more individual drills and two-a-side and three-a-side games, etc., and less eleven-a-side. Everyone has his or her own style of being a star!

5. *Versatility*, which is essential for sportsmanship and comprehensive development. Practising multiple sports is an advantage, and clubs should actively encourage children to do this. If the activities of a given club are of high enough quality and take all the participants into account, the sport(s) it offers will be the subject of a genuine interest. Each child and family has a right to decide the sport(s) they want to practice, and how often they want to do so.

6. *Security*, which comes from parents who understand their role in sports. There are always adults responsible for guided club activities. Favouring the locality and activities close to children's homes increases the feeling of security. Familiar surroundings and the presence of friends are major security factors.

7. *Tolerance*, which means respect of differences. Everyone is different. The international football family includes the whole world, and welcomes everyone without prejudice regarding colour, religion, language, nationality, sex or any other factor.

8. *Non-intoxication*, which is a right for all participants in youth football. Each child has a right to fresh air and a non-toxic environment while practising. This applies to both domestic and foreign events. Alcohol, whether selling beer in a match, advertising it in the stadium or just spending leisure time drinking with teammates, does not belong in events for under-eighteens; nor do drugs or other toxic materials.

The following criteria of the All Stars quality standards are especially stressed, not only to players but also to the parents and other stakeholders:

- Year-around practice facilities
- A high level of coaching

- Bringing up players to be responsible (self-development)

- Player development to district, regional and national teams, connecting school and studies successfully with football and self-development as a football player.

Football marketing and marketing through football

In fact, the core 'product' or 'service' to be marketed in the All Stars Programme is not football itself, but the effects and experience of football. This means not only football marketing to increase the demand for football, but also marketing through football aimed at different resource holders, to increase the different kinds of football resources – physical (facilities), labour (volunteers) and capital (support from society and sponsors). In this kind of situation, marketing is not just a task for football clubs and the FAF but also and especially an important task for everyone involved with the game (Figure 10.3).

The first step in developing a marketing strategy designed to influence different target audiences is to segment audiences and then develop a positioning strategy for the offering. Segmentation helps when making quality, quantity and timing decisions with regard to marketing strategies. Once markets are divided up, one or several of the approaches to market segmentation (such as mass marketing, differentiated marketing, niche marketing or mass customization) can be applied.

The All Stars Programme and marketing related to it have six different target levels, with various offerings and goals regarding each of them:

1. *Children and young people*:
   - to offer interesting games and forms of play in different conditions throughout the year
   - to increase the opportunities for playing football anywhere and at any time
   - to create opportunities for growing into different roles within the football world
   - to increase general football demand.

2. *Club level*:
   - to develop competitions for children and young people
   - to develop the quality of clubs
   - to develop a culture of harmony and support in clubs
   - to develop club resources (supply).

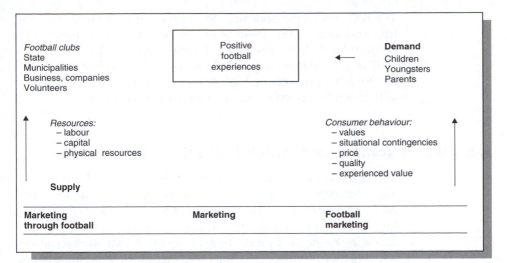

Figure 10.3
The football marketing process

3. *Coach level*:
  - to understand children and young people and their way of thinking within their hobby
  - to invest in coaches' education
  - to activate and motivate by appreciating their work (supply).

4. *Parents/family level*:
  - to provide information on how to support their children in their hobby
  - to activate volunteers by showing the importance of the voluntary work (supply and demand).

5. *Sponsor level*:
  - to increase awareness of all the positive effects of football activities
  - to increase the goodwill of partners
  - to offer a possibility to improve sponsors' corporate image
  - to gain positive publicity and increasing sales
  - to increase football resources (supply).

6. *Society level*:
  - to assume responsibility on a day-to-day basis for children and young people, in cooperation with their homes, schools and other important factors
  - to increase football resources and facilities in general (supply).

The FAF has been responsible for marketing at the national, district and local levels. In spite of the fact that it has used many modern marketing techniques during its events, both on TV as well as in printed media, 'word-of-mouth' has probably been the most effective marketing tool. Also, the 'let the satisfied partners tell' principle has led to new cooperative agreements.

A critical resource for Finnish football – volunteers

One of the key elements during the whole project has been recruiting volunteers. Volunteers are critical to the success of most non-profit organizations. Voluntary work is the cornerstone of activity for traditional club activities. It is a necessary basic element for arranging events, and guarantees the organizer that other resources will be efficiently used and that each one of those giving time or investing in resources will receive profit from their investment. Parents as voluntary workers will provide their children with beneficial recreation. By supporting sport organizations full of voluntary workers the public sector promotes sports activity, which in many ways benefits the society more than other public actions. Even businesses get good publicity when advertising sports events organized by voluntary workers.

Volunteers, by definition, do not earn money for their efforts, but they can be reimbursed for costs. How well an organization functions depends to a large degree on how well it is able to use the resources of the surroundings to fit its functional goals. In this connection the concept of resources is wider, referring to elements other than economic factors. Thus the resources can be divided into three categories – material, energetic and know-how. An organization functions and realizes its goals with the aid of a versatile resource reserve. Material resources include spatial preconditions of different facilities, natural environment, and monetary economy – i.e. available funds to cover functional expenses. Energetic resources include the contribution on which basis the organization functions, as well as the readiness and willingness of the members to exercise and take part in sports activity. The know-how available regulates the quality and outcome of activities.

Beside personal factors, organizational characteristics also affect the level of members' work input – for example, attraction, sanctions available and the decision-making system. These things affect how big a commitment a member is willing to make. Activity can be maintained only if the society organizes new services for its members, or has a fresh, important goal; otherwise, the activity will gradually decrease following initial enthusiasm.

The motives of voluntary workers can be divided into four different categories:

1. Personal satisfaction (keeping fit, an interest in teaching, as a counterbalance to work and a channel to social relations)

2. Being chosen for a task

3. Unselfishness and willingness to help

4. A combination of personal satisfaction (1) and unselfishness (3).

Sport volunteers are by and large a self-help group. They are far more likely, therefore, to be motivated by the benefit for family and friends or by their own needs, as well an interest in improving or assisting a club or federation whilst gaining personal satisfaction.

The typical profile of a voluntary worker is very similar in most countries: a sports club member from an early age, normally male, who when older takes a leading position in the administration – first as a trainer in a club, then as a board member in a club and finally perhaps as a board member in a federation at the national level. Volunteers have normally had a strong involvement in competitive sport as athletes; in general, at a medium or low level, they work as multifunctional officials and are often also members of different non-profit organizations on the local level. They do not normally have substantial financial problems and they are well educated.

It is difficult to find a systematic and particular model for recruiting volunteers; motives are so versatile. Many factors affect how people become members of a sports organization. Sport has to compete with other hobbies. The organization should meet the demands of those interested in physical activity. Moreover, people's personal lives affect their joining a sports organization. These external, individual factors that affect leisure activities include, for instance, an individual's social and economic position, working conditions, education, age, sex, family structure, health status and availability for service depending on the place of residence. There are also various internal motive factors – for example, personal interest; the opportunity to practise sports and competitive sports, for self-development, to meet people, to create new friendships and social interest, and to promote sport; and working with youngsters. Many reports state that finding voluntary workers often happens spontaneously and is more or less a 'lucky hit'. Some authors say that it is very important to have better knowledge and systematic analysis of voluntary work, because this provides a basis that makes recruiting less haphazard and helps with planning it more precisely at all levels.

However, one of the best ways to recruit volunteers is to apply the consumer behaviour model; people will become volunteers in stages, and it is important to figure out what stage they are in at present and then try to tailor a strategy to that stage. Some people are not aware of the volunteering opportunities; some do not realize how important, sensible and desirable volunteering is; some of them have just started; and some of them have already worked several years. The development of the amount and quality of voluntary work in the near future depends on how the organizing bodies for sports activity succeed in volunteer coordination, education, stimulation, motivation and appreciation. During the All Stars Programme, the FAF has followed the following principles when keeping and recruiting new volunteers:

1. *Appreciate*. Appreciation of voluntary work at local, regional as well as national or international level is an essential condition to have even more work input available in the future. Appreciation must be shown in connection with successful events and in official prize ceremonies. Additionally, a more flexible system adapted to modern needs and interests is needed. Voluntary work must not cause excessive cost to its workers; reimbursement of expenses is part of appreciation.

2. *Explain*. The targets and meaning of the needs and effects of voluntary work must be explained not only to volunteers but also to their partners and to political decision-makers. Probably one of the greatest problems just now is the decreasing public support given to sports organizations, which is also having a strong negative effect on recruiting voluntary workers.

3. *Coordinate*. Coordinating voluntary work includes, for example, detailed job descriptions to identify tasks, and long-term planning with detailed schedules.

4. *Educate*. Educational programmes, short training programmes and other possibilities must be developed to achieve merit as well as awards through voluntary work.

5. *Stimulate*. Job satisfaction increases in stimulating working conditions. Modern equipment and rooms in which to work, a pleasant working atmosphere, valuing others' work and encouragement all increase job satisfaction and make the quality of work better.

6. *Motivate*. People are motivated to work if they consider the work important to themselves. Because motives vary from person to person, it is important to emphasize the social aspects of working, the opportunities of education through voluntary work and so on. In other words, it is important to emphasize those things which people themselves consider important.

The significance of voluntary work in Finnish sport clubs is huge, and during the following years it will presumably remain so. Professor Seppänen stated in 1983 that:

> Most Finns have a strong positive opinion about sports and sports club activity. To encourage this positive thinking and allow it to grow stronger we need, however, something we can never buy with money – living interest and self-sacrificing work, which have always been and always will be the heart and core of result-giving sports club activity.

In conclusion, all the football organizations in Finland must, regarding volunteers:

- value their contribution
- appreciate any extra effort they make
- take account of their complaints,
- care about their wellbeing
- care about their opinions
- try to make their jobs as interesting as possible.

Furthermore, persons involved with the All Stars Programme try to treat volunteers as far as possible as professional workers. It is important to assess the volunteers' skills and match those skills to the tasks to be performed in the organization. Job responsibilities must be set out clearly, in detail and in advance. Coordinators must set specific performance goals and benchmarks, and inform the volunteers of the organization's expectations. So far, there has been no need to dismiss volunteers for unsatisfactory work.

Results of the All Stars Programme

The All Stars Programme has been a success story. After just five years (1999–2004) of systematic work, marketing and running the All Stars Programme in Finland, the following goals have already been reached:

1. The number of children and young people playing football weekly as a hobby has risen 180 000 to 261 000 (an increase of 43 per cent; Finnish Sports Survey, 2002/03).

2. The number of licensed players has risen from 88 000 to 110 000 (Register of Licensed Players, FAF).

3. The number of girls has risen from 13 600 to 19 900.

4. The number of people who annually take part in schooling for adults has risen from 5000 to 10 000 (an increase of 100 per cent; The Register of Education Department/FAF).

5. Interest in youth football has risen enormously in the media. Newspapers, radio and TV have noticed the All Stars Programme, and especially its values and activities.

6. Over 2100 comprehensive schools (over 60 per cent of the total) have actively participated in the 'Week for Ball Sports'.

7. Support from the Ministry of Education, especially regarding youth activities, has increased.

8. Public support of successful football clubs at a local level has increased.

9. More artificial-grass football fields have been built.

10. More sponsorship agreements have been made.

11. There are more sponsorship agreement proposals from companies, particularly because of the results gained by and high values of the programme.

12. More full-time workers and volunteers are working in football clubs and district organizations.

The future

The Football Association of Finland wants to improve the quality and increase the quantity of football. With the help of research and logical actions, the aim is to maximize the positive effects and results of football and minimize any negative ones. Hopefully marketing through football will help, especially in developing the football infrastructure and getting new stakeholders. One of the targets is also to develop football awareness among youngsters and to give them positive experiences. The All Stars Programme is only one part, although a successful part, of the Action Plan and Marketing Plan of the Football Association of Finland. The FAF wants a unique view of itself and its role in the marketplace. In the near future, activities must be even more visionary, customer-centred, differentiated and flexible and, in particular, motivate more volunteers.

Bibliography and references

Andreasen, A. R. and Kotler, P. (2003). *Strategic Marketing for Nonprofit Organizations*. Prentice Hall.

FAF (1991–2001). *A Dream of Good Sports, the Ethical Guidelines for Youth Sports*. Young All Stars Publications.

FAF (1999/2001). *All Stars – Publications*. Football Association of Finland.

FAF (2000/01). *All Stars – Educational Material*. Football Association of Finland.

Finland's Ice-Hockey Association (1999). *Spirit of the Game – Guide for Parents of E-D-juniors*. Finland's Ice-Hockey Association.

Football Association in England (2000). *The FA Child Protection Policy*. FA.

Mullin, B. J., Hardy, S. and Sutton, W. A. (1993). *Sport Marketing*. Human Kinetics.

Seppänen, P. (1983). *Suomen urheilujärjestäistä ja niiden toiminnasta 1980-luvun alkaessa*. Jyväskylän yliopisto. Liikuntasuunnittelun laitos. Tutkimuksia no. 28.

Stotlar, D. K. (2001). *Developing Successful Sport Marketing Plans*. Sport Management Library. Fitness Information Technology, Inc.

Young Finland (1998/2001) *Spirit of the Game Guides*. Young Finland.

Young Finland (2000). *Competition Study Group's Recommendations*. Young Finland.

Appendix 10.1

Interview with Timo Huttenen, Director of the All Stars Programme of the Football Association of Finland (FAF), 8 March 2006

Q1: How can you describe in a few words the history of your All Stars Programme?

TH: One of the most important wishes of a parent is that a club provides a good environment for growth. At its best, football can give physical and mental health, as well as lifelong relationships with team-mates and others involved with the team. While practising and playing with a group, a child's ability to focus develops along with the social skills. Football can give joy for life and a feeling of control over one's own life. Sport as a hobby, and membership of a club, is an important and valuable experience for a child. It can become an important part of the growth environment, along with family, school and friends.

Research shows that one of the most important motives for playing football is to make friends. Ability to establish relationships is one of the most important factors defining quality of life. Common rules and ways of doing things are also included in individualism. A child's thoughts as well as the principles of home, school, team and club should be observed in football. Being aware of all that, FAF launched, together with its Districts, annual Game-rule Conversations in youth football. Acting within a club offers an excellent chance to learn social skills. Each member should have an important role in a team.

Q2: According to the latest studies, one of the highest values among Finnish citizens is health. How can you show or prove to the parents that football is a healthy hobby?

TH: Youth sports should always be versatile. This secures the development of basic sports' skills, which enable learning of more specified skills at later age. Too early specialization may harm a child's development. The FAF encourages children to practise multiple sports while they are young, as this creates a good basis for various physical exercises in adulthood. When the quality and quantity of a youth sport is balanced, it creates a good basis for health. Practice should develop and stress the whole body evenly. Sports injuries are often due to increased practice times, weight-lifting or simply because the quality of training is poor. The All Stars quality control system, which we have developed, covers the health aspects at three levels with the aim of aiding and supporting the different club cultures.

Q3: What are the principles the All Stars Programme is based on?
TH: The All Stars Programme is based on eight equal principles which form the basic values of youth football: playfulness, equality, individual approach, individualism, versatility, security, tolerance and non-toxication.

Q4: How have you reached your target audiences?
The All Stars Programme and marketing related to it have comprised six different levels and we have also set different goals on each of these levels: children and young people, club, coach, parents and family, sponsors, and society. At all these levels we have used Campaign Marketing Planning (CMP). We listen to our target customers and learn to know them and understand their thinking, and then translate the learning into concrete programmes of action. Normally we also pre-test our key elements of action with part of the target audience. After some corrections we launch the campaign, make further amendments as necessary during the implementation, and in the end try to learn and improve when starting a new campaign. We are not afraid of mistakes; making mistakes is a way to move ahead and improve.

Q5: What are the critical resources in Finnish football clubs?
TH: Definitely the volunteers; volunteerism is not only our strength but also our weakness. Hundreds of thousands of volunteers work daily in our sports clubs and try both to get resources and to develop football in all possible ways. The biggest part of the volunteer system is parents, which means that it is very difficult to motivate them to continue after their own child has grown up. The Finnish population is getting older, and day after day it's harder to get volunteers involved with sports club activities. That is one reason why we need more professionals and paid staff, to coordinate and motivate the existing volunteers and recruit and manage new ones.

Q6: What are your future plans?
TH: We still want to develop our infrastructure. At the moment [2006] there are 32 fields with artificial grass, and our target is to have 150 altogether by 2010. We also want to develop football awareness among youngsters, give them positive experiences and, finally, create 'a happy marriage' between youngsters and football. Because of that marriage, and hopefully soon, a boy or a girl will be born and that child will lead to a place in the European Championship or World Championship Finals. That day will come, and I want to see it!

PART 2

The development of dedicated football marketing in the rest of the world

CHAPTER 11

The football business in Brazil, and the example of Atlético-PR

Amir Somoggi

Overview

In Brazil, football as a business has developed at a very slow rate when compared with what happened in Europe in the latter half of the 1980s and the 1990s. Since 1993 new sports laws have been created to bring professionalism to Brazilian sports management, these regulations being greatly influenced by the sports laws established in Europe a few years previously. In general, the Brazilian sports laws lay down corporate obligations for the professional clubs, similar to those for public limited companies. This chapter tries to clarify how the football business has developed in the 'country of football', analysing the evolution of Brazilian sport legislation and the reality of Brazilian football clubs' management. The example provided, Atlético-PR, describes how the club from Paraná State has developed its management and strategic long-term plans, becoming the first strategic model in Brazilian football.

Finally, an interview with Luciano Kleiman, Marketing Director of adidas, Brazil, is presented (see Appendix 11.5).

Keywords

Brazilian sports laws, football business, Brazilian sports industry, football club management, Atlético-PR

Introduction

This chapter about the Brazilian football market has two parts. First, it presents the changes in Brazilian sports law and describes the reality of football clubs' management in Brazil, along with their outlook over the next years. Secondly, it describes the development of Atlético-PR's management model, a benchmark in Brazilian football, emerging from the creation and implementation in 1995 of a strategic long-term plan in an environment of crises and difficulties.

The football business in Brazil has a short history when compared with the expansion of the football industry in Europe. The number-one sport in Brazil, which has a huge number of football fans all over the country, has suffered a delay in development of the business aspect, and the football clubs have a long way to go regarding the modern realities of global football and forming a platform to generate opportunities for clubs, sponsors, strategic partners and financial investors.

In Brazil, the sports law regarding the management of professional clubs and sports entities is very new. In the 1980s in Brazil, football management didn't have specific laws; the first one followed the new rules in the football industry in Europe, which were initiated in England and spread throughout the major football countries of the continent. In 1993 Brazil passed its first football law, the Zico Law, named after the ex-player who had become the National Sports Secretary. The Zico Law was the first time in Brazil that a legal environment had been created to develop a new model of administration and organization of clubs, federations and confederations.

In Brazil, football clubs' management had for years been focused solely on performance in the field, in which they invested many financial resources – sport medicine, physiotherapy, physical training and technical preparation – making Brazil a worldwide point of reference in football. From the 1990s until today, the reality of the management of soccer in Brazil has become a paradox.

The clubs play in competitive championships and raise new talents; they have fans attending the matches, and millions of people check the sports news via different media. However, until recently it was the case that each year the clubs sold their best players and the money obtained was always destined to repay debts, to make delayed payments to players and, occasionally, to be invested in physical training and technical preparation. Many clubs have training centres, in the same way as the European clubs, but only a minority are developing their brand and their relationship with consumers to generate new incomes, becoming a business unit supported by modern management based on accountable, financial and marketing policies.

Nevertheless, in 1992 a new club administration model arose in the Brazilian football market: the partnership between clubs and companies in the management of the football clubs. Just one was successful. The Italian company Parmalat created, along with the club SE Palmeiras, the first cooperative 'Co-Gestão' model in Brazilian football. The company began to control the management of professional sports, investing directly in players and their wages and having a major part in the future sale of athletes. In addition, the Italian company used the club as a vehicle for its marketing strategy, through jersey sponsorship and publicity at Palmeiras matches. Parmalat and Palmeiras created an example for the Brazilian market, which was followed by some clubs, which cooperated with different companies; however, after some years they failed. The Palmeiras and Parmalat partnership was the sole success, and became the showcase of an association in Brazilian football. The partnership finished in December 2000, and in the eight years it existed a US$150 million movement was realized.

In 1998, when the ex-player Pelé was the Extraordinary Sports Minister in Brazil, he created a new sports law called the Pelé Law. Again, the political environment gave football clubs an opportunity to transform football management. Among many aspects, the law offered professional clubs the opportunity to change their management, as in a company, and their association with investors.

Associations with banks, investment funds and sport-marketing companies arrived in Brazil, but not all of them were successful. The partners injected millions of US dollars, but they did not administer the clubs; some of the investors just put up the money and didn't have the power to make management decisions. After this period many clubs had to sell players in the middle of championships, owing to contractory obligations to some of these companies.

The model practised by some clubs in Brazil regarding this principle was interesting, but later it was demonstrated that the clubs were not prepared for these associations and that companies that could explore a football club's brand didn't do so as a mutual investment, as happened in the Palmeiras–Parmalat case, with a real partnership providing benefits for both the company and the club. It became clear that there is only one way to success: clubs must be professional administrations, with professional directors remunerated appropriately, and the executive staff must base work on strategic planning management and develop a long-term vision to increase business via the football brand, media and home matches, rather than being dependent on the sale of the best players to pay their debts and equilibrate the budget. The first Brazilian football club that was able to create a professional administration was the Club Atlético Paranaense (Atlético-PR). This arose from a new management model, which concentrated on the development of new business and the evolution of income. Atlético-PR is the main example of management of the football clubs in Brazil, and will be the subject of the second part of this chapter.

After having tried the management model of association with companies, the clubs arrived at 2000 with the European market in crisis, low payments for TV broadcasting rights, and without a plan to develop new sources of income. The clubs entered a time of crisis – they were not ready to convert their business into a profitable force, and they were not able to change the management scheme to provide for the consolidation of their brands, improved relations with their fans and a new generation of new income from different sources, rather than being dependent solely on their sporting success. Nowadays, the clubs' marketing departments are creating small projects to generate new income, but a lot of them don't have a strategic vision or an appreciation that all their actions return value for the brand and their strategic objectives.

At present, the Brazilian football market is presenting many exceptional opportunities for the clubs, with new legislation for the professional clubs going a long way towards developing their turnover diversification projects. The most important resources of the biggest football clubs in Brazil are the trading of players, broadcast rights and sponsorship, which together represent an average of 70 per cent of all income.

The football business in Brazil

Sports laws in Brazil

The first discussions on sport legislation in Brazil began in 1939, when the National Commission of Sports was created. Its principal objective was to make a study of the reality of the sport in Brazil, and to produce new regulations. At that time it was decided that questions regarding each sport would have to be judged in that sport itself, and that the sports organizations that looked for common legislation would be disqualified. The main consequence of this Commission was the creation in 1941 of the CND – National Advice on Sports – which had the objective of establishing the direction for sport in Brazil.

One of the most important of CND's legacies was the creation of a single national organization by sport modality that would represent the regional organizations, of which there would be one for each state of the country. At that moment, the sports' organization in Brazil was created, with national confederations for each sport modality along with regional federations.

This regulation remained in force until 1993, when Law 8,672/93, Zico's Law, was created. In 1976 there was an important change in sports law in Brazil, when legislation came to include regulations regarding conditions of work for the professional football athletes, creating the *passe* – the bond between athlete and club. The *Passe* established that after the contract between the club and the player had expired, the player would remain connected with the club until it decided otherwise.

The most significant changes only arrived with the promulgation of the present Brazilian Constitution in 1988, after the military period of Brazil. The main principles of this were the freedom of people to take part in sport organizations, the prohibition of state interference in the operation of sport organizations, differentiation of the treatment of professional and amateur sport, and the obligation of the government to promote the sport for the community.

Nevertheless, the 1988 Constitution did not have rules for the sports industry, which was an important generator of income with many workers directly involved in it. Simultaneously in Europe, discussion was taking place regarding how countries could include a professional view of the sports management of the National League clubs – clubs with government policies.

Law 8,672/93 – Lei Zico

The creation of the Zico Law, when Artur Antunes Coimbra Zico was Sports National Secretary, was the first time in Brazil that a specific law had been designed with regard to the professional administration of sports entities. This law involved the creation of the 'Clubes-Empresa', companies that generate professional activity in the clubs, and the clubs had the opportunity to change their legal structure to public limited companies or commercial societies of closed capital. In addition, they could remain as clubs but would have to be managed as companies.

The law was innovative, but it included an ambiguity that ended any possibility of implementation by the football management. The idea was to create 'Bingos' – organizations that could explore the betting opportunities of the game, and which must be connected with sports entities that were destined a percentage of the income of the respective Bingo. The Bingos initiative, although born to create resources for the Brazilian sport, was in the end used by people who weren't interested in the development of sport in Brazil and of professional management.

The significance of the Zico Law was that, for the first time in Brazil, there was talk of the creation of a new form of professional sport management, with new rules for the clubs. The clubs' directors must manage the clubs as a company. This was also the first time that the creation of a professional league was suggested. The great legacy of Zico was that his law gave Brazil the opportunity of providing national sports rules with the same professional reality that had been developed a few years earlier in Europe.

Law 9,615/98 – Lei Pelé

The Pelé Law was created by the Extraordinary Minister of Sports in Brazil, Edson Arantes do Nacimento, Pelé, to correct a series of imperfections in the Zico Law. However, it retained 75 per cent of the previous law. The main points included:

1. The obligation for the clubs that participate in competitions with professional athletes to change their legal structure, becoming 'Clubes-Empresa'. There was no option regarding the clubs' juridical structure in the first text of the Law.

2. The end of the *passe*, revoking the 1976 law regarding the work relations of the professional athletes and forcing clubs to adapt to new contracts by March 2001.

3. The creation of the Brazilian National Football League and regional leagues, making it possible for the clubs to organize the competitions.

4. The obligation to convert semi-professionals (aged between fourteen and eighteen years) to professionals when they reach eighteen, while giving the former club the first option to sign a contract with the player.

5. The provision of the same consumers' rights for the spectators at the stadiums in Brazil as for the consumers of other products and services.

The Pelé Law, after its approval, led to many objections from the clubs, mainly owing to the end of the *passe*, the principal clubs' asset, and other obligations such as changes in their legal structure.

The law underwent many changes before being approved, but the first impact of the law was that clubs that negotiated with different partners were to be jointly responsible for the administration of the football. Clubs like Flamengo, Vasco, Bahia, Vitória Corinthians and Cruzeiro signed associations with companies to generate new businesses through football. The Pelé Law allowed this possibility, and these groups created a new business model, but it didn't become profitable.

Nevertheless, in 2000, following strong pressure from groups close to the football clubs, many aspects of the law were modified by Law 9,981/00, which didn't oblige Brazilian clubs to transform into companies and also restricted the companies which formed partnerships with the clubs to one club to each company.

In the years following Law 9,981/00, Brazilian football was in deep crisis and a few clubs that were in associations with companies terminated their contracts and returned to the situation previous to the association – low levels of income, public opinion influencing the clubs' professional management, and clubs with a bad image.

This situation remained unaltered until the government of ex-President Fernando Henrique Cardoso, in its last year (2002), created two new laws: the Law of Football Responsibility and the Code of Defence of the Supporter. These laws were created with the objective of returning to discussion and obliging clubs to follow the norms of professional football management. This new norm was created so that the new government of Luis Inácio Lula da Silva, who had been elected Brazilian President at the end of 2002, had the opportunity to begin its mandate in January 2003 with clear regulations for football management.

Laws 10,671/03 (Supporters) and 10,672/03 (Responsibility)

President Lula's government maintained the directives of its predecessor, and on 15 May 2003, ten years after Zico's Law, Brazil at last had two specific sports laws – one regarding supporters' rights and another relating directly to the management of professional clubs.

Law 10,671/03, called the *Estatuto do Torcedor*, was very well received by Brazilian society, because matchday revenues were unexplored in Brazil, and problems including the violence of some fans, organizational difficulties regarding the competitions, and poor facilities and services for the fans at the Brazilian stadiums were far from the modern reality of football matches, where fans are provided with facilities in the stadium and the services for supporters are based on entertainment.

In general, in Brazil clubs have never worried about taking care of their mass-consumers, who at the moment watch matches on TV. With the new law, the clubs were obliged to change their structure and relationship with their fans, and the legislation provides the same rights for the sports consumer as for consumers of other products and services. In addition, the clubs are required to invest in numbered seating, clean toilets and security services. Moreover, for stadiums with a capacity greater than 20 000 spectators, the clubs must invest in closed-circuit TV to support the police's work. At the same time the Confederation must publish the competition calendar, do sixty days promotion of it, and regulate the competitions.

Law 10,671/03 is a great initiative in the development of the football business in Brazil, because the Brazilian stadiums must be adapted to become modern platforms for entertainment, with facilities for the fans, and must also generate revenue for the football clubs.

Law 10,672/03, the Law of Football Responsibility, forces clubs to follow the same policies as Pelé Law, but is more specific and complete regarding subjects like corporate governance in football clubs. All professional sports entities must have their balance sheet approved, and their directors may be investigated and possibly lose their position in cases of irregularity. The clubs have the same obligations as open capital companies, but it is not necessary for them to change their legal structure.

The perspective of business in Brazilian football is very positive, because the football clubs are undergoing a lengthy development of new income from different sources. The clubs are now obliged to treat their fans as consumers, and the legal environment means that clubs must be managed professionally. The changes in sport legislation in Brazil have formed the basis for clubs to develop their projects and create a new income cycle, but in order to build this model the clubs must have professional management based on a long-term strategic plan.

For a long time in Brazil, clubs haven't known exactly how to develop their management model. They still believe that the changes in sport legislation are a threat to the management of the clubs. However, if the political and legal environment in Brazil were used to develop the business model, Brazilian clubs would become profitable and generate revenues from B2C projects. This would lead to more resources for maintaining the best players for a long time, and create a cycle of income.

The Brazilian sports industry

The Brazilian sports industry has been growing at a rate above that of the Brazilian GDP (see Figure 11.1), and between 1996 and 2000

300

Figure 11.1
General information: Brazil, 2004
(*Source*: IBGE – 2005)

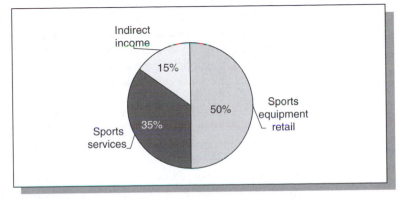

Figure 11.2
Breakdown of the Brazilian sports industry's revenue – total US$11 billion in 2003
(*Source*: FGV-RJ)

the sports economy (according to the FGV-RJ survey) had an average development rate of 12 per cent per year. In 2003, the sports industry in Brazil employed 963 000 direct workers according to the survey 'Atlas do Esporte 2003', and generated US$11 billion in revenues – which represents 1.9 per cent of the Brazilian GDP.

Figure 11.2 breaks down the sports industry revenues into sports equipment retail, sports services and indirect income.

Sports equipment retail – US$5.5 billion

The revenue from equipment retail makes up 50 per cent of the total revenue from the Brazilian sports industry. This is for several reasons – the large consumer base, the many people (60 million) who regularly participate in sport, and the fact that it is a competitive market with international companies as Nike, adidas,

Umbro, Kappa, Diadora, Puma, Kelme and Wilson, and national companies as Olympikus, Penalty, Rainha, Finta and Topper. Sports shoes and sports clothes sales represent US$1 billon/year, and home and professional fitness equipment sales represent another US$1 billion.

The other part of the retail revenue comes from small expenditures by sports spectators, income from sports properties and TV rights (clubs, federations and leagues).

Sports services – US$3.85 billion

Sports services in Brazil show a contradiction in that while people are spending money on sports participation, spectator sports, sports properties and TV rights have only a small value compared with Europe and USA.

The Brazilians, like the rest of the world, are looking for health – there are 3.4 million subscribers to fitness gyms each year, producing US$1.2 billion. However, the spend on spectator sports is just a small part of the sports services sector revenue, caused by the limited level of attendance in stadiums and sports complexes, and the low prices of the tickets.

Sports sponsorship represents US$320 millions, 63 per cent of which comes from sports broadcasting and 37 per cent from direct investment in clubs, venues, events and the selections. TV rights have only been developed in a small way in Brazil, compared to Europe and USA. The contract between TV Globo and Clube dos 13 for the Brazilian First Division football championship TV rights (free-to-air and PPV) provided just US$100 million for the main football clubs in 2004.

Indirect income – US$1.65 billion

Indirect income is represented by sports structures used for spectators and training centres, and transport and accommodation for the professional athletes and spectators.

In the next few years, with big sports events in Brazil – like the 2007 Pan-American Games in Rio de Janeiro, and possibly the 2014 FIFA World Cup – the country has a good opportunity to increase investment in the construction area and spectators' services. Meanwhile, bringing the World Cup to Brazil will need a big investment in Brazilian stadiums.

The Brazilian football industry

In 2004, the nineteen biggest football clubs in Brazil (see Appendix 11.1) generated a consolidated turnover of US$311.08 million

according to a survey, *The Casual List of Brazilian Football Clubs*, carried out by the accounting firm Casual Audiotores Independentes. In Brazil, the professional football clubs generated approximately US$400 million in revenue in the same year.

The Brazilian football market has more than 500 professional clubs and 350 stadiums with an average capacity of 15 000. Some stadiums in Brazil have a capacity of more than 50 000 – such as Maracanã in Rio de Janeiro, Morumbi in São Paulo, Mineirão in Belo Horizonte, Beira Rio in Porto Alegre, Arruda in Recife and Fonte Nova in Salvador. All of these stadiums have been in use for more than twenty years.

Mentioning just the more important competitions, between January and April the biggest clubs play in the regional championship (each state); between April and December is the Brazilian Championship (Série A and Série B); the Third Division, Série C, plays from August to December; from February to July is the Copa do Brasil; and also from February to July is the Libertadores da América.

Since 2003, Série A, the Brazilian Championship, has been a knock-out competition, where all clubs play without play-offs – as in the domestic European leagues. In 2004 Série A had twenty-four clubs, in 2005 there were twenty-two, and in 2006 there are twenty clubs participating.

In Brazil, more than 140 million people support a football club. The fifteen biggest clubs have 71 per cent of this fan base, but the biggest earnings of the market are concentrated on TV deals, sponsorship and player transfers (Appendix 11.2). In 2001, the income from the transfer of international players overseas represented US$114.9 million.

The investment in football club sponsorship reached US$30 million in 2003, and the biggest jersey sponsorship contracts in Brazil are shown in Table 11.1.

Over the next few years the football clubs in Brazil must improve their income from football fans, from the sale of products and services, and from matchday revenue, and must generate value for their brands so they receive more investment from sponsors, commercial partners, TV and different media projects.

Appendix 11.3 shows the revenues, expenses and shareholders' equity of six Brazilian football clubs in 2003.

Football club management in Brazil

The crisis that occurred in 2000 in the football industry in Europe has resulted in very damaging consequences for Brazilian football clubs. The clubs that always used player sales as a management instrument to equilibrate their budgets entered a very complicated

Table 11.1
Sponsorship deals, 2005

Clubs	Sponsors	Deal value (US$ millions)
Corinthians	Samsung	6.5
São Paulo	LG Eletronics	6.5
Flamengo	Petrobrás	5.0
Atlético-PR*	Kyosera	3.0

*Including Kyosera Arena's naming rights contract.
Source: Casual Auditores Independentes.

financial situation. The years of 2000, 2001 and 2002 were very difficult for football in Brazil. In this period the clubs were forced to reduce their wage costs, and this was the first action of the clubs on the closing of the European market to players. Meanwhile, young players moved at very early stages to new markets in Turkey, Russia, Ukraine, Japan, Korea and China. The Asian market even became more interested in Brazilian players following the 2002 World Cup.

This, of course, meant that the Brazilian clubs continued a vicious cycle by continuing to act as an exportation platform for young players. Player-trading in the football industry is an important income generator, but professional football clubs must also be part of a new strategy of management where the clubs develop revenue diversification projects, strategically plan their commercial actions and explore different marketing opportunities.

The most important thing in a professional football club is to install the best professionals in the market as executives – as in companies, clubs must have qualified workers in finance, marketing and promotion, planning, legislation, accounting and professional sport.

After 2002, the football clubs in Brazil could sell their best athletes to the European market and the players' wages increased again. Over the next years the Brazilian football clubs must improve their management and develop their income. Nowadays, the debts in football clubs are caused by low generation of income and the big wage costs, which aren't managed with a wage policy index.

The Brazilian market is singular, and certain data verify the potential environment for the football business in Brazil:

1. There are 45 million addresses in Brazil with TV in 2004, representing 90 per cent of the total homes in Brazil

2. There were 3.7 million subscribers to Pay-TV in 2004, 70 per cent with football broadcasting

3. There were 248 000 consumers of Série A PPV in 2003, at an annual cost of US$113 a year

4. More than 80 million mobile phones were sold and credit-card transactions totalled US$39 billion in 2004

5. More than 22 million Brazilians accessed the Internet in 2004, and e-commerce in Brazil reached US$660 million in 2004, US$1 billion in 2005

6. The advertising market in 2004 represented US$6.3 billion, and in 2003 was US$5 billion (61 per cent on TV advertising)

7. Big football clubs had more than 150 hours of broadcasting in the Brazilian First Division Championship (Série A).

In 2004, TV Globo paid US$100 million for the Brazilian Championship (Série A) broadcasting rights, and these resources come to the clubs. TV Globo sells quotas of static publicity in the field, TV slots and, in some cases, virtual advertisements, the total cost of which can be US$35 million for each advertiser per year.

The information regarding the Brazilian market illustrates how the consumer and business markets are already prepared for the football industry, and how, with radical changes, the clubs can become the most important players in the sports industry in Brazil. The football clubs must adapt to the professional reality of their sponsors and their strategic partners, and must direct their focus onto the relationship with the fans in order to convert them into profitable consumers.

In general, in Brazil football management is focused on the performance at the pitch and on the transference of players, leaving the marketing and sales projects to be tactical operations that are trying to solve the cash-flow problems in the short term. The marketing initiatives, such as new products and services and brand exploration, give a limited vision of the potential of the business that can in many cases be created, thereby reducing the club's brand value and failing to offer the consumer any opportunities to communicate.

A big part of the Brazilian football clubs' revenue depends on money from TV rights sales, sponsorship deals and matchday revenue (based on gate receipts, without season tickets, and other revenues from such things as catering, hospitality and banqueting suites). In this way, the football clubs try to maintain their costs within the maximum limit of their income. This attitude only maintains the clubs in Brazil as training and exporting units of players, but doesn't allow for internal development of the Brazilian football industry – which is indispensable in order for Brazil to be included in the worldwide panorama of the football business.

The new model: strategic management of Brazilian football clubs

The strategic planning of football clubs is the key point in allowing the creation of a profitable Brazilian football industry. Nevertheless, administrative and political aspects of the clubs make it difficult to change the current situation. The first difficulty is the internal statutes of each club, which are not focused on the business perspective and are used to maintain the large number of directors. Many statutes prohibit remuneration for directors, which means that the people in charge of the club often have to have another profession – thus making it difficult to appoint a director who is experienced in long-term strategic planning.

The Council of Partners (*Conselho Deliberativo*) chooses the President, and this Council is formed by the older club's partners and determines the clubs' future. There are between 200 and 400 people involved. This model must now become one of democratic representation, where the football fan in a commercial relationship with the club can see the transparency essential for the success of the business. The best thing for Brazilian football would be to focus the management on a new perspective of income generation, transparency and credibility.

Another point that makes strategic planning difficult is the requirement for initiative and knowledge of the football business. This affirmation can be verified; indeed it is the strategic mission of one of the main players in the football industry – Manchester United:

> Manchester United's aim is to convert our popularity and footballing achievements into long-term value for shareholders by building a sustainable business around a truly global sports brand.
>
> *(Manchester United Annual Report, 2002)*

The Manchester United mission is centred on the generation of business through the consolidation of the club's global brand, and this is the route that Brazilian clubs need to follow. Brazilian clubs, in order to increase the profile of their brands and to extend their income, must use the strategic vision that is observed in Europe in some football clubs.

Many points must be noted and reconstructed in order to implement the strategic management of football clubs in Brazil, and these are in different areas of responsibility of regarding the management activity in each club.

Strategic planning by the management

At some stage the clubs must begin to work on their management plans. The ideal is to begin the new phase early in each club, and directors must create a long-term, dynamic plan that matches the approved budget, the mission and the previously defined strategic objectives.

Each club must create internal committees for marketing and management, and define performance indicators that help to control the strategic planning. The activities and actions created must have a strategic coherence that allows for planning how clubs can develop a profitable business and the management can become really professional.

Brand value

Clubs must develop a process of branding – creating an identity through a strong brand – and create strategies and actions that add value to it. A club's brand must become its most important asset, because in the strategic planning of a football club the brand is the connection between the club, its consumers and the market. A club and its values must be perceived and developed, and add both tangible and intangible aspects to the club's identity. All business generation depends on how the club is positioned with its public, and especially on the relationship between them. In Brazil, this process of brand-value generation and the resultant new income from a brand determines the position that a football club in Brazil holds nowadays (see Figure 11.3).

A marketing director in a football club must develop brand value in the club's brand; with this attitude, more important business and relationships will be possible and revenues will grow.

Three general areas that must be developed by the marketing department are the media, commercial sponsorship and matchday revenues. In Brazil, media projects are just beginning, with the biggest earnings coming from TV deals, and the clubs beginning to work with the Internet, thematic TV and radio, mobile phones, magazines, games and DVD projects. Regarding commercial sponsorship, the clubs in Brazil receive resources from just two or three sponsors, and don't use their brands to generate income with product sales, licensing, campaigns and other commercial projects. Nowadays, the matchday revenue in Brazil is the most important resource from football clubs, and this must be

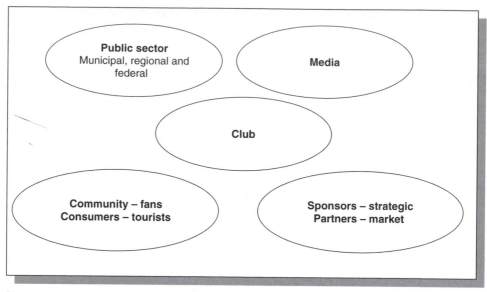

Figure 11.3
Club's positioning

developed further. The average stadium utilization in Brazil is just 20 per cent of the total, and clubs must make their matches an entertainment model in order to generate income from gate receipts and other matchday activities, including all revenues from the football match, with retail activity at different points of sale.

The football clubs in Brazil must improve the following:

1. *Sponsorship.* The sponsors and clubs must be strategic partners. In Brazil the clubs focus their action on brand visibility, and the sponsorship strategy must be a business platform to the companies that have chosen to sponsor the club. The relationship must be based on products and services sales, and different campaigns where the clubs' brands can be used. The clubs can create different propositions for their partners and produce annual actions with the players and matches, and in media projects, to narrow the relationship between the sponsors and the clubs' fans.

2. *Relationships with consumers/fans.* Football fans in Brazil haven't yet entered into the reality of business, where fans stop being only a spectator and instead become product consumers, with the football clubs basing their strategies on them. The clubs in Brazil do not see that more and more young people, who are the primary consumers, have other sports activities and hobbies (fitness, surfing, etc.) as well as their football club. The directors must concentrate on the close relationship with their

consumers and always be looking for new groups of consumers – tourists, executives, students, etc. The first step and the central point of the planning of a club's activities is the quality of the relationship between the club and its fans. It is crucial that each club invests in different communication channels with the consumer, in order to maintain contact and to keep them commercially motivated.

3. *The use of players' images.* As in other markets, in Brazil the clubs pay part of the players' salary as image rights, but they don't exploit this marketing opportunity. The clubs' management must manage these image contracts, using a strategic plan of sales, loyalty and relationships, using the images of their athletes to generate new income and value for the brand, and taking advantage of the charisma and commercial appeal of the players, based on a creative marketing and communication strategy.

4. *Public relations.* In Brazil, as in other parts of the world, the directors of the football clubs, the players and coaches have the facility to speak with their public about club news via different mass media. The marketing director must plan PR strategies in order to ensure that the appearance of the directors and the exhibition of players on the media is a strategic and independent opportunity to communicate campaigns, promotions and the club's news, centred on the expectations of the consumers/readers/viewers.

5. *The use of new media.* Technology can help football clubs a great deal in improving their incomes, but Brazilian clubs have so far made little use of it. The club home page, SMS services, quizzes, games, DVD, cinema and all other media must be controlled by the clubs, and if a company wants to be connected with the club brand it must pay a quota and royalties. All the clubs in Brazil have their own websites, but not one has yet created a virtual community though its brand. The website management must be strategic, with privileged news and promotions, and the website must be the best place in the market to find out everything about the club, its history, product sales, tickets, the annual report, etc. The official website is an excellent vehicle for partners and sponsors, and in particular is the simplest way to use the information regarding the target sector as a source for future strategies, offering a complete platform for the development of all alternative media projects.

6. *The use of stadiums and points of sale.* The most important point of contact with the football fan that must be reorganized in Brazil is the stadium and the varied points of sale (POS), so clubs can offer products and services from a wide variety of outlets – the

clubs' stores, shopping malls and other different POS – directly related with the clubs' brands. The clubs must invest in commercial actions through stadiums and from new points of sale, and with this attitude the football consumer will be able to contribute to the football club's revenues. The club's partners will also be more satisfied with these different sales and relationship channels with the football brand's objective clients.

In Brazil, the football clubs' management have a myopic and short-term view, and this must be changed to strategic planning. With a long-term project clubs could improve their B2B and B2C projects, and efficient strategic planning, although this seems difficult in football, is the escape route for clubs that are in financial trouble or at a critical moment owing to poor sports results and the landslide for the Second Division. At the moment in Brazil, with the clubs having isolated marketing actions, they are way below the level of the professional clubs' management in Europe and the United States.

Marketing reinvention of the sport product in Brazil

Sport offers a strategic business platform throughout the world for companies interested in changing the traditional marketing and communication strategies of their brands. With sports marketing strategies, companies from different markets can involve their business in a goodwill perspective. With sports strategies, the sponsor receives benefits like visibility and added value to the brands, and an intensification of the relationship with stakeholders – such as the final consumers, corporate clients, market, suppliers, intermediaries and employees.

Nevertheless, in the Brazilian market the sponsors, their agencies and the properties have not yet evolved sales strategies to improve the companies' and clubs' revenues, keeping the property associated only with brand visibility.

Sports products in Brazil have in general been a tactical tool used by the sponsors, companies and their respective agencies. In some cases the agencies look at sports properties and don't plan the communication projects of their client together with the sports marketing strategies defined by the same client, and negotiated with sports agencies, clubs or sports entities. This new vision of the relationship between marketing and communication suppliers to develop a global strategy, each agency with its own specialization, has only been verified by public companies like Banco do Brasil, Petrobrás, Caixa Econômica Federal and Correios, and some projects with other sports. Two companies currently have an efficient sponsorship project through football: Ambev with the Brazilian Selection, and the Swiss company Nestlé, with the campaign in Série A 2005, where the deal was closed with 'Clube dos 13', the entity which represents the Série A Championship.

Sports sponsorship in Brazil doesn't generate the same commercial return as the advertising market. An industry that produces more than US$10 billion per year does not generate substantial income in the same way as traditional publicity. Sponsors often cannot find sports properties that maximize marketing.

The sports marketing strategies inside the Brazilian football clubs have managed until now with a short-term perspective, and this has damaged the football product and the clubs' brands, devaluating their brand value and moving away from the true investors in the football clubs' business – the sponsors, the consumers and all other stakeholders. The marketing and communication projects with the football clubs' brands must reach the general advertising market, and the properties must be seen to provide an opportunity for generating business for the companies. This is the vision that football clubs must have in order to be able to position themselves as excellent marketing products in the market (see Figure 11.4).

Clubs' inclusion in the advertising market in Brazil would lead to success as it has done in Europe, where the football clubs encourage the market (agencies, sponsors/advertisers, media and investors) to use the clubs in their global marketing/communication strategies. Correct brand exposition in the media, the relationship with the fans/consumers and, mainly, a club's position as an income generator for sponsors and partners are the marketing reinventions needed for sports products over the next few years in Brazil.

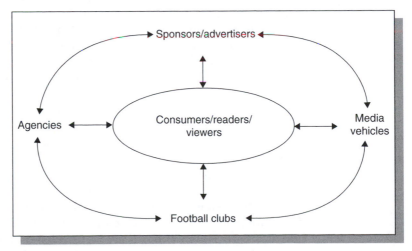

Figure 11.4
The football club as a marketing product

The market and the groups of consumers of football clubs' brands (although many of them don't know yet that they will be consuming) must be identified and worked upon. The core strategies and plans of action must have the same return on investment exigencies that exist nowadays in the advertising market. The conclusion is that the million of football fans and potential consumers, the readers, viewers and all clients must be treated in this way. Sponsors will hope that the clubs are offering a brand with a strong identity that will lead to contact with a lot of objective consumers of the brands' companies.

With this new reality, the sports industry will become bigger because of the football clubs developing into members of the industry. Each club will be responsible for generating business, from its fans, and its sponsors and partners will pay millions of dollars to the clubs for the privilege of being connected with a strong sports brand.

The urgent requirement for revenue diversification projects

The present reality of business generation by the football clubs in Brazil is that it is highly concentrated on just a few sources of earnings. This is the main difficulty for the development of the football industry in Brazil. Most Brazilian clubs depend on few sources of income and need to create a strategic revenue diversification project in order to increase their business model by the development of income sources, in order not to be so dependent on TV deals, player transfers and success in competitions. In general, the clubs have always hoped that the value of broadcasting rights would grow and imagined that the sale of players would be enough to equilibrate their financial situation, because every year they spend more resources to pay players' wages (see Appendix 11.4) and labour contingencies.

Now, football clubs must create a management model that will look for new opportunities for income, converting the club into a sports business platform focused on marketing and financial development. The management must line up with the return of investment required by the sponsors and partners, from a branding process and in consumer satisfaction, with actions previously planned, and together these can generate brand value to the clubs through marketing experiences linked to footballing emotions.

This actual reality is easy to understand, looking at the revenue distribution of four Brazilian clubs as examples. Figure 11.5 shows how, at the present moment, there is a need for strategic management, offering great opportunities to the football clubs in the 'country of the football'.

Analysing the revenue distribution in 2003 of these four clubs shows us how the clubs are depending on a few sources of income. In Brazil, the clubs depend on player transfers, broadcasting, sponsorship and advertising, but in some cases, like Vitória SA, the clubs generate revenues from player sales and the TV deals. The revenue from gate receipts is the unique way to identify the football fan in a club's balance sheet.

Another point that is possible to identify is the income from the social clubs of SPFC, Corinthians and Flamengo. These football clubs, like others in Brazil, have complete social clubs with swimming pools, sports squares, etc., and the financial contribution

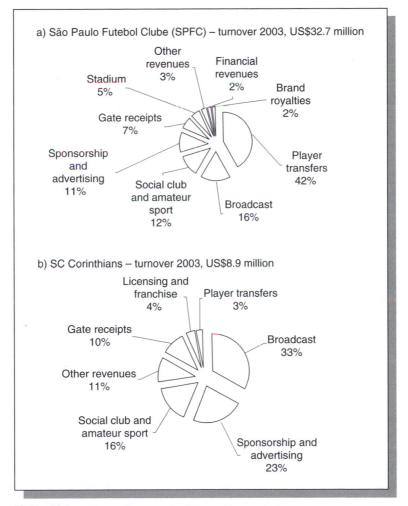

a) São Paulo Futebol Clube (SPFC) – turnover 2003, US$32.7 million

- Other revenues 3%
- Financial revenues 2%
- Brand royalties 2%
- Stadium 5%
- Gate receipts 7%
- Sponsorship and advertising 11%
- Social club and amateur sport 12%
- Broadcast 16%
- Player transfers 42%

b) SC Corinthians – turnover 2003, US$8.9 million

- Licensing and franchise 4%
- Player transfers 3%
- Gate receipts 10%
- Other revenues 11%
- Social club and amateur sport 16%
- Sponsorship and advertising 23%
- Broadcast 33%

Figure 11.5
Revenue breakdown of four Brazilian football clubs
(*Source*: football clubs' financial statements, 2003)

from this source in some cases represents more than traditional football revenues such as gate receipts. Although the social clubs generate income for the clubs, they are very costly to run and far beyond many professional football clubs' means. These must concentrate on football exhibitions, with matchday, brand exploitation and media income.

Clubs like SPFC and Vitória SA, two of the biggest player-sellers in Brazil, enter into negotiations every year regarding their young players and, in some cases, best players – like the Kaká negotiations between São Paulo and Milan. In 2003, São Paulo FC generated US$13.8 million on player transfers, and Vitória SA generated US$6.4 million in the same way. Corinthians and Flamengo, which have the biggest fan bases in Brazil, don't generate so much of their

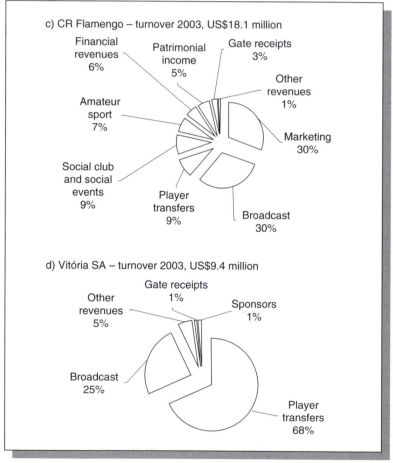

Figure 11.5
(*Continued*)

resources from player transfers, and depend more on TV rights and sponsorship resources.

The changes in football club management in Brazil are the way forward in developing a new model of income generation that considers new sources of independent income. This strategic activity by the management will make it possible for the clubs to obtain financial resources to maintain a high performance in the field, creating a virtuous cycle of revenue generation.

Brazilian clubs must include their consumers in the new strategic management and create products and services with a strong and continuous promotion. A good idea would be season tickets and in this way, as is so common in the USA and Europe, form a relationship with regular attenders. Some clubs in Brazil have started issuing season tickets, but these still represent a small part of the club's income. The European football market shows how season tickets are important to football clubs for direct income, and how the large number of fans at football matches can generate other revenues – from catering, products and services sales. With this relationship with thousands of regular attenders, it is also possible to negotiate better contracts with the sponsors and commercial partners.

Brazilian football must improve matchday revenues, because the development of stadiums and the increasingly full stadiums will bring new income and the maximization of existing sources. With these changes, the revenue distribution of Brazilian football clubs will be more equilibrated.

Considering just the football clubs, the Brazilian football market represents US$400 million. The potential of this market is US$2.5 billion, considering consolidated revenues, and this situation would be improved further if football clubs' business could be converted into a strategic planning model based on the essence of marketing: 'The necessities, desires and expectations of the consumer'.

The next section focuses on a special club, Atlético-PR, which has an original model of development in Brazil.

An original model of football marketing in Brazil: Atlético-PR

The history of Atlético-PR

Clube Atlético Paranaense (Atlético-PR, or CAP) was born on 26 March 1924 of the fusion of two traditional teams at the time, America and International, both of Curitiba-PR. From America, Atlético-PR received its red colour; from International, its black.

The city of Curitiba and the state of Paraná, from which sprouted Atlético-PR, show a true manifestation of passion for a club: the *Furacão* (Hurricane). In a few years the club began to win titles, like the Paranaense Championships of 1925, 1929, 1930, 1934, 1936, 1940, 1943, 1945 and 1949, proving to be a competitive team that year after year attracted more and more fans.

The expression 'Hurricane' arose in the year of 1949, when the club mounted a memorable team for its twenty-fifth anniversary celebrations. In that season, the club made a historical conquest of the Paranaense Championship. The expression 'Hurricane' ended up becoming a symbol of the enthusiastic identity of Atlético-PR, and was the fuel needed to conquer a position in Paranaense's sport and later in the national scene. The following decades (1960s, 1970s and 1980s) were very successful for Atlético-PR, when the club won important championships, attracted new fans and transformed the main derby of the Paraná state – Atlético-PR against Coritiba-PR (Atletiba) – into a significant sporting event in Curitiba and one of the main matches in Brazilian football, full of historic rivalry and passion.

The goal for Atlético-PR, in addition to winning the Paranaense's titles, was to win the Brazilian Championship. In the 1983 Brazilian Championship, the club fell in the semi-finals to Flamengo, which became the champion of that year; thus Atlético-PR became the third best Brazilian club in that year. Nevertheless, in all Atlético-PR's history, the decade of the 1990s was the peak for the club's development, as much in its sport aspects as in the management.

The club had dominated all Paraná State, but also had to be positioned as one of the main clubs in Brazil. In 1995, having won the Série B (Second Division) title, the club regained the right to return to the First Division. At that moment there was the need to adapt the club to new objectives, and the changes were soon obvious, with the modernization of the brand, and the construction of a new stadium – the Arena da Baixada (which in February 2005 became the Kyosera Arena following a contract with the telecom company Kyosera), the most modern stadium in Brazil – and a new training centre. These changes meant that Atlético-PR entered the new millennium positioned as one of the most important football clubs in Brazil, and won the First Division championship – Série A – in 2001.

In 2002, another important factor for the club and its objectives was the player Kleberson, who had started in Atlético-PR's training centre, was selected for the national team after returning from the Korea/Japan World Cup, and was later sold to Manchester United.

Titles of Atlético-PR

Titles of Atlético-PR include:

- Winner of Série A – the Brazilian Championship, First Division – 2001

- Runner up in the Libertadores da América –2005

- Winner of Série B – the Brazilian Championship, Second Division – 1995

- Winner of Paranaense's championship – Estadual – 1925, 1929, 1930, 1934, 1936, 1940, 1943, 1945, 1949, 1958, 1970, 1982, 1983, 1985, 1988, 1990, 1998, 2000, 2001 and 2002

- Winner of the Sesquicentenario Cup – 2003

- Winner of the Paraná's Cup – 1998

- Winner of the Winterthur Cup (Switzerland) – 1991 and 1992.

The stadium

Atlético-PR had a very long history before having its own stadium and what later became the actual Arena. In 1912, Joaquim Américo, the first President of the Football International Club, rented a property in Baixada's Agua Verde district and arranged for the club's matches to be played there (see Figure 11.6).

In 1914 he constructed wooden seats, making it the first football ground in Paraná State to have seating. When in 1924 the clubs International and America merged, the new Clube Atlético Paranaense renewed the rent of the stadium ground for five

Figure 11.6
Joaquim Américo's property in the Baixada Agua Verde district

Figure 11.7
Joaquim Américo Stadium, later to become the Arena da Baixada

years. At the end of this period a major industrialist from the region bought the property and renewed the rental period for the club.

In 1929 the situation was redefined when, in a transaction, Atlético-PR became the owner of the land, and the original stadium with its wooden seats was named the Joaquim Américo Stadium. In 1937 the construction of concrete seats began, and this project was completed in 1939 (see Figure 11.7) – at which time many clubs still did not have their own stadiums. In 1967 there was the first big renovation of the stadium, and in 1980 a new lighting system was installed, but it was always clear that despite the improvements the stadium was inadequate for the club.

Figure 11.8 shows the attendance figures at the Joaquim Américo Stadium between 1976 and 1986.

In 1986 Atlético-PR began to play at the Pinheirão Stadium, abandoning its old area of Baixada. In that period the relations with the fans became distant because Pinheirão did not benefit the fans and had no identification with the club. In 1994 there was a major renovation at Baixada and the club reverted to playing its matches there; this immediately improved relations with the fans, who viewed Baixada as being an identity symbol of Clube Atlético Paranaense.

In 1997, ambitious plans transformed the old stadium at Baixada into the Arena da Baixada, by demolishing the old Joaquim Américo Stadium and constructing the modern Arena – the most modern stadium in Brazil. The first part of the project was completed in record time, just eighteen months, and designed in accordance with the regulations of FIFA, with a structure of services, entertainment and leisure to allow big cultural and sports events.

With the inauguration of the Arena da Baixada in 1999, the club became top news in the national newspapers, magazines and TV

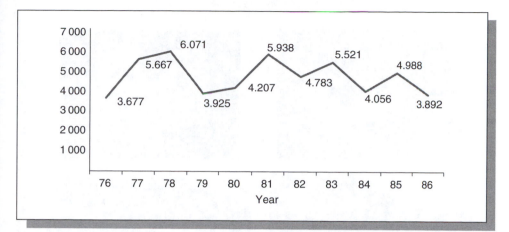

Figure 11.8
Atlético-PR's average attendance figures for the Joaquim Américo Stadium
(*Source*: www.atleticopr.com.br)

programmes, and showed that Atlético-PR was prepared for modern methods of football management, centred on long-term projects and positioning Atlético-PR as an original example to Brazilian football.

Now, the stadium can hold 32 000 seated spectators, but with the second phase of the project its capacity will rise to 51 000 spectators.

The facilities at Kyosera Arena

Kyosera Arena has the following facilities:

- An open arena of 110 m × 70 m

- A capacity of 32 864 spectators, all seated, all covered, divided into various grades of seating and including staterooms and a VIP restaurant

- Ten dressing rooms for players and concert artists

- Six conventional elevators, two panoramic elevators and sixty-eight stores

- Parking for 500 cars

- Twenty-one public toilets, with twelve more planned in the next part of the project

- Ten sponsors' suites each with a capacity of twenty-two people

Figure 11.9
The Arena da Baixada
(*Source*: www.atleticopr.com.br)

- A commercial centre at the front of the stadium, with two panoramic elevators, a fitness gym, and space to build a big convention centre, a museum, a sport store, a visitors' office for tours of the Arena, and two external restaurants.

Figure 11.10 shows the attendance figures at the Arena da Baixada (Kyosera Arena) for the Brazilian Championships, Série A.

The construction of the Arena da Baixada was an important factor in recent Brazilian football business history. While Brazilian clubs generally tried to form partnerships with foreign groups, Atlético-PR invested its own resources in the construction of the stadium and its training centre. This unusual position for Brazil was a consequence of a management model based on strategic principles. People who did not believe that it would be possible to create a new model in a critical environment without a foreign partner criticized Atlético-PR. Nowadays, Atlético-PR can be considered ready for its more ambitious plan – the internationalization of its brand.

The management model

In 1995, with the election of the new President, Mario Celso Petraglia, Atlético-PR entered a new era. Petraglia was elected

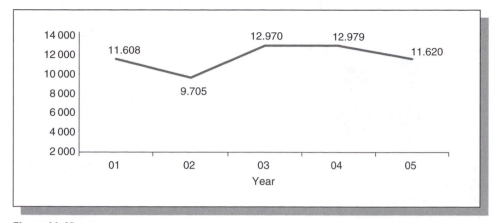

Figure 11.10
Attendance figures at the Arena da Baixada (Kyosera Arena) for the Brazilian Championships, Série A
(*Source*: www.cbfnews.com.br)

President of the club and inherited the same reality as the other big football clubs – a depreciated brand, an old stadium and no professional training structure. At that time the club was playing in the Second Division of the Brazilian Championship, and did not have a national name. Mario Celso Petraglia, with a strategic vision, created a new model of management for Brazilian football.

In the same year he created the strategic planning for Atlético-PR, with a perspective of ten years (until 2005). The most significant point in Petraglia's attitude was that this was the first – and so far the only – time that a Brazilian football club had abandoned short-term action plans with immediate objectives and implemented a modern understanding of the football business, with a strategic vision to be successful both on and off the pitch.

In 2000, Atlético-PR, continuing with its strategic vision and perceiving the football globalization, accompanied by the new sport legislation in Brazil, contracted the services of the consulting company Deloitte Touche Tomatsu. Together they have prepared the execution of the strategic planning that is already on course, which made it possible for Atlético-PR to achieve its current excellent results.

Since 1995 the club has planned its actions, and the ongoing planning and club's development have transformed the recent history of the Hurricane, making the club a reference point in Brazil and Latin America. Currently Atlético-PR doesn't retain Deloitte's help, but the planning and execution of the actions has changed the club's structure and vision and centred the club's management in a model that is original for Brazil.

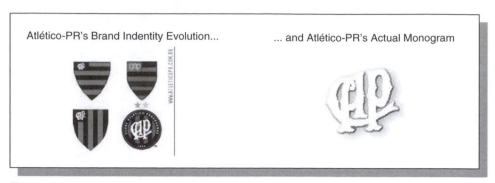

Figure 11.11
The evolution of Atlético-PR's brand logo
(*Source*: www.atleticopr.com.br)

Strategic planning

In 1995, when the President Mario Celso Petraglia was elected, Atlético-PR participated in Série B. There was a need to begin the work of planning a strategy for the club. The strategic plan for Atlético-PR was created, with a perspective of ten years (1995–2005), and considered investment in three big areas:

1. Brand development

2. The establishment of a training centre

3. The construction of the stadium.

Figure 11.11 shows the evolution of Atlético-PR's logo.

The ten-year strategic plan was divided into two parts, the first from 1995 to 2000 and the second from 2001 to 2005.

Between 1995 and 2000 the planning was divided in three parts, with actions that would allow the club to reach its objectives. The first stage included the recovery of the club's image, through its financial and moral credibility; returning to play on its old stadium; and winning access to the First Division through the construction of a competitive team. The second stage consisted of recovering the hegemony of Atlético-PR in the Paraná State, consolidating the club's brand and making investments in structure and assets. Between 2001 and 2005, the third stage included a focus on the total professional management of the club, finding strategic partners, conquering new markets and undergoing a technical reconnaissance in Brazilian football.

In 1995, Atlético-PR was able to return to the First Division after winning the Série B title. With the club's return to its old stadium, Baixada, the execution of the planning was already on course.

In 1997, the Arena's project began transforming it into a modern stadium – an important factor in order to achieve the results that were defined in the strategic plan. After eighteen months and an investment of the club's own resources of US$18 million, the first stage of the new Arena da Baixada was completed, with a capacity of 32 000 spectators and following all the exigencies of FIFA. It was FIFA-standard stadium in Brazil, and placed Atlético-PR as the precursor of a new model of management for football clubs.

In the same month, the club inaugurated its new training centre, the CT do Caju, and this, together with the new stadium, was indispensable for the club to achieve good financial results. Between 1998 and 2001 the total of income of Atlético-PR grew by about 130 per cent, and in 2001 Atlético-PR won Série A, putting the Hurricane back with the biggest clubs in Brazil.

Atlético-PR's strategic management included different areas of the club, and was focused on strategic principles with an understanding of how the club should be managed professionally. Atlético-PR proved once again that strategic management is as important to the development of a football club as its performance in the field. The strategic focus and plan of Atlético-PR provide an example to be followed by all Brazilian football clubs.

Figure 11.12 provides a diagrammatic representation of the strategic focus and vision of Atlético-PR.

Atlético-PR's strategic vision and the correct execution of the actions defined in the strategic planning have transformed the club's recent history. While the big Brazilian clubs were recovering following the crisis in football, the Hurricane put in course the continuation of its ambitious plans and moved away from the situation in Brazilian football, where actions are being produced without a strategic perspective.

Atlético-PR, like other football clubs, must improve its different sources of income, but the Hurricane has the base to grow, through the stadium, training centre, media and brand development, and with this new model maintain its best players to develop the Brazilian market.

Figure 11.13 shows the turnover for Atlético-PR in 2003.

Following the strategic planning, Atlético-PR constructed a training centre of the highest quality that quickly became a reference for the progression of players and transformed the club into an important centre of athlete's formation. The CT do Caju was inaugurated officially in June 1999, two days after the opening of the stadium, and was at that time the most modern training centre in Brazil (Figure 11.14). Located in the Umbará district, about fifteen kilometres away from Curitiba and with an area of 246 577 square metres, it was constructed to hotel norms, with seventy suites for professional and amateur athletes, a nutrition centre that develops

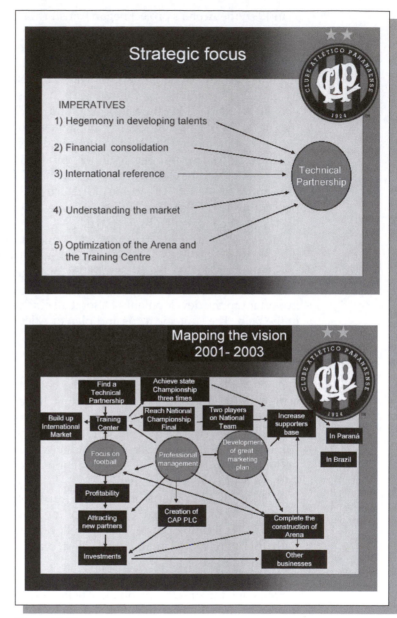

Figure 11.12
The strategic focus and vision of Atlético-PR
(*Source*: Atlético-PR Direction)

specific diets for each athlete, a physiology and educational centre, a TV and games room, a restaurant with a capacity of 100 people, a kitchen that provides 600 meals daily, a laundry, a data processing centre and a theatre that can hold 1700 spectators.

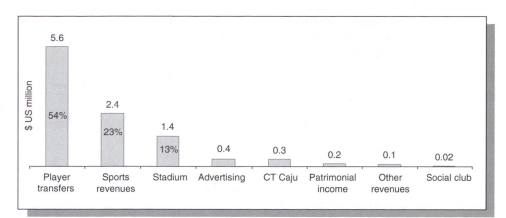

Figure 11.13
Atlético-PR, turnover 2003 – US$10.4 million
(*Source*: Atlético-PR financial statement, 2003)

Figure 11.14
Atlético-PR's training centre – CT do Caju

The CT do Caju works like an incubator, and its extremely professional work has already brought excellent results to the club, with the formation of many players of the highest level. Every year more of Atlético-PR's athletes are called for Brazilian selection, in all the different categories, and many have transferred to big European clubs. Well-known graduates of the training centre include Oséas, Varley, Adriano Lucas, Alessandro, Kleberson, Ilan, Dagoberto, Fernandinho, Evandro and Paulo Rink.

Recent actions

Atlético-PR has continued with its strategic work that was initiated in 1995. It perceived that other battles would have to be conducted in order to further its growth over the future years. The club has identified problems that need immediate action and divided them into three main areas:

1. The cultivation and recovery of the fans and internationalization of the club's brand

2. The cultivation of players

3. Brand internationalization.

The cultivation and recovery of the fans and the internationalization of the club's brand

The first goal for the next years was to obtain more fans in Paraná State. The club created a Football School, which led to the consequent conquest of new fans besides contributing the opportunity for more young people to play football.

The Atlético schools don't pretend to form professional athletes; they are centred on encouraging football practice and the loyalty of fans in more than nine cities and, after launching the expansion project, on planning marketing actions. The evolution of the schools project was incredible; by the end of 2003 the number of students enrolled surpassed 1600 students, and in 2004 there were more than 4000 students.

The club created another activity, the Atlético-PR Kids, to reach more fans among children. Atlético-PR Kids offers a loyalty card to children who come to the club's matches. At the moment, the mailing list of Atlético-PR Kis has 3000 names on it. Another action that the club created was Atlético-PR News, which was a set of press releases to the cities of Paraná with the objective of keeping the fans outside Curitiba informed. The local radio stations and city newspapers receive daily releases from the club, so they can update the content regarding Atlético-PR.

Cultivation of players

The second goal that the club had to achieve was to discover new potential athletes. For that reason it extended the project for cultivating athletes to looking for new talent for the club throughout Brazil. The club invested in new training centres in Paraná and other states – for example, Minas Gerais. The objective is that when a new talent arises from one of these nucleuses of sport training, the athlete is automatically directed to the club. At the moment, the club is maintaining nearly 600 athletes in 4 different nucleuses.

In CT do Caju, the club has developed a structure for its players' cultivation, focused on sport and physical training and also on the personal development of the young players, in order to produce athletes who are also good citizens. The athletes who are part of Atlético-PR train in the CT and have the support of psychologists, sociologists and educational organizations near to the CT. These activities have given the club a different formation to other Brazilian clubs, and have contributed to the club's image by the technical quality of its players.

Brand internationalization

Another important goal to be reached is brand internationalization in different markets all over the world. The club utilizes the CT building to receive foreign selection camps, where the teams pay for the accommodation and can use the club's facilities. The club has received different selections, including China, Japan, Korea, Brazil, USA, Angola, etc.

Synchronized with these international programmes, the club's training centre also carries out an exchange programme with young athletes and managers of different clubs from different countries. These international athletes and managers are training with the same methodology of Atlético-PR's teams, and after completing their course they all receive a certificate verifying that they were trained in Brazil, by the Atlético-PR method. These international relationships are really important, both to internationalize the club's brand and also as an excellent source of new income.

The results of Atlético-PR's actions

- The club has the biggest fan base in Paraná State, with nearly 52 per cent of the fans, predominantly of the higher socio-economic classes, leading to great potential regarding the club's brand

- Nearly 40 per cent of fans that attend the matches at Atlético-PR's stadium are women

- From the success of the football schools of the club was born schools for women, where the objective is to increase the number of female fans of Atlético-PR

- The club won the Top of Mind six times, four times consecutively (2000–2003)

- The players cultivated in the Atlético-PR training centre are constantly called to the different Brazilian selections

- The players cultivated in the club transfer overseas at higher values than players of other big Brazilian clubs

- The success of the foreign training programmes has led to anticipation of an extension and construction of a new area for the international teams.

Conclusions

This chapter has provided an excellent opportunity to clarify how the football business in Brazil is doing. All over the world, professionals in sport marketing and management are asking why Brazil, the only five-times World FIFA Championship winner, is not able to transform its sport success and technical quality into fuel for the generation of new income to the football clubs.

The reasons for the delay in the management development of Brazilian clubs are related to the short-term view of the clubs' directors, who have always tried to evade the new sports law in Brazil. The aspects of control and the regulation of football business have not been used to develop the Brazilian market, and changes in the political and legal environment are not being used to alter this situation. This delay of more than ten years means that the football clubs in Brazil remain as exportation platforms for young players rather than keeping them in a potent domestic football industry.

The change to this is shown by Atlético-PR. The club, which is outside the Rio de Janeiro–São Paulo axis, verified that the escape route is to change the limited vision of football business practised by most Brazilian clubs. While creating its strategic plan, Atlético-PR looked to generate value for the club's brand and use the consequent income to invest in a training structure and the reformulation of the stadium, while the others continued to use only the sale of players to equilibrate their budgets.

The vicious cycle will only be changed when Brazilian clubs, through professional strategic management, can practise budgetary control and management centred on new sources of independent income. This must be centred on the clubs' long-term strategic plan. The objective is to generate new income, so that clubs can obtain further resources and financial tranquillity as well as achieving their sporting objectives and a high performance on the pitch. This new income must be used to invest in clubs' own structure and to create a virtuous cycle of generation of income, already used successfully in some European clubs.

The success of Brazilian clubs' management is directly related to the fans, and management must centre their actions on the expectations of football clients, filling the stadiums with an entertainment, generating value for the clubs' brands and creating different resources of income. The financial success of the clubs will depend on how the directors will achieve professional management. Besides this, they must also consider the consumers' satisfaction with sporting aspects and the quality of their relationship with the clubs. That's how they will realize the triumph of their business and become main players in the sports industry in Brazil, and one of the most important markets for the football industry in the world.

Acknowledgements

I would like to thank Atlético-PR, and especially its Director of International Affairs, Alexandre da Rocha Loures, for the information provided, without which this chapter would not have been possible. It is clear from the transparency and professionalism shown that Atlético-PR provides an example of successful club management in Brazil.

Bibliography and references

Aaker, D. A. (1996). *Building Strong Brands*. Editora Futura.
Atkearney (2001). *Your Customer, Your Boss*. Atkearney, Chicago.
Atkearney (2003). *The New Sports Consumer*. Atkearney, Chicago.
August, S. (2002). In the ball world. *Carta Capital Magazine*, 25 November.
BCG (2003). *Discovering the 'C' Class*. BCG, São Paulo.
Caspistegui, F. J. and Walton, J. K. (2001). *Football and Local Identity in Europe*. EUNASA – Universidad de Navarra.
Conn, D. (1998). *The Football Business – Fair Game in the 90s?* Mainstream Publishing.
Casual Auditores S/S (2005). *Casual List of Brazilian Football Clubs*. Casual Auditores, São Paulo.
FGV-RJ (2000). *Modernization Plan of Brazilian Football (CBF)*. FGV-RJ, Rio de Janeiro.
Kfouri Aidar, A. C., Leoncini, M. F. and Oliveira, J. J. (2000). *The New Football Management*. Editora FGV.
Krieger, M. (1999). *Pelé Law and Sports Law in Brazil*. Editoras Forense e Gryphus.
McKenna, R. (1993). *Relationship Marketing*. Editora Campus.
Melo Neto, F. P. (2000). *Sponsorship Marketing*. Editora Sprint.
Mullin, B., Hardy, S. and Sutton,W. (1999). *Sport Marketing*, 2nd edn. Editorial Pai do Tribo.
Paris Roche, F. (2002). *Sports Management – Strategic Planning of Sports Organizations*. Artmed Editora.
Porter, M. E. (1989). *Competitive Advantage*. Editora Campus.
Pozzi, L. F. (1998). *Theory and Practice of Sports Marketing*. Editora Globo.
Ries, A. and Ries, L. (2000). *The 22 Immutable Laws of Branding*. Makron Books.

Roberts, K. (2003). Ad men show the way. *Sport Business Magazine*, **August**.

Shank, M. D. (2001). *Sports Marketing: a strategic perspective*. Prentice Hall.

Siviero, R. and Rocha Loures, A. (2002). Nuts about football. *Stadia Magazine – Showcase Special*.

Somoggi, A. (2003). Football clubs' management in the client era. *EsporteBizz*, 12 May (available at www.esportebizz.com.br).

Taylor, R. (2002). Talking to football fans. *Britcham-Brasil Magazine*, **May/June**.

Varea Sanz, M. (1999). *The SAD Administration*. Editora Civitas.

Websites

www.cbfnews.com.br
www.esportebizz.com.br
www.lancenet.com.br
www.atleticopr.com.br
www.soccerinvestor.com
www.sportbusiness.com
www.atkearney.com
www.ibope.com.br
www.bcg.com
www.mmonline.com.br
www.casualauditores.com.br

Appendix 11.1

Football fans in Brazil – 2004

Table 11.2
The informants and the data collection methods

Ranking	Teams	%	Fan base (millions)
1	Flemengo-RJ	18.1	32.9
2	Corinthinas-SP	13.1	23.8
3	São Paulo-SP	7.3	13.3
4	Palmeiras-SP	6.5	11.8
5	Vasco da Gama-RJ	5.5	10.0
6	Cruzeiro-MG	3.7	6.7
7	Grêmio-RS	3.5	6.4
8	Santos-SP	2.7	4.9
9	Internacional-RS	2.6	4.7
10	Atlético-MG	2.0	3.6
11	Botafogo-RJ	1.5	2.7
12	Fluminense	1.2	2.2
13	Bahia-BA	1.1	2.0
14	Sport-PE	1.0	1.8
15	Vitória-BA	1.0	1.8
16	Remo-PA	0.7	1.3
17	Paysandu-PA	0.6	1.1
18	Atlético-PR	0.5	0.9
19	Santa Cruz-PE	0.5	0.9
	Top nineteen teams	73.1	133.0
	Others	4.8	8.7
	Without a team	22.1	50.2
	Total Brazilians (2004)	100.0	182.0

Source: Research IBOPE/Lance! 2004.

Appendix 11.2

International player transfers

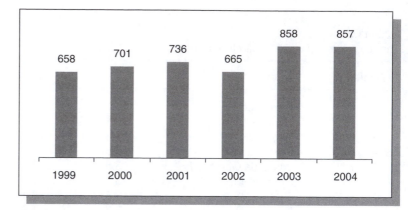

Figure A11.1
International player transfers – Brazil (US $ million)
(*Source*: CBF, www.cbfnews.com.br)

Appendix 11.3

Revenues, expenses and shareholder equity of Brazilian clubs

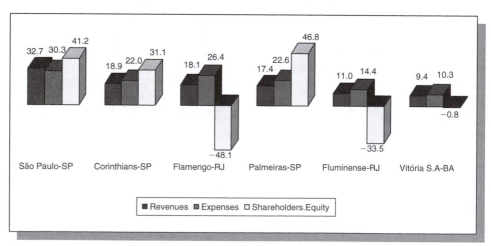

Figure A11.2
Total revenue, expenses and shareholder equity of some Brazilian football clubs (US$ million), 2003
(*Source*: Casual Auditores Independentes)

Appendix 11.4

Brazilian professional football players' wages, 2002

Table 11.3
The informants and the data collection methods

Wage per month (US$)	Number of players	Percentage
< 83	8638	52.9
83–166	4987	30.5
166–415	1289	7.9
415–830	436	2.7
830–1660	293	1.8
> 1660	701	4.3
Total	16 344	100

Source: CBF (Confederação Brasileira de Futebol) 2002.

Appendix 11.5

Interview with Luciano Kleiman, Marketing Director, adidas, Brazil

Part I – Football clubs and adidas in Brazil

Q1: Which are the main modalities and business areas of adidas in Brazil? How much does football represent to the company in Brazil?

LK: adidas is present in more than thirty sports worldwide, and has as its main business the categories of running and football. Football is and always was part of adidas' soul and history. Football is distinguished not only as an excellent business but also as one that is more intensely related to the passion of the Brazilians, and therefore this sport has a visibility incomparable to any another sport in our country.

Q2: Brazil is the 'country of football'; it has big clubs and the professional championships have intense media coverage. In your opinion, what is required to make football in Brazil become

more profitable, as in the European, the American and the Asian markets?

LK: There is no doubt that the difference in economic realities between Europe and Brazil are considerable. In my opinion, the question is not how to become as profitable as Europe – for this, Brazil needs a long period of structural and complex changes – but rather, how to maximize the potential business in the football clubs our country possesses nowadays. I think that movement in this direction exists, if it reduces the dependence on resources from the broadcast rights. This does not mean reducing this income, but rather developing other sources such as licensing, ticket offices and sponsorship. Obviously, strong clubs and attractive championships increase the interest in the football business as a whole. Everybody gains: clubs, companies and fans.

Q3: Nowadays in Brazil, adidas sponsors two big clubs – Fluminense-RJ and, more recently, Palmeiras-SP. Do the biggest football clubs in Brazil offer a good commercial return on the invested value?

LK: With Fluminense, from the state of Rio de Janeiro, adidas has the longest partnership in current Brazilian football, now in its tenth year. In this period we have created very successful projects, such as the launch of the first shirt particularly for Fluminense's own fans through the Internet. The chosen colour was orange, and this has become one of the all-time favourites of the fans in all the times – today it is seen as an icon in the Fluminense tradition.

We have also returned to the relationship with Palmeiras from the state of São Paulo, a club with which we had the first sponsorship contract in Brazilian football, in the 1970s.

These two partnerships have a main objective: to associate adidas with the values that these clubs represent – superior performance, tradition and victories. This is the biggest concern, because we are speaking of protagonists in the national football scene. Added to this, the clubs have millions of football fans and these are beginning to link with the adidas brand, which generates business at a significant order of scale. It can be said that regarding sales of a single item, clubs' shirts are almost insuperable in the textile business. It is also still necessary to indicate that, in visibility terms, the brand exposition generated by football sponsorship exceeds the biggest media packages in the market.

Q4: According to information provided, the shirts of the Brazilian idols of Milan and Real Madrid generate more revenue for adidas in Brazil than do the sales of Fluminense's shirts. Does this represent a weakness of the Brazilian market, or a business opportunity for global football?

LK: This is uncommon, but shows the impact of the transfers of Brazilian international players to big European clubs. Local weakness does not exist; what this demonstrates is that the football in Europe has increased its local influence to a form that has not been seen before. I understand that broadcasting of the European championships and the Internet have great relevance to this, and the presence of Brazilians idols is a component in this process of football globalization. I also add the impact of huge projects, such as at Real Madrid, which give the club's brand an extra perspective.

Q5: Palmeiras is a club with 12 million fans in Brazil, and good proportion of the richest fans are concentrated in the state of São Paulo. What does adidas, together with the club, plan for the next few years, to generate business with the 'Palmeirense' consumer?
LK: Our aim is to associate the adidas brand as far as possible with the values of the club. Our intention is to include all the moments at which the fan interacts with the club – on TV, in the store and on the Internet. It is necessary to use creativity and know how to stay close to the football fans.

Q6: How do you predict the business generation will be for the football clubs in Brazil in future years? What are the profile and characteristics of the clubs that are of interest to adidas in Brazil?
LK: The football business in Brazil will never fail to represent enormous potential and still has much growth ahead. I expect the clubs, in the medium and long term, even for survival, to understand that there will be a reduction on the dependence of the TV revenues and that they must create conditions of growth in other sources of income. As well as investment in the football base, licensing and even ticket revenues have great potential for development, as things stand. I am optimistic that the new mentality of the clubs – through modernization of the management vision of the current managers and, without a doubt, the contribution of a new generation – will bring many fruits to Brazilian football. adidas has the strategy to make partnerships in qualitative terms in each market. More important than sponsoring a large number of clubs, the priority is to select the best and the biggest ones. Any club with this profile is a potential partner for adidas. This is the case in Europe, with Real Madrid in Spain and Milan in Italy, among others. It's the same in Brazil.

Q7: How do you believe that adidas can contribute to future Brazilian football clubs' projects of brand internationalization?
LK: adidas is present in more than 100 countries in all the continents. The company's brand is the leader worldwide in the football world, and it has a portfolio of sponsored clubs in different nations. This is a great example of internationalization: displaying the biggest icon of a club, its official shirt, to consumers throughout

the world. Moreover, there is always the possibility of diverse forms of interchange, through marketing actions, friendly games or championships. In summary, a presence throughout the world is adidas' strength, and can be a great vehicle for a club outside its native country.

Part II – adidas, a FIFA World Cup sponsor in Brazil

Q8: What activities is adidas planning for the 2006 FIFA World Cup in Germany?

LK: adidas is an official sponsor of the 2006 FIFA World Cup, and will in this have reaffirmation as the worldwide leader in football. Through the most complete project of marketing, including properties like the World Cup's ball, we have a great media campaign. In terms of products, since October 2005 we have presented a major launch each month, with the Teamgeist+, the ball of the 2006 World Cup, and the Tunit, the first customized football shoes already being produced. We are only initiating the impact of our campaign +10 based primarily on the collective force, rather than a good performance in the football. The matches are not the main focus; the strength of the group in the football teams is the focus of this campaign.

Q9: How did adidas develop its strategies related to the World Cup in Brazil, when its main competitor is the official sponsor of the Brazilian selection?

LK: adidas is an official sponsor of 2006 FIFA World Cup, therefore the company's brand will be exposed all over the world through the media, and through activities in Germany in the stadiums – both around the pitch and on the pitch, with our six elections, the referees' clothing and the match balls. We have some of the most important idols in the football event – David Beckham, Zinedine Zidane and Juan Riquelme, among others, will wear our products. In other words, the universe of a World Cup is bigger than the sponsorship of one of thirty-two selections. Remembering our campaign +10, as well as shining players – such as Kaká, for example – the game must have complete teams, a football field, a ball. Whoever has passion for the football must be linked with this entire universe.

Q10: What are adidas' strategies to improve its business in a World Cup year? What has been the economic impact of the World Cup on adidas' business in Brazil?

LK: As in the rest of the world, in Brazil everybody is awaiting a great jump in the football business category. The offers of complete product lines are an example. adidas not only has official products of the selections, but also a fan line focused on the fans' interest in following the matches in the stadium or on TV. The media campaign searches to stimulate the biggest attention, which of course in a World Cup year is on football, and use this to strengthen the linking of the adidas brand with football. It is important to mention that adidas has a presence in many other sports, and not just the World Cup is important to us. For example, adidas_One, the first intelligent tennis, continues to be successful throughout the world, and our technology continues to bring growth performance in the running and the originals clothing lines, directed to casual use. This is the big challenge for a brand like adidas – to work with as many innovations and as many types of consumer as possible at the same time. It is part of the prescription of the success of the brand over many decades.

The football business in Japan

Yoshinori Okubo

Overview

The successful operation of the J. League and the 2002 World Cup has reformed Japanese football into a more sustainable business. Despite some difficulties over the past decade, overall the clubs and the league show some improvement in their management, and the local fan base is gradually expanding. Football now seems to be the second most popular professional sport in Japan after baseball.

The 2002 World Cup has left a legacy of excellent football facilities. However, due to their enormous maintenance costs, efficient use of the facilities is the task for the future. Nonetheless, these facilities will support the further continuous development of Japanese football.

Today, Japanese footballers go to play in Europe while European clubs come to Asia, both in order to develop their business and also to enhance their popularity in this emerging market. For the players, clubs and companies involved in such international business operations, there are many obstacles to get over – such as cultural difference and the considerable physical distance. However, even so both sides are likely to gain some mutual benefits, as the international football business is becoming increasingly competitive and teams always try to gain some advantages in order to outdo their competitors. Developing regional football and practising with more international corporations will eventually promote the global integration of the football business.

Keywords

J. League, Japan (Japan national team), Football World Cup 2002, establishing the brand (brand), consistent development (consistent)

Introduction

Since the formation of the J. League and the successful operation of the 2002 FIFA World Cup, the development of Japanese football has been significant and remarkable. Today, football in Japan is largely recognized by the entire nation, and because of this emerging football popularity in the Far East, some of the big European clubs are also considering Asia as a new and potentially lucrative market. In this chapter, the development of Japanese football and the international business relationship between Japan and Europe will be examined from a statistical and socio-cultural point of view.

The final part of this chapter is based on interviews with Sadao Suzuki, the CEO of Kashima Antlers, and Takaaki Shimazu, the Senior Managing Director of Sapporo Dome Stadium (see Appendix 12.1).

The emergence of Japanese professional football

Formation of the J. League

It is said that football first came to Japan in the late nineteenth century, introduced by an Englishman, Lieutenant Commander Douglas of the Royal Navy. Since then, football has gradually spread throughout the country, particularly as a school sport. However, the Japan Soccer League (JSL), Japan's first nationwide amateur football league, eventually began in 1965, just a year after the Tokyo Olympics (Sugden and Tomlinson, 1998: 170).

The traditional concept of Japanese sports has been dominated by a corporate-oriented idea and amateurism. Football, basketball and volleyball had only non-professional leagues, consisting of the amateur teams owned by the major companies such as Nissan and Toyota. Therefore, almost all the players were the employees of the company, and they worked in the morning and had training in the afternoon. Not surprisingly, Japan's level of football itself was relatively low in Asia around this time, and the team never managed to pass the Asian qualifier for the World Cup finals. Baseball was Japan's only major professional team sport at the time. It was consistently popular and successful, but had a strong corporate image as all the teams held their parent company's (sponsor's) names – for example, the Tokyo Yomiuri Giants and the Osaka Hanshin Tigers.

In 1993 Saburo Kawabuchi, the then J. League Chairman, led an operation to launch Japan's first professional football league. Back in 1960, as a young player in Japan's national side, Kawabuchi had toured around Europe with his team for the forthcoming Tokyo Olympics and stayed at an impressive sports club complex in Duisburg, West Germany. He was very impressed by the way the Germans had built a total sports club within their local community, having seen the excellent facilities – the grass pitches, gymnasiums, swimming pool, and people taking part in various sporting activities. Kawabuchi therefore had an ambition to create many of these total sports clubs in Japan, so that anybody could participate in their local community through sports activities. This was quite a challenge to Japan's traditional, corporate-oriented notion.

The structure of the J. League

The J. League started its inaugural season in 1993, with the ten founding members. It then affiliated further members every year, reaching sixteen teams by 1997. From 1999, the league formed two professional divisions – J1 and J2. As of 2005, basically the league automatically relegates the two bottom teams of J1 and promotes the two top teams of J2. The team placed sixteenth in J1 also has to win play-offs against the team placed third in J2 so as not to be relegated (see Figure 12.1).

Currently, there is no promotion/relegation between J2 and JFL (the Japan Football League, an amateur nationwide league). However, according to a report from the J. League future vision committee of JFA (Sanspo.com 2006), the ideal number of J2 clubs would be twenty-two but they are intending to increase J2 clubs to more than eighteen by 2010. The current J. League Chairman, Masaru Suzuki, has also stated that the movement of teams between J2 and JFL will take place regularly. The JFA report also says that currently thirty to fifty clubs in Japan are interested in joining the J. League in the future. In order to join J2, the clubs will have to comply with the criteria required by the JFA, such as an average attendance per game of over 3000 and an operational revenue per year of around 150 million yen (£748 500).

The football season in Japan begins in the spring, in March, and finishes in December – so it is different to Europe's football season, which extends from September to June. Since the start of the J. League, J1 had always played a two-stage championship, deciding the annual champions by the final two-leg play-off in

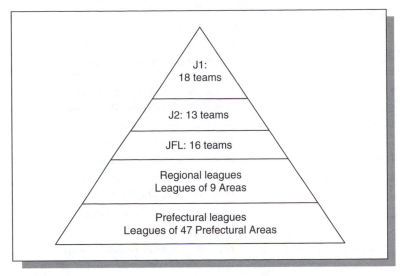

Figure 12.1
The structure of Japanese football in 2005

December – apart from 1996, when there was a solo championship throughout the season. J2, the Second Division, began with eleven teams in 1996, and always plays one championship a year in order to decide which will be the two or three promoted teams.

However, in the 2002 and 2003 seasons, Júbilo Iwata and Yokohama F. Marinos won both stages in the year respectively, and therefore the play-off was not held. From the 2005 season, J1 has finally started a one-season championship and this will continue into the future. The top league, with eighteen teams, was won by Gamba Osaka for the first time, and J2 will play the 2006 season with a total of thirteen teams, as it has added Ehime FC, a new team from JFL.

Regarding the revenue of the J. League, the league distributes its income equally to its eighteen clubs so that many more clubs will be able to compete rather than allowing the domination of a few. This concept has come from the revenue structure of the NFL, as J. League saw the American professional leagues as being extremely successful models. Regarding club management, all the J. League clubs are limited companies apart from a single exception. Throughout the past decade, some of the big J. League clubs have been dependent on a single big company; however, today the J. League and the clubs are making efforts to find more sponsors, and greater variety in the companies (see Table 12.1), so they can be more independent of their parent companies (i.e. main sponsors).

Table 12.1

J. League first division (J1) and club sponsors, 2005 season

Club	Sponsors/founding funder
Kashima Antlers	Local government and companies Sumitomo Metal Industries Ltd
JEF United Ichihara Chiba	Furukawa Electric Company Ltd East Japan Railway Company
Kashiwa Reysol*	Hitachi Ltd, Hitachi Group and local government
Omiya Ardija	Consortium of the local companies including, NTT Data, NEC Mobiling Inc. TV Saitama
Urawa Red Diamonds	Mitsubishi Motor Corporation Local companies
Tokyo Verdy 1969*	Nippon Television Network Corp Local government and companies
FC Tokyo	Consortium of local government, bodies and companies including Tokyo Gus, Tokyo Electric Power, and TV Tokyo
Kawasaki Frontale	Consortium of local companies, including Fujitsu, Ajinomoto
Yokohama F. Marinos	Nissan Motor Co. Ltd
Shimizu S-Pulse	Local companies
Júbilo Iwata	Yamaha Corporation Local government and the companies including The Shizuoka Broadcasting System
Albirex Niigata	Consortium of local companies and bodies
Nagoya Grampus Eight	Consortium of twenty major local companies (core, Toyota Motor Co. Ltd)
Gamba Osaka	Matsushita Electronic Industrial Co. Ltd
Cerezo Osaka	Consortium of seventeen Osaka companies, including Nippon Meat Packers Inc, Yanmar Diesel Engine Co. Ltd
Vissel Kobe*	Crimson Group Ltd (Tokyo, owner of Rakuten Inc.), Ito Ham Foods Inc., Noritsu Ltd. Local bodies and companies
Sanfrecce Hiroshima	Consortium of fifty-nine companies, including Hiroshima Prefecture, Hiroshima City, Mazda Motor Corporation, Chugoku Electric Power and Hiroshima Bank
Oita Trinita	Consortium of local bodies and companies

Source: Sugden and Tomlinson (1998: 172; also the Geocities website (http://www.geocities.co.jp/HeartLand-Gaien/7502/football/teams.html).
*At the end of 2005 Vissel Kobe, Tokyo Verdy and Kashiwa Reysol were all relegated, the former two automatically and the latter on losing the play-off. Kyoto Purple Sanga, Avispa Fukuoka and Vantforet Kofu (which won the play-off) will be promoted from J2.

The early J. League boom

The J. League had an extraordinarily successful start. The key to the outstanding start was the league's well-organized marketing strategy, thanks to its exclusive partners, including Hakuhodo (Japan's second largest advertising agency) and Sony Creative Products (merchandising experts).

Football, an unpopular sport around that time in Japan, suddenly became surprisingly fashionable for the consumers. The teams emphasized their local identity and created a more sophisticated and attractive marketing appearance than at any time previously. Sumitomo Metal became the Kashima Antlers, Nissan became the Yokohama Marinos and Mitsubishi became the Urawa Red Diamonds. Their new fashionable kits and related merchandising goods strongly attracted young people. In fact, Sony Creative Products (the league's exclusive merchandising coordinator at that time) sold J. League goods worth a staggering 3.6 billion yen (£21.6 million) in 1993, the first year of the J. League, and the total sales of licensed products were estimated at 100 billion yen (£659.3 million) (Birchall, 2000: 12, 15).

The media also contributed hugely to the J. League's success. Hakuhodo's proactive advertising and frequent media exposure of football almost won a landslide victory. The price of the television rights for J. League coverage rocketed to 10 million yen (£59 962) per game, from the previous paltry sum of 300 000 yen (£1349) for JSL games. In the following year, the fee was doubled to 20 million yen (£127 860) per game.

However, to maximize this media and marketing effect, another important factor was the star players. Just before the J. League started, some of the international big names joined – such as Zico from Brazil (Kashima Antlers), Gary Lineker from England (Nagoya Grampus), Pierre Littbarski from Germany (JEF United) and Ramon Diaz from Argentina (Yokohama Marinos), as well as a Japanese national, Kazuyoshi Miura (Verdy Kawasaki), who had been playing for Santos in Brazil as a professional. To harness their fame, the media advertised these stars as far as possible, and a large number of people were ready to watch them on TV, at the stadiums and at the training grounds.

Therefore, almost all the stadiums were full of supporters who were a mixture of the traditional fans and newly emerged football fans, and the latter group was much larger in size. In the stadiums, in the media and at the city corners, football was suddenly everywhere in society. Japanese football has dramatically transformed itself in a very short period of time, in terms of its commercial value and attractiveness to consumers. In 1989, the JSL's average attendance per game was a mere 3972, despite its cheap admission fees (children 100 yen, students 400 yen and adults 700 yen, where £1≈225 yen; today, the cheapest J. League ticket for adults is about 2500 yen). Having seen the poor state of the JSL, the new league operation was an almost revolutionary transformation. Marketing, media, clubs and people – all of these factors contributed to create the J. League boom.

This social phenomenon attracted a great number of people, especially the young, to football. The new young football fans were probably attracted by the idea of participating in their local clubs or communities through playing the sport in a casual manner. Presumably, this also occurred because they were a generation looking for an identity and trying to enjoy their daily lives by participating in this new community.

However, about three years after the league was launched, the J. League boom faded rapidly. The attendance numbers at league matches and sales of relevant goods declined steadily, while many people lost their interest in football. This episode shows a characteristic aspect of the temperament of Japanese consumers. They are very sensitive to any new trend in the market environment; however, they are also easily bored and quickly direct their attention elsewhere. Therefore, the J. League suffered from a slump as this type of consumer left the football market. This also meant that the football culture in Japan was not yet established among the people. The recession lasted for the latter half of the 1990s, until football was saved by 2002 World Cup fever.

Constructing professionalism

From the final years of the JSL (amateur league) to the early J. League years, Tokyo Verdy 1969 (formerly Yomiuri Club, Verdy Kawasaki) and Yokohama F. Marinos (Nissan Motors) were the two stronger sides and major rivals.

However, from 1996 to 2002, two of the most successful J. League clubs, Kashima Antlers and Júbilo Iwata, competed fiercely for the title. In fact, Kashima won four and Iwata won three championships within those seven years. Their remarkable success brought the professional league to fruition. Kashima and Iwata, both from relatively small cities, succeeded in establishing the ideal model of the football club closely related to its local community. Careful management, such as sensible acquisition of players and sustained youth development, enabled the teams consistently to show excellent performance. This led the clubs rapidly to create loyal fan bases, and to keep their fans on their side.

However, the key factor in the success of these clubs was acquisition of the two influential Brazilian players, Zico (Kashima Antlers 1992–93 player; 1994–2002, technical director; since 2002,

Japan's national team coach) and Dunga (Júbilo Iwata 1995–98). They brought a professional attitude to the club, along with technical and tactical improvement, firm teamwork and Brazilian skill. Their vast experience in top international football largely helped the clubs to establish a professional attitude and management. Their advice ranged from how to deal with fans and the further acquisition of players, to a long-term vision for club development. Even since the Brazilians have left the clubs they have maintained a good relationship, while the clubs themselves are still using the Brazilians' managerial philosophy. The two clubs seem to be constructing a football culture in their regions, and the Brazilian legends are still precious assets.

Current sports in Japan

Popularity-wise, Japanese sport has been dominated by professional baseball for more than half a century (the sport has been professional for nearly seventy years). According to a report by a Japanese research company, Central Research Services Inc. (www.asahi.com, 2003), in 2003 people's favourite sport in Japan was still baseball, which attracted 60 per cent of the vote. It was well ahead of the second sport, football, which had 28.6 per cent. Professional Sumo wrestling, Japan's traditional sport that was ranked second until 1996, was third in 2003, with 22.9 per cent of the vote, followed by golf (14.2 per cent), boxing (12.4 per cent) and motor racing (Formula 1) (10.4 per cent).

With regard to the age of the sports fans, baseball is supported by a much wider range of ages because of its long, successful history as entertainment. As can be seen in Figure 12.2, more than 60 per cent of male and 40 per cent of female voters of all ages supported baseball in 2001. Significantly, people aged over forty support baseball more than the younger generation. In fact, just ten years ago Japan's only major professional team sport was baseball, and Figure 12.2 indicates how baseball has been a familiar sport in people's lives in Japan for an extended period.

In contrast to baseball, Figure 12.2 shows that football is supported by a younger generation, and especially by young males – 40 per cent of men in their twenties supported the sport in 2001. This is probably because the J. League's fresh and active image and its concept of creating the local community-based sports clubs has attracted the young generation who are seeking a new identity. Moreover, football's international and global nature appeals strongly to those of the Japanese youth who eagerly follow Euro-American culture.

In addition, football goods such as shirts and kits are quite popular among young football fans in Japan, as they consider these to

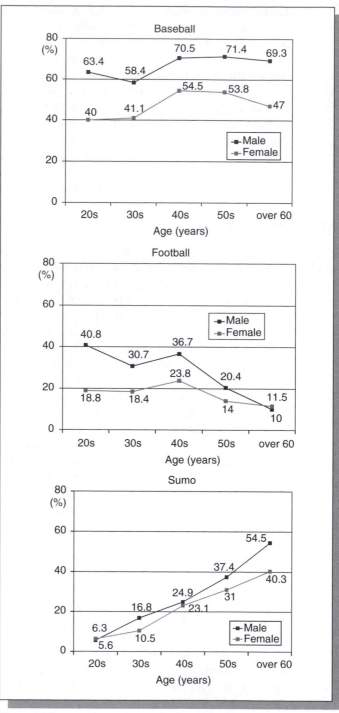

Figure 12.2
Preference for various sports in Japan, by age, in 2001

be fashionable – as do fans in Europe. In fact, in the World Cup 2002 countless Japanese and Korean young supporters wore their national team kits, and many Japanese also enjoyed supporting countries such as Brazil and England by wearing the national team shirts. This clearly shows how football in Japan is becoming popular, and also indicates Asia's potential in football marketing.

With respect to Sumo wrestling fans, Figure 12.2 shows that, remarkably, the older people got, the more they supported sport. This is because Sumo, Japan's national sport, has more than a thousand years of history. Its tradition and identity are profoundly embedded in the people's soul.

The turning point – Japanese professional sports

Japanese baseball's traditionally predominant popularity can be seen in Figure 12.3. However, in 2005 its average attendance suddenly dropped. This is because from 2005 onwards, baseball will disclose the actual figures of attendance as opposed to estimates, as was previously the case. In addition, baseball, which consists of two top leagues, seems to be facing a turning point in its history. In fact, in 2004 the Pacific League's Osaka Kintetsu Buffaloes merged with Kobe Orix Bluewave, becoming Orix Buffaloes

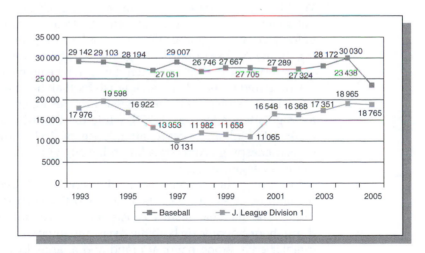

Figure 12.3

Average attendance at baseball and football in Japan, 1993–2005
(*Sources*: www.j-league.or.jp; www.sanspo.com; www.d7.dion.ne.jp;
http://www.j-league.or.jp/; http://www.sanspo.com/baseball/data/2001guest.html;
http://www.sanspo.com/baseball/data/2002guest.html;
http://www.sanspo.com/baseball/data/2003guest.html;
http://www.sanspo.com/baseball/data/data.html;
http://www.d7.dion.ne.jp/~xmot/kankyakudoin.html)

based in Kobe. The Crimson Group, led by businessman Hiroshi Mikitani, then won the bid to enter the professional baseball market with a brand-new team. (H. Mikitani is also the owner of Vissel Kobe, a J. League club since 2004.)

The Rakuten Golden Eagles, based in the city of Sendai, joined the same league in the 2005 season. This turmoil obviously shocked the Japanese, following nearly forty years of stable management in baseball, and this might explain the sudden drop in attendance.

Moreover, in November 2005 basketball also joined the Japanese professional sports, launching its first ever professional league, the bj League (Basketball Japan League). Basketball is also potentially a very popular sport, particularly among Japanese youth. Therefore, Japan's current situation regarding the sport's popularity will also change gradually. However, it looks as though basketball was encouraged by the J. League's consistent success over a decade to start Japan's first pro-basketball league.

With respect to football attendance in Figure 12.3, in the first three seasons J. League enjoyed adequate attendance, recording an average of over 15 000 spectators per game. However, from 1996 to 2000 the league's average attendance suffered a severe recession. As mentioned above, this is presumably because young people who are sensitive to trends quickly lost interest and left football. Football's attendance finally revived in 2001, synchronizing with the 2002 World Cup preparation. Subsequent World Cup success and its national fever were largely supported by frequent media exposure of football, and ubiquitous World Cup advertising and merchandising. In the 2005 season, J1s 306 games attracted a total of 5 742 233 spectators – the highest total attendance in J. League history.

Compared to the J. League, English football has a far bigger fan base. In December 2003 the English Premier League's (2003/04) average attendance was 34 778, while the English First Division (2003/04) had an average attendance of 15 147 (htt;://www.soccernet.espn.go.com/stats/attendance), which is a similar size to the J. League average.

Regarding the national team, the story is different. Japan's national team always attracts 40 000–50 000 spectators to the stadium. The national team's consistently successful performance throughout a decade on both the Asian and international stages has established a strong national brand and a large, loyal fan base in Japan. In fact, when the national team performs well, people also tend to pay more attention to the domestic league – for example, following the 1992, 2000 and 2004 Asia Cup triumphs, the 1996 and 2000 Olympic Games and, of course, the World Cup. In addition, nowadays even people who are not interested in J. League teams follow the national team, as supporting the national team is becoming a vehicle for experiencing the nationalism in a positive way.

The regional development of football and the 2002 World Cup legacy

Urawa (Saitama)

Saitama city was one of the World Cup venues, and its Urawa Red Diamonds is one of the best supported clubs in the country. Urawa is about fifteen miles north of Tokyo, in the middle of a densely populated commuter residential area. Despite the team struggling at the bottom of the league at the beginning of the J. League, the Urawa Reds soon became a well-supported club, as traditionally football has been a popular sport in that region. Today, the team attracts an average attendance of 39 000 per game and the Saitama Stadium – the World Cup venue, with a capacity of 60 000 – is its home ground. In the 2003 season, the Urawa Reds finally won a J. League title, the League Cup, ten years after the launch of the league. In 2004 the team became 2nd stage Champions, although it was beaten in the final play-off by Yokohama F. Marinos.

Kashima (Ibaraki)

In contrast to Urawa, Kashima is a small city with a population of 60 000, famous for its steel industry and an old Shinto shrine. It is located about 100 kilometres east of Tokyo. The Kashima Antlers team was managed by the famous Brazilian Zico, and the club won several titles in a decade. It therefore established a relatively solid fan base for the size of the city. Moreover, Kashima won the 2002 World Cup bid and expanded the Antlers' home Kashima Stadium (built for the J. League) from a capacity of 15 000 (football only) to one of 40 000. The Antlers team has become the proud symbol and identity of its local community, which did not have many leisure facilities or a particular identity previously.

Sapporo

Sapporo city in the northern island of Hokkaido has a population of more than a million. The Sapporo Dome hosted three World Cup games, and is an impressive multipurpose stadium. The dome itself does not move at all, but the huge plate of pitch can slide (hover) out of the dome so that the grass always gets the sunshine. As the shape of the inside of the dome can also be transformed, different kinds of sporting events (such as baseball and American football) and concerts and exhibitions can take place. The stadium is now the home ground for two professional teams – the Nipponham (sponsor name) Fighters (baseball) and Consadole Sapporo (football, J2).

Table 12.2
J. League average home attendance, 2005

Team	Attendance
J1 (seventeen home games)	
Albirex Niigata	40 114
Urawa Red Diamonds	39 357
FC Tokyo	27 101
Yokohama F. Marinos	25 713
Oita Trinita	22 080
Kashima Antlers	18 641
Cerezo Osaka	17 648
Júbilo Iwata	17 296
Gamba Osaka	15 966
Vissel Kobe	14 913
Tokyo Verdy 1969	14 716
Kawasaki Frontale	13 658
Nagoya Grampus Eight	13 288
Kashiwa Reysol	12 492
Shimizu S-Pulse	12 752
Sanfrecce Hiroshima	12 527
Omiya Ardija	9980
JEF United Ichihara Chiba	9535
Average	18 765

Niigata

Albirex Niigata was established in 1996 and joined the J. League in 1999. The team was launched because in 1996 Niigata City won the bid for becoming a World Cup venue. As can be seen in Tables 12.2 and 12.3, Albirex Niigata records one of the highest average attendances in the J. League. The World Cup Stadium, Niigata Big Swan, is the perfect venue for supporting the local team once the tournament had finished. In the few years since the World Cup, a staggering 40 000 fan base has emerged. This has totally changed the Japanese public's perception, as it had viewed Niigata as being a place where no professional sporting franchise could grow and blossom.

The remaining legacy

The J. League made a huge impact on the development of regional football culture in Japan. However, another important force for the development was the success of the World Cup 2002. The advertising agency Dentsu has estimated that the World Cup had an economic impact of approximately 3 trillion yen on the country.

Table 12.3
Albirex Niigata: average attendance per game

Year	Attendance
1999 (J2)	4211
2000	4007
2001	16 659
2002	21 478
2003	30 339
2004 (promoted to J1)	37 864
2005	40 114

Japan invested approximately US$3 billion in 10 stadiums with an average capacity of about 40 000. In addition, Japan built or upgraded the official preparation camps of the eighty-four candidate sites throughout the country, including the twenty-five campsites officially selected for the World Cup.

The problem with these facilities, especially the huge stadiums, is the enormous maintenance costs. It is understood that the stadiums are costing 460 million yen (£2.3 million) per year to maintain. However the revenue they are generating is 40–60 million yen (£200 000–£300 000). Currently, the Sapporo Dome and Kobe Wing Stadium are run by independent companies while the other eight stadiums are owned by local governments. They will therefore have to cover the large annual loss in some way. In addition, some stadiums were built far from the city centre, and there are not sufficient commercial facilities to generate revenue throughout the year, including on non-match days.

However, in 2005, with the regulations slightly modified regarding local government, the Kashima Antlers won the bid to become the appointed owner of the Kashima Stadium. This means that the local government still owns the stadium, but the Antlers now can use its facility much more freely to organize the team's own events. Presumably such a scheme is one of the possible solutions to reduce the annual deficit of the stadium, and the JFA, J. League, local authority and community must all work together for this to be successful.

Even though it is a difficult situation, the stadiums and facilities left in the country as a consequence of the J. League and the World Cup provide brilliant long-term assets for Japanese football. Once, Japan's only major international football event, the Toyota Cup (Inter-Continental Cup) used to be held on a pitch with a yellow scorched lawn at the National Stadium. Today, vivid green grass can be seen throughout the year in every stadium and training ground.

There is a greater number of improved football grounds available to the general public throughout the country. Some of the J. League clubs have created a regional identity that they can be proud of, attracting a large number of supporters. These grounds have also stimulated the regional development and economy, as well as improving people's lifestyle. All of these aspects were part of Kawabuchi's (the JFA President) initial ambition and dream.

J. League revenue

Television rights

Since it began, the J. League has been selling its broadcasting rights to both terrestrial and satellite TV. From 2002 to 2006, for five seasons, the J1 and J2 matches will be mainly broadcast by NHK, the national broadcaster (terrestrial/satellite); TBS (terrestrial/satellite); Nihon TV (terrestrial, delayed matches); and J Sports and Sky PerfecTV! (both satellite). For example, in 2004 at least fourteen live matches were contracted to be broadcast by the terrestrial channels, while the NHK-BS (satellite) broadcast ninety-two games and J Sports broadcast all the J. League matches. In addition, local TV stations also broadcast some of the games, focusing on their local teams.

Regarding the revenue from the TV rights to the J. League, Figure 12.4 shows the progress over the past decade. The league's

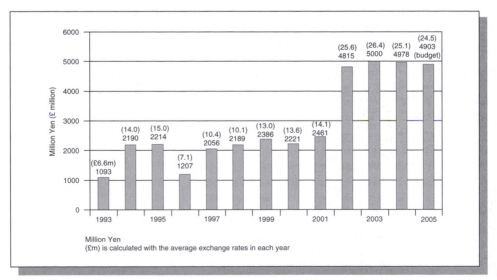

Figure 12.4
Revenue from broadcasting rights, 1993–2005
(*Source*: www.j-league.or.jp)

income from the TV rights almost doubled from 2641 million yen (£14.1 million) in 2001 to 4815 million yen (£25.6 million) in 2002. Clearly, World Cup fever increased the value of football broadcasting. In fact, during the tournament the Japan–Russia match recorded 58.1 per cent (in the Kansai area, around Osaka) and 66.1 per cent (in the Kanto area, around Tokyo) of the TV ratings, which was the highest in football and the second highest in the entire sports broadcasting history of Japan.

The revenue from the broadcasting right is very important for the league, as it makes up a considerable percentage of the league's total revenue. In fact, TV rights sales in 2002 and 2003 – 4815 million yen (£25.6 million) and 5000 million yen (£26.4 million) – made up 43 per cent and 46 per cent respectively of the league's total income for those years, jumping from 28 per cent in 2001.

Other income streams

The revenue sources for J. League clubs over the past decade can be seen in Figure 12.5. A significant feature is that in 1994 and 1995 clubs enjoyed staggering ticket sales (£24.4 million and £24.9 million respectively) because of the J. League boom, although their advertising income over the first three years were relatively low. Regarding advertising income, since 1996 it has been fairly stable at around £5 million and £7 million per year.

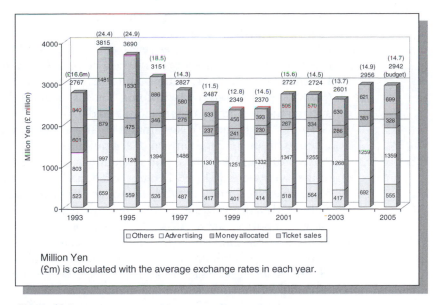

Figure 12.5
J. League clubs' average revenue breakdown, 1993–2005
(*Source*: www.j-league.or.jp)

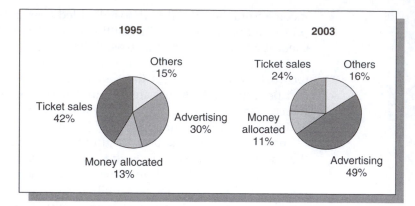

Figure 12.6
Revenue breakdown of J. League clubs, 1995 and 2003
(*Source*: www.j-league.or.jp)

Figure 12.6 shows clearly that the percentage of income from advertising in 2003 has increased dramatically compared to that in 1995, while the percentage of income from ticket sales decreased by 18 per cent. It is evident that clubs are now depending more on advertising income.

The economic future of the J. League

According to the Managing Director of FC Tokyo, Yutaka Murabayashi, the average income of J. League clubs is around 2.6 billion yen (£13.7 million) per year (see also Figure 12.5), which is one-tenth of that of the world's richest club, Manchester United, which had an annual income about £130 million in 2001/02 (*Source*: www.wasedawillwin.com). The J. League's 'big clubs', such as the Kashima Antlers, Urawa Reds, Júbilo Iwata, Nagoya Grampus Eight and Yokohama F. Marinos, generate annual incomes around 3.5 billion yen (£18.4 million).

According to J. League reports (headlines.yahoo.co.jp), in 2001, of the twenty-eight J1 and J2 clubs, nine made profits of over 40 million yen (£0.2 million) while ten made losses. In 2002, fourteen clubs made a profit while eleven clubs made losses. The J. League has also reported that in 2004, J1's eight clubs had the opportunity to become big clubs in term of their business, recording sales income of over 3 billion yen (about £15 million). This is similar to Murabayashi's estimate. In addition, in 2004 twenty-six clubs made a profit and no clubs made a loss. From J. League information and from Figure 12.5 it can be seen that since 2001, overall the J. League clubs have shown a gradual increase in revenue.

However, regarding J. League's future income, Japan's difficult economic situation must be remembered. In 1990, the Japanese economy suffered badly and then entered a long period of stagnation from which it has not yet recovered. Under such difficult circumstances, the league and clubs must be prudent in their business management. In fact, over the past decade some clubs have faced serious financial crises, spending more than they could afford, and a few eventually went out of business.

Securing diversified and sustainable revenue sources for the league and the clubs is crucial for the future of the business. Currently, the business depends largely on the income from TV rights and advertising. In 1998 Yokohama Flügels was forced out of business, and the main reason for this was the sudden withdrawal of the main sponsor. Therefore, in order to have a balance in the revenue structure, ticket sales need to be increased and further expansion of the fan base is necessary. In order to increase the fan base, construction of an attractive club and team is vital. Long-term plans for club development, including sustainable youth development and enhancing the bond with the local community, take a long time to achieve, but will support the club's finance for long into the future.

Promoting merchandise and selling video contents through new media is also an underdeveloped revenue area for the league and clubs. Nowadays, the streaming of football content through mobile handsets and the Internet is potentially an extremely attractive product for the users all over the world. The J. League is also broadcasting free goal video clips on its official site. However, there are still many technical problems ahead, and the profitability of these methods has yet to be established. Nevertheless, Japan, where the new media infrastructure is well developed, has a good opportunity to begin a new media business. This can be one of the important revenue sources in the future, for both clubs and federations.

The effective use of stadiums is also important in maximizing revenue. As of 2006, England's New Wembley Stadium is still under construction. However, when complete it will have good transport access and a state-of-the-art commercial complex inside the stadium that can generate revenue throughout the year. When considering the management of Japanese stadiums this concept should be remembered, as venues always have to organize events and generate income in order to pay for their maintenance fee. Therefore, Japanese stadiums must improve their usage by holding various kinds of events, and regulation changes, as in the case of Kashima Stadium, can help to achieve an increase in revenue.

The business relationship between Japan and Europe

Japanese players in Europe

At the beginning of 2006 twelve Japanese footballers are playing for the European clubs (see Table 12.4), and other players always have the opportunity to head for Europe. Most of them are in Japan's national team, and players like Nakata, Nakamura and Inamoto already have important roles in their current European clubs.

Among these players, Nakata's case may be the most successful business-wise for both the club and the player. According to Hayward (2001: 23), in 1998 Hidetoshi Nakata signed for Italian Série A side Perugia for 5 billion Lira (£1.7 million). The Japan International midfielder showed an excellent performance during the season, and was a major factor in helping the club to remain in Série A. While he was in Perugia, a large number of the Japanese press, tourists from Japan and Japanese living in Italy keenly followed him. Moreover, the club sold around 100 000 Nakata shirts all over the world, and 80 per cent of the total sales were made in Japan (Boldrini, 2000: 57). The Japanese star was then sold to AS Roma in January 2000 for about 50 billion Lira (£15.7 million). Perugia, Italy's relatively small provincial club, had been almost unknown in Japan previously, and had by now become one of the most well-known Italian clubs.

After playing for Roma, Nakata joined AC Parma for 60 billion Lira (£19.3 million) in the summer of 2001. The contracts with Parma included selling 10 000 Nakata jerseys in Japan, and the

Table 12.4
Japanese players in Europe, February 2006

Player	Country	Club
Shunsuke Nakamura	Scotland	Celtic FC
Hidetoshi Nakata	England	Bolton Wanderers FC
Junichi Inamoto	England	West Bromwich Albion
Naohiro Takahara	Germany	Hamburger SV
Sota Hirayama	The Netherlands	Heracules Almelo
Daisuke Matsui	France	Le Mans
Masashi Oguro	France	Glenoble (Ligue 2)
Yoshito Okubo	Spain	RCD Mallorca
Kenji Fukuda	Spain	Castellón (Second Division)
Atsushi Yanagisawa	Italy	FC Messina
Koji Nakata	Switzerland	FC Basel
Takayuki Suzuki	Serbia & Montenegro	Red Star Belgrade

broadcasting of live Parma matches on Japanese cable/satellite Channel SkyPerfecTV!.

Within those three years, his commercial value as a player grew to ten times the fee initially paid by Perugia. The economic impact of a single Japanese player on the club's business was enormous.

However, there are some negative aspects in the acquisition of Japanese players. For example, according to FA rules, every non-EEA (European Economic Area) player must obtain a work permit to play in English football. To qualify, the player must have played 75 per cent of games for his national team. For the permit to remain valid, the player must play at least 75 per cent of his English club's games a year, although this second criterion is more relaxed (www.ukfootballfaq.org.uk/).

In addition, as mentioned before, the different football calendars in Europe and Japan also make it difficult for Japanese players to go to Europe. When the Japanese season finishes Europe is still in the middle of its season, and this complicates the players' smooth move to Europe. Moreover, when the Japanese players in Europe are called up by their national team, they have to travel to Japan or to other parts of the world. It takes a long time to travel to the Far East and then more time to re-adapt to their European teams. Owing to these difficulties, European clubs must be prudent about purchasing Japanese players.

The obstacles, including strict regulations along with incompatible calendars and schedules limit the business opportunities between the clubs. However, the main concern about Japanese players is their level of play. In fact, in Europe not many Japanese players have become regular team players who participate in the whole of every game, helping the team to win. For example, in Table 12.4 the real regular players are just Nakamura (Celtic) and Matsui (Le Mans), who had both played in more than fifteen matches in the 2005/06 season by the end of 2005.

Another concern is that when Japanese players come to play in Europe, most of them are physically less able than the European, South American and African players. They need to improve their physical strength and technique in order to survive in the severe competitions in their team and in the league. In addition, they have to learn a new language, and it takes a great deal of time and effort to be able to communicate with their team-mates and managers.

The communication problems in particular are a cause of stress for Japanese players, as the European culture and languages are totally different from those of Japan. Therefore, before improving their football skills the players have to struggle to adapt to the European way of life. Culture, language, food, people's mentality, muddy pitches during the dark cold winters and severe press criticism are all contributory factors. Even so, for the players it is worth the challenge to play in Europe, as its leagues have the world's highest levels of competition, prestige and remuneration.

Therefore, European clubs need to be careful about buying players just because of their commercial value. They must remember the difficulties for Japanese players, and that the commercial benefit brought in by those players can be just an extra bonus. Regarding the club's management, the first priority is to build a strong team that is able to win against strong competition. Nonetheless, many European clubs are still continuing to search for Asian young talent because their commercial impact is desirable.

European players in the J. League

In 2005 only eight European players belonged to the J. League, while the country that sent the biggest number of foreign players (thirty-three) to Japan was Brazil. As can be seen in Table 12.5, those eight European players are less well-known ones. However, in the brief J. League history some of the European big names have made a great impact on the teams' performance by showing excellent leadership, technical ability and professional attitude. These include Salvatore Schillaci from Italy (Júbilo Iwata 1994–97), Guido Buchwald from Germany (Urawa Reds 1994–98), Gerald Vanenburg from The Netherlands (Júbilo Iwata 1993–96) and Dragan Stojkovic from Serbia and Montenegro (Nagoya Grampus Eight 1994–2001).

Some of the European coaches have also contributed hugely to J. League development by creating some excellent teams. For example, Arsène Wenger from France (Nagoya Grampus Eight 1995–96), Hans Ooft from The Netherlands (who coached teams including Iwata, Kyoto, Urawa and Japan's national team 1984–2003) and Ivica Osim from Bosnia-Herzegovina (JEF United 2002–2005), have brought discipline to the teams. They managed

Table 12.5
European players in the J. League, 2005

Player	Country	Club
Tomislav Maric	Croatia	Urawa Red Diamonds
Mario Haas	Austria	JEF United Ichihara
Ilian Stoyanov	Bulgaria	JEF United Ichihara
Gabriel Popescu	Romania	JEF United Ichihara
Martin Muller	Czech Republic	Vissel Kobe
Ivo Ulich	Czech Republic	Vissel Kobe
Pavel Horvath	Czech Republic	Vissel Kobe
Patrick Zwanwike	The Netherlands	Oita Trinita

to train their team to make efficient passes and consolidated their teamwork by improving players' communication, judgement and spontaneous decisions.

European clubs' business in Japan and Asia

Today, Europe's big clubs travel to Asia almost every summer in order to enhance their popularity in the region. In particular, the Asia Pacific region, including Japan, has a large number of potential European-football fans. In the summer of 2005, some of Europe's biggest names were in Japan – Manchester United, Real Madrid (toured 2003, 2004 and 2005), FC Barcelona (toured 2004 and 2005), Bayern Munich, and Juventus playing the J. League teams. In particular, Real Madrid enjoys considerable commercial success in Asia, although its 2005 tour was controversial because of its hard schedule. In the summer of 2003, Real Madrid went on a four-match Asian tour of China, Japan and Thailand. The Galacticos gained around €2.7 million (£1.7 million) in revenue just from the match in Beijing and the training sessions in Kunming, both in China (*China Daily*, 2003).

European clubs' other way of approaching the Asian market is by corporate club partnerships. Since 2003 the Eredivisie giant Feyenoord and the J1 club Omiya Ardija have had a corporate partnership, while the Spanish Primera Liga club Atlético Osasuna and the J2 club Shonan Bellmare have had an ongoing partnership since 2004. In addition, in 2006 J1's Urawa Red Diamonds and the Bundesliga side Bayern Munich also signed a partnership. Here, the partnership includes exchange of management, coaching staff and youth players, and of scouting information. Osasuna and Shonan in particular are trying to learn from one another regarding their different management styles so that they will be able to improve their own business. In addition, Urawa and Bayern are planning to hold friendly matches and training camps for their teams of different age categories. They are also trying to incorporate one another in the areas of merchandising and promotion. In the case of Feyenoord, its partnership includes a deal with Omiya's sponsor, NTT DoCoMo. NTT, the Japanese telecommunication expert, will assist with the commercial and technological development of the Dutch club in Asia.

In the spring of 2003, the Italian Série A giant Inter Milan signed a partnership with JSV the Japanese sports retailer, Dentsu, Japan's largest advertising agency and professional events Asian football promoter/marketing consultants. With this partnership, Inter is trying to implement various kinds of commercial activities in a well-organized manner in Asia. The key business areas of the partnership include developing Inter merchandise; identifying regional licensing and sponsorship; setting up Inter stores, an official e-commerce site, fan clubs and a football clinic/school; scouting for talented Asian youth players; and promoting links with local football association and teams.

Summarizing the corporate business between Japanese clubs and companies, and European clubs, both sides have mutual benefits. European clubs can expect Japanese companies' technical support in telecommunications, e-commerce and knowledge of the local market, so that they can develop their business in Asia more efficiently. Japanese teams can learn important aspects from European clubs' traditional managerial style. In addition, the exchange of youth players, management and coaching staff, and two different clubs working together in the areas of merchandising and promotion, will, providing those relationships are sustainable, lead to expansion of business opportunities for both the Japanese and European partners in the long term.

In 2005 the FIFA World Club Championship Toyota Cup was finally held in Japan, following the 2000 tournament in Brazil. This tournament, still an underdeveloped commercial area for FIFA, is again to be held in 2006 in Japan. In 2005 the tournament attracted average attendance of 37 351 per game, and 66 821 spectators watched the Final, São Paulo – Liverpool, at the Yokohama International Stadium. The average attendance at this tournament surpassed that of 2000 in Brazil (35 942). It is estimated that Japan's 2005 tournament financial balance could be slightly minus or break even. There were no Japanese clubs participating in the tournament this time, whereas in Brazil in 2000, two big local clubs (Corinthians and Vasco da Gama) were in the final. Bearing this in mind, it can be said that the 2005 tournament was successful.

Conclusions

The birth of the professional football league encouraged the Japanese football culture to grow again. Professional club management and a firm fan base will be established gradually. In Eastern Asia football business is also improving, led by countries such as South Korea and China, with the operation of the professional leagues. These trends synchronize with the globalization of football to some extent.

Today, European clubs are keen to join the lucrative Asian market in order to enhance their popularity in the region. Under these circumstances, corporate business activities among Japanese and European clubs, organizations and enterprises will increase gradually in the future. In that process, the operation of corporate business and organizing international major events such as the World Cup and World Club Championship will provide valuable experience and also necessary practice for the Japanese business. Such experiences will allow the clubs and organizations to be more interactive and sophisticated in arranging their business activities at the international level.

Eastern Asia's football leaders – Japan, South Korea and China – have to try to develop international business within the region. These countries have or will have excellent facilities as a result of holding the 2002 World Cup and the forthcoming Beijing Olympics 2008. However, despite the status of being Asia's premium competition, the AFC Champions League is still very much an underdeveloped commercial area compared to the successful UEFA Champions League. Improving international business operations in key regions can help the Asian Champions League to become a more attractive and valuable event.

The professional leagues in these three countries, the AFC (Asia Football Confederation) and the EAFF (East Asia Football Federation) must work together in order to improve tournaments. If they can create sustainable market condition for Asian local events, with better commercial value and far more sophisticated business operations and event organizers, it is more likely that they will be able to hold top international events such as the FIFA World Club Championship in a more successful and sustainable manner.

Bibliography and references

Birchall, J. (2000). *Ultra Nippon*, pp. 12, 15. Headline.

Boldrini, S. (2000). *NAKATA Un giapponese nel pallone* (trans. Michiro Katano). Asahi Shimbun Co.

Central Research Services Inc. (2003). Research into the popularity of the professional sports in Japan (available at www.asahi.com).

Hayward, C. (2001). *Soccer Analyst*, **2(12)**, 23.

Sugden, J. and Tomlinson, A. (1998). *FIFA & the Contest for World Football*. Polity Press.

Websites

http://www.sponichi.co.jp/society/kiji/2002/08/19/08.html (article about the World Cup Facilities).

http://www.wasedawillwin.com/series/030322_kyodan/ (lecture by Yutaka Murabayashi, Managing Director, FC Tokyo).

http://headlins.yahoo.co.jp/hl?a=20031214-00002055-mai-spo (J. League disclosure about the clubs' profits and losses, reported by *Mainichi* newspaper).

http://www.ukfootballfaq.org.uk/ (FAQ on British Football, 5.4 The Bosman ruling, 5.4.1 Foreign players).

http://www.sanspo.com/soccer/top/st200601/st2006011809.html (news about the J. League's future vision, Committee of JFA).

Appendix 12.1

Interviews with Sadao Suzuki (CEO, Kashima Antlers) and Takaaki Shimazu (Senior Managing Director, Sapporo Dome)

The interviews with Sadao Suzuki and Takaaki Shimazu took place in September 2005. The eight questions were provided by the author, and the answers were submitted via e-mail by the interviewees. The interviews were initially in Japanese, and were then translated into English.

Interview with Sadao Suzuki, Kashima Antlers

Q1: In your opinion, has hosting the World Cup made people more aware of football? Are more people now interested in football than before the tournament took place?

SS: I think that Japanese nationals have now become more interested in football. In fact, the 2006 World Cup Asian qualification match (where Japan played against North Korea in Bangkok; Japan qualified in that game) recorded high TV ratings despite the late-night broadcast. This proves that the people's interest in football is rising.

Q2: Has hosting the World Cup been good for football players? Was there a massive increase in people playing football after the World Cup?

SS: The number of registered players is a matter for the federations, so we at the clubs do not fully understand the situation. However, the number of the children joining our club's apprentice and youth course is increasing. The interest of their parents in football also seems quite high.

Q3: What about for the professional leagues? Has hosting the World Cup improved crowds, sponsorship opportunities and finances for them?

SS: Since the World Cup was held, the finances of the club have not shown much difference. However, we can probably say that our international knowledge in the operation has been significantly improved.

Q4: Has hosting the World Cup resulted in more people in other countries becoming interested in Japanese football?

SS: Not only just after the event, but consistently until today, overseas clubs have been paying attention to the improvement in the ability of our players. As the interest in the national team is also rising, we are involved in the world's football market.

Q5: Many expensive stadiums were built to host the 2002 tournament, with clubs moved to the stadiums. Has this proved to be a success for the clubs involved?

SS: All the World Cup stadiums are facilities owned by the local governments, so this is not a question for the clubs. But I presume that in the future it will increasingly be the case that J. clubs own the stadiums as the regulations for the management of public facilities will probably be modified.

Q6: Will the stadiums be used to host future international events?

SS: As I mentioned before, because of the aggravation of the financial conditions for the local government, their policy for stadium use is taking the direction of harnessing the vitality of the private sector. This is a common problem for all the local governments who own the World Cup stadiums. I think that the improvement in the stadium use, not just limiting it to international events, is the first priority in order to reduce the running costs of the stadiums.

Q7: Have the stadiums proved to be a financial success?

SS: They are all suffering severe financial difficulties, except for the competitive stadiums with a large capacity located in capital cities such as Yokohama and Saitama. In addition, Sapporo Stadium is also a rare successful case, where the stadium use for post-World Cup events was considered at the planning stage.

Q8: In your opinion, was hosting the World Cup a success for football in Japan?

SS: It depends on what we mean by success. Kashima Soccer Stadium is a football-only stadium capable of holding 40 000 people. It is the only sports facility of that size for the people in our prefecture, and in the future it will be impossible to have such a huge facility built in the region. When we talk about success, it is a question of how we are going to use the facility from now on.

Interview with Takaaki Shimazu, Sapporo Dome

Q1: In your opinion, has hosting the World Cup made people more aware of football? Are more people now interested in football than before the tournament took place?

TS: Having the common experience, by living in the same era, I feel that the Japanese interest in football has risen further, beyond the generation. I think the Japan national team's excellent performance contributed to this a lot, but, especially in Sapporo, people experienced huge excitement and delight in watching such games as England–Argentina and David Beckham's excellent performance. Experiencing the Olympic Games (in Athens, Japan played football) and moving towards the World Cup in Germany 2006, I think that the people's interest in football is again rising, including the way the media are focusing on the sport.

Q2: Has hosting the World Cup been good for football players? Was there a massive increase in people playing football after the World Cup?

TS: The questions about 'for the players', and the football population, we cannot answer, as we do not know. What about asking Hokkaido FA or Consadole Sapporo about this matter?

Q3: What about for the professional leagues? Has hosting the World Cup improved crowds, sponsorship opportunities and finances for them?

TS: Sapporo Dome has been the home stadium of a current J2 club, Consadole Sapporo. However, it looks as though there has been no direct relationship between the effect of the World Cup 2002 and the number of J. League attendances. In the case of Sapporo, Consadole, who were playing in J1 in 2002 (the World Cup year), were relegated to J2 in that season because of their slack performance. Since then, you can see that the numbers attending have changed depending on the club's performance. Regarding the sponsors' opportunities and other details, please contact Hokkaido Football Club Inc., the management of Consadole Sapporo.

Q4: Has hosting the World Cup resulted in more people in other countries becoming interested in Japanese football?

TS: We do not know about this as well, so please ask the entity such as JFA.

Q5: Many expensive stadiums were built to host the 2002 tournament, with clubs moved to the stadiums. Has this proved to be a success for the clubs involved?

TS: In case of the Sapporo Dome, the facility owner is Sapporo city and Sapporo Dome Inc. is managing the Dome on the instructions of the city, as it is defined by the regulation of the local government. With respect to the fee for stadium use, we have a system with an 'excess' fee, which means a basic fee plus an extra fee if the attendance reaches a certain number set by us. As Sapporo Dome is a football stadium but also can transform itself into a baseball stadium, with the astro-turf, it is also the home of the professional baseball team, Hokkaido Nipponham Fighters. In addition, as a multipurpose all-weather facility, apart from those sports, various sorts of events such as live concerts and exhibitions are being held. With the only function being football, I think probably it couldn't make it in terms of management. However, by making an effort in sales as a multipurpose facility in order to increase the number of the days it is used each year, our management is showing a rather satisfactory performance. Regarding the business side of the teams using our facilities, we cannot comment; please contact those teams.

Q6: Will the stadiums be used to host future international events?

TS: From now, we would like to bid for the domestic and international events proactively as a multipurpose event venue, so that we can make the citizens in Hokkaido and nationwide happy through the variety of events. As an example, in February 2007 the FIS Nordic Ski World Championship will be held in Sapporo. Sapporo Dome is going to hold the opening ceremony, and we are also discussing holding an indoor competition by setting up a course covered with snow inside the stadium.

Q7: Have the stadiums proved to be a financial success?

TS: Sapporo Dome has been able to manage the facility as a multipurpose stadium that includes football and baseball, rather than just a World Cup football stadium. Therefore, at present we consider that our business is going well.

Q8: In your opinion, was hosting the World Cup a success for football in Japan?

TS: Before talking about the technical improvement in the football in the contest, the event was hugely meaningful because it has brought a dream to a great number of citizens, particularly the youth and children.

CHAPTER 13

Marketing professional soccer in the United States: the successes and failures of MLS and the WUSA

Richard M. Southall and
Mark S. Nagel

Overview

This chapter examines the past successes and failures of professional soccer in the United States, specifically focusing on Major League Soccer (MLS) and the Women's United Soccer Association (WUSA) as the most recent examples of successful and unsuccessful US professional soccer leagues. Since both MLS and the WUSA have been largely ignored by sport-management scholars, it is hoped that this chapter will increase the knowledge and understanding of these leagues and their marketing successes and shortcomings. To place the examination of the leagues in a proper context, the chapter will also present an overview of professional soccer's history in the United States, as well as the two leagues' structures. Within this context, the leagues' marketing strategies and plans are then examined through the lenses of exchange theory, cause-related marketing (CRM), and strategic philanthropy.

Keywords

United States, soccer, exchange theory, cause-related marketing (CRM), strategic philanthropy, single entity

Introduction

The 1994 Men's World Cup generated near-capacity crowds at stadiums around the United States, and resulted in relatively large domestic television audiences. Buoyed by this success, Major League Soccer (MLS) was founded in 1996, with several wealthy and influential owners among the league's investors (National Soccer Hall of Fame, n.d.). Similarly, the unprecedented media coverage (11.4 Nielsen rating for the final), record-breaking attendance figures (90 000 at the Rose Bowl for the Women's World Cup Finals) and the United States Women's national team's 1999 World Cup shootout victory over China paved the way for the founding of the Women's United Soccer Association (WUSA) in 2001 (Women's United Soccer Association, 2000a). Each league's inception was hailed – to various degrees – as proof that soccer was no longer just a fringe or *niche* American activity, but had finally arrived as a major professional US sport.

For any new or existing sports league successfully to make the transition from niche to major professional sport league, it must have sufficient capitalization to sustain itself until sufficient revenue is generated to cover operating expenses. This economic fact of life requires not only that league or individual team owners are financially and emotionally committed to long-term incremental growth, but also that sponsors, league administrators and players are cognizant of the sport's and/or league's growth potential. It is important to remember that all sport leagues, niche or major, are supported by the same revenue sources (i.e. ticket sales, broadcast rights, sponsorship and merchandise). However, for a niche league – with its more limited fan base – to be successful, it is critical that existing revenue sources are effectively cultivated and harvested. Additionally, potential revenue sources must be identified, prospected and obtained if the league is to experience growth in sponsorship, merchandising, attendance and broadcast rights.

Since both MLS and the WUSA have been largely ignored by sport-management scholars, this chapter is designed to increase knowledge and understanding of these leagues. The leagues' marketing successes and failures are examined through the lenses of *exchange theory, cause-related marketing* (CRM) and *strategic philanthropy*. To place the examination of the leagues in the proper context, this chapter will also present an outline of professional soccer's history and the two league's financial and organizational structures.

Finally, Appendix 13.1 is based on an interview with Eddie Rockwell, Former Vice President (Operations) of Columbus Crew (MLS) and Former General Manager of Atlanta Beat (WUSA).

Theoretical frameworks

Exchange theory applies to any successful business transaction. For any transaction to succeed, all parties must agree that a satisfactory value exchange has occurred (Howard and Crompton, 2004). A desired outcome is only achieved when each party is willing to act in the best interest of all stakeholders or participants (Blalock and Wilken, 1979). Exchange theory is based upon three elements: rationality, marginal utility and fairness (McCarville and Copeland, 1994). McCarville and Copeland contended that rationality in marketing or sponsorship agreements focuses on the elucidation of all parties' goals, the achievement of stated goals and that past favourable outcomes for participants increase the likelihood of future agreements. Conversely, if a previous agreement has not fulfilled participants' expectations, the likelihood of any future agreement being finalized is diminished. In exchange theory, fairness involves equitable reward distribution (McCarville and Copeland, 1994). If specific and identifiable benefits sought by an organization can be met through other more cost-effective means, it will be unlikely to agree to an initial agreement or renew an existing one (Kuzma *et al.*, 1993; Stotlar, 2001).

Cause-related marketing is a strategic positioning and marketing tool that publicly associates a for-profit company with a non-profit organization and a relevant social cause or issue. Such an association links the company and the company's product(s) directly to a social cause or organization through the implementation of a strategic marketing plan while also raising money for the non-profit entity, thus mutually benefiting both (Polonsky and Macdonald, 2000; Pringle and Thompson, 2001). American Express'1983 involvement in the restoration of the Statue of Liberty is an example of a cause-related marketing campaign. Generally, an organization prefers to support 'causes' that are of interest to its target market. While there may be a philanthropic motive to cause-related marketing, the efforts of a cause-related marketing campaign tend to produce relatively short-term, product-related outcomes (LeClair and Ferrell, 2000).

Strategic philanthropy involves a long-term investment by a company in a cause that provides societal benefits while also enhancing the company's reputation (Stotlar, 2001). Such a long-term investment may require a company to endure short-term business losses for the good of the cause and for the fulfilment of the organization's social responsibilities and long-term gain. It requires support from top management and shareholders, and coordination of corporate giving and employee volunteer programmes with the overall corporate mission. This redefinition of philanthropy recognizes that while businesses should be good corporate citizens, they must not forget their fundamental obligation to their shareholders and employees, and to the company's profit-and-loss statement.

Overview of United States professional soccer

Prior to Major League Soccer's 1996 commencement, there had been two legitimate major professional leagues in the United States (Litterer, 2003a). In 1921 the American Soccer League (ASL) was founded, and was a viable league that successfully competed for European players ('The golden era, 1921–1933,' 2005). The league often attracted over 10 000 spectators for games – figures rivalling the fledgling National Football League's (NFL) attendance ('The golden era, 1921–1933'). The league's greatest strength, backing of strong local businesses, eventually contributed to its 1933 demise, since the Great Depression depleted most businesses' team-sponsorship, as well as most fans' ticket-purchasing abilities.

The next major professional league – the North American Soccer League (NASL) – resulted from the 1968 merger of the United Soccer Association and the National Professional Soccer League (Litterer, 2003b). Despite nearly going bankrupt in 1969, in 1975 the league made international news when one of its teams, the New York Cosmos, signed Pelé to a contract (Litterer, 2003b). Pelé's arrival attracted other well-known and well-compensated international soccer stars to the league. Despite dramatic increases in attendance (with some games drawing over 70 000 fans), spiralling salaries eventually forced many teams to cease operations (Litterer, 2003b). By 1981, both the star players and most the NASL's teams were gone. By 1985, the league had disbanded (Litterer, 2003b).

The impetus to the establishment of another major soccer league in the US began when the US men's soccer team unexpectedly qualified for the 1990 World Cup. Despite the teams' limited success in the tournament, the United States had established itself as a viable participant on the world soccer stage ('US soccer history', 2005). In 1993, in preparation for hosting the 1994 World Cup, the US men's national team embarked on an ambitious worldwide schedule. The US had a successful 1994 World Cup, both on the field and in the stands. Not only did the US team advance beyond round-robin play (including a 1–0 loss to eventual champion Brazil), but the average game attendance was 67 000 ('US soccer history', 2005). More significantly, the tournament netted a (then record) $60 million profit (Trecker, 1998a). By 1995, MLS executives had obtained Federation Internationale de Football Association (FIFA) sanctioning as a Division I League, but lacked investors, players and team locations. Despite these issues, preparations went ahead for the league's 1996 inaugural draft and opening season.

While the foundation for men's professional soccer in the US was taking place in 1994–95, several concurrent developments reflected the growth of US women's soccer. The founding of the United States Interregional Soccer League (USISL) and its establishment of the W-League, a national amateur league that provided playing time for many top female players, in 1994 was an important first step. The league played a brief exhibition schedule in 1994 and launched a full-fledged schedule in 1995, with nineteen teams spread nationwide (National Soccer Hall of Fame, n.d.).

In 1995, the US Women's National Team was placed third at the Women's World Cup in Sweden, falling to eventual champion Norway in the semifinals 1–0, but defeating China (National Soccer Hall of Fame, n.d.). In February 1995, US soccer announced its intention to host the 1999 Women's World Cup and began the formal bid process with FIFA. Reflecting the growing prowess of the women's national team, at the 1996 Atlanta Olympics the US women captured the gold medal before a crowd of 76 000 (National Soccer Hall of Fame, n.d.). However, the National Broadcasting Company (NBC) did not broadcast the game – an indication of the lack of significance placed upon women's soccer by media and corporate entities.

The United States Soccer Federation's (USSF) ambitious plans for hosting the 1999 Women's World Cup, including utilizing large stadiums across the United States and developing advertising and marketing campaigns to insure adequate press coverage and fan support, was contrary to the wishes and advice of FIFA, which envisioned a small regional tournament, ideally held in high-school stadiums (National Soccer Hall of Fame, n.d.). The USSF expressed the goal of making the tournament the most successful and largest women's sporting event in history (National Soccer Hall of Fame, n.d.).

The tournament was a resounding success, with much larger than expected crowds and national television coverage for many matches (Southall *et al.*, 2005). The final match was played before over 90000 Rose Bowl fans and a large national television audience (11.4 Nielsen rating) (Southall *et al.*, 2005). The US victory over China (5–4 on penalties) resulted in unprecedented media coverage – most notably for Brandi Chastain's celebration. Team members appeared on top news programmes, visited the White House and graced the covers of *Time*, *Sports Illustrated*, *Newsweek* and *People* (Southall *et al.*, 2005). The media attention generated by the 1999 Women's World Cup appeared to signal the emergence of women's soccer as more than just a niche sport.

Major League Soccer

From its inception, MLS owners knew it would take years or even decades for the league to become financially successful. The league initially implemented a *single-entity* structure to retain control of league expenses – particularly player salaries. (In a single-entity model, there are no individual team owners. Investors may be assigned a particular team, but ultimate authority for player movement, marketing strategies, television contracts, and sponsorship acquisition and retention lies with the league office (Zimbalist, 2005). While the adoption of a single-entity model allows the league to control labour costs and ensure a more competitive league through league assignment of players, such top-down control may have the unintended consequence of alienating an individual team's fans, who may feel 'their' team is not doing everything it can to win (Sweet, 2001a).) With an initial salary cap of $1.3 million (Trecker, 1998b), the league's investors were confident losses would not exceed the initial business plan projections. Even with player-salary cost containment, the league lost over $100 million in its first three years' of operation (Trecker, 1998b). Despite these losses, in 1998 then league commissioner Doug Logan noted (Trecker, 1998a: 21):

> We have a stable of investors who believe this is a wise, prudent, long-term investment. We have a solid business plan and we're sticking with it, and that plan is reinforced by the knowledge that our backers bring to the table.

Among the league's initial investors was one of the greatest American sports entrepreneurs, Lamar Hunt. With Hunt's dedication, commitment and financial resources, MLS had an initial advantage over many start-up sport properties. Hunt had long been a sport pioneer, founding the American Football League as well as maintaining ownership positions in the Chicago Bulls, NASL's Dallas Tornadoes and the World Championship Tennis Tour (Harris, 1986).

Hunt's financial resources and his willingness to use them were legendary. *In 1960* (authors' emphasis), when Hunt's father was asked to comment on the first-year $1 million dollar operating loss of Lamar's Dallas Texans (later renamed the Kansas City Chiefs) AFL football franchise, he responded that at that rate, 'the boy only has 123 years to go' (Harris, 1986: 105). Hunt has continued to proclaim his willingness to see MLS succeed, in spite of short-term financial losses: 'I know soccer's going to get there eventually. It has done things that tell you that inevitably it is going to be big ... ' (Schoenfeld, 2003: 29).

In addition to Hunt, MLS's other primary investor is Philip Anschuntz of Anschuntz Entertainment Group (AEG). Originally a $5 million investor and operator of the Colorado Rapids, Anschuntz has since directly invested over $100 to maintain the league (Sweet, 2001b; Lisi, 2002). In 2001, MLS faced several challenges – yearly losses in the millions, cessation of team operations in Miami and Tampa Bay, and the decisions by several investors (including Kenneth Horowitz, John Kluge and Stuart Subotnick) to leave the league (Sweet, 2001c). In spite of these negative developments, Anschuntz reemphasized his commitment to MLS (Sweet, 2001a). Anschuntz's commitment to the league is so deep that other league executives have begun calling him 'Uncle Phil' (Plagenhoef, 2003: para. 5).

In 2002, MLS Commissioner Don Garber noted the importance of Anschuntz's and AEG's commitment to MLS' future (Lisi, 2002: para. 11):

> Having a small group of committed investors is better for the long-term success of the sport than a large number of (backers) who are unwilling to reach our goals ... Anschuntz and his group have made a massive commitment to the sport. Soccer needed someone to tell the naysayers, 'I'm right, and you're wrong. I've made bets on businesses that everyone said wouldn't work and I've proved to be right. My next bet is on soccer.' Anschuntz is that person.

Until 2004, Hunt and Anschuntz controlled nine of ten MLS teams. The only other owner was Robert Kraft, operator of the New England Revolution (and, more famously, the owner of the

NFL's New England Patriots) (Plagenhoef, 2003). Although so few owners could conceivably control trades, draft selections, etc., greater concern has been the effect of losses being concentrated among so few investors. However, the willingness of the three league investors/owners to assume league losses totalling $250–$300 million has actually kept the league from bankruptcy (Carney, 2001). Richard Motzkin of SportsNet LLC noted, 'At one end, it [teams run by one group] sounds absurd ... But it would be even more absurd to have the league go bankrupt' (Sweet, 2001d: 24). Robert Kraft recently explained his long-term commitment to MLS, noting that his organization 'does not stay with businesses that either aren't profitable or we don't feel have the potential to be profitable' (Warfield, 2005a: 17).

The willingness of league investors to sustain losses in anticipation of long-term rewards appeared to be nearer to reality when, at the conclusion of the 2002 season, three MLS teams posted losses totalling less than $500 000 apiece (Trecker, 2002). More notably, in 2003, after moving into the $150 million Home Depot Center, the Los Angeles Galaxy was profitable (Warfield, 2004, 2005a). In addition, according to league sources, lack of a naming rights deal for their new stadium was the only factor preventing the Columbus Crew from being profitable (Warfield, 2005a).

League owners had long sought new soccer-only facilities to enhance revenue streams, and the Home Depot Center solidified the importance of playing-facility control. The league has since agreed to build new facilities in Dallas and Denver. Significantly, the city of Chicago has agreed to build the first publicly-financed, professional soccer-only facility in the United States (Warfield, 2005a). With plans to have six of its twelve teams in soccer-only facilities by 2007, MLS investors see their sport as being at a 'tipping point' (Lefton, 2005; Warfield, 2005a).

Building upon its recent financial success, MLS announced league expansion to twelve teams and new investors for the 2005 season. Dave Checketts, long-time President of the National Basketball Association's (NBA) New York Knicks, purchased the rights to operate the Real Salt Lake franchise, located in Salt Lake City, UT. Checketts explained his interest: 'I think we are on the cusp of the tipping point for soccer and MLS in the US. There's real upside here ... Soccer is still expanding, we have opportunity and labour peace' (Lefton, 2005: 32). Real Salt Lake has already announced plans for a new 25 000-seat facility to open in 2007 or 2008 (*Sports Business Daily*, 2005). Signalling the growth and acceptance of MLS in North America, legendary Mexican Soccer Club CD Guadalajara, known as Chivas, was the second 2005 entry to MLS. Jorge Vergera's Chivas USA will play in the Home Depot Center and should turn a profit in its first season (Lefton, 2005).

MLS investors have consistently focused on maintaining player salaries at affordable levels. During its inaugural season, each MLS team had a salary cap of $1.25 million, with an individual player cap of $175 000 ('U.S. soccer history', 2005). Initially, four 'marquee' league players were allowed to exceed the individual and team salary caps to pursue valuable sponsorship deals. In addition, each team was allowed a maximum of five foreign nationals per team. This restriction was designed to encourage the development and marketing of American players. In 1997, one year after the league's inception, MLS players unionized and sued the league – claiming the single-entity structure violated antitrust laws (Sweet, 2001e). MLS' eventual legal victory (*Fraser v. MLS*, 2002) led to the 2005 Collective Bargaining Agreement (CBA) between the league and the players' union. This initial CBA does not expire until 2009, ensuring long-term labour peace (Warfield, 2005a).

Since its inception, MLS has increasingly been willing and able to sign higher-priced star players and increase team salaries. In 2004 forty-six players made more than $100 000, but by 2005, the first year of the new CBA, that number had increased to sixty-three (Warfield, 2005b). In addition, by 2005 the twenty-seven players making the league minimums saw their salaries increase from $24 000 to $28 000 (Warfield, 2005b). The league has also recently signed world-class players, such as Landon Donovan ($900 000) and Eddie Johnson ($875 000), by paying salaries comparable to those of established leagues around the globe (Warfield, 2005b). In another 2005 move that many feel is critical to the future marketing of US soccer, MLS signed teenage star, Freddie Adu, to a base salary of $500 000 (Warfield, 2005b). Doug Quinn, Executive Vice President of MLS, described 2005 as the first season where 'part of our whole approach to the business … is building stars' (Warfield, 2005c: 33). By 2005, the twelve-team MLS had player salaries totalling $23.1 million (Warfield, 2005b).

The growth of any American sport enterprise requires an ability to deliver content through various media outlets. During the initial 1996 season, MLS knew it could not expect to receive large television broadcast-rights fees, so it paid the American Broadcast Company (ABC) $450 000 (plus production costs) to broadcast its championship game (Trecker, 1998a). However, the league was able to sell all of the in-game advertising inventory, prompting The Disney Company – parent company of ABC, ESPN (Entertainment and Sports Programming Network) and ESPN2 – to negotiate a partnership in which ABC, ESPN, ESPN2 and MLS would share production costs and sales revenue (Frank, 2001). Although overall the year 2000 broadcast ratings declined from 1999 levels (ABC, 0.9–0.7; ESPN, 0.34–0.34; ESPN2, 0.26–0.22), the 2000 ratings for 18–34 year-old males increased, indicating a potential for future ratings' growth. In 2002, ABC and ESPN agreed to continue broadcasting MLS games, but MLS assumed responsibility for advertisement sales ('General overview', 2005; Warfield, 2005a).

The 2004 ESPN2 ratings for MLS games, which increased 11.1 per cent from 2003, reflected the league's increased popularity. ABC's sole broadcast produced a 1.3 rating (4 share), a 30 per cent increase from 2003 (Warfield, 2005a). Although not equal to other sports broadcasts, such as MLB, NBA or NFL games, the 1.3 rating was still significant. This increased demand prompted ESPN2 to implement a split-screen commercial format so viewers would not miss any game action (Warfield, 2005a).

MLS has seen progress in other broadcast agreements. MLS games have consistently enjoyed strong viewership on Spanish-language stations. As early as 1998, MLS games were the highest rated programming on Univision – drawing a 3.8 rating (Trecker, 1998a). Recently, the league announced additional soccer-specific, regional cable-television and local-radio deals (Brockington, 2003a, 2003b). David Sternberg, Executive Vice President and General Manager of the Fox Soccer Channel (FSC), noted his company's interest in regional broadcasts: 'We think there is a lot of upside. It is going to take time and it's not going to happen overnight, but the indicators are pointing in the right direction' (Warfield, 2005a: 17).

By the 2005 season, between national and regional television deals, 95 per cent of MLS games were broadcast on live television ('General overview', 2005). In addition, MLS attempted to focus media attention on 'Soccer Saturdays', by scheduling 'doubleheaders' throughout the season. While clearly MLS' stature on the US sports' scene has increased, Commissioner Garber anticipated continued growth (Lewis, 2000: para. 7):

> In tie, we should be able to achieve the significant import-
> ance that the other four established sports league have
> achieved. When you look at demographic changes, eth-
> nic changes, and global communication changes that
> are taking place, we believe soccer is poised to capital-
> ize on those ... The question is: When? And our investors
> are committed until that happens. I see no reason why
> we shouldn't be able to achieve some of that signifi-
> cance in time.

Television broadcasts of a league's contests allow for increased market reach and saturation of the league's product (games). Any effort to increase the significant importance and perceived value of a league's brand is influenced by the stadium aesthetics, including perceived crowd size and fan enthusiasm at its games (Southall et al., 2005). It is not essential that games are played in massive stadiums, but it is important that facilities appear to be near capacity and that fans are engaged. Since MLS per-game attendance (an average of 15 008 from 1996–2004) is appreciably less than the capacity of most major professional/collegiate 'football' stadiums, the construction of smaller, soccer-specific stadiums is critical if MLS crowds are to overcome being overwhelmed, or lost, in such cavernous facilities (Canevari, 2005). MLS attendance has been sufficient to sustain the league, and compares favourably to NBA and National Hockey League (NHL) figures (Canevari, 2005). In fact, MLS' attendance growth has outpaced that of the NBA during its early years. MLS commissioner Don Garber has noted that it took the NBA over twenty-nine years before it exceeded 10 000 in average game attendance (Trecker, 2000). The league's attendance figures are more significant, considering that MLS clearly cannot market itself as the world's premier professional soccer product (Trecker, 1998b).

In addition to the construction of new, soccer-specific facilities, the acquisition and retention of star players, which in turn leads to higher quality games, appears to be critical to MLS attendance. Quality teams with star players (i.e. winning teams), including the Colorado Rapids, DC United and LA Galaxy, more often draw larger crowds. Conversely, despite initial promise and a large Latino fan-base, a poor 2–14–3 record to start the 2005 season resulted in poor attendance figures of 17 080 per game for Chivas USA (Warfield, 2005d). Although Chivas had the fourth highest MLS attendance, it was anticipated that the team would potentially lead the league.

Since MLS generates more revenue from sponsorships than from media contracts, sponsorship is a critical revenue component (Sweet, 2001f). From its inception, the league has successfully attracted corporate sponsors. In 1996 alone, sponsors committed over $80 million – an average of $2 million per sponsorship (*Sport Business Journal*, 1998; Trecker, 1998a). According to Tom Haidinger, MLS Vice President of Corporate Partnerships, the league's success in sponsorship acquisition and retention is due to dedicating staff resources to the task and also a personal-service approach. In a 2001 interview, Haidinger declared, 'We're going out and sitting down with every one of our clients' (Sweet, 2001f). MLS annually generates $20 million from sponsorships, and has a 90–100 per cent renewal rate (Sweet, 2001f). Corporate sponsors include Honda, Kraft, Anheuser Busch and, most recently, adidas – which signed a $150 million deal in 2005 (Warfield, 2005a). Kevin Ross, American Soccer Director for adidas, said 'It's probably one of the biggest (deals) for the entire company in the last three or four years, at least in the US' (Warfield, 2005e: para. 18). Companies, such as Pepsi, that have been involved with MLS since its inception, appreciate the league's unique demographics. John Galloway, Pepsi's Youth Marketing Vice-President, remarked: 'It's about reaching out to an emerging multicultural demographic in the United States. And, of all sports, soccer is a melting pot in terms of the audience that it delivers' (Warfield, 2005a: 17).

One fan demographic group that league and individual team marketing efforts have focused on is the burgeoning US Latino market. By 2000, the 35.3 million Latinos in the US reflected a 58 per cent increase from 1990 figures (Stone, 2001). In order to tap into this market, MLS has implemented 'Hispanic Heritage Nights', which involve pre-match festivals, recognition of local Latino heroes, and donations of a portion of ticket revenues to specific local Latino scholarship funds (Stone, 2001). However, not all marketing efforts toward the Latino population have been success-ful. While the league has successful teams in heavily-populated Latino areas (Los Angeles, Chicago, New York), its marketing strategies were unsuccessful in Miami. MLS Manager of Hispanic Partnerships, Laina de Lima, noted: 'I think people are first and foremost fans of their home country, but our goal is to make them fans of the soccer that they can watch every week in this country – and that's MLS' (Stone, 2001: para. 15).

Since its founding, MLS has repeatedly undertaken new mar-keting efforts in an attempt better to control and direct product distribution. In 2002, AEG, in coordination with MLS, established Soccer United Marketing (SUM) (Warfield, 2005f). SUM was initi-ated to negotiate both Men's and Women's World Cup media con-tracts and establish marketing plans for all aspects of American soccer, particularly MLS' marketing and merchandising activities.

MLS' initial plan for licensed merchandise was to implement a 'slow-growth plan' to prevent unsold inventory accumulation (*SportsBusiness Journal*, 1998). As a result, the league only made $9 million in 1997 – a small sum in comparison to other American sports leagues' merchandising revenues (Trecker, 1998c). However, by 2001, MLS merchandise sales of $50 million suggested an increase in fan loyalty (Graham, 2001). Stu Crystal, MLS Vice-President of Consumer Products, highlighted the league's intention to continue fan loyalty development through increased merchandise sales: 'We want soccer fans to be closer to our game, to wear a DC United or Columbus Crew jersey, and to play with our new ball' (Graham, 2001: 26).

One area in which MLS has been able to generate positive pub-licity and fan awareness is through the development of MLS-asso-ciated youth-soccer camps. The league has established over 1300 youth camps for children five to twelve years of age, and these camps are attended by over 68000 children annually (Bernstein, 2001). In addition, MLS soccer camps are sponsored by Lego®

(manufacturer of children's building blocks and toys). This symbiotic sponsorship agreement is not only a revenue source for MLS, but also allows MLS to build long-term relationships, designed to increase fan awareness and loyalty, with both parents and children (Bernstein, 2001).

The Women's United Soccer Association

In their business plan, the WUSA league founders highlighted several factors they felt supported the league's viability:

- the limited, but steady, growth in men's professional soccer in the United States

- the continued popularity of youth soccer among young girls

- overall strong Women's World Cup attendance (660 000) at various US cities

- a core group of recognizable and marketable female soccer players, led by Mia Hamm, Brandi Chastain and Julie Foudy

(Relive 1999, n.d.; Women's United Soccer Association, 2000b). WUSA founders developed an ambitious five-year business plan predicated on their ability to develop a fan-base sufficient for the league to become a viable television commodity attractive to advertisers and/or corporate sponsors (Women's United Soccer Association, 2000b).

With an eight-team, single-entity structure, the WUSA was the premier women's league in the world, sanctioned by the USSF (Women's United Soccer Association, 2000a). The initial league investor-operators were Jim Robbins-Cox Communications, Amos Hostetter-Pilot House Associates, LLC, Amy Banse-Comcast Corporation, Mel Huey-Time Warner Cable, Jerome Ramsey-Time Warner Cable and John Hendricks-Women's Professional Soccer, LLC (Women's United Soccer Association, 2000b). In addition, founding players had an equity stake in the league and a player representative on the WUSA Board of Governors (Women's United Soccer Association).

Understanding the league would not be profitable initially; WUSA's founders anticipated operational losses of nearly $15 million dollars from 2000 to 2003. However, in September 2003, when the WUSA announced cessation of operations, it was revealed by John Hendricks, CEO of Discovery Communications and one of the league's founders, that 'investors ... found out after the first season that they had $20 million in expenses that were not covered by revenue and realized that gap could not be bridged by increased ticket sales and merchandise sales' (Lee, 2003a: 4). Lynn Morgan, WUSA President, announced the league's demise, saying: 'The original business plan had some revenue assumptions built in that have proven to be unrealistic' (Lee, 2003a: 4). League sources consistently identified that the ingredient preventing the league's survival was its inability to attract corporate sponsors (Fisher, 2003).

WUSA founders anticipated broadcast revenues from a national television contract at $3 million per year for the first four years of league competition (Women's United Soccer Association, 2000b). In 2000, the WUSA signed an initial four-year television broadcast contract with Turner Network Television (TNT) (*CNN Sports Illustrated*, 2000). While the terms of the agreement were not made public, it was reported that the WUSA actually paid TNT to broadcast a total of twenty-two games during the inaugural 2001 season (Isidore, 2003). First-year TNT ratings of WUSA games averaged 0.4, equalling roughly 425 000 households (Lee, 2003a).

Dissatisfied with an irregular TNT broadcast schedule, WUSA executives chose to negotiate an end to the TNT agreement and, prior to the 2002 season, announced a new deal with Paxson Communications Corporation (PAX TV). During the 2002 and 2003 seasons, WUSA games were broadcast during the 4–6 pm Saturday time-slot on PAX. Recognizing that PAX TV did not have the national recognition of TNT, Lynn Morgan still expressed satisfaction with PAX TV as a broadcast partner: 'Our continuation on PAX is also a very positive step. We have a season under our belt where we have had the opportunity to educate our fans on where they can find PAX in their local markets' ('Quotesheet: WUSA season preview', 2003: para. 13). Contrary to league claims, during the 2002 and 2003 seasons evidently only a limited number of fans found WUSA games on PAX TV, since WUSA game broadcasts averaged a 0.1 rating (Lee, 2003a), equating to approximately 100 000 households nationwide.

Upon initial examination, it appeared the WUSA had in place a substantial stable of sponsorship partners and an adequate sponsorship pool from which to draw. With an initial $5 million investments from such companies as Cox Communications, Comcast Corporation, Time-Warner and Discovery Communications, the league appeared to have adopted a *vertical integration* model (i.e. one in which a sport product's creation, marketing and distribution is controlled by a single entity) patterned after those found in other US professional sports. However, since these corporate sponsors were also league founders/investors, the initial investors' capital investments were used to determine the perceived value of anticipated league sponsorship packages.

League founders anticipated being able to secure eight $5 million sponsorship packages from the lucrative beverage, apparel, home improvement, financial services and athletic shoe sponsorship pool characterized by deals between the National Football League and such companies as Pepsi ($560 million over eight years), Gatorade ($384 million over seven years) and Reebok ($250 million over ten years) (Lee, 2003a; Lefton, 2004). However, while initial investors had *equity* in the league, prospective *charter* sponsors were not offered ownership benefits. The few viable large-scale sponsors – or prospective sponsors – were reticent about purchasing $5 million dollar sponsorship packages, recognizing the lack of league equity, the low broadcast numbers and a limited fan base. League attendance figures for 2001 (8104 average per game attendance), 2002 (6957 – a 14.2 per cent decrease over the previous year) and 2003 (6667 – a 4.2 per cent decrease) substantiated these weaknesses (Lee, 2003b). In fact, only Hyundai and Johnson & Johnson purchased $2.5 million charter sponsorships (Lee, 2003a; 'WUSA folds', 2003). Four companies capable of investing in a charter sponsorship (Coca-Cola, McDonald's, Maytag and Gillette) chose to invest only $500 000 annually (Lee, 2003a).

Conclusion

From its inception, the viability of MLS has inextricably been bound to the fact that it is an extremely well-capitalized and well-supported league – in other words, league owners have extremely 'deep pockets'. In 2000, one of the two principal league owners, Philip Anschuntz, was among America's richest individuals (sixth in the Forbes 400), with a net worth of $18 billion (www. Forbes.com, n.d.). In addition to being extremely wealthy, Lamar Hunt is also incredibly committed to US professional soccer, having been involved as both an owner and a proponent since 1967. Prior to his MLS involvement, Hunt had ownership interests in both the United Soccer Association (USA) and the NASL (Harris, 1986). Even though both of MLS' principal investors have deep pockets, the league has consistently maintained a much lower profile among sports-entertainment properties and has not allowed expenses significantly to outpace revenues, thus allowing the league to meet its financial obligations. MLS has implemented strategies similar to those employed by the early NBA and NFL, which built national followings over decades, not a few years. A slow-and-steady approach to MLS expansion, solid capitalization and a decades-long commitment to professional soccer have all contributed to MLS's success. The steady approach to building MLS has seen recent increases in media attention and attendance. The solid ten-year foundation established by the league has resulted in two new investors and new soccer-specific facilities across the US. With new investors and new facilities, the risks of future financial insolvency are diminished. Clearly, the future of MLS, though not secured, is on a solid path of growth and long-term success.

Analysing WUSA marketing efforts involves examining the activation and non-activation of marketing strategies involving two core market sectors: (1) the youth soccer community (soccer moms/dads and female youth soccer players) and (2) adult females – including lesbians. The league's ability to penetrate the youth soccer market was constrained by many young girls (players) and women (soccer mothers) – not being sport entertainment consumers to the same degree as young boys and men, who constitute the primary fan base of the major male professional sport leagues (Eitzen and Sage, 2003; Southall et al., 2005). While the WUSA's marketing efforts did reach members of the youth soccer community, unfortunately these spectators, on average, were only persuaded to attend one to two games per season, resulting in a fan base insufficient to generate ticket revenue to meet league expenses or secure and maintain league sponsors (Southall et al., 2005). In addition, fears of alienating a significant percentage of the youth soccer community impeded significant activation of marketing strategies aimed at the lesbian community (Hollis Kosco, personal communication, 8 April 2002; Eddie Rockwell, personal communication, 21 March 2004).

The WUSA's demise can be traced to a flawed business model, similar to the failed United States Football League (USFL), in which league expenditures far outpaced revenues and committed financial reserves. While the WUSA had secured most, if not all, of the best female soccer players in the world, the league was unable immediately to compete with other established sport/entertainment options, particularly with male sport/entertainment properties. Given the WUSA's cost structure and the marketplaces in which it was located, league investors lacked either the financial ability or the willingness to sustain operations on the 'big-league' level to which they aspired. The WUSA did control player salaries, but was unable or unwilling to keep a tight rein on other associated league expenses. Seemingly blinded by the sight of 90 000 fans in the Rose Bowl for the Women's World Cup finals, the league attempted to buy its way into the US sport consciousness, amassing close to $100 million in operating losses during its three years of existence (Isidore, 2003).

The WUSA's lack of adequate capitalization and its product's diminished perceived value led to exactly the results predicted by exchange theory. As the league attempted to sell sponsorships at reduced rates, prospective sponsors recognized that the ease and availability reflected the lower value of such sponsorships. As a result, existing and prospective corporate partners demanded new, more valued, benefits as part of any new agreement. Unfortunately, the league had no additional valued benefits to offer sponsors. In a last ditch effort to survive, and recognizing its decreased value as a traditional professional sports property, the WUSA attempted to utilize strategic philanthropy as a stop-gap marketing strategy.

As the league continued to be unprofitable, WUSA executives seemed convinced that CRM and strategic philanthropy, which have been used by non-profits to solidify already strong and developed relationships with for-profit corporations, would also work for the league. The league initially positioned itself as a strictly for-profit professional sport league and utilized exchange theory principles. Recognizing that it was not a viable, for-profit entity, the WUSA futilely attempted to switch tactics and utilize strategic philanthropy (LeClair and Ferrell, 2000). What the WUSA failed fully to grasp was that most prospective sponsors or fans did not perceive it as a charitable cause, but simply as a fledgling league struggling to survive. Since the league did not have strong fan or sponsor 'psychic attachment', which established 'male' sport leagues such as the NFL and MLB enjoy, it did not possess a sufficient reservoir of sponsorship goodwill, based upon a history of revenue generation and broadcast reach. As a result, the WUSA could not utilize strategic philanthropy to develop any long-range cooperative ventures with existing or potential sponsors.

While the surge of patriotism surrounding the United States' women's national team's 1999 Women's World Cup victory was remarkable, WUSA founders seemed to confuse (or attempt to use interchangeably) three marketing theories – exchange theory, cause marketing and strategic philanthropy – in developing their business and marketing plans. As can be seen by the demise of the WUSA, fans and sponsors consciously or subconsciously understood the basic premises of exchange theory, and the nuanced difference between philanthropy and strategic philanthropy. As a result, the WUSA was doomed to failure from its inception. The league never made the leap from a novelty item that spectators went to see once a year to a sport that had enough true fans to support it.

The MLS, in addition to having substantially greater capitalization than the WUSA, has seemingly recognized its lower perceived value among both American sports fans and prospective partners. It has operated within the confines of exchange theory and, while it has utilized CRM and strategic philanthropy, it has not resorted to these marketing strategies as the primary tool to insure the league's survival.

Hopefully, in the future the WUSA will be seen as women's professional soccer's equivalent of the men's NASL: a noble but failed experiment that laid the groundwork for a future successful women's league. Currently, it appears MLS has matured into a viable US sports property positioned for continued long-term success.

Bibliography and references

Bernstein, A. (2001). Camps – Lego builds on MLS link, will sponsor camps. *SportsBusiness Journal*, **3(39)**, 4.

Blalock, H. M. and Wilken, P. H. (1979). *Intergroup Processes: A Micro–Macro Perspective*. Free Press.

Brockington, L. (2003a). Chicago Fire, Fox deal for 3 more years. *SportsBusiness Journal*, **5(44)**, 6.

Brockington, L. (2003b). Galaxy will have weekly show on LA radio. *SportsBusiness Journal*, **5(44)**, 7.

Canevari, R. (2005). Canevari: build it and they will come (available at http://www.mlsnet.com/MLS/news/team on 21 October 2005).

Carney, S. (2001). New TV deal gives MLS hope in pivotal year. *SportsBusiness Journal*, **4(49)**, 23.

CNN Sports Illustrated (2000). A league of their own. *CNN Sports Illustrated*, 10 April (available at http://sportsillustrated.cnn.com/soccer/news/2000/04/10/wusa_cities/ on 1 April 2004).

Eitzen, D. S. and Sage, G. H. (2003). *Sociology of North American Sport*, 7th edn. McGraw-Hill.

Fisher, E. (2003). Troubled WUSA folds. *Washington Times* (available at http://www.washingtontimes.com/functions/print.php?storyid=200030916-121457-9052r on 10 December 2003).

Forbes.com. (n.d.). *Forbes 400 Richest in America – 2000* (available at http://www.forbes.com/lists/home.jhtml?passListId=54&passYear=2000&passListType=Person 6 August 2005).

Frank, M. (2001). Demographics, not ratings, the focus of national broadcast renewal talks. *SportsBusiness Journal*, **3(46)**, 23–24.

Fraser v. MLS, 284 F.3d 47; 2002 US App (2002).

'General overview' (2005) (available at http://www.mlsnet.com/MLS/about/on 30 October 2005.

Graham, S. (2001). Licensed products still a tough sell. *SportsBusiness Journal*, **3(46)**, 26.

Harris, D. (1986). *The League: The rise and decline of the NFL*. Bantam Books.

Howard, D. and Crompton, J. (2004). *Financing Sport*, 2nd edn. Fitness Information Technology, Inc.

Isidore, C. (2003). Cup no kick for women's soccer. *CNN Money* (available at http://money.cnn.com/2003/09/19/commentary/column_sportsbiz/sportsbiz/ on 1 April 2004).

Kuzma, J. R., Shanklin, W. L. and McCally, J. F. (1993). Number one principle for sporting events seeking corporate sponsors: meet benefactor's objectives. *Sport Marketing Quarterly*, **2(3)**, 27–32.

LeClair, D. T. and Ferrell, L. (2000). The role of strategic philanthropy in marketing strategy (available at http://www.e-businessethics.com/lf/strategic.html on 9 June 2004).

Lee, J. (2003a). Thin ratings, lack of sponsors trip WUSA. *SportsBusiness Journal*, **6(22)**, 4–5.

Lee, J. (2003b). WUSA to seek individual owners. *SportsBusiness Journal*, **6(16)**, 1, 29.

Lefton, T. (2004). Reebok, NFL near 10-year renewal deal. *Sports Business Journal*, **7(2)**, 1, 34.

Lefton, T. (2005). MLS investors see their sport at 'tipping point'. *SportsBusiness Journal*, **7(47)**, 32–33.

Lewis, M. (2000). Major League Struggle – Major League Soccer. *Soccer Digest* (available at http://www.findarticles.com/p/articles/mi_m0FCN/is_5_23/ai_67492177 on 30 October 2005).

Lisi, C. (2002). The man behind the curtain: patience is most certainly a virtue for MLS's mysterious patriarch Philip Anschutz. *Soccer Digest* (available at http://www.findarticles.com/p/articles/mi_m0FCN/is_4_25/ai_92201934 on 24 October 2005).

Litterer, D. (2003a). The American soccer history archives (available at http://www.sover.net/~spectrum on 19 February 2004).

Litterer, D. (2003b). North American Soccer League (NASL) 1967–1984 (available at http://www.sover.net/-spectrum/nasl/naslhist.html, 25 October 2005).

McCarville, R. E. and Copeland, R. P. (1994). Understanding sport sponsorship through exchange theory. *Journal of Sport Management*, **8(2)**, 102–114.

National Soccer Hall of Fame (n.d.). *American Soccer History Timeline* (available at http://www.soccerhall.org/history/us_soccer_history.htm on 16 September 2005).

Plagenhoef, S. (2003). MLS must invite others to invest in its future (available at http://www.findarticles.com/p/articles/mi_m0fCN/is_3_26/ai_106143229 on 24 October 2005).

Polonsky, M. J. and Macdonald, E. K. (2000). Exploring the link between cause-related marketing and brand building. *International Journal of Nonprofit and Voluntary Sector Marketing*, **5**, 46–57.

Pringle, H. and Thompson, W. (2001). *Brand Spirit: How cause-related marketing builds brands*. Wiley Publishing, Inc.

Quotesheet: WUSA season preview (2003). Available at http://www.cnnsi.printthis.clickability.com/pt/cpt?action=cpt&expire=&urlID=5896951&fb=Y on 10 December 2003.

Relive 1999 (n.d.). Available at http://www.fifaworldcup.yahoo.com/03/en/d/fottball/1999/overview.html on 12 May 2004.

Schoenfeld, B. (2003). Hunt owns a legacy as a sports innovator. *SportsBusiness Journal*, **5(44)**, 1, 28–29.

Southall, R. M., Nagel, M. S. and LeGrande, D. (2005). Build it and they will come? The Women's United Soccer Association: a collision of exchange theory and strategic philanthropy. *Sport Marketing Quarterly*, **14(2)**, 158–167.

SportsBusiness Daily (2005). Politically motivated? RSL to build new stadium in Sandy. *SportsBusiness Daily* (available at http://www.sportsbusinessdaily.com/index.cfm?fuseaction=print Article.main&articleId=97566 on 12 October 2005).

SportsBusiness Journal (1998). Q&A: Doug Logan. *SportsBusiness Journal*, **1(6)**, 32–33.

Stone, D. (2001). Pledge of allegiance – attracting Hispanic Americans to Major League Soccer (available at http://www.findarticles.com/p/articles/mi_m0FCN/is_3_24/ai_76 487121 on 26 October 2005).

Stotlar, D. K. (2001). *Developing Successful Sport Sponsorship Plans*. Fitness Information Technology, Inc.

Sweet, D. (2001a). Anschutz group buys rights to Metrostars, its fifth MLS team. *SportsBusiness Journal*, **4(32)**, 39.

Sweet, D. (2001b). Anschutz a rock for MLS. *SportsBusiness Journal*, **4(35)**, 44.

Sweet, D. (2001c). MLS cuts to save investors $10M. *SportsBusiness Journal*, **4(39)**, 3.

Sweet, D. (2001d). Anschutz has soccer world at his feet. *SportsBusiness Journal*, **4(49)**, 21, 24.

Sweet, D. (2001e). Can we have business that succeeds? *SportsBusiness Journal*, **4(30)**, 21, 27.

Sweet, D. (2001f). MLS applies personal touch to court sponsors during tough economic times. *SportsBusiness Journal*, **4(30)**, 24.

'The golden era, 1921–1933' (2005). Available at http://www.soccer-for-parents.com/us-soccer-history2.html on 23 October 2005.

Trecker, J. (1998a). Soccer gets its foot in the door. *SportsBusiness Journal*, **1(6)**, 19–21.

Trecker, J. (1998b). Problems, losses mounting for MLS. *SportsBusiness Journal*, **1(26)**, 17.

Trecker, J. (1998c). MLS' brief history: hits and misses. *SportsBusiness Journal*, **1(6)**, 22–23.

Trecker, J. (2000). MLS Commissioner says remember the NBA when looking at attendance. *SportsBusiness Journal*, **3(16)**, 20.

Trecker, J. (2002). Cup and cuts brighten the outlook for MLS. *SportsBusiness Journal*, **5(32)**, 5.

'US soccer history' (2005). Soccer for parents (available at www.soccer-for-parents.com/us-soccer-history5.html on 24 October 2005).

Warfield, S. (2004). Home improves Galaxy sponsorships. *SportsBusiness Journal*, **7(10)**, 38.

Warfield, S. (2005a). Playing to win. *SportsBusiness Journal*, **7(45)**, 17.

Warfield, S. (2005b). Labor deal boosts MLS salaries (available at http://sportsbusinessjournal.com/index.cfm?fuseaction=article.printArticle&articleId=45984 on 24 October 2005).

Warfield, S. (2005c). Donovan's return a kick for league. *SportsBusiness Journal*, **7(47)**, 33.

Warfield, S. (2005d). Slow start on the field hinders MLS' Chivas (available at http://www.sportsbusinessjournal.com/index.cfm?fuseaction=search.show_article&articleId=46186&keyword=yearly, per cent20attendance, per cent20figures, per cent20mls on 25 October 2005).

Warfield, S. (2005e). Selling soccer. *SportsBusiness Journal*, **7(45)**, 32.

Warfield, S. (2005f). SUM of all parts: marketing arm boosts awareness of soccer. *SportsBusiness Journal*, **7(45)**, 30.

'WUSA folds' (2003). Available at http://www.soccergamenight.com/wusa/news2003/0915folds.htm on 24 October 2003.

Women's United Soccer Association (2000a). *Coca-Cola and WUSA Women's United Soccer Association: A charter partnership preview*. Author.

Women's United Soccer Association (2000b). *Memorandum*. Author.

Zimbalist, A. (2005). Single entity ownership too simple to solve NHL's complex problems. *SportsBusiness Journal*, **7(46)**, 23.

Appendix 13.1

Meeting with Eddie Rockwell, Former Vice President (Operations) of Columbus Crew (MLS), and Former General Manager of Atlanta Beat (WUSA)

Q1: In your opinion, what is the current state of professional soccer in the United States?

ER: There are really two states of soccer in the United States. Women's professional soccer is unfortunately non-existent. Although there is the W-league, few of the players are actually paid. Most of the US professional soccer players are playing in Europe or Japan. Although women's amateur soccer is still very popular in the US, there are no true professional leagues.

Men's professional soccer is still growing and progressing. Although it took a few steps back with some teams folding a few years ago, a few have been added recently. There is optimism, as some teams are making a profit. There is still a need to grow, but there are signs of a positive future.

Q2: Do you see the growth of men's soccer ever reaching the level of American professional baseball, football, or basketball?

ER: It will probably not ever reach that level in this country, but it doesn't need to in order to be considered highly successful. If you look at the model for Major League Soccer right now, teams are building stadiums that seat 20 000–25 000 people, not the 60 000-seat facilities for baseball or football. They are developing a model where success is measured by filling smaller facilities. What is especially encouraging for the MLS is the potential for a better television deal. ESPN saw that MLS ratings were better than NHL (hockey) ratings, so instead of paying the NHL $100 million for the rights, they went after the MLS rights for considerably less money. I don't think they will get to the level of baseball and certainly not the NFL, but hockey maybe.

Q3: What has enabled the MLS to build, sustain, and achieve the success they have?

ER: It starts with a long-term outlook. They had committed owners (not very many of them) like Lamar Hunt, Phil Anschuntz and Robert Kraft as the primaries. They were willing to withstand losses over a long period of time because they had the vision to see that there was success around the corner, and the key to that is building stadiums where you control the revenue. So they recognized that early on and eventually got some of those stadiums built or in the final planning stages to be constructed. Once those stadiums have been built, it changes the financial outlook for the team. When I was with the Columbus Crew, we didn't turn a profit in the first year in the new stadium, but we came very, very close to turning a profit. When the other owners saw what Lamar Hunt was able to do with that, their commitment to build their own stadiums was higher than ever. Los Angeles now has its own stadium, Dallas has its own stadium, Chicago and New York both have new stadiums coming on-line. New England actually does not need to build one because Kraft already owns the stadium there and they already have that revenue model in place. Although it has 70 000 seats (The NFL's New England Patriots also play there), they do not have to fill it to be profitable. Every team has either built, is in the planning stages to build, or is trying to devise a way to build a new stadium.

Q4: Do you think other sports investors are going to look at Kraft, Anschuntz and Hunt and want to be involved with the MLS in the future?
ER: Yes, I think that they have built a good model that will attract future investors. Much of the most difficult work in starting the league has been completed. Now they need to continue to build upon that initial vision and attract other investors to provide a wider financial base.

Q5: The MLS is still growing and getting stronger, and you mentioned the importance of facilities. What other areas provide the best opportunities for growth? What things should they be doing?
ER: In the very short term, the United States needs to be successful in the 2006 World Cup. The US performance (reaching the quarterfinals in 2002) generated great exposure for the sport and demonstrated the ability of the league to develop stars who could play at the highest international level. If they can repeat that success and get to the quarterfinals, then that would be a great short-term accomplishment for all of US soccer. In the long term, the MLS needs to continue to develop players as well as sign international players from different countries. The MLS needs to develop stars as well as bring in enough international stars so that people who are here from other countries can follow their hometown heroes, if you will. Then the quality of play on the field will improve and hard-core soccer fans become part of the marketing mix as they are a potential fan segment the MLS is not reaching, since too many other leagues currently have a higher quality soccer product. Those people are certainly not the only ones that MLS needs to attract, but they are an important part of the mix. With FOX Soccer Channel and Gol TV and some of the Hispanic channels, like Telemundo and Univision, televising games, it is critical to have a high-quality product to position the MLS as a player in the professional soccer landscape. Currently, I think that the MLS is

at least as good, if not better, than most of the Central and South American leagues, but when we have been able to broadcast games from English, Italian, Spanish and German leagues, viewers in the US notice the difference in quality of play. A person can watch ten games a week now without having to pay much for it and the difference in the quality of play is significant. So when they can improve their quality of play to a level where people are satisfied watching that instead of having to watch other leagues to see the highest quality of soccer, that will help a lot.

Q6: With the facilities completed and the emphasis on signifi-cantly raising the quality of play in place, what other marketing challenges does MLS face?
ER: Certainly developing sponsorships is a key point of empha-sis. When [Commissioner] Don Garber took over he made a lot of changes quickly that helped a lot. The approach for marketers will be to maximize sponsorship dollars at the new facilities. The MLS needs to continue to build a core sponsorship base and then enhance it by expanding into different categories.

Q7: With soccer not having a tremendous historical following in the US, what must MLS do to help change the culture?
ER: The MLS's biggest future challenge will be the same issue that soccer has faced here for thirtyyears: turning younger players who stop playing after high school into fans. Soccer is arguably the largest participation sport in the US, and is certainly the largest from a team-sport standpoint. Historically, many of the younger soccer players have not had the opportunity to consume soccer as a fan since US professional soccer has not been successful until recently. The MLS needs to figure out how to turn those kids who stop play-ing soccer into fans when they get older. The biggest challenge there is tradition. The tradition of Major League Baseball and the NFL is amazing. The NFL just had two days of live coverage of their player draft. The MLS will certainly not have that type of attention, but if they can capture the interest of the hundreds of thousands of kids who play soccer, they could really build their brand. So many more kids play soccer than [American] football, but the consumption of football is enormous. Soccer needs to estab-lish just a small piece of that type of tradition.

Q8: What specific actions will MLS take to attempt to make that a reality?
ER: The development has begun with soccer leagues and families with kids playing soccer. The goal has to be to create soccer fans and soccer consumers who follow the sport at the professional level with a passion. The MLS has been focusing money and atten-tion to attract soccer leagues to MLS games. They have also tried to

generate excitement for the games. It's a matter of getting the kids to tell their parents that is what they want to do and providing a family-driven experience when they go to a game. Those fans must have a great experience once they attend a game. If the league can improve the quality of play to attract the hard-core soccer fan, and change the perception of soccer as a viable consumer sport among kids and parents, then attendance and viewership will grow. Certainly the MLS must continue to develop the entertainment model that the American sports consumer has come to expect. The MLS has marketed the game, but also has used entertainment to create excitement. During breaks they have promotions, music and other things like that. The casual fan or the parents taking their kids to the game likely needs these types of ancillary activities to keep their interest. But as kids come to more games, they will develop a greater understanding and appreciation for watching the sport. And certainly as the MLS increases the quality of play, fan passion and loyalty will be developed.

Q9: When you were working with the Crew how did you determine your level of success?
ER: Success really is the financial bottom line when you look at it from the ownership standpoint. But you certainly build in other areas that are components of the bottom line. Market penetration is important – having coverage within the market. One of the issues we had with the Crew as well as with the Atlanta Beat was that we had on-field success, as well as 'marketing success' in attracting fans, but the media often would ignore us. Too often the media would focus on other sports that often did not have nearly the attendance numbers we had. It is difficult to be successful when the media isn't following what a significant number of people are following. So often it became an issue that we not only strived to be successful on the field, but we also worked to attempt to market our successes.

Q10: What are some examples of the media challenges?
ER: When we were with the Atlanta Beat, we often outdrew the Atlanta Hawks (of the NBA). But we could not get into the local newspaper or on the local news. It was somewhat of a weird situation because the Hawks were often perceived in the Atlanta market as a struggling franchise that had few fans that actually showed up for games. Meanwhile, we had winning teams and, more importantly, fans who came to our games and by every measure had a good time.

Q11: How, then, do you convince the media that the fans are here?
ER: It's a long-term process, and it is partly about the history of the sport and also the success of the overall league. While we

were doing better drawing fans for selected games, the media was focusing on the overall league and the NBA has a powerful presence in the US, even if the Hawks have not been successful in the Atlanta market. And it was not strictly any one form of media, but they would all pay most of their attention to the traditional four sports. At times it became frustrating, not because we expected or even hoped to get a large media following, but because we knew we had some great stories worth reporting.

Q12: Do you see that media attention changing in the United States?
ER: Yes, you now actually see television paying more attention to a lot of the non-traditional American sports; it is just that there has been a very slow development process for that trend to continue on radio, newspaper or the Internet. Convincing long-time journalists of the potential and the following of what they perceive as a second-tier or third-tier sport or an 'ethnic' or 'female' sport is a challenge. Much of this will only change with time and by convincing younger journalists that soccer is a sport that has 'media' value.

Q13: If the perception of the non-big four sports is slowly changing and the MLS has shown a commitment to assume financial losses until better times arrive, why couldn't the WUSA follow the same model?
ER: Unfortunately, the owners did not anticipate losing as much money as they did. The losses for some of the owners were too great to sustain, as they may have had an unrealistic revenue and expense model. In Atlanta, the local ownership, Cox Enterprises, was dedicated and willing to continue. The difference was that some of the other companies involved, like AOL/Time Warner and Comcast, were publicly owned and were much less willing to withstand the losses in the short term. The financial losses had continued to drop on a league-wide level each year, and I think we were two to four years away from being able to get close to breaking even for some teams and then another two to three years for the entire league. It was unfortunate that the league didn't have an opportunity to get through the initial growing pains and come to a point where they could then attempt to overcome some of the media and marketing issues as MLS has been able to do.

Q14: Besides ownership commitment and financial solvency, what else could have been done differently?
ER: Certainly, any time there is a failure, there are numerous areas that could have been changed. Unfortunately, the league did not develop revenue sources quickly enough, and at the same time was losing too much money. Although there were some successes

at the local level, nationally the league could not afford many of the expenses. It certainly will be many years until another league is attempted, but another women's soccer league would likely need to use a grassroots model rather than a top-down national format. The WUSA's emphasis on paying for national television exposure as well as the production fees associated with it could not be justified. Although some additional sponsorship dollars were generated, it was not nearly enough to cover all of the fees and it quickly became apparent that it was a losing proposition. What also became a problem in sustaining a money-losing operation was the perception of some of those involved. By the time many of the owners realized how much money they were losing and would likely continue to lose, concessions needed to be made. Another issue was the player salaries. While they did take a pay cut from year one to year two, the player representatives tried to put too much pressure on the league from year three to year four to get salaries back up. The league made an offer that increased the salaries, but there was pressure to push that to a level that the ownership group would not approve. Here's a league that has lost $100 million in three years and now has labour issues to deal with as well. I think the ownership group lost patience on that issue. And while I think that the people representing the players thought they were doing the right thing, that position ultimately had a very negative effect and probably contributed to the league's demise. Making this part of the situation more disturbing was that many of our players told me, after the league ceased operations, that they would have played for free. They were upset with how it all shook out. I think a better model, and one that may work in the future, involves players who do not get paid year round. The revenues simply don't justify that approach. So with the large financial losses in multiple areas, it simply became too difficult to keep the league going for an additional year. Professional women's sports is currently a difficult proposition, and even in the case of a more popular sport such as basketball, only the marketing and financial power of the NBA keeps that alive.

Q15: Despite the failure of the WUSA, are there positive things you accomplished with the Atlanta Beat?
ER: Certainly our sponsorship was outstanding. We grew revenues each year and in fact doubled some of our individual sponsor commitments each year. Sponsors had a lot of opportunities to activate with our fans. We also implemented creative marketing plans that attracted fans. One of our greatest achievements was only having to follow through on our 'money-back guarantee' one time. Fans enjoyed their experiences when they arrived, and in fact the one time we refunded money was due to Atlanta traffic

issues rather than our facility or on-field product. Even though you cannot always control the outcome on the field, it was great to have such a successful team. We made the finals two of the three years, and were in the semifinals the other season. We also committed to over 200 player appearances each year and developed strong bonds with the local community. We took pride in providing a great place to watch a game and to be entertained. This was especially valuable for us since we had to take a deteriorating college football stadium and convert it to a soccer venue. In fact, US Soccer nominated our stadium as one of the best venues in the US to watch a soccer game.

Q16: Who were your greatest marketing competitors while you worked with the Beat?

ER: The biggest problem besides the lack of media support was actually people's time. Our typical fan was family oriented and actually had a high household income level. So where many sports have issues with ticket prices being a deterrent; that was not an issue for us. What became a huge challenge for us was getting people to come to multiple games. Market research continually showed that our fans enjoyed their experience, but would rarely come to more than two or three games since they tended to have so many other things to do. In trying to sell for an eleven-game season, we found many fans just did not have, or make, the time to devote to our games, since they had other interests and responsibilities. We needed to develop a following like other traditional sports, but we just didn't have enough seasons to build that following.

Q17: With such an affluent fan base, did you utilize the Internet for marketing purposes?

ER: We actually utilized the Internet extensively. We constantly attempted to expand our database, and we used email blasts extensively. One issue we had was the limit on sending marketing or commercial-related emails to children under the age of fourteen. If we did not know if the child was fourteen years old, we did not take the risk and send an email. This left many names in our database who we never attempted to contact via email. And this was especially difficult because such a large portion of our fan base were kids. We also spent considerable time developing our website and utilized a variety of creative methods to get visitors to return to the website after their initial visit.

Q18: Do you see women's professional soccer ever returning to the United States?

ER: Certainly it could, but it likely will be many years in the future. One issue that anyone attempting to start a women's soccer league should consider is maintaining close ties to the MLS. Unfortunately, when the WUSA was formed, due to ego issues in both leagues, there was little discussion of pooling resources, conducting joint marketing efforts, etc. If another women's league is to be developed, they would greatly improve their potential for success if they would use the knowledge, data, and marketing experience of the MLS. The marketing intelligence of the MLS is too strong to ignore. A new league may have some MLS investors or it might not. It certainly does not need to be called the WMLS, but it should have a close enough relationship that valuable information and resources can be utilized to increase the chance for success.

Marketing of professional soccer in the US: some lessons to be learned

Frank Pons and
Stephen Standifird

Overview

Using secondary data (websites, academic and professional publications) as well as interviews conducted with
two General Managers of US professional soccer teams,
this chapter presents how professional soccer is marketed
in the United States. After a short description of the history
of professional soccer in the US, we discuss specific sports
marketing strategies used by US professional soccer teams'
managers to address issues such as fan loyalty, segmentation and branding issues. In light of the complexity of the

US sports and entertainment market, our discussion shows that US professional soccer leagues have to be far more aggressive in their marketing efforts than is seen throughout much of the world of soccer.

Keywords

segmentation, branding, strategy, fan loyalty, Major League Soccer

Introduction

As a born and raised French soccer-addict and a Midwesterner from Indiana, the authors of this chapter originally shared negative opinions about the potential success of soccer in the United States, albeit for very different reasons. On one hand, the Frenchman was very judgemental when he first moved to North America in 1994. In his mind, as for a lot of Europeans, Americans could not compete in any way with European football. They did not understand or respect football. For instance, how could they dare to rename football 'soccer'? In his mind, there was only one football. It had been played worldwide by millions of people for over a hundred years, and its legends were Pelé, Cruyff and Platini – not Elway, Marino or Smith. On the other hand, the Midwesterner saw soccer in the same light as many Americans – as a participant sport played by young kids and supported by a fleet of soccer parent volunteers. Professional soccer didn't exist in the minds of most Americans, and was considered amateurish at best when compared to real professional sports such as baseball, basketball and American-style football.

What both of us failed to realize at the time is that our positions were the reflection of ignorance and stereotypes. In fact, we totally misevaluated the amazing sports marketing machine that US soccer leagues and professional teams were about to release. The purpose of this chapter is to move away from the traditional on-field comparisons to bring an alternative angle to studying professional European football (henceforth referred to as soccer) in the US. Instead, we focus on marketing strategies pursued by US soccer establishments. Indeed, an on-field performances comparison of US versus European or South American soccer teams and players would be somewhat inappropriate, given that professional soccer is a relatively new concept in the US. Even if American players now play in leagues across the world and the national team regularly performs well during the World Cup, the level of professional football played in the US is still significantly below that of most European leagues. However, the level of sophistication of marketing strategies, the overall business orientation and the tenacity and innovativeness of professional soccer teams in the US could serve as an important benchmark for teams throughout the world whose current survival is based solely on winning seasons or state/local support.

US professional soccer teams compete in one of the toughest sports business environments on the planet. In this environment, professional soccer teams face tremendous competition from other major sports and entertainment offers; they continuously fight for media exposure and sponsorships and, unlike European teams, they face a quasi inexistent loyal fan base. For these teams, marketing cannot be an afterthought; it is critical to their survival.

Using secondary data (websites, academic and professional publications) as well as interviews conducted with the General Managers of the Real Salt Lake (Major League Soccer, MLS) and the Atlanta Beat (former Women's United Soccer Association, WUSA) (see Appendices 14.1 and 14.2), this chapter presents the nature of professional soccer in the US and, more specifically, how professional soccer is marketed in the US. In particular, the chapter describes how two teams envisioned and implemented their marketing strategies in the difficult US context, and how ultimately they fared in their respective markets. The first section of the chapter focuses on the history of professional soccer in the United States. This includes an in-depth description of the Major League Soccer, and also a brief discussion of the now dissolved Women's United Soccer Association (WUSA). In the second section, we discuss specific sports marketing strategies used by US professional soccer team managers to address issues such as fan loyalty, segmentation and branding issues. Finally, we include an integral version of the interviews conducted to write this chapter.

Overview of the US professional soccer leagues

The early years

Professional soccer was launched in the United States in 1967, following the important exposure given to soccer in the English-speaking world after England's 1966 World Cup victory. The first two professional leagues were the Fédération Internationale de Football Association (FIFA)-sanctioned United Soccer League and the unsanctioned National Professional Soccer League (NASL). These two leagues quickly merged into a single entity, keeping the NASL brand name. Despite some early national exposure through the CBS network, the NASL did not draw a lot of followers early on, and television contracts were terminated. In fact, the league was facing huge challenges, as it was trying to sell a sport that was almost unknown – or at least not understood nor appreciated – by Americans. To resolve this issue, the NASL decided to focus on its offering and to alter its product through the 'Americanization' of the rules in an attempt to make the game more exciting for the average American sports fan. For instance, these changes included a countdown clock, a 35-yard offside line, and a shootout to decide matches that ended in a draw. As a short-term result, these changes attracted more fans. However, in the long run, the changes only widened the gap between US soccer and the rest of the soccer football world (Wikipedia, 2006).

Once the league started growing, new franchises were awarded quickly and it reached twenty-four teams in only a few years. This apparent success hid structural issues that would later set the stage for league failure. In fact, this overexpansion brought in owners who did not have a common vision or the knowledge of soccer or sports marketing. It also resulted in the talent level being spread too thin. In addition, several teams in small markets lost huge amounts of money in paying aging stars in an effort to match the success of the Cosmos New York (one of the top franchises that recruited Pelé) and on rental of football stadiums that were way too big for the crowds the teams were able to attract. The average attendance of the league never reached 15 000 spectators. As a result, The NASL suspended its operations in 1984. From 1984 to 1992, the Major Indoor Soccer League (MISL) was the only First Division soccer league operating in the United States. Although successful in a new niche of fans who loved the high pace/intense nature of the games, the MISL was disdained by soccer purists and faced many of the same problems as the NASL. After the MISL folded in 1992 and was replaced by second-tier leagues (the Continental Indoor Soccer League, for example), there was no major First Division league in the United States until the start of Major League Soccer in 1996.

The World Cup effect I: the MLS is born

The MLS started as a condition for the staging of the World Cup 1994 in the United States. The US Soccer Association had to fulfil the FIFA requirement to establish a 'Division 1' professional soccer league to host this event. Therefore, MLS was launched in 1996, with ten teams divided among the Eastern and Western conferences.

During the last ten years the league has been through expansions and contractions, with twelve teams and three geographic divisions in 1998 and ten teams and two conferences in 2001, finally adding Real Salt Lake City and Club Deportivo Chivas USA, a team playing in Los Angeles but owned by Jorge Vergara, President of the club Chivas de Guadalajara in the Mexican professional league (Warfield, 2005a). While the NASL may have failed, it introduced professional soccer to North America and provided lessons for its successor, Major League Soccer. Unlike the NASL's unruly and non-strategic approach, the structural decisions regarding MLS were always made with the overall survival and prosperity of the league in mind. Specifically, the latest expansions were business decisions aimed at tapping into markets with great potential (such as the Hispanic, with the Mexican affiliation and the fast-growing youth market in Salt Lake City). MLS is also expected to expand further in 2007, with the addition of two more teams, including one in Toronto, Canada. Unlike most other soccer nations around the world, there is currently no system of promotion and relegation in the MLS. In fact, such an organization does not exist in any sport in the United States both because of lack of popularity in minor league (except in Baseball) or reserve teams, and strong opposition from top-level managers in professional teams or leagues who fear the loss of control to the uncertainty of sport in deciding which city (or team) would be promoted or relegated.

In addition to the lack of a promotion/relegation system, MLS presents another striking organizational feature. In contrast to most other professional sports leagues in the United States and abroad, MLS is a 'single-entity' organization. In this framework, the league (rather than individual teams) contracts directly with the players, in an effort to control spending and labour costs, share revenue, promote parity and maximize exposure. This organizational model dictates a strong central power that sets practical rules to ensure the league viability and development (Robinson, 2005).

For instance, the full roster for each MLS team is limited to eighteen players, plus a maximum of ten roster-protected (reserve) players. Of the eighteen main players, MLS teams are allowed a maximum of four senior (over the age of twenty-five) international players on their active roster, as well as three youth international players (under the age of twenty-five). These quotas allow prominent names in European football (such as Stoichkov and Djorkaeff) to spend a few years in the MLS, but the rule also prevents the league from being seen as a 'retirement' league for European players. In addition, since several MLS players have signed with wealthier teams in Europe following their stay in MLS, MLS now appears as an opportunity to develop young American players (such as Carlos Bocanegra and DaMarcus Beasley). Most of the players in the league are from the United States, ensuring an outlet for a growing number of young athletes finishing their college years in the National Collegiate Athletic Association (NCAA). The league aims to bank on the unprecedented level of participation achieved in youth sports, as 80 per cent of all soccer players are under eighteen years of age. Soccer is the number one sport in the youth category, with over 15 million participants in the US (*SoccerNova*, 2003). Until recently, the lack of local professional soccer options created a void for young adults, who had to turn to international broadcasts in order to satisfy their soccer interests. MLS hopes to build an attachment with fans in order to allow them a regional offering for quality local professional soccer.

The central decision was made to allow the league to sign a new collective bargain agreement in early 2005. This contract with the players' union set the minimum salary at $US28 000 per year. Still, there are significant salary disparities at both the league and team levels. Table 14.1 features top players' salaries and labour costs for MLS teams (Warfield, 2005b).

Table 14.1
Salaries and payrolls in the MLS in 2005 (US$)

Top 10 MLS players	Salary (US$)
Player guaranteed compensation	
Landon Donovan	900 000
Eddie Johnson	875 000
Freddy Adu	550 000
Ramon Ramirez	500 000
Josh Wolff	420 357
Clint Mathis	410 000
Eddie Pope	378 949
Tony Sanneh	365 000
Chris Armas	325 000
Jovan Kirovski	290 000
Team payrolls	
Team total payroll*	($US million)
Los Angeles Galaxy	2.70
FC Dallas	2.61
Chicago Fire	2.20
DC United	2.17
Real Salt Lake	2.07
Kansas City Wizards	1.76
MetroStars	1.75
Columbus Crew	1.75
Chivas USA	1.73
San José Earthquakes	1.70
Colorado Rapids	1.46
New England Revolution	1.22

Source: Major League Soccer Players' Union document (Warfield, 2005b).

Even though professional soccer in the US has not been able to reach the status of the major professional leagues, the organizational structure of the MLS provides a strong foundation to secure the survival and development of the league in the coming years. By building a solid business model, the league has tried to change stereotypical issues often blamed for the lack of popular success of soccer in the United States. The continual nature of soccer, with relatively few set plays or fixed positions, the low-scoring nature of the game and the perception of soccer as a 'foreign' sport are all negative attitudes that hinder the sport in the US. Consistency, patience and grassroots techniques aim at solving these issues, and MLS is on the right track for a relatively young league only ten years in existence.

The World Cup effect II: the rise and fall of the women's professional league

If soccer became the fastest growing participant sport in the US in 2002, it was mainly because of its popularity among young girls. In fact, female soccer players were estimated to reach 9 million in early 2002, and more than 90 per cent of these players were under eighteen years of age (SGMA, 2002). Partly to reward these high levels of participation and to establish women's soccer, but mainly to open up potential coverage and sponsor deals in the US markets, the FIFA awarded the 1999 Women's World Cup to the United States. This 1999 World Cup was a huge success, drawing more than 660 000 spectators overall and 413 000 for the US games. The US and the entire world came to understand the great potential that women's soccer, played at this level, has.

The 1999 Women's World Cup final, in particular, elevated US players as icons, not only for a generation of young boys and girls but also for the whole country. The players were everywhere, from TV shows to magazines. Attempting to build on their popularity, and despite the fact that the US sport consumers had not been particularly receptive to women's professional sports leagues, the twenty US players sought out the investors, markets and players necessary to form the first USSF-sanctioned, Division 1, professional women's soccer league (Southall *et al.*, 2005). Similar to the MLS, the Women's United Soccer Association (WUSA) was structured as a single entity formed from eight teams. However, the similarity stopped there. The WUSA was structured in a way that gave a tremendous power to the players. In fact, the twenty founding players received an equity stake in the league and a representative on the Board of Directors (Southall *et al.*, 2005). Sponsors and investors rushed to support the league, hoping to tap into the female audience – an audience that traditionally it

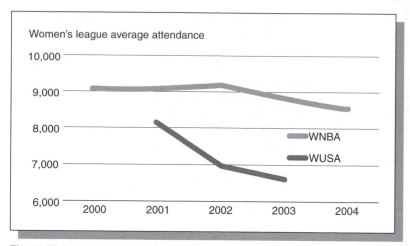

Figure 14.1
Attendance at WUSA and WNBA games, 2000–2004
(*Source: SportsBusiness Journal* research)

has been difficult to reach through major league sports. Using inspiring athletes such as Mia Hamm, the league and sponsors empowered the players, and as a result the league was positioned as a trendy 'first-class' product compared to other major US sports. However, by emphasizing the athletes first it was difficult for the league to build its own identity and brand, as more importance was placed on personal stories than on the competition. This early positioning was a gamble, and significantly different from the conservative approach used by MLS.

The WUSA played for three full seasons, but failed to attract viewers and sponsors or to draw the type of crowds experienced during the Women's World Cup. In fact, the WUSA was never able to achieve the level of attendance experienced by the only other US women's professional sports league, the Women's National Basketball Association (WNBA) (see Figure 14.1). Plagued by huge operating expenses (Figure 14.2), the league suspended its operations in September 2003. There is much conjecture suggesting that the unique business form of the WUSA (especially the central role of players) is what in large measure led to its suspension of operations. There have been several attempts to revive the league, with the latest being the 'Women's Soccer Initiative, Inc.'. The initiative's intention is to 'guide the re-launch of women's professional soccer in the United States'. There is little doubt in the mind of sponsors and former officials of the league that there is a market for professional women's soccer in the US. What is needed is a business approach capable of attracting consumers who are not the usual sport entertainment consumers (i.e. women and children),

Projected Expense	Amount ($)
Projected Player Costs	
Salaries	6,460,000.00
Benefits	1,292,000.00
Total Projected Player Costs	7,752,000.00
Projected League Office Expenses	
Sales & Marketing	
Advertising	2,000,000.00
Corporate Sales	175,000.00
Consumer Products	150,000.00
Sponsor Services	400,000.00
Public Relations	200,000.00
Total Sales & Marketing	2,925,000.00
Administrative	
General Expenses	3,710,100.00
Player Administration	400,000.00
Insurance	200,000.00
Total Administrative	4,310,100.00
Total Projected League Office Expenses	7,235,100.00
Projected Game Day Operations Costs	
Stadium Rental	1,004,500.00
Game Day Expenses	1,274,000.00
Ticket Expense	183,181.00
Other Operating Costs	200,000.00
Total Projected Game Day Operations Costs	2,661,681.00
Total WUSA 2001 Projected League Expenses	17,648,781.00

Figure 14.2
WUSA's projected expenses for 2001
(*Source*: Southall *et al.*, 2005)

thereby establishing a viable niche for the survival and development of a professional women's soccer league (King, 2005).

Marketing at work: where US soccer teams got it right!

The previous section described the US professional soccer leagues in their early stages of development, and in the case of the WUSA through a period of decline. This portrait presents a rather gloomy picture of professional soccer in the US, an industry plagued by financial and organizational issues. Despite these complications, professional soccer in the US has shown a high level of marketing conscience with corresponding strategies designed to conquer the complicated and challenging markets in which it operates. In this section we discuss some of the marketing challenges facing the sport and entertainment industry in the US, and present the approaches used by US professional soccer teams as potential benchmarks for other professional soccer leagues.

Market research and segmentation issues

Understanding consumers' needs is the key to establishing a marketing strategy, and this becomes even more critical when dealing with the complex nature of sporting events (Holt, 1995; Shank, 2002). This approach must enable the creation of an offering, desired by consumers, in order to optimize the sporting event–fan–marketing strategy triad. The fan/consumer must be at the centre of any decision made by marketing managers (Gladden and Funk, 2002).

A sporting event is intangible, short-lived, unpredictable and subjective in nature (Gladden *et al.*, 1998). Yet, despite these unfriendly characteristics, it is actively sought by consumers. This underlines the importance for managers of listening to their consumers and monitoring on a consistent basis their preferences and reactions, particularly in a field as competitive as the sports and entertainment industries. Moreover, fans' segmentation should be taken seriously, as the sport and entertainment business is very fragmented (Richelieu and Pons, 2005). Socio-demographic variables can be used as bases for segmentation, but they should represent the minimum level of sophistication of the segmentation strategies. The analysis of the consumers' specific needs and motives should also be considered. These needs should be monitored on a regular basis so as to avoid moving away from the customer's reality and concentrating on the quest for winning records (which may or may not be of critical importance to customers). Once the needs of customers have been clearly identified, only then should the organization start developing carefully targeted marketing tactics designed to reach specific segments of consumers. In conclusion, sports teams should be managed as real businesses, where marketing is not an afterthought or a simple sales tool. This approach is not usual in most professional soccer teams except for the big European names … and some MLS teams. In fact, many average teams in European leagues do not actively seek information about their consumers, instead assuming that all consumers want the same thing from their experience. Real Salt Lake is an interesting example that shows that some MLS teams have acknowledged the fact that market research is essential to understanding, segmenting and better serving their target market. We had the opportunity to discuss this issue with Steve Pastorino, Real Salt Lake General Manager (see Appendix 14.1). He highlighted for us the importance of the information gathered from consumers and how they implement market research in their organization:

> We are always asking for feedback … we want to hear what they think. We constantly are asking them for ideas, we actually survey not the entire group at once, but

> segments of the group, weekly. We also, through the league, have partnered with a company in Baltimore, called 'Fan Track', to do some surveying ... and we're thinking that this year that we will add a web element instead of just doing in-stadium surveys.

He even admitted that these are only the early steps of a more comprehensive approach to research in his organization. His hope is to add more qualitative research in the future, so as to develop a better understanding of the market.

We were surprised by the level of marketing sophistication at Real compared to other sport business organizations. The information gathered by Real through research enables both Real and the league to have a better understanding of their market. In particular, it allows them to have an accurate description of the different segments that form this market. This, in turn, allows them to develop different marketing tactics that may be used to reach different segments. For instance, the league tracks basic demographics for its fans, and their evolution year after year, to adapt communication campaigns to their national and local markets. Figure 14.3 gives a demographic profile of MLS fans.

We also had the opportunity to discuss marketing strategy with the former General Manager of the Atlanta Beat (WUSA), Eddie Rockwell. He also emphasized the importance of knowing fans better, stating:

> We really drove the family atmosphere more than anything because that was our main demographic, but our secondary demographic was the twenty-one to thirty-five-year-olds of both sexes ... there were a lot of guys down there just having a good time ... However, our first focus was on families, and even more so on families with kids who played soccer. We really learned a lot there, in that we thought that the soccer-playing crowd would be older but it ended up that the under-fourteens were the majority of the fans. Anywhere from six to fourteen, those were the kids that were most active as far as our audience goes, and as soon as they got to be fourteen it wasn't cool anymore ... We did not target women; we did target families and, like I said, the secondary market, the twenty-one to twenty-fives, was really more guys ... I would not say that women were ever our primary target audience, and we did very little to try to market strictly to them.

Careful research and segmentation has helped US professional soccer to fine-tune its approach to specific consumer needs. However, market research is only a part of a full scope marketing and

Scarborough Research surveys consumers in 75 U.S. metropolitan markets on hundreds of demographic and purchasing habits. Among those markets are the 11 that are home to MLS clubs.

For the data presented below, the number listed in each year's column shows the percentage of MLS fans that fits the specific measure. The index columns compare MLS fans within that specific category to the national average. Par equals 100. For example: 21.9 percent of the survey respondents in 2004 who identified themselves as MLS fans are of Spanish/Hispanic origin. That's 64 percent higher than the percentage of the general U.S. population that is of Spanish/Hispanic origin. Conversely, 8.9 percent are African-American, a figure that's 16 percent lower than the percentage of the general population.

	2002 Pct.	Index	2003 Pct.	Index	2004 Pct.	Index
Gender						
Male	61.1	127	60.6	126	61.7	128
Female	38.9	75	39.4	76	38.3	74
Ethnicity						
White	63	88	63.1	89	62.5	89
Spanish/Hispanic origin	20.8	166	21	161	21.9	164
African-American	10.1	91	9.5	86	8.9	84
Asian	3.2	130	3.3	129	3.6	144
Other	2.9	111	3.1	115	3.1	105
Marital status						
Married	55.7	100	54.9	100	55.4	100
Never married (single)	30.5	123	30.5	120	30.9	121
Widowed/separated/ divorced	13.9	71	14.6	75	13.7	72
Age						
18–24	16.6	136	16.4	131	17.7	139
25–34	24.4	131	23.2	125	22.3	122
35–44	24.4	114	23.7	113	23.5	114
45–54	17.3	90	17.7	93	17.7	94
55–64	8.7	71	9.3	75	9.5	74
Age 65+	8.7	53	9.7	59	9.3	56
No. of children in household (17 or younger)						
None	51.1	87	50.7	87	50.8	87
1 or more	48.9	118	49.3	119	49.2	119
2 or more	30.1	125	30	123	29.9	123
3 or more	11.3	126	11.8	129	11.9	127
No. of teenagers in household (ages 12–17)						
None	76	94	76	95	75.8	95
1 or more	24	123	24	120	24.2	121

Figure 14.3
MLS fan demographics
(*Source*: Warfield, 2005a)

branding strategy. The importance of having a clear-cut branding strategy in particular is described below.

Branding issues

Through its brand, a firm creates and manages customers' expectations (Aaker, 1994). A brand is a promise a company makes to its customers, and this promise is built on the coherence and continuity of the brand's products (Kapferer, 2001). Consumers use brand names and product attributes as retrieval cues for information on product performance. A brand is a differentiating asset for a company (Kapferer, 2001), and high levels of brand awareness as well as a positive brand image increases the probability of brand choice, generates higher consumer loyalty and reduces vulnerability to competitive marketing actions (Keller, 1993). Successful brands are able to establish a strong emotional and personal relationship with the customer, and as a result trigger trust and loyalty toward the brand (Richelieu and Pons, 2005). It is only with a clear identity and strong positioning that marketing actions become relevant and can then serve the purpose of leveraging the brand equity of an organization.

For professional sports teams, the power of a brand often determines the degree to which spectators will turn into paying consumers or fans, buying items such as memorabilia or clothing items that enable them to identify publicly with their team (Pons and Richelieu, 2004). The brand also determines the fit with corporate sponsors and thus determines which companies will be willing to pay to associate themselves with the brand (Desbordes *et al.*, 2001). The strength and meaning of any sport franchise is based on the core values (both tangible and intangible) associated with the brand itself. Some franchises are more successful than others in developing an identity based on values that are unique to their brand, and in implementing actions that reflect these values. Real Salt Lake is a good example of a professional team with this marketing and branding vision, which understands that a strong brand identity is critical for the survival of the team and league. For instance, Steve Pastorino stated:

> We want to build a legacy of soccer through a fun, winning world-class organization ... World-class, we don't want to be the best and then the less – that's just not good enough ... we want Real Salt Lake to be the American soccer team that really dominates the scene ... we should also be a leader in gender equity ... girls play soccer just as much as boys, so we have no excuse not to really be a gender-neutral sport and appeal to everybody. This is not a short-term project.

Real Salt Lake puts these words into action by implementing a series of decisions that convey this positioning to the team's fans and the general public. For example, the choice of the name for the team, the equipment and the team presentation routines are all in direct alignment with the brand image chosen by the team owner. These actions are detailed in the interview in Appendix 14.1, but some examples are provided hereafter. As noted by Steve Pastorino:

> we used a very traditional soccer name … Real stands for royalty, it stands for greatness, for certain expectation or aspiration, so Dave made it very clear from his expectation of how we present ourselves publicly, whether it's what the fans experienced with customer service, with the stadium, with the high-end hospitality, with affordable tickets for young families … It has to be first-class … The colors are traditional, very rich and bold. Through the consistent way in which we presented the name, we introduced the jersey, we introduced the team on opening day, and we decorated the stadium, I think our fans are sort of caught up in it without really realizing that we had a master plan. All these things became a reflection of what we are trying to do.

If the case of Real Salt Lake shows how effective branding can be implemented through a great vision, adequate media coverage and appropriate actions, branding strategies at the league level (MLS) are only slowly coming around. This situation is often the opposite in Europe, where only prominent leagues (such as the English Premier League, the Spanish Liga, the Calcio in Italy or clubs such as Real Madrid, Manchester United and other G14 clubs) have picked up on the importance of branding and have gained fame through strong central branding leadership. This approach has left some of the more average clubs/leagues in a branding no man's land. In the US, MLS does not lead branding efforts. Clubs are the driving force, and the league is urged to follow for the overall development of professional soccer. Steve Pastorino noted:

> MLS doesn't have the history, tradition or respect of all these other leagues, people are realizing that is a very viable business partner but we need huge branding effort on the league's part domestically or internationally.

Poor media coverage contributes to the weak exposure and positioning of the MLS brand on the national sport scene. However, a recent agreement for 2007 with broadcasters ABC/ESPN and

Univision may help to increase MLS's visibility and facilitate branding actions.

The case of the Atlanta Beat and the WUSA also provides important insight into the importance of branding for professional soccer teams. The failure of the WUSA has been mainly attributed to the financial burden that the league organization was carrying. However, as suggested by Eddie Rockwell, poor branding may also have been one of the reasons for the disappearance of the league:

> [about branding, having a brand strategy/identity] I think that is something we tried to constantly discover, and I think the main part of the brand was fun, entertainment, family-oriented, world-class athletes. I mean we had the best athletes in the world on our field, so those were the key focuses. I can't speak for the league as much, because I think they were striving. I think it was very similar, but I think different teams approached it differently. I think that was part of the problem at the beginning. Each team was trying to identify exactly what the league brand was, and I think that was one reason they made the change at the top of the management structure.

In fact, it seems that the Atlanta Beat was one of the most successful teams in the league because they had at least a general idea of what their brand identity was. They delivered this fun, entertainment, family-oriented positioning. Eddie Rockwell went on to suggest that:

> Game day experience was everything to us … We had everything you can imagine: face-painters, balloon clowns, all kinds of interactive games … You know all the entertainment factors, the music, everything from how you introduce a team to how the game ends … it was all a scripted show … We tied a lot of sponsorship elements into that. People on stilts and anything we could do to entertain the kids … and it was all free … We even had, in our second season, a beer garden down on the field behind one of the goals, which was a lot of fun. We did it intentionally away from where the families were sitting so people could choose to be there or not … The game was not secondary by any means, and it was certainly the primary thing that was going on, but we had to have a lot of ancillary activities to keep people entertained … I think, our crowd was not the type that you would find in a European soccer market where they come strictly to watch the game … In fact … if you watched everybody as

they left the stadium and you looked at their faces, you would have no idea that we had lost a game ... Sport entertainment, that's what it was.

This reinforces the importance of brand identity and positioning. Regardless of the identity chosen, if the market is receptive and the team is able to deliver this positioning, the team may be able to prosper or at least survive. Each team should be able to develop its individual brand to rally consumers and fans behind its values. Only a few soccer teams in the world can claim to have developed a strong global brand identity (for example, Chelsea FC, Real Madrid and FC Barcelona). Most of the teams that have developed a strong brand internationally have done so through a history of winning performance. However, only a handful of teams can effectively adopt the same high-class, traditional winning positioning. It is critical to follow the example of Real Salt Lake and to develop a particular identity if the team wants to prosper. That identity need not (and in many cases cannot) be based solely on winning performance. Regardless, offering an identity around which fans can rally is the first step toward building loyalty.

Loyalty issues

In consumer behaviour, loyalty is a 'deeply held commitment to rebuy or repatronize a preferred product/service consistently in the future' (Oliver, 1999). Loyalty is a key component of studies dealing with customer retention (Dick and Basu, 1994). Retention costs are estimated to be five times less than the costs of new customer acquisition (Fornell and Wernerfelt, 1987). Thus, increasing loyalty usually leads to higher profits. In the context of sporting events, loyalty has been shown to depend on variables such as consumers' identification with the team (Wakefield, 1995; Funk, 1998) and commitment to it (Bee *et al.*, 2003).

Developing loyalty and turning spectators into avid fans and season-ticket holders are key priorities for US professional soccer teams. Loyal fans provide a steady flow of revenue, and guarantee the stadium atmosphere and experience to newcomers. Once again, in this area MLS teams appear to understand that spectators will only become fans if they are involved in the team/brand and find ways to increase their commitment to the team. The creativity used by Real Salt Lake and the Atlanta Beat are good examples that may be adopted by teams around the world. As noted by Steve Pastorino:

We develop strong ties and relationship with the community through personalized events ... We've done a lot of these, you can call them whatever you want – grass-roots events, town hall meeting types – but I think that's been one of our points of difference – when 300 people take their lunch hour and come to these offices, just to be with other soccer fans, buy merchandise and watch the World Cup Draw, which you can do on your computer… it's a great sign that people care about us … The access that we provide to our fans from our owners, our CEO, our GM, our coaches, our players is very different from what other professional teams offer to this community and, I think, very different from what the other MLS teams offer, and that's just something that helped us cement a quicker, stronger bond with our fans. … I really think that we can build a fan base one at a time like that, and I do it, and I encourage my staff to do it. Most time people want to have a relationship with the team, they don't just want to write cheques, they want to get something in return, they want to voice their opinions, they want to say the coach is terrible or the striker needs to be replaced, or whatever …

Eddie Rockwell also described some of the actions undertaken by the Atlanta Beat:

How do we get the person that's coming to four of five just to come to the whole season? We had to really strive to come up with extra benefits for our season-ticket holders. The last two years we had fan parties at the stadium where we would bring all the season-ticket holders on a day after a game to come down to the stadium to play games with the players down on the field.

These approaches require a certain level of proximity between fans, players and team management that might not be appropriate for all sports franchises. What's important here is the emphasis placed on fan involvement. This involvement could take a variety of forms. The key is to develop ways for fans to become connected to the team brand, thereby turning average fans into loyal customers.

Lessons to be learned from professional soccer in the US

Major League Soccer has yet to gain significant market share in the complicated US sports market. It may be years before soccer becomes a significant spectator sport in the US, if it ever does. It would be tempting to conclude from the lack of success in the US market that there is little to be learned from US professional soccer leagues; however, it would be a mistake to make such an assumption. In fact, the complexity of the US market has forced US professional soccer leagues to be far more aggressive in their marketing efforts than is seen throughout much of the world of soccer.

In our discussion with the managers of professional soccer franchises in the US, we discovered that the franchises have been very focused on the marketing side of their business. Specifically, these franchises have been quite proactive in performing basic market research by listening to customers and segmenting their markets accordingly. Real Salt Lake specifically has been diligent in its efforts to create a uniform franchise brand. Everything the franchise does, from ticket pricing to the use of team colours, revolves around its branding efforts. Perhaps most importantly, these franchises see fan involvement as being critical to their long-term success. As noted by Steve Pastorino, 'people want to have a relationship with the team, they don't just want to write cheques, they want to get something in return'. The focus is on making a connection with fans so as to develop a cadre of customers that will be with the team for better or for worse.

Perhaps Americans will never be able to compete at the same level as Europeans in the arena of soccer, and it's entirely possible that Americans will never develop the same level of respect for soccer that there is in Europe. There is little doubt that soccer will continue to be an important participant sport for young children and that soccer parents will continue to play an important role in the evolution of soccer in the US. However, based on our interview with managers from US professional soccer franchises, we have come to realize that none of this precludes the development of professional soccer in the US. In fact, by understanding the importance of market research and branding, and by focusing on customer involvement, US professional soccer franchises have distinguished themselves in the world of spectator sports. Moreover, while the level of play in the US may never match that of Europe, the level of professionalism seen in the marketing of US professional soccer is something to be noticed throughout the world.

Acknowledgements

The authors would like to thank the Real Salt Lake organization (most particularly Steve Pastorino, Trey Fitz-Gerald and Greg Zaskowski) and Eddie Rockwell for their participation in this work. They would also like to thank Richard Southall and Matt Shank for their help in securing interviews.

Bibliography and references

Aaker, D. A. (1994). *Le management du capital-marque: analyser, développer et exploiter la valeur des marques*. Dalloz.

Bee, C., Jones, S. and Stinson, J. (2003). *Loyal Spectators: The Mediating Role of Psychological Commitment and Resistance to Change*. AMA Proceedings.

Desbordes, M., Ohl, F. and Tribou, G. (2001). *Marketing du sport*, 2nd edn. Economica.

Dick, A. S. and Kunal, B. (1994). Customer loyalty: toward an integrated conceptual framework. *Journal of the Academy of Marketing Science*, **22(2)**, 99–113.

Fornell, C. and Wernerfelt, B. (1987). Defensive marketing strategy by customer complaint management: a theoretical analysis. *Journal of Marketing Research*, **24(4)**, 337–347.

Funk, D. (1998). Fan loyalty: the structure and stability of an individual's loyalty toward an athletic team. Doctoral dissertation, The Ohio State University. *Dissertation Abstracts International*.

Gladden, J. M. and Funk, D. (2002). Developing an understanding of brand associations in team sport: empirical evidence from consumers of professional sports. *Journal of Sport Management*, **16(1)**, 54–81.

Gladden, J. M., Milne, G. R. and Sutton, W. A. (1998). A conceptual framework for evaluating brand equity in Division I college athletics. *Journal of Sport Management*, **12(1)**, 1–19.

Holt, D. B. (1995). How consumers consume: a typology of consumption practices. *Journal of Consumer Research*, **22(1)**, 1–16.

Kapferer, J.-N. (2001). Is there really no hope for local brands? *Brand Management*, **9(3)**, 163–170.

Keller, K. L. (1993). Conceptualizing, measuring, and managing customer-based brand equity. *Journal of Marketing*, **57(1)**, 1–22.

King, B. (2005). What's up with women's sports? *SportsBusiness Journal*, **25 April**, 18.

Oliver, R. L. (1999). Whence consumer loyalty? *Journal of Marketing* (Special Issue), 33–44.

Pons, F. and Richelieu, A. (2004). Marketing stratégique du sport: le cas d'une franchise de la Ligue Nationale de Hockey (LNH). *Revue Française de Gestion*, **30(150)**, 161–174.

Richelieu, A. and Pons, F. (2005). Reconciling managers' strategic vision with fans' expectations. *International Journal of Sport Marketing & Sponsorship*, **6(3)**, 150–163.

Robinson, M. (2005). Interview with Don Garber, MLS Commissioner. *Sport Marketing Quarterly*, **14(2)**, 69–70.

SGMA International (2002). Youth reigns supreme in the world's sport (available at http://www.sgma.com/press/2002/press 1023217230-10882.html).

Shank, M. (2002). *Sports Marketing: A Strategic Perspective.* Prentice Hall.

SoccerNova (2003). Youth Soccer in the USA structure (available at http://www.soccernova.com/working/youth.htm).

Southall, R. M., Nagel, S. M. and LeGrande, D. J. (2005). Build it and they will come? The WUSA: a collision of exchange theory and strategic philanthropy. *Sport Marketing Quarterly*, **14(3)**, 159–167.

Wakefield, K. A. (1995). The pervasive effects of social influence on sporting event attendance. *Journal of Sport and Social Issues*, **19**, 4.

Warfield, S. (2005a). Playing to win. *SportsBusiness Journal*, **21 March,** 17.

Warfield, S. (2005b). Labor deal boosts salaries. *SportsBusiness Journal*, **11 July**, 6.

Wikipedia (2006). (available at http://www.answers.com/topic/major-league-soccer).

Appendix 14.1

Interview with Steve Pastorino, General Manager of Real Salt Lake (MLS)

Q1: Could you please briefly describe your professional background/career path?

SP: I attended Northwestern University in Chicago. I studied journalism. While I was in college, I considered a career in newspapers, a career in television, a career in radio, and after I spent some time in each one, I decided I didn't want to do that. I got my start in minor league baseball at the recommendation of several friends who were working in the sport. I spent six years in California leagues, and I think that minor league baseball is a fantastic learning experience with a very small staff, a very limited budget. You learn to do everything on your own. With most of the teams, we had no advertising budget, so you figure out ways to be creative and get the word out. After six years of that, I felt I was ready for a bigger challenge and I wanted to get back to a big city. The Chicago Fire (MLS) was just starting so I contacted Peter Wilt, and by the end of the first conversation he told me I was hired. I hadn't even sent him a resumé and I hadn't even talked about money, timing and relocation. So for seven years I put everything I had into the Fire. My initial scope was marketing, advertising and sponsorship sales. I sort of took it as a personal mission to be the brand builder/brand organizer because we had some very talented people, but everybody had their own idea of what the team was going to be. And nobody was trying to put it all together. By the end of the seventh year, I was also overseeing broadcasting, much of the sales, including tickets, most aspects of the business, and I had spent as much as five years working out of four different stadium projects. I didn't know what the next opportunity would be. I considered leaving sports. I considered different industries. Then Salt Lake was announced, it was an expansion team so I came here for the opportunity to run the ship.

Q2: So what is your business? How would you describe that? Is it sports? Is it entertainment?

SP: I have always considered it as a lot of promotion, like Barnum & Bailey's circus is a promotion ... like Cirque de Soleil is entertainment ... it's not just about soccer. What differentiates soccer from the circus or arena football is that the game has a hundred plus years of history. It also has a rich history in this country. There's a tremendous level of participation among kids, but, unless you use every tool you have to get the word out, use every ability in your organization to sell and build the relationships, you will not succeed. Then, once you've got people hooked, you've got to entertain them and keep them coming back. So there's a great aspect of entertainment. Think about music and mascots, what you see when you walk about to the stadium, what you feel when you're sitting in the stands … so it's all of that. In a start-up environment like we've got here, you also have to build up a brand and decide what you're going to be, and what you're going to stand for. Fortunately, we have a very visionary owner who has been at this for a long time, and has a track record for what he wants to stand for and has a name that we can kind of rally around.

Q3: Would you say that you have a formalized marketing strategy in your organization? Could you please describe this strategy in few words?
SP: Our mission statement is to build a legacy of soccer through a fun, winning world-class organization. We want to win. World-class, we don't want to be the best and then the less – that's just not good enough. We don't want to be the most exciting team in Utah. We want to be the name on the tip of people's tongues everywhere. At some point in the future … five years, ten years, twenty years from now, we want Real Salt Lake to be the American soccer team that really dominates the scene. We want to belong up there with the great clubs of the world, for whatever reason, business, on-field success … we want to build a legacy. This is not a short-term project. We're still very much at the beginning of things, but our sport in general tends to be more youthful in this country than some of the other major sports. We should also be a leader in gender equity … girls play soccer just as much as boys, so we have no excuse not to really be a gender-neutral sport and appeal to everybody. I think as a league and as a team, we should be a little bit cutting-edge or modern or advanced or just a little bit different. Times have changed too much, we can't just recreate the New York Yankees for the 50s, 60s, 70s, 80s … we have to be something entirely different.

Q4: Do you consider that your organization has a clear brand strategy? Could you describe the Real brand identity? For instance, what messages, values, signs (brand attributes) do you want to communicate to the fans?
SP: We built it. Dave Checketts [the owner] knew what he wanted. He chose the name so that there was no question we were a soccer team. This is not football, baseball, hockey, arena football … it's not the Dragons, Warriors or Blast Offs. So we used a very traditional soccer name, and we have seen Dallas do the same things and DC United has it in our league. I don't think all the teams in our league are going down that same path, but there is still a

place in this country, in this league, for some more traditional name, and I think this is a good mixture/positioning for us. Real stands for royalty, it stands for greatness, for certain expectations or aspirations, so Dave made it very clear from his expectation of how we present ourselves publicly, whether it's what the fans experience with customer service, with the stadium, with the high-end hospitality, with affordable tickets for young families. Dave had a pretty good idea of how to put it all into place. This is where I let all my brilliant people, come up with great ideas, and put it all together. We were a little concerned with the name and we felt there would be some immediate pushback because we used a Spanish word in Utah, and in fact, within a day, we got very positive reactions. People loved the badge – it looks like a traditional soccer badge that has been around for a long, long time – it's not just something we invented a year and a half ago, even if that is the case. The colours are traditional, very rich and bold. Through the consistent way in which we presented the name, we introduced the jersey, we introduced the team on opening day, and we decorated the stadium, I think our fans were sort of caught up in it without really realizing that we had a master plan. All these things became a reflection of what we were trying to do. We found that Salt Lake and Utah was much more cosmopolitan, much more multilingual, much more multicultural than we ever imagined, and part of that is because of the missionaries from the Church going overseas to South America, Asia, Europe and coming back, and along the way they developed an affinity for the sport ... so it wasn't a hard sell – it is also a very educated community, its very highly wired, very technologically savvy community, so we just sort of tapped into it all those things.

Q5: What about the other teams in the league?
SP: Columbus wants to be America's hardest working team, that's great, they can conquer the country, we can conquer the world. The Metro Stars have never had a coherent brand, in ten-plus years in this league. The Miami Fusion probably had a pretty good platform to build upon, but they didn't have the business model or the resources to pull it off; the Galaxy strives to be a little bit like the Lakers or the Dodgers, and the glamour somehow forming big name players like a galaxy of stars, I would say they are pretty effective at it, and they have won some championships, so they can hold that up. I don't feel that the Revolution has ever had a strong identity; the Dallas Burn was an abject failure and now they are rebranded as FC Dallas. They are taking steps in the right direction. Colorado Rapids have no identity whatsoever so, overall, I would say some teams have done well, and some haven't. But they all try to differentiate themselves with a clear

brand strategy. I have been fortunate to be in two different situations where we had the resources and we had the money, and the staff to have a chance to be successful and I think some teams never had a chance in this league.

Q6: At the league level, is there a homogeneous approach to branding and marketing strategy?
SP: The league's transformed quite a bit from 1996 to 2005. I think we were the beneficiary of an evolution of single entity. In the early years of the league, I really think the league tried to control everything, and it created a bottleneck. Through the middle years of the league, you really only had three owner groups and they all had different philosophies, and the soccer team honestly had a different priority within their overall organizational structure. As Steve mentioned, I think we are fortunate to have an owner, a visionary, as we call him, in Dave Checketts, who in his career as a sports entrepreneur has been successful everywhere he's been – with the Jazz, the Knicks, Madison Square Garden, the Rangers, Radio City Music Hall – so from a league level that is one of the complaints that a lot of teams have, that there's not a clear meaning to what the MLS means on a national stage. I think Don Garber, the Second Commissioner, coming from the NFL, understands branding as well as anybody, but at the league level resources are really limited to build this brand. The league's marketing budget is smaller than that of three or four of the teams, so right now we are a league where the teams are responsible for all branding and, being such a small number of teams and being such a large geographic area, branding, national branding has been a problem.

Q7: How would you compare your team/league with major soccer leagues around the world? What kind of relationships do you have with these leagues?
SP: When you compare MLS to la Liga or the English Premier League, we don't have the history, the tradition, and we're not taken seriously competitively. However, I think that, in the last five years, we have started to see some MLS players be successful overseas. The players really need to make a name for themselves. In addition, I really think there is a significant curiosity level overseas and, I hope, an underlying begrudging respect for what we are doing as a business. If ten years later we are still around, we must be doing something right because our national team is performing well, our league players are slowly becoming sought after, and there's continual interest from foreign clubs in what we're doing. Very wealthy teams in England, Italy or Spain are trying to figure out what their strategy is going to be in the USA. In an open dialogue between us and Hanover when we acquired Clint Mathis, their General Manager gave his take on American soccer.

He is well ahead of the curve in terms of understanding what is happening to American soccer. He has been to the Home Depot Center, he has been to our games, he knows that, if for no other selfish reason, they can steal our young talent, that there's an opportunity here. But there are just countless clubs like that, that are suddenly trying to figure out how to do business with MLS, and even though MLS doesn't have the history, tradition or respect of all these other leagues, people are realizing that is a very viable business partner but we need huge branding effort on the league's part domestically or internationally. We begrudgingly earn respect, because a lot of people still think that America is the leader in the sports marketing, and if we can build stadiums like the Home Depot Center and monetize them, then we must be doing something right.

Q8: What is the latest big change in the business plan of the league?
SP: Probably the biggest thing the league has done, just recently, is we have a rights fee now, starting in 2007 for ABC/ESPN for our television package. So that'll start next year and I believe that's a five-year deal and then Univision is coming back with a modest rights fee as well. We've been buying time during the early days of the league, then it went to a kind of hybrid, when the time was given to us by ESPN, but we paid all production, so that's a big step forward.

Q9: In the league there is the trend to build new stadiums with smaller capacities (20 000–25 000 seats). What is your take on that? How does it contribute to your business plan?
SP: When we bring Real Madrid and we need to sell 90 000 tickets, there's a venue like the University of Utah, the Rose Bowl, the Coliseum, Soldier Field, that we can take games like that to. We need a 20 000-seat stadium for twenty to twenty-five games a year. That is critical to provide a real soccer entertaining experience to our fans and to control operating costs. You only need a 50 000-seat stadium once a year, twice a year if you're lucky. This is Salt Lake – we're not exactly the first choice for European teams. They want to go to New York, they want to go to Los Angeles to go to the beach. We're gonna have to really fight to put Salt Lake on the map, but one of the things that we are doing is that we have a arranged accommodation and practice fields in Park City, so about 20 minutes away, about 6900 feet above sea-level, 2100 metres, in July and August of this year, and we are inviting clubs from around the world to come and train and play with us. If we get two or three teams to Salt Lake this summer, that will be a huge success. They have never considered Utah until now, but we are at a world-class Olympic venue. We saw it during the

Olympics in 2002 – fantastic hospitality – and our long-term goal is to turn this into a business and make this a real destination for soccer teams in the summer. We'll see how it goes.

Q10: You have to use your assets, and that is one of your assets. Just to come back to your marketing strategy, what is the role of market research in your organization and the way you market your product?

SP: 'It's limited right now ... we've chosen to put our resources into other areas, but where we can do research, we are. Just in the last three months, we've been doing a lot of surveying of our season-ticket holders and other kind-of opt-in databases ... such as our kids club, we are creating an advisory board from our 5000 season tickets, there are about 250 people we periodically throw ideas to. We are always asking for feedback, we want to make sure that those lines of communication between our most important, well, all fans are open. For those who have invested in us on a season basis, and really have quickly attached themselves and their lifestyles to our brand, we want to hear what they think. We constantly are asking them for ideas, we actually survey not the entire group at once, but segments of the group, weekly. We also, through the league, have partnered a company in Baltimore, called 'Fan Track', they're actually in Philadelphia now, to do some surveying. Again, it's where you work with all the other teams in the league as a whole to kind of maximize our resources, and we're thinking that this year we will add a web element instead of just doing in-stadium surveys. So we're in the nascent stages of our research. And then the other thing, our radio partner, which is the number one station in the market, has been performing focus groups, so it put in some real Salt Lake-related questions and the feedback was fantastic. Right toward the end of the season last year we actually ran a survey and the incentive to fill this out was the opportunity to win a lunch with the General Manager. We picked five names just right out of the hat and had them each invite a guest and took them all out to lunch. We talked about everything under the sun, and very openly; I don't worry that there are trade secrets you tell the fans that it is somehow going back to bite you. We develop strong ties and relationships with the community through these personalized events. You'll see a lot of this tonight at our event; we've done a large number of these types of events where it's a watch party, whether for our games or the US games. We did a World Cup draw where you try to tie things in together, so we ask season-ticket holders to come pick up their renewal gifts at the World Cup Draw party, we had players here signing autographs and the media showed up. We've done a lot of these, you can call them whatever you want – grassroots events, town hall meeting types – but I think that's been one of our points of difference – when 300 people take their lunch hour and come to these offices, just to be with other soccer fans, buy merchandise and watch the World Cup Draw, which you can do on your computer … it's a great sign that people care about us and know that we're connected to the greater soccer world. The access that we provide to our fans from our owners, our CEO, our GM, our coaches, our players is very different from what other professional teams such as the Jazz offer to this community and, I think, very different from what the other MLS teams offer, and that's just something that helped us cement a quicker, stronger bond with our fans.

Q11: How would you describe your market? What does the market look like, and how do you satisfy this market in each of the segments?

SP: I've always felt that we can't spend too much time trying to convert a football fan to a soccer fan, or a baseball fan to a soccer fan. There are enough people that love the game in every market to make it successful. If we just get the people involved in soccer, their kids, players in college and their friends, people who you like to watch the Premier League on Saturdays, there are enough people that care about the sport of soccer. One of the first things that I think is important to us is that we stay true to what I think we all agree is the history, tradition, and what the sport of soccer is really all about. So we don't try to change the game for Americans, we don't try to change the presentation for Americans, we don't play silly music during the game. Everything else comes from the fans. We have a scoreboard and we use it, but soccer fans don't want their sport presented like arena football or like an arena hockey match where there are spotlights and music. I'd rather stay true to the core of what our sport is all about and let people gravitate to us. I'm not going to change how I present things just for one segment of the fan base – that said, we have programmes for kids, we communicate electronically, we do lots of grassroots things out on the soccer fields, we do things like parties where our fans come out and watch the USA play, and so they do appeal to different segments. We don't mess with our core business. We reach the soccer community through the state associations for both youth and adults, through various means, we go to their annual banquets, we go to Field Club Saturdays, we have them down on the field every game. Somebody is receiving something, so we get to the soccer community. Some of our media actually go after men eighteen to thirty-four listening to sports radio, and we're gonna get some crossover and reach some people that aren't the core demographic. Anything you do in radio or television is going to crossover and attract women, except for sports radio, but we'll do some post-game concerts this year to attract different people that wouldn't normally come out, so we do have some specific programmes. We're not very effective yet at reaching the affluent, high-end corporate customer for two reasons, and one is a flaw in our league, that isn't a negative, it's just something that we'll have to deal with … if you have a suite at The Jazz or The Padres or whoever, 75–80 per cent of their games are on week nights, so you meet your client for dinner, you're a law firm you meet your client at 5.30 take them out for steak and seafood and then you go to the arena and you sit in your suite and you do whatever, and it's a corporate adult environment. Ninety per cent of our games are on a Saturday night, so I have said for years that we need to come up with a brand of corporate hospitality that is different. We're still doing it, it's just gonna feel a little different. It just might be the CEO taking his best friend CEO of another company, but it's 'bring your family and lets go hang out' and have a relaxing Saturday night – it costs about a tenth as much as that Jazz or Padres experience … But we haven't quite gotten there yet, and this stadium is not particularly well set up for that. I was just in a sports conference last week listening to these incredible innovations the NBA and NHL teams are doing in terms of high-end hospitality and these half-a-million dollar membership clubs and private rooms and all these things, and cigar bars and porto wine. I don't think we're ever going to get that in our league, but I don't think we have to. I think there are other ways we can do it.

Q12: How important is the proximity between the organization and the fans to you?
SP: I will just give you a personal example to answer this question. I try to spend about half of every game in the stands and I walk around and I just sit and I listen to conversations and people will see me and ask questions, or I'll go seek out specific people. Somebody called me on the way today, and complained about something, I asked, 'Are you coming to the game Saturday?' 'Yes.' 'Where are you sitting?', and after they told me and I said, 'Why don't I just come by and then we can talk about it at the game'. And they said, 'REALLY? You'll do that?' Most of the time I can, and when we announced on the last game of the season last year that we were building the stadium in Sandy, big announcement, beautiful venue, beautiful drawings, there were some fans who live here in Salt Lake and felt upset and wanted us to play here and they had banners saying 'Sold out to Sandy'. I'm standing on the field, during the anthem and I see this sign, and the game wasn't on television, but I felt we had just committed $50 million to build this stadium and this $100-million venue, and

fans have a right to be upset, but I don't think they have the right to embarrass me and our owner. It should be a day to celebrate – it's taken every other MLS team three to ten-plus years to build a stadium, and on the last day or our first season, we announced that we're building a stadium. These fans had bags over their heads, and I said 'Is that your sign?' and they said, 'yes'. I'm talking to these guys with bags over their heads, and I said, 'I respect your opinion, for us this is an incredibly proud day, and I'd like to ask you to remove the sign, it's kind of insulting to Dave and all he has done for this organization,' and we were sort of talking back and forth and I said, 'well, let's do this, you take the sign down, call me Monday and come to my office, with or without the bags, and we'll talk this through, I want to hear what you say, I know what some of your arguments are, I want you to hear my end of the story, will you do that for me?' And they said, 'One minute' and so the three guys in bags moved over about ten feet and have this little conversation and then they come back and say, 'okay, we've agreed – we'll take the sign down', and so we took the sign down and I never heard from them again. There was another section of fans that every time, all season long that I would walk by that section, they would start yelling at me, 'Build in Salt Lake City, build in Salt Lake City, keep the team in Salt Lake City', and all this kind of stuff, so I had to go talk to them, so I went and sat down next to them, and said, 'Isn't this the group that's been yelling at me all year of how the stadium needs to be built in Salt Lake City?' and they said, 'yes', and I said, 'well, then you're probably not happy with our plans to build in Sandy?' and they said, 'No'. And I spent twenty minutes of the first half talking with them and why we felt the way we did, and why we decided on what we did, and I believe that everyone of those season-ticket holders have renewed and are coming back, and they have said thank you for coming to talk to us, thanks for explaining your side of the story, and I said 'if it takes five years for Salt Lake to get around to deciding it's a priority to build a stadium instead of one, like in Sandy, we lose 3, 4, 5 million dollars a year, there just as much of a chance that in five years if this team is playing in Portland, as it is in Salt Lake, and is that what you want?' And they'll say, 'no, no, we want to keep it here'. Well, that's part of the reality, every game we play in this stadium, we lose money, and we write big cheques, and we can't go on doing this. So they sort of heard that … and I know that those thirty people that were most upset probably had thirty friends that were upset, they also went home after that game to say, 'you won't believe what happened at the game … the GM came down and sat next to us in our seats, and let us scream at him, and a couple of people were uh, that's stuff that you can't buy' … I really think that we can build a fan base one at a time like that, and I do it, and I encourage my staff to do it. Most time people want to have a relationship with the team, they don't just want to write cheques, they want to get something in return, they want to voice their opinions, they want to say the coach is terrible or the striker needs to be replaced, or whatever.

Q13: How do try to convert your fan base into season-ticket holders? Are there specific ways in which you do that?
SP: We had 500 season-ticket holders last year, two months before our first game; 4500 are on board for this coming season, so we've done something right, and remember we were 5–22 last year. It really starts in every transaction and every interaction that we have with these people. This survey told me that 91 per cent of our fans thought that our ticket customer service was excellent or above average. That was one person last year doing the majority of that as her job description. It's really everybody involved with tickets who I call, who ever I know in the office to say, I've got this problem where I either want to add tickets or exchange tickets, and everybody answers the questions but there is really only one person where that is her job description and serves our season-ticket holders. Obviously, she has done a pretty good job. It's a all that little stuff … there's no magic programme, we don't have a loyalty card, we don't have a punch card, we're not keeping track of how many … we don't have the technology to barcode and check every ticket and to know exactly who's coming and who's not, and which tickets go unused; we're still old-fashioned. It's old-fashioned hard work in my opinion. We had 3000 or 3500 of our season-ticket holders renew before Christmas, and we asked them to renew in August, and we told them their deadline is in November or else you are going to lose your seats. Many MLS teams are afraid to ask their faithful people on the spot, they don't want to offend people, they don't want to give people's seats away, and then it's 14 April and you start to see them the next day, and you get people saying where's my seat, why didn't you hold them? I credit our director of ticket sales, Chris, for establishing a mentality from the beginning that we're not going to be one of those teams that is constantly going to be chasing. You've got to come back now because when you're in the situation of having a new stadium, you're going to have to be renewed as soon as the season ends, or you'll lose your seats because there will be a waiting list. The capacity is going to be lower and the demand is going to be increased, so we might as well start training that out.

Q14: Who would you say your main competitors are?
SP: From a media standpoint, the fact that the Jazz is the only other professional team in town is a fantastic situation for us to be

in because we get much more coverage than any of the other MLS teams do. This is really a football state, Utah football and BYU football are the dominant entities here, but if you've been around UCLA, USC, Notre Dame, Michigan, it's silly in comparison, it's just not that developed. More than anything it's competition for someone's time, you can go to the movies, you can go to Zion National Park, you can go up to the mountains, you can go to a ton of great parks and outdoor activities here, you can stay home and watch TV, you can play video games – a modern family has a million choices every weekend. We're trying to be the first appointment on people's social lives or family calendars. We work closely with youth soccer and try to schedule our games at times that make sense for them; this year we open on a Saturday before Easter, which we were initially concerned about, but youth soccer doesn't play that day, so nobody in youth soccer has a game obligation so theoretically everybody can come to the first game of the season. A lot of people watch Mexican soccer, but I don't think that anyone is going to skip an opportunity to watch live soccer because they videoed fourteen taped games that they want to watch, and people do make time to watch those games, but if you love the sport, at some point you want to experience it in person. In context of the Hispanic community, Mexican fans have not accepted that MLS is of the same level as the professional league in Mexico – and quite frankly, in every international competition, very rarely does an MLS team win. We will bring one to two Mexican teams to Salt Lake every year, ideally; that we were not able to last year is one of my disappointments – just to showcase the game, and remind people that we are playing the same game, guys, that you watch on Saturday in Mexico or up here. I think that will lead to meaningful competitions between our leagues, just kind of grudging respect. I would never ask a Mexican fan in Salt Lake to abandon their support of Chivas. You're supporting a team that is thousands of miles away and that is fine, but you can experience a lot of that with a team that is right here in your backyard, where you know a lot of the players, and you can really get involved in the same way that you got sort of sucked in Mexico. Give us the chance, too and don't write us off.

Appendix 14.2

Transcript of interview with Eddie Rockwell, former General Manager of Atlanta Beat (WUSA)

Q1: Could you please briefly describe your professional background/career path and your relationship with soccer?

ER: I played soccer all my life. I was involved in a bunch of other sports as well – skiing, swimming, volleyball. I've always been very athletic-oriented. I went to University of California-Irvine, but UC Irvine does not have business programmes. So I got a psychology degree. I graduated in '92, and the World Cup was in '94. You know, it was one of those things where you can't get a job without experience … but you can't get experience without a job, so I had to go volunteer for them. I volunteered two days a week for six months. And then a job became available so I started working for them. And then from there, I came here to Atlanta and started working for the Olympics. After doing that, I started doing some freelance work for Nike Sports Entertainment and Coke. And as I was waiting for the next deal, I got an offer from Columbus Crew, Ohio (MLS). I was their VP of operations and then I came back here when the WUSA started. I came down as a director of operations, but our General Manager at the time, Lynn Morgan, was promoted after the first season to the President of the league, and she asked me to be the General Manager of the Atlanta Beat.

Q2: Please describe the Beat organizational structure and marketing more specially.

ER: I think with any smaller organization, like we were, you had to be willing to wear many hats. So all of us were involved to some extent with marketing. I did have a person that was just in charge of marketing. We had another guy who handled more of the PR stuff. But basically, I had one guy who was in charge of marketing and PR, and then our ticket sales guy.

Q3: Who would you say your main competitors were?

ER: Just other forms of entertainment. I wouldn't say we competed against the Atlanta Braves (MLB). I don't think we can really consider them competition. I just think entertainment in general was our main competitor. I mean anything from movies to attraction parks. Sometimes, we were as cheap as a movie. You could get a ticket from $8–20. I think our highest-price ticket was $24 for a club seat.

Q4: What stadium did you play in?

ER: Well … that was our biggest challenge after the first year – the stadium. Because we started out playing on the campus of

Georgia Tech, which has a huge, huge stadium, we had challenges there with the size of the stadium. Parking was also an issue. You know field issues and access to the field was always a challenge, and we knew it was only a one-year deal. We moved to the stadium on the campus of Morris Brown College. This stadium was much better for us from the fan entertainment standpoint. The problem was, it was in an area of town that our fans weren't familiar with and weren't comfortable with. You know they were uncomfortable, and we understood why. I mean, a few blocks from there you get into some bad housing areas and some crime-ridden neighbourhoods and, you know, you had to go a couple of blocks to get there, but because people were unfamiliar with the stadium, it triggered a negative perception. You knew people wouldn't necessarily come down. So we had to really find a solution. It cost us an enormous amount to put on a game, a lot more than it would to play in a stadium with parking on site, because we had to hire security, police, to control about four different intersections and to run shuttle buses, and that is more than you want to do. It was a very expensive part of the game. So that was one of the big issues. You know we did a lot of refurbishments to the stadium, so we didn't have to pay rent. We paid rent by putting in a new field, and by upgrading the stadium – it was built for field hockey for the Olympics, and it hadn't been kept up well. So, we had to do everything from repairing bathrooms to water fountains to painting and seats, and press box … we just had to do a tremendous amount of upgrades to the facility … at a pretty substantial cost.

Q5: What about the game-day experience? What market segments did you target?
ER: Game day experience was everything to us. It wasn't just the action on the field, which was, obviously, extremely important from our standpoint. We had everything you can imagine: face-painters, balloon clowns, all kinds of interactive games. We tied a lot of sponsorship elements into that. People on stilts and anything we could do to entertain the kids … and it was all free. You know, we would never charge anyone for face-painting or anything like that. Everything we did was part of the price of admission, if you will. We even had, in our second season, a beer garden, down on the field behind one of the goals, which was a lot of fun. We did it intentionally away from where the families were sitting so people could choose to be there or not. We really drove the family atmosphere more than anything, because that was very important – that was our main demographic, but our secondary demographic was the twenty-one- to thirty-five-year-olds of both sexes … there were a lot of guys down there just having a

good time, and it was inexpensive, and the games on Saturday night were early enough that that was the first thing you did. You know, 7 o'clock game, you're out of there by 9, 9.30, so then you can go to the bars, so we tried to hit that element as well. However, our first focus was on families, and even more so on families with kids who played soccer. We really learned a lot there, in that we thought that the soccer playing crowd would be older but it ended up that the under-fourteens were the majority of the fans. Anywhere from six to fourteen, those were the kids that were most active as far as our audience goes, and as soon as they got to be fourteen it wasn't cool anymore. Like I said, we thought initially the audience would be a little older. But we were wrong. I guess the thinking was that, if you're going to develop players, the best way to do it is to let them watch the game played at the highest level. So, we really tried to use this as a strategy and tried to think about the players that are most eager to improve their game. They are probably in the fourteen- to eighteen-year-old range as they try to get into college and beyond. But we didn't get a whole lot of that market, so yeah, the strategy changed when we realized that it wasn't working – that that was a much smaller age group of our audience. And the younger ones were the ones that were more attracted to all the stuff we were doing. There's constant music, and we obviously had a few fans that didn't like all the music we played, but the majority did. All you had to do was to look at the crowd, and as soon as we played music they started getting up and moving around … it was one of those no-brainers.

Q6: What about the female market?
ER: We did not target women; we did target families and, like I said, the secondary market, the twenty-ones to thirty-fives, was really more guys … we would go to bars, especially during the World Cup and soccer events, and stuff like that, and we'd go to bars and try to get information out and try to let people know what was going on. So from that aspect, we tried to promote more of the soccer side of things, but I would not say that women were ever our primary target audience, and we did very little to try to market strictly to them. What we discovered very early on is that women do not necessarily support women's sports just for the sake of it. In fact, I think, and I don't know this for sure, but women's tennis, for example, has more men viewers than it does women.

Q7: What attributes were you selling to fans?
ER: I came from an MLS team and I was in operations the first year, so it was my responsibility to put the game-day experience on. So I did pull a lot of that stuff … you know, all the entertainment

factors, the music, everything from how you introduce a team to how the game ends … it was all a scripted show. Basically, my whole thing was to make sure that people were having an incredible time from the time they got to the parking lot till the time they left the parking lot. Sport entertainment, that what it was. The game was not secondary by any means, and it was certainly the primary thing that was going on, but we had to have a lot of ancillary activities to keep people entertained. Because, I think, our crowd was not the type that you would find in a European soccer market, where they come strictly to watch the game … In fact, one of the things I noticed which was unusual, and I have not seen in any other sporting event, EVER, is that very frequently, especially with the younger crowd, if you watched everybody as they left the stadium and you looked at their faces, you would have no idea that we had lost a game. If you go to a Thrashers or a Hawks game, and the team loses, you're gonna see it on people's faces when they're leaving the stadium.

Q8: You speak a lot about the entertainment segments … what about the actual game itself?
ER: Well, we were the best team in the league for three years. We cared about it immensely, even to the point where we tried to develop our players to be recognizable faces. We had our marquee name players as far as Brianna Scurry, Cindy Parlow and Charmaine Hooper, but we tried to develop some of our other younger players. We really did put some emphasis on trying to develop our players as faces, and a silly example is whenever we had pictures of our players, whether in ads or programmes or whatever, we always had their name and number on everything. And again it seems like common sense, but it doesn't happen all that often … there's a lot times that people don't identify who the players are.

Q9: How did you try to convert your fan base into season-ticket holders? Are there specific ways in which you do that?
ER: You always want to get people to come to more games, and one strategy was how to get a person who comes to one game to come to two or three, and how to get the person who comes to two or three to come to five or six. And how do we get the person that's coming to four of five just to come to the whole season? And in that case, our biggest competition was time, people's time … you know, we were playing during the summer, so that's when people have vacations, there's not a tremendous amount of incentive to buy season tickets, because the discounts weren't significant – there were discounts, but they weren't significant, and we had to really strive to come up with extra benefits for our season-ticket holders. The last two years we had fan parties at the

stadium, where we would bring all the season-ticket holders on a day after a game to come down to the stadium to play games with the players down on the field.

Q10: What was average attendance?
ER: Oh, about 9000 the second two years ... about 11 000 the first year. We were second overall to DC – DC had the Mia Hamm factor so, yeah, DC had the best attendance over the three years, I'm pretty sure. That's kind of where we went with our marketing strategy, a lot of it was tied with trying to get our players out into the community.

Q11: How did you try to establish yourself in the community?
ER: Well, we had relationships with the Georgia State Soccer Association as well as most of the bigger clubs in town. And the partnership that we had with Georgia Soccer was excellent, but we didn't get as much return on the things we did with them as the things that we did with other clubs, and I think that has a lot to do with the loyalty factor. The best example I can draw from that is if you're a fan of the Washington Redskins and the NFL sends you a letter saying 'Attend the game', you're not necessarily going to do it, but if you're a fan of the Redskins and the Redskins sends you a letter that says 'Attend the game', then you're probably going to do it. So when the parent organization of these other member clubs says, 'Yeah you should go out and get this discount', people are not necessarily going to act on it. But when their own club says 'Hey, we're gonna do this as part of our own club', then there's more ownership, and this is our deal ... so we get a lot of that. We actually had a programme our third year with the member clubs where if they committed to buying a certain amount of tickets, we would bring the whole team out to their field.

Q12: Was it successful?
ER: Well, we went from 8000 group tickets in our second year to about 20 000 group tickets in our third year, primarily from that programme, so yeah, it was very, very successful. The challenge with that programme was that the ticket price was not very high because we let them use that as a fundraiser; they could buy the tickets for six bucks and then sell them for about eight or ten. So, the return wasn't excessive, you know, it was a low-priced ticket, but at the same time it got a lot of people out to experience it.

Q13: More and more people say that the biggest asset of a professional sport franchise is its brand. What do you think? Did you consider that your organization/league had a clear brand strategy?
ER: That is a tough question, but it shouldn't be. I think that is something we tried to constantly discover, and I think the main

part of the brand is fun, entertainment, family-oriented, world-class athletes. I mean, we had the best athletes in the world on our field, so those were the key focuses. Yes, we had the best soccer players in the world, we had a fun, interactive family-centred environment that was a good time for all.

Q14: Was this brand definition only good for the Beat? Or for the league?
ER: I can't speak for the league as much, because I think they were striving. I think it was very similar, but I think different teams approached it differently. I think that was part of the problem at the beginning. Each team was trying to identify exactly what the league brand was, and I think that was one reason they made the change at the top of the management structure – because Lynn Morgan had a much better idea on how to drive the thing than the people that were in charge before.

Q15: The league was based on the founding players. Don't you think it was somewhat dangerous to build a league mainly around personal stories and athletes?
ER: Well, that's one of the reasons we were trying to build the image of other players. Like I said, we knew who our marquee players were, but we were trying to make a lot of the other ones more popular, get them better known. But yeah, that was a tremendous challenge that, if the league would have stayed in existence, we would have had to be struggling with right now as the bigger names start to retire. At the time, we didn't have to worry about it quite as much, but it was definitely something that when we had our league meetings and discussions we would try to figure out. And strategize, how are we going to build the next wave of name players?

Q16: Do you think that the WUSA could come back?
ER: Unfortunately, I don't think so … especially not to the level that it was before. We had $5 billion companies behind the league, and I don't think it will ever come back at that level and it certainly, absolutely will never start at that level … if it's ever back, it will be from the ground up … as opposed from the top … or starting out big like that. And that was probably one of those things that if you were ever to go back and do it again, you would say, alright let's start a little more modestly … not spend quite so much money, and build it brick by brick. If it gets back, it will be something that takes years and years to develop and starts much smaller and gets bigger over time, and you can look at the WNBA as an example – that's come close to being extinct several times. I think that if the WUSA comes back, it might be as an affiliate of the MLS. And I think that would be a good thing, because they

could take advantage of a lot of similar resources, like stadiums and front-office staff and ticket-sales plans and operations. I think that has probably the greatest potential for success for a women's league, if they are affiliated with the Major League Soccer. And I think the fact that they didn't cooperate as well is unfortunate and doing so probably could have led to greater success. I don't have 100 per cent of the background, but I believe that MLS, in the very beginning, was interested in helping out, but the people involved on the women's side – especially the players, from what I have heard – were not interested in that type of an arrangement. Like I said, I think it started out too big. I agree that there was too much emphasis placed on a national TV contract ... it cost a whole lot of money ... but at the same time, that's what helps get the national sponsors interested, and again, these were cable companies that were founding this thing, and a cable company wants to see its product on cable. Again that was important from a national sponsor standpoint but it was hard and costly to build with only eight teams. I agree that it started out too big, and it might have been more successful if it had started out smaller and grown as opposed to just been so big. And yeah the front offices might have been too big, we spent a lot of money as players costs were significant as well.

Q17: Is there a market for women's professional soccer in the US and its sponsors?

ER: Well the market's not as big as cable companies may think it is. Also, one of the issues with the sponsorship element is, the sponsors couldn't determine if this was sports marketing or cause marketing ... and they're not going to spend that much on cause marketing, but that's where it made more sense to them. I think there was a quote from one potential sponsor, I believe it was Coca-Cola, and he told our CEO, 'I love your league; I'm just not crazy about your business plan' because they just couldn't see the financial return ... that quickly. The return wasn't there because there was no clearly defined target market or the initial target market was a little off target. Also, the business plan thought that TV ratings would be greater based on WC99 ... but America loves a big event for soccer not leagues ... look at the World Cup in '94, over 3.5 million tickets sold in the United States ... and now, MLS is averaging 16 or 17 thousand a game. I think that forecasting based on the success of an event was not necessarily a good strategy ... because an event is usually going to be successful. It is easier to market an event, but it's much harder to market something that has to be sustained.

CHAPTER 15

The beginning of a new beginning? How to expand soccer in Canada – a look at the federation and one club

André Richelieu

Overview

This chapter highlights the reasons for past failures and some guidelines for the long-term growth of soccer in Canada. Obviously, the lack of infra-structure (playing facilities, coaches and referees) and the absence of quality ownership are the two main reasons behind the past failure of soc-cer in Canada. However, overall, several intrinsic and extrinsic factors explain the problems associated with the diffusion and adoption processes of soccer in the country – the nature and rules of the game, as well as his-tory (intrinsic), political factors, the weak promotion of the game, the lack of local stars, the absence of financial means, the geography and the weather (extrinsic).

In fact, Canada is facing the challenge of managing the growth of the sport and translating strong participation into successful performances at both the clubs' and the national team's levels. Undoubtedly, there is the need for a more aggressive marketing approach: first, to promote the game and the local product offered by the clubs and the national teams; and second, to generate new streams of revenue through, among others, merchandising.

Furthermore, in order for soccer to grow in this country on a long-term basis, the Canadian soccer community will need to work in the same direction.

Keywords

soccer, Canada, diffusion and adoption processes, branding, merchandising

Introduction

Canada prides itself on its hockey heritage and its success on the world stage. Epic moments are cherished and relived as glorious moments of sports history, but also of *our* history – Paul Henderson's goal against the Soviets at the 1972 Summit Series in Moscow, Mario Lemieux's winning goal in the finale of the 1987 Canada Cup, the Gold Medal at the 2002 Winter Olympics, the 2004 World Cup title, etc.

Compared to hockey and, to a lesser degree, US football and baseball, soccer in Canada looks like a poor little duck lost in the pond; our performances, at the club and the national team levels, are a far cry from those in other major sports. This might be seen as paradoxical, considering that soccer is the worldwide sport and Canada is a country of immigration. More intriguing is the fact that, as the interest in and practice of soccer both increase in the country, Canada is sinking even further in the FIFA rankings – deeper than seems possible. So what is wrong with soccer in Canada? Is the last frontier of soccer such a unique case?

This chapter intends to uncover some of the mystery of the situation of soccer in Canada, while providing some guidelines in order to see how the main actors of the soccer community in Canada, essentially the national and provincial federations and professional teams, might help ensure the long-term growth of the sport in the country. This is why the chapter is based on two interviews: one with the Chief Operating Officer of the Canadian federation (see Appendix 15.1) and the other with managers of the Montreal Impact soccer club (see Appendix 15.2). Furthermore, print and electronic references from both the media and the parties involved in the study were consulted.

We will start with a brief history of soccer in Canada. Secondly, we will present the state of soccer today and the causes of past failures. Thirdly, we will try to identify some guidelines for the development and viability of soccer in Canada. We will end this chapter with a conclusion and discussion.

A brief history of soccer in Canada

The history of soccer in Canada dates back to the second half of the nineteenth century (Soccer Canada, 2006). The first recorded game was played in 1876 in Toronto, and from that point on various football associations spread across the country and organized play took root. However, it was only in 1907 that the closest thing to a national championship was created, with the People's Shield.

Very seldom remembered is the first international title won by a Canadian national team – a gold medal at the St Louis Olympic Games in 1904. However, this does not really count, as soccer was a demonstration sport then.

The ancestor of the Canadian federation, the Dominion of Canada Football Association, known as Soccer Canada today, was created in 1912 before becoming a member of FIFA in 1913. The federation withdrew from FIFA between 1928 and 1946 because of a dispute over broken time payments to amateurs.

The first true national championship was held in 1913, but it was not until 1926 that the National Soccer League was formed, with teams from Ontario and Quebec. Unfortunately, the Second World War had a devastating effect on soccer in Canada: the national federation, along with several provincial ones, ceased its operations.

In 1946 the North American Professional Soccer League was launched, with teams from Canada and the United States. However, the League lasted for only two years. In 1961 the Eastern Canada Professional Soccer League was created, with teams from Toronto (two), Montreal and Hamilton. This League lasted until 1966.

In 1967, two coast-to-coast professional leagues were formed in the United States; the National Professional Soccer League (NPSL) had a team in Toronto, and the United Soccer Association (USA) had teams in Vancouver and Toronto. In 1968, the North American Soccer League (NASL) was created following the merger of the NPSL and the USA. The teams in Vancouver and Toronto lasted for just one year, and it was only in 1971 that Canadian teams re-entered the NASL with the Toronto Metros and the Montreal Olympique. Eventually there would be five Canadian teams in the NASL: the Toronto Blizzard, the Montreal Manic, the Edmonton Drillers, the Calgary Boomers and the Vancouver Whitecaps. The latter were the only Canadian team to win a NASL championship, in 1979. The NASL folded in 1985 and the Canadian Soccer League (CSL) took up the baton in 1987, expanding to eleven teams coast to coast before folding in 1992.

As far as Team Canada is concerned, the men's national team reached the quarter finals at the 1984 Olympics in Los Angeles, losing to Brazil on penalty kicks. Canada also qualified for the 1986 World Cup in Mexico, losing all three games – to France, Hungary and the Soviet Union – without scoring a single goal.

Team Canada was more prolific in 2000, when it won the CONCACAF Gold Cup, beating Colombia 2–0 in the finals. Canada finished third at the 2002 event – a small consolation, considering that the men's national team has still not qualified for a World Cup since 1986. The women's national team won the silver medal at the CONCACAF Gold Cup in 2002, losing on a golden goal to the Americans.

Regarding clubs, three Canadian teams are now part of the United Soccer League (USL), a second-tier North American soccer League: the Montreal Impact, the Toronto Lynx and the Vancouver Whitecaps. Toronto is expected to join the Division 1 soccer league in North America, Major League Soccer (MLS), in 2007, with the other two Canadian teams following suit by 2010, according to plans by Soccer Canada.

The state of soccer today and the causes of past failures

Soccer in Canada combines a rich history and strong participation – there are 850 000 registered players in Canada in 2005, compared to 544 000 hockey players (Hockey Canada, 2006) – with endless experience of failure at the club level and poor performances by the men's national team. However, between 1983 and 1987 Canada saw a rise on the world stage, and a true national championship was launched: the Canadian Soccer League (CSL).

Other than this, Canada cannot seem to get its act together when it comes to soccer. As Joey Saputo, President of the Montreal Impact (launched in 1993) says:

> If we look at the registration and attendance numbers, the state of the game is good. However, as far as the professional game is concerned, and even though there is more stability than in the past, it does not translate into good results for the national team.

Every time there is a ray of hope on the horizon, something somehow goes wrong and Canada needs to start from scratch all over again. Why?

Apparently, there seem to be two key factors that have prevented the stability and long-term growth of soccer in Canada: the lack of infrastructure and the absence of quality ownership with financial strength. These were both underlined in a study conducted by KPMG in 2000 on the future of professional soccer in Canada (KPMG, 2000).

The lack of infrastructure

Truly, the lack of infrastructure (playing facilities) prevents the emergence of a nucleus of quality players that will continue to play beyond university at the highest level and feed the national team. This is especially critical in the case of Canada, which has a relatively limited pool of players because of its population of 32 million, and also six months of harsh winter weather. In Quebec City, 50 playing fields are needed just to keep up with the increasing demand of over 22 000 soccer players (Dumas, 2004); right now, some baseball fields are being transformed into soccer pitches.

Additionally, most of the talented players leave for Europe because Canada is unable to provide them with the training and playing facilities that would avoid the exodus. Canada has already lost Owen Heargraves – Canadian born but now playing for England – and is in danger of losing more in the coming years if serious action is not taken.

Furthermore, as far as the fans attending games are concerned, the Chief Operating Officer of Soccer Canada, Kevan Pipe, says: 'Consumers of the twenty-first century want to attend sporting events in first-class locations. Plus, first-class stadiums help generate higher revenues with sky boxes and/or luxury seats.'

Indeed, a new stadium can be associated with modernity and refreshment of the brand, as sports clubs around the world soon realize after opening new facilities (Richelieu, 2004). Even the legendary New York Yankees are planning on opening the new Yankees' stadium by the 2009 season. Not to mention that a new stadium, with sky boxes and VIP seats, helps to generate substantial revenues – US$15–20 million a year in the United States for baseball and American football teams with the highest revenues from luxury suites (Anonymous, 1998; Barra, 2005). However, some teams generate less than 3 million dollars a year (Anonymous, 1998).

Furthermore, when focusing on the infrastructure issue we should not overlook the lack of coaches and referees, who are essential actors in the player development programme. There are more and more soccer players in the country (850 000 in 2005; rising to a predicted 1.2 million by 2010), but quality coaches and referees are still lacking nationwide.

The absence of quality ownership

As for the absence of quality ownership, Kevan Pipe starts by referring to the North American Soccer League (NASL) experience:

> The NASL allowed us to develop high-calibre Canadian soccer players (Gray, Lenarduzzi, Lettieri, Mitchell, Segota, etc.) because these players were facing the best in the world, even though they were not in their prime anymore (Beckenbauer, Neeskens, Pelé, etc.). However, the NASL was not financially structured to survive. The NASL experience carried us until 1997, after which there was a sharp decline in our men's national team performance.

However, beyond the specific case of the NASL, which is one among many failures in Canada, what can be said? According to the Chief Operating Officer of Soccer Canada:

> What we have failed to do up until now is to convince entrepreneurs to bet on the development of soccer in Canada, compared to what happened in the United States. We have convinced the public sector; now we must convince the private sector to jump on board with us.

Indeed, the fact that soccer (at least the local product) is not considered of major-league calibre makes investors worry about the return on investment they might achieve by being associated with soccer: soccer will not give a company the same reach as a major league sport such as hockey, American football, baseball or basketball. Additionally, the decline of professional clubs in

Canada, first with the NASL and then with the Canadian Soccer League, has definitely damaged the performance of the men's national team at world level. As a result, companies are even less inclined to support soccer in Canada.

This might explain why North America in general, and Canada in particular, are untapped markets for soccer, and why the diffusion and adoption processes of soccer have been unsuccessful until now.

The diffusion and adoption of soccer in Canada

The diffusion process is a concept originally described by Rogers (1983: 5):

> Diffusion is the process by which an innovation is communicated through certain channels over time among the members of a social system. It is a special type of communication in that the messages are concerned with new ideas.

According to a study undertaken by Baccouche (2004), there are two sets of factors that might explain the problems of diffusion and adoption of soccer in Canada:

1. *Intrinsic*:
   - nature and rules of the game
   - history of soccer in Canada

2. *Extrinsic*:
   - political factors (the relationship between Soccer Canada and the clubs/provincial federations)
   - the promotion of soccer
   - the lack of local stars
   - the absence of financial means (stable ownership)
   - insufficient infrastructure (stadiums, coaches, referees)
   - geography and weather.

Intrinsic factors refer to the nature and rules of the game and history. On the one hand, the rhythm of the game of soccer and its format are not adapted to the requirements for speed, physical involvement, an abundance of goals and the TV commercial breaks in North America. On the other hand, as emphasized previously, soccer in Canada has experienced situations where teams and leagues were disappearing, prohibiting any continuity of the game and a chance to establish it as part of the socio-cultural scene. Furthermore, increasing nationalism in the province of

Quebec pushed people away from soccer – a sport that was considered alien because of the number of European- (especially, but not only, British) born players. Instead, they favoured hockey, football and baseball, where local stars were more common (Schwartz and Gagnon, 2003). As a matter of fact, Strang and Soule (1998) and Rogers (1995) show that practices are more likely to be adopted when they are culturally consistent with local conventions or frames of reference, and as such make them familiar and attractive.

Extrinsic factors are mainly related to the environment. First, there are political factors. These refer to the relationship between the national federation and its provincial counterparts. According to Schwartz and Gagnon (2003), it is very difficult to build cooperative relationships between the different administrative bodies in Canada: the national federation seems to have a centralized approach and the bureaucracy prevents any changes. This argument is reinforced by Joey Saputo, President of the Montreal Impact:

> We wish there would be a better dialogue with Soccer Canada on how to develop our players. There was no consultation with Canadian professional teams when Soccer Canada decided to build the stadium in Toronto with public funds. We expect more transparency from Soccer Canada. Because there is no synergy between the different actors [involved in soccer in Canada], it's difficult to feed the development of players and establish the game in Canada.

Secondly, the promotion of soccer in Canada has been deteriorating until recently. Admittedly, more games from abroad are available on cable TV today than in the past, and people follow the World Cup, the European Championship and the Champions League, but the national game doesn't get a lot of attention from the media. Some men's national team matches are even broadcast at midnight, after the baseball game and the late news! Obviously, the lack of a televised presence does not help to develop the interest of the fans in the local product, or an allegiance to local clubs or the national team (Mullin *et al.*, 2000).

Thirdly, and in line with the previous element, the lack of local stars and their promotion has failed to establish a true sense of belonging from fans regarding local players and teams. The Montreal Impact tries to provide a remedy for this at its own level by working with the grassroots (young soccer) players and building a pyramid of player development, starting with children and going all the way to the big club via a farm team.

Fourthly, financial problems have led to repeated failures of initiatives to implement soccer in Canada. It is worth noting that in 1986 Canada was the only World Cup team not to have a national championship. As mentioned in this chapter, Canada has a great need for qualified coaches, referees and soccer stadiums. The problem is recognized by most actors involved in soccer in Canada, but people do not seem to agree on how to overcome this difficulty. Indeed, as explained in the next section, and based on our interviews (see Appendices 15.1 and 15.2), the federation seems to have one vision and the clubs another.

Fifthly, as the infrastructures are limited and soccer is not yet a major sport, there are very few opportunities to transform a passion into a profession for Canadian players unless they move to Europe – as is the case for the most talented ones (such as de Guzman, Radzinski and Staltieri). Says Joey Saputo: 'You lose some of the kids who play soccer because of the lack of coaching, management and infrastructure'.

Finally, geography and the weather are important hurdles: winter reduces the length of the soccer season, and this situation is aggravated by the lack of indoor facilities, even though the decision by FIFA to allow the use of artificial turf for games should, according to Kevan Pipe, help Canada in this regard.

Could there be some cultural reasons that are preventing the development of soccer in Canada? This theory is dismissed by the Chief Operating Officer of Soccer Canada:

> In fact, I believe it is the direct opposite: Canada is a very multicultural society. The face of Canada is changing and more and more open to the world; so is the interest for soccer in this country […] Soccer brings people from all over the world together; it is the only sport that achieves that, especially during the World Cup. This is particularly appealing in Canada because of our multicultural background.

How, then, can the current situation, with women's soccer thriving and men's soccer in disarray, be explained? The lack of infrastructure and quality ownership is no different in men's and women's soccer; in fact, the resources allocated to women's sport tend to be less abundant than those for men's (Sport Canada, 1999; Lopiano, 2004).

Could it be because Canada has long been a leader in women's sports, as with most Nordic countries (Forde, 1996), and this gives Canada a relative edge when it comes to competitive soccer on the world stage? Indeed, in 1977 Canada held its first national women's championship – ahead of any other country in the world. Right now, 400 000 of the 850 000 soccer players in the country are female. However, if the infrastructure and ownership issues are not solved soon, women's soccer may face the same collapse as men's soccer.

In this regard, the comments of the President of the Montreal Impact are interesting:

> We need more infrastructures: coaching, management, stadiums, etc. Building the proper infrastructure, having the right coaching staff, will provide the foundations of a pyramid, for both men and women, we could then grow to ensure the development and growth of soccer in Canada.

Should we believe that things will be different this time around and that soccer in Canada will finally take off? Some people do, like the Chief Operating Officer of Soccer Canada:

> With the MLS, which is a tier-one league, and the world-class events Canada will stage in the coming years, we have the opportunity to change things for the better in Canada. We have a *rendezvous* with History.

Could we be at the beginning of a new beginning?

How to grow soccer in Canada: the beginning of a new beginning?

Obviously, soccer in Canada has had a rough time and the durability of the game over time is a major concern. Admittedly, there is a long history of soccer in Canada, and registered soccer players outnumber their hockey counterparts. At the same time, the lack of infrastructure and quality ownership, which could help teams and leagues survive beyond the short term, are major hurdles. How is this going to change, if indeed it is possible to change it?

Tackling the infrastructure issue

First, there are the facilities. In 2006, two soccer-specific stadiums of 20 000 seats will be built in Toronto and Montreal. By 2010, there should be three soccer-specific stadiums, with Vancouver the third beneficiary. The plan is to have these three cities in the MLS by 2010: 'Everybody involved in soccer in this country should understand that we need to bring the calibre of play to the top; we cannot stand still!', says Kevan Pipe. Joey Saputo agrees: 'When we look at the FIFA rankings, there's obviously only one way to go for soccer in Canada, and it's up!' (Canada was eighty-fourth, between Albania and the United Arab Emirates, on 2 February 2006; FIFA, 2006).

That said, facilities alone are not enough. Canada needs resources to allocate money for training coaches and referees, and developing young players, as well as for promoting the game. With the revenue coming from several world events the country will stage in the coming years, Soccer Canada hopes to generate enough money to sustain its development plan for the sport in Canada and ensure its long-term growth. For instance, Soccer Canada has a gross budget of $30 million for the Under-20 World Cup in 2007. Says the Chief Operating Officer of Soccer Canada:

> By 2010, our budget should be the biggest of any sports federation in Canada. [...] One of our goals is to generate enough revenue to sustain a budget of 12–13 million dollars, with only 1 million coming from the government.

This is a realistic project, considering the actual budget of $11 million. The Canadian federation is counting on the spill-over effects of the several international tournaments Canada will host between 2006 and 2011: the Under-20 World Cup in 2007, the CONCACAF Olympic qualifying tournament for both men and women in 2008, the men's Gold Cup in 2009 and the women's World Cup in 2011. According to the Chief Operating Officer, Soccer Canada:

> We need to develop professional clubs in Canada, in order to increase media coverage, attract new partners and generate new revenue streams through merchandising.

Ownership issues

As far as ownership goes, it seems that Montreal, Toronto and Vancouver can count on three solid groups: Saputo in Montreal, the Hartrell family in Toronto and Greg Kerfoot in Vancouver. This could enable all three franchises to move from the USL to the MLS and be both competitive and viable in a tier-one division. Says Kevan Pipe:

> The MLS coming to Canada will in fact give us the opportunity to develop high-calibre players, as the NASL did in the 1980s, but with the financial strength we didn't have back then. We need to react to our North American

environment if we want to compete at the World Cup. And with a very limited pool of players, we must develop more players that will help us be competitive on the world stage.

And what role does Kevan Pipe see for Soccer Canada?

Soccer Canada will be the initiator, conductor, traffic cop, in order to convince new partners to get involved in the game. We need to instil leadership among high-calibre professional clubs: they will be the ones developing and training players on a day-to-day basis, and helping Canada be competitive at the international level. [...] We don't want to ship young kids to Europe anymore because we don't have the infrastructure (professional clubs, coaching staff, physical infrastructure, etc.) to develop them here!

Managing the growth

This is especially important now, because Canada can count on more young and talented players than ever before. If we relate to Shank's model of the lifecycle of a sport (Shank, 1999), soccer in Canada is in a phase of growth, with the influx of more and more local players. However, developing a critical mass of players should be accompanied by a marketing approach toward the consumer in order to promote the game and help teams to generate new streams of revenue (e.g. merchandising). In this regard, the Montreal Impact managers are right when they underline the fact that their biggest challenge consists of managing the growth of soccer in Canada: 'The national programme has not been able to manage the growth of soccer in this country, as far as player development, coaching and infrastructures are concerned'.

That is why, in 2002, the Impact launched a five-year plan in order to build the foundations that will help to develop local talent, implement the infrastructure, provide a competitive soccer environment and solidify the team presence at all levels. This five-year plan should provide the foundations for the development and growth of both soccer and the Montreal Impact (Figure 15.1). According to Joey Saputo:

The idea is to build a pyramid, starting with youth teams, going through the high-performance centre, the farm team, ending with the Impact, which will help sustain soccer at the highest level in the province of Quebec. In this regard, the Impact works hand in hand with the Quebec

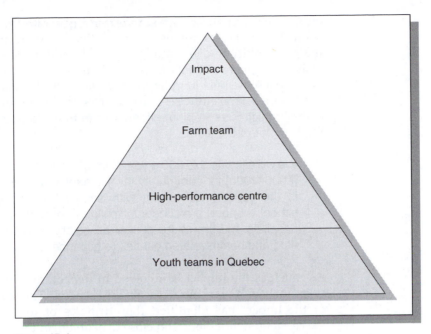

Figure 15.1
The pyramid of player development according to the Montreal Impact

Soccer Association in order to be in line with the needs of the provincial federation. [...] In fact, we should have two pyramids: one for men and one for women, which will provide us with the infrastructure we must have [to develop soccer in Canada].

The need for more aggressive marketing

The Impact should complement the pyramid of player development with more aggressive marketing of the club and game. Right now, the team allocates a mere $150 000 to marketing, including media coverage, which represents 7 per cent of the club's budget. As a non-profit organization, the team seems very constrained in the funds allocated to marketing: 'we are careful and creative [...] we don't want to take a giant step that would hurt us very badly if we failed', says Joey Saputo.

The management of the Impact counts on reciprocity agreements with partners to promote the team in the media or through special events, and the accessibility of players to connect with the fans: 'As players are available, we get free publicity', says Joey Saputo. This is especially true when more than 50 per cent of the team is made up of Quebec players: having on its roster a local player who has a certain reputation and has become established on the field can attract fan support and generate loyalty to the team. These players are also more inclined to be recognized by the community and become involved locally, which helps the team to implement roots in its community and have the fans develop a sense of belonging toward the team (Richelieu, 2004).

Also, there is an entire section dedicated to community relations at the Impact. Says Stéphane Banfi, Communications and Marketing Director of the team:

> We will allocate $75 000 a year during the next three years [2006–2008] for community involvement. Our main focus is the youth (involvement with school boards against school dropout, breakfasts for children in need, visits to hospitals and grants for soccer associations in Quebec, etc.) and health-related causes (e.g. cancer).

As much as the Impact is involved in the community, the team does not have a brand strategy or CRM scheme. The management of the Impact has identified the attributes of the team brand ('accessible, sympathetic and close to people'), but recognize they have not articulated the strategy around a true 'Impact' brand: 'It is more in the way we are and what we do that we express our branding. The Impact is more of a trademark than a brand *per se*.'

This is unfortunate, as branding is considered to be a strategic tool for sports teams when it comes to capitalizing on the emotional attachment of fans. Indeed, the development of a strong brand often allows a sports team to instil trust and trigger fan loyalty. In return, this trust and loyalty help the team to leverage its brand equity and generate additional revenues through the sale of goods and services, within and outside the sports arena (Richelieu and Pons, 2005). This is especially true in a period of growth (Shank, 1999), as Canada is experiencing nowadays. Right now, merchandising represents only 5 per cent of the Impact budget.

Even though the level of success on the field of a professional team has an impact on brand development, ultimately strong brand equity should overcome losing records through the establishment of a strong identity. For instance, the symbolic benefits generally attached to a sports team (the need for social approval or personal expression and outer-directed self-esteem) or a unique identity (Chicago Cubs, Oakland Raiders) of the team may represent the benefits of the brand for the fan (Richelieu and Pons, 2006). The Canadian federation and clubs should seize the growth period of soccer in Canada as an opportunity to build their respective brands that will grow with the development of the sport in the country.

Improving communication and knowing where soccer is heading in Canada

Beyond the lack of marketing initiatives, there seems to be a communication problem between the national federation and Canadian soccer teams. The federation seems to have its vision and the clubs another. While the federation believes it's time to push for an entry into MLS, Joey Saputo, President of the Montreal Impact, is cautious, keeping in mind the failures of the NASL and the CSL because of poor foundations:

> We need to solidify the game provincially before thinking of joining MLS. It doesn't matter which cities are in MLS, but the game must be healthy at the provincial level first. I would like to see a professional team in every province in order to increase the pool of players from which the national team could draw and improve its performance.

Joey Saputo even believes that Soccer Canada wants to create a national team to play in MLS in Toronto, with the rest of the country feeding the team. If this were the case, it wouldn't make much sense and would be akin to admitting the failure of the national programme.

Whether we are facing two different visions of the development of soccer in Canada or lack of communication, there is a problem which, at the end of the day, prevents the long-term growth of soccer in the country. Without a shared vision within the soccer community in Canada, and especially among the key actors (national and provincial federations, professional clubs, coaches, private sponsors, etc.), soccer will never have the healthy foundations to take root and grow as a major sport. As a result, Canada will be condemned to live with perpetual failure and remain stuck in the basement of the FIFA rankings.

Potential avenues for the long-term growth of soccer in Canada include:

1. Implementing the right infrastructure by building stadiums, training coaches and referees

2. Counting on financially stable ownership

3. Developing a more aggressive marketing approach by promoting soccer and the local product in the media (clubs and national teams), and generating new streams of revenue (merchandising)

4. Improving communication between the different actors of the Canadian soccer community and knowing in which direction soccer is heading in Canada.

Conclusions

This chapter has presented an overview of soccer in Canada, the reasons for past failures and some guidelines for the long-term growth of the sport in the country. Admittedly, we should take into consideration the fact that this chapter was written following only two interviews and an analysis of secondary data (published and electronic references from both the media and the parties involved in the study); in itself, this leads us to remain careful in our conclusions.

The lack of infrastructure (playing facilities, coaches and referees) and the absence of quality ownership are the two mains reasons behind the past failure of soccer in Canada. However, overall, several intrinsic and extrinsic factors explain the problems associated with the diffusion and adoption processes of soccer in Canada: the nature and rules of the game, as well as the history (intrinsic); and political factors, weak promotion of the game, the lack of local stars, the absence of financial means, the geography and weather (extrinsic).

As Kevan Pipe, of the Canadian soccer federation states, Canada is at the crossroads:

> We must make sure that we do not mess up in the eighteen months ahead, which means: successfully stage the 2007 Youth World Cup, with sold-out stadiums and a worldwide TV audience; build three new soccer-specific facilities in the country (Toronto, Montreal and Vancouver); expand First Division professional soccer clubs in Canada with entry in MLS; and put together competitive men's and women's national teams.

In fact, Canada is facing the challenge of managing the growth of the sport and translating strong participation into successful performances at both club and national team levels. In this regard, implementing the right infrastructure and counting on financially stable ownership are key. The President of the Montreal Impact refers to the pyramid of player development when considering these two factors.

However, as mentioned in this chapter, referring to Shank's work (1999), there is need for a more aggressive marketing approach: first, to promote the game and the local product offered by the clubs and the national teams; and secondly, to generate new streams of revenues through, among others, merchandising, as merchandise sales in Canada and the United States in 2008 will exceed ticket sales for the first time in history, reaching more than US$19 billion (PWC, 2004). In addition, the sales of merchandising products feed themselves through the reinforcement of the emotional connection between fans and the team by offering signs, displays and rituals to the 'tribe' of fans (Holt, 1995, 2002; Chaudhuri and Holbrook, 2001). This could prove useful in making soccer more entrenched in people's lives.

Furthermore, in order for soccer to grow in Canada on a long-term basis, the Canadian soccer community will need to work together in the same direction. As Joey Saputo puts it:

> The Canadian federation is the General and we are the soldiers. But if we are not given the proper directions and the right tools, it is a battle we are destined to lose.

Hopefully, Canada will get its act together and be able successfully to have its *rendezvous* with history. Looking back at some of the failures of the past could help the different actors to avoid making the same mistakes that resulted from hasty decisions or fear of the unknown. That way, the period we are going through could in the future be remembered as a turning point: 'the beginning of a new beginning', as Kevan Pipe says.

Acknowledgements

The author would like to thank sincerely Kevan Pipe, Chief Operating Officer of Soccer Canada, as well as Joey Saputo and Stéphane Banfi, respectively President and Communications and Marketing Director of the Montreal Impact Soccer Club, for their precious collaboration. The author hopes that his analysis may feed the reflection on the development of soccer in Canada.

Bibliography and references

Anonymous (1998). Suite dreams: rating the boxes. *The Wall Street Journal*, 30 October, W6.

Baccouche, B. (2004). *La diffusion et l'adoption du soccer au Québec: problèmes et pistes de solutions*. MBA Essay, Fall 2004, Université Laval, Quebec City.

Barra, A. (2005). And very sweet for the Yankees. *The Wall Street Journal*, 22 June, D12.

Chaudhuri, A. and Holbrook, M. B. (2001). The chain of effects from brand trust and brand affect to brand performance: the role of brand loyalty. *Journal of Marketing*, **65(2)**, 81–93.

Dumas, G. (2004). La rançon de la gloire. La ville manque de terrains de soccer. *Le Soleil*, 15 November, S7.

FIFA (2006). www.fifa.com.

Forde, O. (1996). Le sport en Norvège (available at http://odin.
 dep.no/odin/fransk/om_odin/stillinger/032005-990371/
 dok-bn.html).

Hockey Canada (2006). www.hockeycanada.ca.

Holt, D. B. (1995). How consumers consume: a typology of consumption practices. *Journal of Consumer Research*, **22(1)**, 1–16.

Holt, D. B. (2002). Why do brands cause trouble? A dialectical theory of consumer culture and branding. *Journal of Consumer
 Research*, **29**, 70–90.

KPMG (2000). *Business Plan for a Canadian Professional League. A
 review of key findings.* KPMG, Ottawa.

Lopiano, D. (2004). Gender equity in sport. *Diversity Factor*, **12(1)**,
 24–29.

Montreal Impact Soccer Club (2006). www.impactmontreal.com.

Mullin, B. J., Hardy, S. and Sutton, W. A. (2000). *Sport Marketing*,
 2nd edn. Human Kinetics.

Price Waterhouse Coopers (PWC) (2004). *Global Outlook for the
 Sports Market: global entertainment and media outlook, 2004–2008.*
 PWC New York.

Richelieu, A. (2004). Building the brand equity of professional
 sports teams. In: B. Pitts (ed.), *Sharing Best Practices in Sport
 Marketing*, pp. 3–21. Fitness Information Technology Inc.

Richelieu, A. and Pons, F. (2005). Reconciling managers' strategic
 vision with fans' expectations. *International Journal of Sports
 Marketing & Sponsorship*, **6(3)**, 150–163.

Richelieu, A. and Pons, F. (2006). Toronto Maple Leafs vs. Football
 Club Barcelona: how two legendary sports teams built their brand
 equity. *International Journal of Sports Marketing & Sponsorship*,
 April (Special issue).

Rogers, E. M. (1983). *Diffusion of Innovations*, 3rd edn. *The Free
 Press*.

Rogers, E. M. (1995). *Diffusion of Innovations*, 4th edn. *The Free
 Press*.

Schwartz, G. and Gagnon, J. (2003). *Histoire du soccer québécois.*
 Socbec.

Shank, M. D. (1999). *Sports Marketing: A Strategic Perspective.*
 Prentice Hall.

Soccer Canada (2006). www.canadasoccer.com.

Sport Canada (1999). Analyse comparative entre les sexes dans le
 sport (1997–1998) (available at www.pch.gc.ca/progs/sc/
 pubs/sexe-gender/index_f.cfm).

Strang, D. and Soule, S. (1998). Diffusion in organizations and
 social movements: from hybrid corn to poison pills. *Annual
 Review of Sociology*, **24**, 265–290.

Appendix 15.1

Interview with Kevan Pipe, Chief Operating Officer of the Canadian Soccer Association (CSA), 20 December 2005

The federation and soccer

Q1: In your opinion, what is the current status of soccer in Canada?
KP: We are at the crossroads. The next six years in Canada will be unique for the history of soccer in this country. We either make it or break it!

- In 2006, two soccer-specific stadiums will be built in Toronto and Montreal

- In 2007, Canada will host the under 20 World Cup and Toronto will enter Major League Soccer (MLS)

- In 2008, we will host the CONCACAF Olympic qualifying tournament for both men and women

- In 2009, Canada will play host to the CONCACAF Gold Cup

- In 2012, we will celebrate the centennial of the Canadian Soccer Association.

We have taken the right direction to make soccer grow in this country.

Q2: What are the factors that might account for the decline of soccer in Canada (many experiences ending in loss, poor performance by the men's national team, etc.)?
KP: The North American Soccer League (NASL) allowed us to develop high-calibre Canadian soccer players (Gray, Lenarduzzi, Lettieri, Segota, etc.), because these players were facing the best in the world, even though these were not in their prime anymore (Beckenbauer, Neeskens, Pelé, etc.). However, the NASL was not financially structured to survive. The NASL experience carried us until 1997, after which there was a sharp decline in our men's national team performance.

MLS coming to Canada will in fact give us the opportunity to develop high-calibre players, as the NASL did in the 1980s, but with the financial strength we didn't have back then.

We need to react to our North American environment if we want to compete at the World Cup. With a very limited pool of players, we must develop more players that will help us be competitive at the world stage. The decline of professional clubs in Canada, first with the NASL, then with the Canadian Soccer League (CSL), now with the United Soccer League (USL), has definitely damaged our performances at the world level.

Q3: Where do you think the federation and soccer will be in five or ten years from now in Canada, compared to where they are currently?
KP: By 2010, the federation should have 1.2 million players registered. There will be more girls playing soccer than people playing hockey in this country. We will have three new soccer-specific facilities and three new teams in the MLS. Our budget should be bigger than any sports federation in Canada. In 2010, Canada should take part at the World Cup and by 2014, be competitive. In 2011, Canada should host the Women's World Cup and hopefully win it.

Q4: In your opinion, what are the greatest challenges, present and future, that Canadian soccer is facing?
KP: Generating enough revenue to sustain a budget of $12–13 million ($1 million from the government), in order to allocate money to players' development, referee development, promotion of the game, etc.

We need to develop professional clubs in Canada, in order to increase media coverage, attract new partners, generate new revenue streams (merchandising).

As far as women are concerned, we need to take advantage of the programme in order to establish ourselves as a true force in the game.

Q5: In your opinion, what are the greatest opportunities for Canadian soccer in the next years?
KP: Staging world events, such as the Under-20 World Cup in 2007, the MLS All-Star game in Toronto in 2008, etc. We want to bring soccer to the next level in Canada. We can count on more young, talented players than ever before in this country. We just do not want to lose them to other countries anymore (e.g. Heargraves, Canadian-born, but now playing for England).

Q6: In your opinion, what are the main steps to be taken to ensure the development and growth of soccer in Canada?
KP: Being competitive at the 2007 Youth World Cup could give a dramatic boost to attendance and practice of soccer in Canada, as the 2002 Women's World Cup did for women soccer practice and interest.

The CSA needs to (1) maintain good relations with international bodies, primarily with FIFA, in order to attract major events to Canada; (2) generate and maintain new partnerships with the private sector; (3) help build new soccer-specific facilities (in Toronto, Montreal and Vancouver); and (4) generate more revenue.

Q7: What role can the federation play to contribute to the development of soccer in Canada?
KP: The CSA will be the initiator, conductor and traffic cop, in order to convince new partners to get involved in the game. We need to instil leadership among high-calibre professional clubs, which will be the ones developing and training players on a day-to-day basis, and help Canada be competitive at the international level.

We don't want to ship young kids to Europe anymore because we don't have the infrastructure (professional clubs, coaching staff, physical infrastructure, etc.) to develop them here!

Q8: Are there cultural reasons that are preventing, or that may prevent, the development of soccer in Canada or, at the very least, force it to be a minor sport (vs. hockey, American football, baseball, etc.)?
KP: In fact, I believe it is the direct opposite: Canada is a very multicultural society! The face of Canada is changing and is more and more open to the world; so is the interest in soccer in this country.

What we have failed to do up until now is to convince entrepreneurs to bet on the development of soccer in Canada, compared to what happened in the United States. We have convinced the public sector; now we must convince the private sector to jump on board with us.

Right now, we have around 850 000 registered players in Canada (compared to 544 000 hockey players). Soccer is played anywhere. With MLS (potentially a tier-one league) and the world-class events we will stage in the coming years, we have the opportunity to change things for the better in Canada. We have a *rendezvous* with history!

Q9: In your opinion, how important is the development of national elite players? What is being done by the Canadian federation in this regard?
KP: It is incredibly important if we want to compete at the highest level. Being able to compete at the World Cup comes from developing elite clubs with elite players. The World Cup qualifiers are cutthroat; if you want to compete, you need elite players.

We broke the mould by having a team in MLS (Toronto in 2007); more Canadian clubs will follow and we will be able to develop high-calibre players.

Q10: How do you explain the low participation of people aged eighteen years or over (5 per cent) and the expansion of women's soccer (36 per cent) in Canada?

KP: For eighteen years old and older, it is a lifestyle phenomenon that affects all sports and all countries. But admittedly, the lack of clubs and infrastructure in Canada does not help in this regard.

Right now, there are 400 000 women playing soccer in Canada. The success of women's soccer is proper to northern hemisphere countries, where women's sport is strongly encouraged (there is no discrimination).

Canada is a leader in introducing female sports and promoting women in sports: in 1977 Canada held its first national championship, ahead of any other country in the world.

Q11: How would you rate the existing relationship between the Canadian Soccer Association and all the professional teams in Canada?

KP: It has been shaky recently, because we wanted professional clubs in this country to understand that we need to bring the calibre of play to the top; we cannot stand still! Now, the peace is restored, and we move ahead with our plans to build three new soccer-specific facilities and have three new teams in MLS by 2010.

Marketing and brand

Q12: In your opinion, how important are marketing activities in contributing to the development of Canadian soccer? How do you think that marketing will help you to reach your objectives (such as ensuring the long-term growth of soccer in Canada)?

KP: It is essential! In 2006, we will get $3 million in cash from partnership with the corporate sector. This will be three times what we get from the public sector. Revenue from partnerships and other streams of revenue (merchandising) will help us generate the money for players' development, for instance.

In 2007, the youth World Cup of soccer will give exposure to soccer in Canada and draw money toward soccer in Canada. Let's not forget that the 2002 Women's World Cup gave credibility to soccer in Canada!

North America is still an untapped market, an uncharted territory; FIFA wants to promote the game in North America on a continuous basis. Canada will do its part, with the help of its stakeholders and partners, the number one being FIFA.

Q13: It is being said more and more that a sports organization can be seen as a brand. Do you consider the Canadian soccer federation as a brand?

KP: A few months ago, we undertook a branding exercise in order to define what Canadian soccer was. We came up with this acronym: PITCH:

P: Pride in ourselves, the game of soccer

I: Initiative; take initiative to grow the game of soccer in Canada

T: Team work; the growth of soccer is a team effort, with the CSA, professional clubs, public and private partners, international bodies (FIFA)

C: Commitment to the development of soccer

H: Hope for the growth of soccer in this country and what the game of soccer brings to people around the world.

Q14: Have you adopted a true brand strategy? If so, since when? If not, are you planning on doing so? When?

KP: Yes, we are a brand, but it is a work in progress. We have not really formalized it yet. We initiated some work eighteen months ago.

Q15: What messages and values do you want your brand to convey (brand attributes)?

KP: See Question 13. We also have a responsibility toward children: we help develop future citizens for tomorrow. That is why we partner with SOS Charity, which provides foster homes under professional guidance in developing countries.

Q16: Do you believe that there is a link between the brand identity that defines the federation and the brand image perceived by fans? What are you doing to help draw the brand image as close as possible to the federation's brand identity?

KP: We need to do a better job in order to get the message out more as a socially responsible association; partnering with institutions like Unicef is a move in the right direction. It is also a work in progress.

Q17: Which attributes are underlined by your logo? Are you satisfied?

KP: We undertook some work on our logo a few months ago, but people finally preferred the old one. So we will keep it, while updating it (font, colours), as well as the name of the federation (Soccer Canada in 2006). We want to modernize our federation through, among others, our logo.

The branding of the CSA is done at the national (developing the sport in Canada) and international levels (staging international events and competing well on the field at international tournaments).

Q18: To what extent do you exploit merchandise that bears the name of the federation? In what way do you think merchandise could help you develop your brand image?
KP: Like for tier 1 leagues, it could help us develop new revenue streams by proliferation of our logo and merchandise with our logo.

However, Hockey Canada is the only successful Canadian association with its logo and merchandise.

Q19: How are your merchandising activities developing? Where do you market your merchandise?
KP: Winning is important to sell merchandise. We had some sporadic initiatives with adidas, retailers and during events, in order to help our fans reinforce their sense of belonging. We expect to do more in the future.

Q20: Do you attach importance to the impact and brand image of your sponsors on your federation's brand?
KP: It would be nice to say that we choose our partners carefully. As far as our national sponsors are concerned, it has stepped up in quantity and quality in the last few years, and it will improve with the Youth World Cup in 2007. We have good and stable partnerships.

We are also associated with FIFA partners, which are mostly blue-chip companies.

Q21: In your opinion, does the infrastructure currently enjoyed by Canadian soccer help to provide fans with a positive entertainment experience? Why? Is this infrastructure sufficient?
KP: No! A study undertaken by KPMG in 1999 underlined that we need state-of-the-art stadiums and state-of-the-art ownership in order to grow soccer in Canada.

It is the same in any sport worldwide: consumers in the twenty-first century want to attend games in first-class locations (with some exceptions which confirm the rule). Plus, first-class stadiums help to generate higher revenues with sky boxes and/or luxury seats.

Two of our biggest challenges are upgrading our stadiums and improving ownership in Canada.

Furthermore, the decision by FIFA to allow artificial grass to be used for international games was crucial for the development of the game in Canada, because the operational cost of natural grass on a user-pay basis would be prohibitive in Canada, due to the weather.

External catalysts

Q22: Do you think that market size (size of fan base and agreements made with television networks) is a factor that promotes the brand development of the federation and Canadian soccer in general?

KP: Yes, realizing that for the next ten years, at least, we will be competing in a North American environment. We have three or four cities in Canada that could compete in MLS, because of their size (over 1 million people). Other cities could join the USL (Second Division).

The CSL failed mainly because of a lack of good ownership (not enough money), no proper infrastructure and not enough teams.

Q23: What role do you think that the Internet should play in the development of your brand and that of soccer in Canada? What is done in this regard by the federation?

KP: We embrace new technologies. We intend to use it more for better communications, ticket sales and web-casting of games in the future. New technologies open up new opportunities for the CSA and soccer in Canada.

Constraints

Q24: How do you perceive the competition of different entertainment offers for soccer? What kinds of commercial competition worry you the most?

KP: We compete with other sports and other entertainment options for the disposable income of consumers. Our positioning is that we provide connectivity to the world through one sport, which is played by people around the world. Soccer brings people from all over the world together; it is the only sport that achieves that, especially during the World Cup. This is particularly appealing in Canada because of our multicultural background.

Synthesis

Q25: What are the key points that will ensure the development and growth of soccer in Canada?

KP: We must make sure that we do not mess up in the eighteen months ahead. We must successfully stage the 2007 Youth World

Cup, with sold-out stadiums, a worldwide TV audience; build three new soccer-specific facilities in the country; expand First Division professional soccer clubs in Canada with entry in MLS; put together competitive men and women national teams.

It is the dawn of a new era: 'the beginning of the beginning' (Churchill). On 22 July 2007 (at the end of the 2007 Youth World Cup), we hope to be able to say that it is the end of the beginning.

Appendix 15.2

Interview with Joey Saputo, President, and Mr. Stéphane Banfi, Communications and Marketing Director, Montreal Impact, 27 January 2006

The club, the federation and soccer

Q1: In your opinion, what is the current status of soccer in Canada?

JS/SB: If we look at the registration and attendance numbers, the state of the game is good. However, as far as the professional game is concerned, and even though there is more stability than in the past, it does not translate into good results for the national team.

Q2: What are the factors that might account for the decline of soccer in Canada (many experiences ending in loss, poor performance by the men's national team, etc.)?

JS/SB: The challenge is in managing the growth of soccer in Canada. Right now, the national programme has not been able to manage the growth of soccer in this country, as far as player development, coaching and infrastructure are concerned.

You lose some of the kids who play soccer because of the lack of coaching, management and infrastructure.

Also, soccer is played on a six-month basis in Canada and we don't have the infrastructure to play in winter.

Q3: Where do you think your club and soccer in Canada will be in five or ten years, compared to where they are currently?

JS/SB: In 2002, the Impact launched a five-year plan in order to build the foundations that will help develop local talent, implement the infrastructure and solidify the team presence at all levels. This five-year plan will provide the foundations for the development and growth of both soccer and the Montreal Impact.

The Impact is now a non-profit organization. All profits from the Impact operations are put back into the development of soccer.

The founding partners (Saputo, the Quebec Government, Hydro Quebec) of the Impact plus two other partners that have committed for five years (Bell Canada and the National Bank) are working together to ensure the viability of the team.

The idea is to build a pyramid, starting with youth teams, going through the high-performance centre, the farm team, ending with the Impact, which will help sustain soccer at the highest level in the province. In this regard, the Impact works hand in hand with the Quebec Soccer Association in order to be in line with the needs of the provincial federation.

Where we are now is beyond our expectations, as far as attendance and corporate support are concerned: we have an average of more than 10 000 fans per game, and the corporate support is $1.3 million a year. But we need to have a presence all year round in order to be more entrenched in the community and be considered as a major league team. When you are considered as a major league team, you have the credibility to develop relations with soccer teams in Europe and South America.

I would like to see a professional team in every province in order to increase the pool of players from which the national team could draw and improve its performance.

Q4: In your opinion, what are the greatest challenges, present and future, that Canadian soccer is facing?
JS/SB: To manage the growth of soccer and support it. We need more infrastructures: coaching, management, stadiums, etc. It is a work in progress.

Q5: In your opinion, what are the greatest opportunities for soccer in Canada in the next years?
JS/SB: We need to solidify the pyramid approach in order to improve the level of play. When we look at the FIFA rankings, there's obviously only one way to go for soccer in Canada, and it's up!

We want to position soccer as the sport of the future, which is accessible, affordable and healthy, and which inspires great values.

As you build the proper structure, you start getting the sense of belonging of fans, because the team will be more entrenched in its community.

Q6: In your opinion, what are the main steps to be taken to ensure the development and growth of soccer in Canada?
JS/SB: Continue the development with a farm team for men and support the growth of women's soccer; this will give us two pyramids of talent development and provide us with the infrastructures we must have.

Q7: What role can your club play to contribute to the development of soccer in Canada?
JS/SB: The Impact offers the best environment it can to its players, so they can develop to their full potential and hopefully feed the national team. The Impact reintroduces the players that were with the team back in different programmes (coaches, technical directors, referees, etc.). We even lend former players to develop players, coaches, referees, etc.

Q8: Are there cultural reasons that are preventing, or that may prevent, the development of soccer in Canada or, at the very least, force it to be a minor sport (vs. hockey, American football, baseball, etc.)?
JS/SB: No, not really. But you need to be able to assemble a soccer community. Very often in Canada it is fragmented, and because there is no synergy between the different actors involved, it's difficult to feed the development of players through the pyramid. In this regard, Canada is at a disadvantage compared to Europe.

Q9: How would you rate the existing relationship between the Canadian Soccer Association and the professional teams in Canada? How could this relationship be improved?
JS/SB: It is a working relationship. The Impact tries to develop players for Team Canada. We wish there would be a better dialogue with Soccer Canada on how to develop our players.

There was no consultation with Canadian professional teams when Soccer Canada decided to build the stadium in Toronto with public funds. We expect more transparency from Soccer Canada.

Also, we need to solidify the game provincially before thinking of joining MLS. Soccer Canada wants to create a national team to play in MLS, with the rest of the country feeding the team. It doesn't make sense, and it would be like admitting the failure of the national programme.

It doesn't matter which cities are in MLS, but the game must be healthy at the provincial level first.

Marketing and brand

Q10: In your opinion, how important are marketing activities in contributing to the development of the club and Canadian

soccer? How do you think that marketing will help you reach your objectives?

JS/SB: As we are a non-profit organization, we are careful and creative with the funds allocated to marketing ($150 000 for marketing, including media, for a total budget of $22 million, roughly 7 per cent of the budget).

It helps that we win, as more people want to be in contact with the team, players, management, etc.

The accessibility of players is very important to connect with the fans and help them develop a sense of belonging. As players are available, we get free publicity.

We also have commercial deals with the media to help the visibility of the team (reciprocity agreements).

Q11: It is being said more and more that a sports organization can be seen as a brand. Do you consider your club as a brand?

JS/SB: The attributes exist, but it's more in the way we are and what we do that we express our branding. The Impact is more of a trademark than a brand *per se*.

Q12: Have you adopted a true brand strategy? If yes, since when? If not, are you planning on doing so? When?

JS/SB: No and no.

Q13: What messages and values do you want your brand to convey (brand attributes)?

JS/SB: Accessible, sympathetic and close to people.

Q14: Do you believe that there is a link between the brand identity that defines your club and the brand image perceived by consumer fans? What are you doing to help draw the brand image as close as possible to the club's brand identity?

JS/SB: Yes. We have been successful in this regard. Fans perceive the Impact as we want it to be perceived.

Marketing actions

Q15: Which attributes are underlined by your logo? Are you satisfied?

JS/SB: We changed our logo in 2002, as part of the five-year plan for the team. It encompasses more who we are and it represents the team that works toward the development of soccer in the province. That's why we have a *fleur de lys* on our jersey. We want to become the Impact of Quebec. More than 50 per cent of our players and coaches are from Quebec. We play games and organize practices in the entire province and the turnout is very good.

Q16: To what extent do you exploit merchandise that bears the name of your club? In what way do you think merchandise could help you develop your brand image? Where do you market your merchandise?

JS/SB: The merchandising programme is in its infancy, but we realize we must find new ways to market the team and generate revenues from other sources. Right now, merchandising represents 5–6 per cent of our budget. We want to be cautious: we don't want to take a giant step that would hurt us very badly if we were to fail.

We use merchandising to get our brand out in the market; opportunities exist, but we must be careful in the choices we make as we manage our growth.

We sell on our website and have a partnership with Sports Experts.

Q17: Do you attach importance to the impact and brand image of your sponsors on your club's brand?

JS/SB: The Impact has five key partners: three founding partners (Saputo, Government of Quebec and Hydro-Quebec) and two partners that committed for five years (Bell Canada and National Bank).

The programme with the Impact services their need, which is to maximize their exposure. We have to give security to our partners for the investment they make in the team.

Q18: Are you influenced by marketing considerations in the way that you recruit and manage your players?

JS/SB: We can have five foreign players on the field and seven on the active roster. In a way, it is a subconscious decision: it is easier to manage a local player than a player from outside the province, especially financially, when you have limited means. Also, we have the opportunity to monitor local players, their progress all year long. But we do not only hire Quebec players; merit is key when we take our decision.

Q19: What place do advertising campaigns have in your marketing plan? Which media do you use for communication and what is your message?

JS/SB: There are two main axes: season-ticket campaigns before the season through partnership with the media (print and electronic), and promotions for individual games during the season with partners for event promotions. We also organize soccer schools with partners.

Q20: Have you developed a Customer Relationship Management programme? If yes, since when, and what are its main features? If not, are you planning on starting one soon?

JS/SB: We know our clients, but we do not have a CRM. We have 1700 full season-ticket holders; our goal is to have 2100 for the 2006 season.

We take care of our clients: there is a banquet before and after the season for President and Prestige season-ticket holders. This helps develop the sense of belonging of fans toward the team.

We have a 100 per cent renewal rate.

The entertainment experience of fans and community involvement

Q21: How does the club promote the entertainment experience for fans? Have you helped establish rituals for your supporters during games?

JS/SB: We do not have rituals *per se*. We know we compete with other entertainment options available in the summer in Montreal, most of them being free.

The game is one aspect of the entertainment: we have activities during the game, at half-time and after the game (draws, contests, etc.). We want to encourage the interaction with our fans in order to reinforce the sense of belonging of our fans toward the team.

Q23: In your opinion, is the team's involvement in the community important? Describe its involvement.

JS/SB: There is an entire section dedicated to community relation at the Impact. We will allocate $75 000 a year during the next three years for community involvement.

Our main focus is the youth (school boards against school dropout, breakfast for children in need, visits to hospitals and grants for soccer associations in Quebec) and health-related causes (e.g. cancer). But we cannot be everywhere: we have to choose!

External catalysts

Q24: Do you think that market size (size of fan base and agreements made with television networks) is a factor that promotes the brand development of your team and Canadian soccer in general?

JS/SB: Everything is relative: we have limited dates with a limited capacity in a city of 3 million people, with 160 000 kids playing soccer. We have success working with the grassroots; we have not tapped the full potential of our market yet.

463

Q25: What role do you think that the Internet and new technologies should play in the development of your brand and that of soccer in Canada?

JS/SB: Youth have strong affinities with new technologies and we want to reach the youth.

The Internet is a source of information for a lot of people. In this regard, we develop specific material for the Internet (interviews, contests, etc.). Our website got 1.7 million hits in 2005, with 500 000 users.

Constraints

Q26: How do you perceive the competition of different entertainment offers for soccer or your club? What kinds of commercial competition worry you the most?

JS/SB: There is room in Montreal for everything that goes on. We compete for the entertainment dollars of families: we must be priced accordingly in order to compete.

Moderating variables

Q27: Does a team's performance seem to strongly influence the club's commercial success? Do you think that the current style of play positively affects your club's image or soccer in general?

JS/SB: Yes! We work around the fact that in Montreal there are a lot of walk-ups and people support a winner. There is more demand for tickets now that the team is successful.

Q28: What measures have been implemented to ensure the club's sports performance?

JS/SB: If you treat players like professionals, they will perform like ones. We do that for catering, medical attention, psychological support, etc.

We want to instil professionalism into our players and fill the stadium, because players play beyond their expectations when they are in front of a sell-out crowd.

There is camaraderie in the team: they play for each other.

Synthesis

Q29: What are the key points that will ensure the development and growth of soccer in Canada?

JS/SB: The structure. Building the base with proper infrastructure, having the right coaching staff will provide the foundations of the pyramid we could then grow to ensure the development and growth of soccer in Canada.

CHAPTER 16

Marketing in Argentine football: a snapshot

Santiago Ramallo and Francisco Aguiar

Overview

In order to illustrate the existing relationship, by action or omission, between marketing and football in Argentina, it is necessary not only to show theoretical aspects of marketing, so as to share consensus or to generate an open debate on the subject, but also to provide sociological elements that contribute to the understanding of football as a social and an entertainment sport, as well as its actors and followers as consumers.

We start from the premise that sport marketing is the discipline that has to take care of transforming the sport in a product. Sport marketing is a management tool that aims to look for a strategic position and add value to it. However, the most important aspect to understand is that sport marketing must take the approach of looking at everything from a consumer's perspective. Describing the country–football relationship is undoubtedly a task that goes beyond our knowledge, but we provide a few elements for those who do not know much about our history.

This chapter traces the structural (legal) and administrative (management) characteristics of football clubs with proven data such as TV revenues and merchandising sales. However, first it explains the organizational structure of football clubs, showing the most developed line of businesses, the role of its amateur executives in charge of the management, and the incidence of outsourcing as a business developer factor.

The choice and description of the data used show the action required for and implications of sport marketing; which methods influence and contribute and which still have to take a more active role. In fact, this presence or absence of marketing is the main topic of this chapter, as the absence is due to two main reasons: demographic, social and economic barriers; and the lack of vision and professional management. Interviews with José María Aguilar, President of Club Atlético River Plate, and Mauricio Macri, President of Boca Juniors (Appendices 16.1 and 16.2) also provide relevant examples of football marketing in Argentina today.

The management model of Argentine football is disappearing, and in this chapter we try to portray its strengths and weaknesses in order to measure the business potential and discern which are the different areas where sport marketing can be a tool for a positive change, not only as a marker of satisfaction for consumers but also as a revenue stream for those who manage it.

Keywords

sports institutions, Board of Directors, agents, professional manager, outsource

Introduction

In order to illustrate the existing relationship, by action or omission, between marketing and football in Argentina, it is necessary not only to show theoretical aspects of marketing, so as to share consensus or to generate an open debate on the subject, but also to provide sociological elements that contribute to the understanding of football as a social and an entertainment sport, as well as its actors and followers as consumers.

Sport marketing is the science that should control the transformation of sport into a product. It is a management tool that aims to look for a strategic position and make it valuable. However, perhaps the most important thing here is to understand that sport marketing's approach should be thinking about consumers.

To describe the relationship between the country and football is undoubtedly too big a task here, but it is important to provide some information about its history. Towards the end of the nineteenth century, Argentina had a strong exporting model from the farming sector and Europe was its main market. This interchange was the one that motivated, through the higher social classes, the import of football from England. At the same time, Argentina's population was expanding as the country provided shelter to immigrants from almost every country in Europe, who, just by landing in Argentina, acquired the same rights as a citizen, apart from the right to vote. Immigrants formed the working class and began to meet and form associations that linked leisure with their own characteristics and needs. Thus, the popular classes began to found football clubs and today's most popular sport in the world began to be played in all social strata.

The widespread popularity of football in Argentina denotes its choice as the 'national sport', being the only discipline capable of paralyzing (literally) the whole country, which happens during the World Cup.

Demography, culture, resources and roles

Demography and culture

Without doubt, football is not unaffected by the demographic problems of a country with a lack of federalization. In an area of 2 780 403 square kilometres there are around 37 million inhabitants, averaging 13 inhabitants per square kilometres. The paradox is that every province, every city, every town and even every corner of the country has a football club which is followed by millions, thousands, hundreds or only a few fans.

Football clubs, whether a part of or far from the sport business, have a common denominator. Even nowadays they are still organized by the same laws established when they were first created, at the end of the nineteenth century, as non-profit civil associations, and these laws state that this club's Board of Directors cannot be remunerated.

Perhaps the most universal cultural aspect football has is that when it comes to sharing a passion for the same team, social barriers collapse and symbolic integration of all the fans of the same team takes place. However, the cultural characteristics of Argentine fans' behaviour could be described in a generic way by saying that Argentina is a country that lives for football, and therefore reflects it errors and successes. This means that, at the same time that a football match is being played, other matches are at stake – among others:

- a match between football and politics (football has often been used as a cover-up for dubious political activities, and the most 'passionate' fans – the *Barras Bravas* in Argentina, hooligans in the UK, *Torcida* in Brazil and *Ultra* in Spain – have sometimes been paid by politicians)

- a match of violence (a reflection of a non-integrated society)
- a match of economy (with empty or filled stages).

Physical and organizational structure

As an aside, we must mention that football stadiums are very old, unsafe and uncomfortable. Clubs, in spite of playing a key social and community role as civil associations, have not moved with the change in tastes, preferences and consumption habits that have taken place in society. The most important clubs, Club Atlético Boca Juniors (with 13 million fans) and Club Atlético River Plate (with a very similar number of fans) have around 45 000 members, while others have far less – for example, Veléz Sarsfield (with 200 000 fans) used to have 60 000 members but has just 10 000 nowadays. Perhaps this situation shows the mixture of obsolescence, passion and potential in Argentine football.

In this chapter we move away from the heated discussion that goes on in Argentina regarding the privatization of clubs or their continuation as civil associations, and focus on the need to make management professional. In order to achieve this it is necessary to break the present model. The day-to-day activity of any Argentine football director or leader is to work in paid employment for eight hours a day to be able to pay his bills and, after that, to labour in the club until late at night just because of his passion for football. Very praiseworthy. However, the truth is that working for the club is very demanding, and therefore that leader cannot perform at his best in one of his two jobs (either paid or voluntary), with the terrible personal and external consequences (for the club) that this entails.

It is necessary to say, as well, that a club's Board of Directors comprises the officials – President, Vice-President, Secretary, etc. – and, depending on the club, between eighteen and thirty directors with the same vote. Being civil associations, the Board of Directors is elected solely by the club's members, and it has been proved that only 10 per cent of these members actually vote. Thus, returning to our previous example of Boca, it may have approximately 13 million fans and 60 000 members, but only around 6000 decide the club's destiny. Moreover, talking of the need for professionalism, it is important to emphasize that the great majority of directors may be experts in their daily paid employment, but are not necessarily so in the football business. Nevertheless, they are the ones who must make decisions on hugely expensive sales of television rights and players.

The sport marketing match

Which match must sport marketing play? As stated at the beginning of this chapter, sport marketing must focus on consumers and transform football into a product.

Sport marketing's main task in Argentina is initially to make the structures professional, measure the potential market of each club and act consequently. The marketing department of a football club is the management tool that creates plans, drives the activities and provides services regarding the traditional and non-traditional sources of income of the club. Therefore, a marketing professional in the present organizational structure of an Argentine club must contribute to the professional management, assist the directors by providing information and precise analysis for decision-making, and know the fans in order to create demand.

It is marketing's task to provide better stadiums which offer good services so as to raise the attendance index, to promote actions that increase the registration of members, to work hard to convince fans to buy official merchandise and not 'pirate' versions, to promote brands to attract sponsors, and to commercialize all the club's marketing rights.

Throughout the chapter we will see how marketing works in football. The distinctive characteristic in Argentina is that, in 95 per cent of cases, marketing is not applied from within the clubs and aimed at the market, but rather comes from external actors linked to the club, back towards the club and then the market. This means that the companies to which clubs outsource their rights – the sponsors and TV companies – are in charge of designing and applying the strategies protected by the attributes and values, for better or worse, operated by each club (see Figures 16.1 and 16.2).

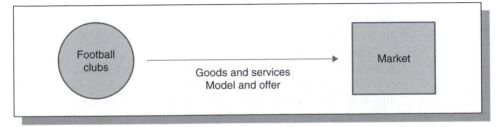

Figure 16.1
Image projection and offer of sports goods and services in the sport business and in European football

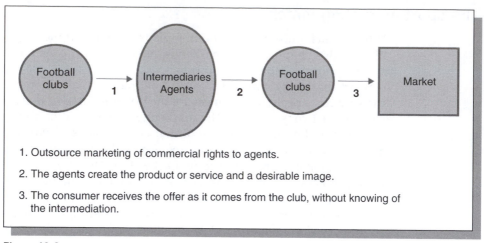

1. Outsource marketing of commercial rights to agents.

2. The agents create the product or service and a desirable image.

3. The consumer receives the offer as it comes from the club, without knowing of the intermediation.

Figure 16.2
Image projection and offer of sports goods and services in the sport business and in Argentine football

The problem

Until the end of the 1960s, football was played more out of love than for commercial purposes. There was some kind of autonomy between means of communication and the sport, where the sport institutions that had been created with social objectives subsisted by the members' contributions.

Nowadays, due to the participation of mass media, everything has radically changed. Football business has grown incredibly, making it into the world's most popular sports. Big media groups have become, with their live transmissions and spectacular images, co-authors of the sport; pitches and grounds have become TV studios, and interference from the media has even managed to modify match schedules as they look for a greater audience share, forcing players to offer a better show and even amending regulations. The sport's popularity no longer comes just from the sport as such, but from the spectacular TV images. The same thing has happened in Argentina; *Televisión Satelital Codificada SA* (TSC) owns the rights to domestic football and, through its control of matches and competitions, has altered the tradition whereby all teams played their matches on Sundays so that particular matches are now played on Fridays, Saturdays or Sundays (at different times) to diversify TV transmission and promote pay-per-view TV.

This is why sport institutions must now be prepared to administer a real show, based on the emotions of hundreds, thousands and millions of individuals. The colours and names of the sport clubs have inherent characteristics that are envied by the most important companies, since they have a brand force, a seduction, mysticism and recognition that any brand would wish to acquire.

Two decades ago, 'sport as a product' started to grow, hand in hand with football, as a combination of show business, passion and health. The concept of business brought in by globalization, the new rules and the worldwide exchange process started in Argentina as well.

Thus, structural changes and different ways of managing club prevail, in order to handle efficiently the fans' demands. They, who used to go to the stadium motivated only by their unconditional fanaticism and folklore, still continue to do so with the same passion but now expect additional services such as security, catering, purchasing opportunities and show quality.

Facing these structural and management changes is the new challenge for Argentine football and also for marketing as a strategic impeller and income generator.

Inadequate management

We emphasize that football clubs in Argentina do not deal exclusively with football; they are also social organizations where a highly professionalized sport coexists with dozens of amateurs sports and where several social and cultural activities (choirs, dancing, theatre, libraries, etc.) are promoted and developed.

Football is becoming more and more professionalized, but the business is being operated inadequately: there is poor administrations, structural failures and non-professional management schemes from the old times when budgets were radically smaller and markets much less complex and competitive. Thus it is clinging to the past ideas of 'a rising industry'.

There must therefore be a managerial focus on continuous and progressive improvement, looking for greater competitiveness from those who administer this business, based on medium- and long-term objectives that outline a local and, depending on the brand, worldwide positioning, knowing that without adequate professional management this industry will not be developed to its highest potential.

Within the sports institutions, amateur directors and executive leaders with an academic background must coexist and communicate with each other in order to provide efficient administration for those institutions.

Most sports institutions in Argentina do not have a defined organizational mission, or a medium- and long-term vision and strategies; they do not have business plans or even marketing plans. There are at the most, four or five marketing managers in the whole of the First Division. There are no audits and panel controls;

there is confusion over responsibilities in marketing development and commercial management, dispersion of marketing and yielding of TV/radio commercial rights; and absolute absence of communication between directors (where relationships are infected by political struggles).

There is a need of marketing plans focused on generating new income, increasing existing sources and looking for major competitiveness regarding the sportsmen (requiring interrelation between the marketing and sports departments) in order to generate greater interest from the media, the audience and the sponsors.

That's why, in order to be able to develop the business of sport in Argentina in an efficient way, an organizational model that aims at achieving success must be followed, professionalizing the structures and using technology and suitable human resources as a way to back this up.

It is necessary to eradicate any resistance to the idea that a professional manager can take impartial decisions in a passionate sport. It is difficult for some to accept that a professional can make detached decisions, looking for the right mix of sports successes, financial balance and economic profitability. If the club is losing money but wins a Championship, the fans will be satisfied; however, there must definitively be a full-time professional staff who can deal with balancing the economic and financial situation, the purchase of players, establishing the wages, negotiating TV rights, merchandising sales, etc.

The export model

Just like its macroeconomic model, Argentina, with a big development in the primary sector, keeps on producing excellent quality and very low-cost 'raw material' (in this case, footballers). Argentina exports to entertainment-producing countries (especially Europe), and Argentine clubs often think that they can save their critical financial and economic situation by loaning or selling young players who starting to excel. The common problem sports entities face is how to finance their operations with their own generated resources. Loan of players leads to the inability to reinforce team squads with new players, since most of them are away; thus clubs are forced to sell their young players to other markets in order to cancel their debts, and this damages the overall level of competition in the country.

Stadiums

Stadiums provide one of the best venues for the production of mega-events, and therefore it is necessary that they start developing and evolving together with the new technological advances so that they serve as a marketing instrument to satisfy the spectators' needs, as well as the participants' and sponsors' demands. Currently, it is unthinkable in Argentina that a football club could consider the possibility of using the stadium for other sources of income – such as renting the premises for conventions, congresses, events, weddings, dinners or managerial meetings, or holding an event not related to football that demands some complexity – beyond a musical concert or a charity match.

Geographical concentration

Clearly, in order to generate an income an entertaining 'show' which targets the biggest quantity of spectators' must be provided. Football in Argentina cannot always achieve this by itself, since it is always the same favourite teams winning the titles. Stadiums are not filled, except for the 'Derbys', and people follow their teams moved by tradition rather than by other attributes.

Nowadays the Argentine First Division Championship has the following distribution of clubs (see Figure 16.3):

- Cordoba – one club
- Santa Fé – one club
- Capital city and suburbs – thirteen clubs
- La Plata – two clubs
- Rosario – three clubs
- Bahía Blanca – one club
- Jujuy – one club.

Figure 16.3
The geographical distribution of football clubs in Argentina

The great majority of the clubs are concentrated in a relatively small area of Argentina (see Figure 16.3). This does not change greatly when the teams are relegated to or promoted from lower divisions. There are five teams in the capital city and eight from the suburbs – that is, thirteen teams out of twenty (65 per cent) are based in the capital city and its suburbs. Moreover, of First Division teams, 70 per cent are within the Buenos Aires Province.

To support a team, there is a need for a fan base able to generate income. It is necessary also to sell television rights, advertising, sponsorships, tickets and merchandising; otherwise, it is impossible to support a football team.

For all the abovementioned reasons, we can infer that nowadays the critical potential mass of other regions is wasted and there is an overconcentration in certain regions. This does not benefit the business of sport, and consequently it is necessary to learn about this phenomenon so as to manage the necessary change in football. Currently, the business is only profitable for sports agents, 'star' players and big clubs.

Sponsorship

Sponsors, together with participants and spectators, form the group of consumers. Sponsors exchange money or goods for the right to link their brands, products or services with a certain event, club, league or athlete. Becoming a sponsor implies several responsibilities.

Sponsor companies

Sponsor companies in Argentina do not yet have one sports marketing manager, like Vodafone, O2, Network Bull, Orange, etc. and as a consequence:

- sponsorships are chosen reactively rather than proactively – i.e. companies generally provide sponsorship according to expected results and not based on a thorough study focused on associating their name with a whole set of values, beliefs and commercial targets

- companies do not sign long- or medium-term contracts based on a particular plan

- companies do not provide any extra budget over that exclusively mentioned in the contract.

It is also common to see managers signing sponsorship agreements based on emotional aspects rather than on a strategic or commercial plan.

The clubs

Currently, clubs:

- do not offer opportunities to develop innovative or creative actions

- worry more about the money than the possibility of being able to promote the brand

- because of the lack of studies in order to determine market values, demand much more than their real worth

- do not offer additional benefits which would differentiate them from other clubs, such as hospitality, greater media exhibition through alliances, etc.

Very few clubs have developed a department that is responsible for attending to sponsors. Sponsors must be looked after and treated in a particular way, since they constitute one of the three components of the sport consumer chain; without them, those events that gather the participants and capture the audience cannot be financed and promoted.

Income and outsourcing in Argentine clubs

Figure 16.4 shows marketing intervention in spite of the sport having an income far less than that of the European market, especially due to the difference in value between Argentine currency (the Argentine peso) and the euro or sterling.

This information, which was published in an article in *Sports and Brands Report Magazine* (Vol. 9) in 2005, shows that 45 per cent of the income comes from selling players, confirming that Argentina both generates and exports talent. TV rights income was 90 million

ARG $320 million Income, First Division Argentine clubs

- ▣ Selling players (45%)
- ■ Local TV rights (29%)
- ☐ Collections (13%)
- ▢ Other income (13%)

Note
1 Argentine peso = 3.5 euros.
1 Argentine peso = 3.0 USD.

Figure 16.4
Argentine football – income
(*Source*: Deloitte & Touche Argentina)

pesos, making up 29 per cent of income; 13 per cent came from collections; and the remaining 13 per cent from ticket sales, advertising and merchandising.

According to Deloitte & Touche Argentina's Corporate Finance Director, Victor Lamberti, the clubs' outgoings reach approximately 230 million pesos per year and 50 per cent of this number is related to players' expenses. This shows 90 million pesos profit. (At the time of writing, 1 Argentine peso = 3.5 euros = US$3.0).

Outsourcing

Outsourcing in Argentina had its moment of climax and splendour in the 1990s, and today, approximately ten years later, we can analyse its benefits and shortcomings.

Merchandising

An emblematic case is the outsourcing of clubs' merchandising:

- Club Atlético Boca Juniors did this in association with the Grupo Clarín through Boca Crece SA; eight years later, it is handling merchandising on its own

- Racing Club also associated with Grupo Clarín for approximately five years; today, merchandising is being handled internally, transferring specific contracts to agents

- Club Atlético River Plate, San Lorenzo de Almagro, Club Atlético Independiente and other First Division clubs outsource via Pro Entertainment, a company that is part of Torneos y Competencias SA (which owns 50 per cent of local football television rights).

All these experiences have been successful because:

- they have opened up a market that did not exist, for both consumers and producers

- they have achieved a new and genuine source of income for the clubs

- they have contributed to the positioning of each club's image.

Perhaps today there is saturation in this market due to the absence of innovation in the offer of products and to the lack of image renewal, but without doubt it is a successful and integrated business; its only big pending account is the export sector.

Table 16.1
Market share for merchandising in Argentina

Club	Minimum guaranteed revenue ($ millions)	Market share (%)
Boca	6.00	56.34
River	2.50	23.47
Others	2.15	20.19
Total	10.65	100.00

In terms of income, Boca and River account for 80 per cent of the market due to their critical mass of fans, and the remaining 20 per cent is split between the other clubs – the majority of which do not have any marketing strategy (see Table 16.1).

Table 16.2
Actual income

Business volume ($)	Average retail mark-up (%)	Gross business income ($)
10 650 000	2.8	29 820 000

Source: interviews with managers of the clubs.

TV rights

With regard to television rights, in 1985 the Argentine Football Association transferred its rights to Carlos Avila who, in 1991, associated his company Torneos y Competencias SA to Grupo Clarín and, obtaining successive renewals through his controlled Television Satelital Codificada (TSC), now possesses the rights until 2014.

The company TSC is contracted to pay 90 million pesos per year to the AFA. This varies according to the basic nominal valuation index (the cost of the average credit of the large cable operators) and is distributed the following way:

- Club Atlético River Plate – 10.5 million pesos
- Club Atlético Boca Juniors – 10.5 million pesos
- Club Atlético Independiente – 7 million pesos
- Racing Club – 7 million pesos

- San Lorenzo de Almagro – 7 million pesos

- Club Atlético Vélez Sarsfield – 7 million pesos

- Each of the ten remaining teams in the First Division – 3 million pesos

- Newly promoted clubs or those with less than one season in the First Division – 2.5 million pesos

- Clubs that are relegated directly from the category – 250 000 pesos.

Regarding static advertising, all clubs have outsourced their selling with the company Estática Internacional SA, and save for themselves selling spaces of above a metre and a half in height in the perimeter and outside the stadium spaces. It is believed that the total business volume is of approximately 35 million pesos.

Benefits and shortcomings of outsourcing

Third parties appear to provide an excellent opportunity for developing those businesses the football club cannot implement owing to lack of knowledge and time; to the need to assure fixed anticipated revenue without taking major risks; and to the requirement to reduce the internal costs of personnel.

However, this returns to a previous subject: the need for a full-time professional structure able to:

- coordinate activities and communication

- control management and propose work targets

- audit accounting

- offer image and communication outlines

- learn the agent forms and procedures

- generate new contacts.

Any shortcomings are not due to outsourcing itself, but because the clubs just give way their rights. The most common faults are:

- exceeding terms – as a result of capital needs by the clubs, there is greater negotiating power for the agents

- unfair contracts – clubs allowing abusive clauses

- income assessment – in some cases it is better to have an adequate internal structure capable of operating certain rights and that results in the same level of income or even higher than those achieved when conceding the rights to an agent.

Pending issues

Basic tools

Even though there have been proven efforts by some clubs and excellent work by some external agents, there is still a greater need to use basic tools that can generate income and increase the value of the brand. We call these tools the 'ABC', emphasizing the idea that they cannot be forgotten if a good marketing plan is to be developed and executed. These tools include the following.

1. *Brand value creation*. Football clubs, more than brands, have almost unbreakable icon-brands, and their great mistake is not adding value to it other than on the sports side (i.e. team roster reinforcements in order to win a championship). There is no corporate image renewal, and any innovation or changes come from sponsors without any alignment on behalf of the club.

2. *Integrated communications*. Every club has a press department that does a good job in terms of checking in with and attending the press during the games at home, but there is no unity regarding the institutional speech or the end product due to a lack of both knowledge and responsible people. There are three speeches that, depending on the situation, are used with some degree of difference: the institutional speech through the team's management; the brand speech through the team's products, services and retail stores; and the team's speech through the team's players and coaches. This is why integrated marketing communications (press, publicity and public relations) must not only be a tactical management instrument but also a strategic tool that integrates the institutional, sports and commercial areas.

3. *Image rights*. When a player signs a contract with his club, he does not transfer his image rights. Thus, when initiating a commercial action using this player's images it is either necessary to pay the player what can be a very large fee, or for the President to petition the player to allow his image to be used as a gesture. The truth is that in Argentina it is difficult to generate income by the image of only one player as a consequence of the fleeting logic of the market. Big players rarely remain in their club for longer than three or four seasons, and that makes it impossible to develop a business that requires long production and rotation times. However, it is no less true that there has never been a definite proposal that impels testing. For example, in Argentina new incorporations into the team are not introduced in either press conferences or stadiums, and therefore no merchandising or shirts with the new stars' names are produced.

4. *Customer relationship marketing.* We might ironically say that a database is almost instantly out of fashion. However, it is necessary to generate and build a database with information that will allow fruitful actions in the future, not only for the purpose of selling but also for the opportunity of better relationships with the fans. A simple and very effective relationship example is the action of the Boca Juniors Club on the occasion of a member's birthday – the club sends a congratulatory letter signed by the club's President. However, it is hard to understand why the member does not also get a merchandise catalogue or the possibility of taking part in T-shirt drawing by filling in a voucher that will provide valuable information about himself, his friends and his family group.

5. *Official Internet site.* It seems that official websites are there just because everyone knows there must be one. However, 90 per cent of these websites lack updating, services, promotions, sales opportunities and the generation of virtual communities – and therefore they do not fulfil their purpose. This situation is made worse by the existence of dozens of unofficial websites, against which no legal action is taken and which in some cases are better designed and have more visitors than the official sites.

New methods

Finally, we make brief mention of specific difficulties in Argentina that are being addressed by new business methods in Europe.

1. *Ticketing.* In classic, traditional ticket sales, season tickets are sold for certain periods or individual tickets are sold beforehand or in the same day of the event. In Argentina, clubs do not implement strategies for encouraging attendance at matches where there will be empty seats – for example, by setting different prices according to the importance of the match. There is also no incentive for members who buy season tickets or special ticket packages.

2. *Hospitality.* As already stated, stadiums in Argentina do not have the infrastructure necessary to offer big events or an alternative product to that which people sitting in the stalls get. The closest thing to this can be the annual or weekly purchase of a corporate theatre box where the company is in charge of the whole set of services.

3. *Services.* Car parking is not even considered. People park the car where they can and the big majority use public transport. With

regard to gastronomy, there is the club's buffet, or hamburgers and hotdog stalls that involve long and tiresome queuing for often poor-quality goods. This is part of the tradition.

4. *Naming rights*. Stadiums still carry the name of their founders, who were generally famous leaders, players or politicians. Additionally, the press often fails to mention the brand that sponsors a particular championship with its name.

5. *Community marketing*. Community marketing is not new, but there must be a major effort to bridge the gap between the difficult life and poor educational conditions of some youngsters and their dream of reputation and glory through sport. They must be offered the opportunity to develop athletic capacities and take part in sports competitions. To date, very few clubs are working on this aspect; however, it should be a goal for all clubs – to aim to improve community wellbeing and thus gain recognition and prestige.

Conclusion

This chapter reflects the actual situation in Argentine football and highlights some real and specific cases in order to evaluate the business being handled, the actors taking part, the areas exploited and the role that marketing as a generating nucleus plays.

The glass is either half full or half empty, and we believe it has the potential to be full. There are some very good examples of success in Argentine football marketing; there are aspects related to the present situation, linked to state policies and to the clubs themselves, that will start being modified; and, especially, that there is a small bunch of young people who are becoming professionals in the sport industry rather than just amateur volunteers.

There is a sports marketing boom, perhaps not yet fully understood, but without doubt advocates will give their best. There is awareness from certain leaders who are starting to adjust to professional structures, and there are initiatives from traditional and new agents that can contribute to the growth of the business.

We dare not say that Argentina is an area of opportunity in sports marketing, but there is initiative, talent, a thirst for victory and excellent possibilities.

Acknowledgements

The authors offer special thanks to Javier De Ancizar for his help in translation and concepts; Adriana Terlesky for her investigations;

and the Presidents of Boca Juniors and River Plate for their interviews.

Bibliography and references

Aguiar, F. and Molina, G. (2003). *Marketing Deportivo. El negocio del deporte y sus claves*. Norma.

Beech, J. and Chadwick, S. (eds) (2004). *The Business of Sport Management*. Financial Times Prentice Hall.

Shank, M. D. (1999). *Sports Marketing. A Strategic Perspective*. Prentice Hall.

Appendix 16.1

Interview with José María Aguilar, President of Club Atlético River Plate, 24 February 2006

Q1: What is the additional value that marketing gives to football?

JMA: In the football industry, marketing is a subject that is just starting to grow and, currently, offers a field that has to do more with hope, with being original, with what has to be developed on top of any attractive speeches.

Today, marketing is a tool for anyone who pretends to manage this brand phenomenon, such as football clubs. Undoubtedly Argentina, as several other countries, has a lot of complex barriers that one has to face, the main one being cultural, or not knowing the meaning of the subject, or fighting against piracy – a frontal enemy in any brand development. Anyway, I think that today clubs in Argentina are beginning to follow the right path. I think that marketing is not a short-term subject, but in our football this is difficult to understand. We use a lot of international examples, but it is very difficult to apply them to our reality. I remember Manchester United's tour in the late 1950s in Eastern Asia; there is no causal fact on the territory expansion and here everybody pretends that by having a good marketing manager or by hiring a good consulting company, in just twenty-four months you will achieve good economic results that will turnaround your financial books. I don't believe it works that way, but I do realize that in the medium term it is a tool that will surely bring along positive results.

Q2: Do you believe that marketing can be coordinated by a leader?

JMA: I believe leaders, generally, come to the clubs, for vocational reasons and they do not necessarily have enough academic preparation to accomplish these type of tasks.

There can be some exceptions, but in general they come to the club to contribute their personal experience from a certain activity they already know. But it is not expected or usual for a Marketing Bachelor to be part of a managing commission.

I do not consider it appropriate to mix different items, but it is clear that although this is a club department it must hold a political control. Everything in a club becomes political actions. And it needs to have as the head and members of that department specialized professionals who can keep themselves apart and beyond the political affairs that a club of these characteristics might have.

Q3: What does the outsourcing of the services handled by Pro or Museum River contribute?

JMA: It gives us the chance and possibility of having specialized associates who can generate important productivity, as they do not have a fixed performance fund, but have to deal with the quality of the merchandise they offer and the importance of the business.

This releases you from the political issues, from the unsubstantial part of electoral changes as far as it works, and in this case it does work. It gives you the chance of feeling supported as well, because in general any club, especially a football club, does not have specialization in these topics. I believe that to rely on a partly external professional gives you the chance to devote yourself, in full, to what you should be doing.

Q4: What are the changes that should be made to improve the structure of income?

JMA: Merchandising and marketing are the fields and resources I consider to have better chances in the medium and long term. Today, River must have a merchandising income of approximately $3 million per year.

Today, in River, we are still tied to the possibility of transferring players, which provides a very important flow of money, but there is usually a shortage of this type of entity.

At present there are different ways of generating income, and world markets make football an attractive business at the time of deciding where to put the money. But, on the other hand, it is a topic which is not clearly developed.

Today we coexist with many investing funds with which, although we do not have ideological barriers, we must have institutional care.

Q5: Do you believe that a phenomenon such as Michel Jordan, where people go to see a show or an idol independently from the team, is feasible in football?

JMA: There is a certain culture in Argentina which indicates, at least in relation to sport brands, that the addiction is to the shirt and not to the sportsman. Magnetism is provided by the passionate phenomenon; I come to see my shirt and come to see the team winning, no matter who is wearing the actual shirt. It is obvious that we consider the illusion of the idol and the sense of belonging, but in my opinion this feeling of belonging is given by the team and the passion itself.

Q6: What do you believe is the advantage of being a social club instead of a private club dedicated only to football?

JMA: I think that we are fulfilling a commitment the club has with society. River was founded more than 100 years ago with this aim in mind, and while we are able to support it, it is good, and besides we have to deal with a society undergoing a very deep crisis. The club and River, in particular, are national and popular names, and therefore cannot ignore the needs of those who have less, and through football I believe there are many things that can be done. The best example is the *Red Solidaria* (United network) that we have been working on since December 2001, and there are more than 1200 pupils who come to our educational institute here in River every day, and sportsmen who come to practise their activities when in other clubs it is very expensive for them to do so or they are simply closed.

Bowls is played in River and there is a philately club, apart from volleyball, handball and swimming. All the things previously mentioned produce a *strange mysticism* that contributes to creating an addiction to the team.

Q7: Do you believe that this replaces the concept of community marketing?
JMA: They are concurrent; to support this business it is necessary to cover social needs, and to support the social structure of the club it is necessary to carry on big business. To allow River to have these activities, which are in general limited, it must have great management aptitude to be able to achieve the resources that support them. I am convinced that this is the big challenge.

Today, when River talks to its Sponsors, generally one of the first things the manager asks is about the relationship with the *Red Solidaria*.

Q8: How does River get to know the fans and associates better? Does it carry out market research or compile information somehow?
JMA: River fundamentally has two proper performance tools; its own web page, which is highly developed, has almost a million visits monthly and allows associates to give their opinions and to do opinion polls. Secondly, we use outsourcing. River has a polling agency called *Arezco*, with which we usually work. I believe that football is one of few subjects where one can receive opinions on an ongoing basis, because there are so many TV programmes, newspapers and magazines, and so much pressure from public opinion, that it is difficult not to know the real opinion of the people.

Nevertheless, we keep working hard on this topic, especially knowing that football is a field where customers are always unsatisfied.

Q9: Can the administration of the clubs become more efficient and more professional? How?

JMA: First of all we must make a historic reference: if we were to make a virtual trip from the 1970s up to now, we can see that the development of football has been better than that of society.

Our football is one of the only things where Argentina is very strong and very competitive compared to other countries, and I think that we can compete against other countries' teams in a football match, but we can't do this regarding society, which has had a lot of problems and has not had the chance to develop itself as football had done.

We can play any match against any country, but we can't compare our PBI or way of living with those of any of the stronger national teams of the world. Although football still have lot more to offer and to develop. And if we can get the formula right to run the spectacle the same way as the cinema or the theatre, it will be a serious economic case to study!

Appendix 16.2

Interview with Mauricio Macri, President of Boca Juniors, 16 March 2006

Q1: What do you think sport marketing gives to Argentine football?

MM: It expresses the feelings, the passion, in a commercial way that could be transformed into income for the clubs.

Q2: Who runs the sports marketing of Boca Juniors? Is it the institution or the company Boca Crece?

MM: Actually, we are much more organized and the club's General Department has a Marketing Department. On the other hand, everything related to merchandising and the licensing of Boca products is managed by Boca Crece SA.

Q3: Do you think marketing could be coordinated by a Director?

MM: If the Director knows about marketing duties exclusively, yes. If not, no way. It has to be run by a specialist.

Q4: What does outsourcing (the museum and the experience with Clarin) give to Boca Juniors?

MM: They are very good, if you choose good operators, they are very efficient. Boca has the most modern and impressive museum in the world football, which in February 2006 had 50 000 visitors. This is a record of visitors who paid for their tickets.

Outsourcing is especially useful if you don't have internal professional structures, but is also useful if you have them because you can count on specialists dedicated to an area or business. You can obtain better results compared to those achieved using multifunctional staff.

Q5: What changes are necessary in order to raise stadium incomes in Argentina?
MM: Stadiums must be adapted in order to be able to offer better access and security at a fundamental level. This is because if you organize the show in a better way, it's more attractive and your income will increase for sure, also from advertising and sponsorship.

Q6: Can you tell me why in this country the players' image rights are not commercialized whereas in Europe they are?
MM: In Argentina the players manage their own rights, and there is special self-training in this subject to help them to transform themselves into products and know how to sell themselves.

A club can mix the player's image and the 'colours' of the team or symbols from Boca and generate income from each part.

Q7: What do you believe is the advantage of being a social club instead of a private club dedicated only to football?
MM: I think they are two different animals. The social part of a club has nothing to do with the commercial side. In Boca both can coexist together, not in the same way as in other clubs, which has been destructive for the institutions.

Q8: Can they coexist?
MM: Yes, they can, but it requires great effort from both parts. In other words, it's achievable only if the club works as a commercial company.

Q9: How does Boca get to know its fans and associates better? Does it carry out market research or compile information somehow?
MM: It carries out market research.

Q10: Can the administration of the clubs become more efficient and more professional? How?
MM: Yes, by having a control structure in order to help the club avoid shortages. This must be external so that it can make objective decisions and be independent.

Q11: Where do you think football is going in Argentina?
MM: Football must become a massive passion for women as well. Football is having a hard time with teenagers, which generates a need for continued inclusion of women in the stadiums.

Q12: In business terms, will football marketing improve, or continue as it is, with the great business logic run in an inefficient way?

MM: Football must be reorganized, because it can't survive just the way it is today. Boca has combined ten years of successful performance with continuous economic development. We have increased our assets from $10 million to $40 million. Together with thirteen Championships titles, we have broken the rule that 'He who wins in the sports arena loses in the economic one'.

Q13: Which are the two or three basic props for this change?

MM: Internal organization, austerity, limiting expenses, commercial strategy and taking the team into the international stratosphere.

Sponsorship marketing and professional football: the case of Korea

Dae Ryun Chang

Overview

This chapter examines the relationship between sponsorship marketing and professional football in South Korea. Sponsorship marketing contributed to the success of FIFA 2002 Korea–Japan, and the chapter highlights some of the key official FIFA partners, such as KT, Hyundai and POSCO. On the other hand, unofficial sponsors (also known as 'ambush marketers') such as SK Telecom, Nike, and Samsung also achieved notable success. The chapter discusses the lessons to be learned for official as well as unofficial sponsors. It then goes on to look into the impact of corporate sponsorship on the Korean professional football league and teams. Although there have been some positive aspects, these are tempered by some significant negative impacts – such as low self-reliance and underdevelopment of territorial support. These problems are exacerbated by the general mindset and football system that is oriented toward achieving good World Cup results. The chapter includes interviews with corporate sponsors such as Samsung and the Marketing Manager of a professional team in the Korean football league, Inchon United.

Keywords

World Cup, sponsorship, Red Devils, ambush marketing, Korean football league

Introduction

The World Cup for football can be safely regarded as being also the 'World Cup' for corporate sponsors. Every four years, as the top footballing nations vie for the Jules Rimet trophy, many more companies converge on the event to grab the attention of the billions of potential consumers for their products. The FIFA 2002 World Cup, jointly held by Korea and Japan, highlighted some new aspects of football marketing that could be benchmarked by other countries and companies in future similar venues. This chapter also examines sponsorship marketing and the effects it has had on professional football in Korea.

The FIFA World Cup: a sponsorship bonanza

It is estimated that the sponsorship revenue earned by the 2002 FIFA World Cup was about $676 million (Kim, 2002a: 113–125). What is important to note here is that this figure only accounts for official sponsorship; it does not include the marketing and the sales generated from the unofficial tie-ins with the big event by non-sponsors. The notable official sponsors in Korea were KT (Korea Telecom), Coca-Cola, Hyundai, POSCO and adidas. Some noteworthy unofficial sponsors were SK Telecom, Nike and Samsung.

A closer inspection of some of these companies will indicate the viability issues that have to be examined by potential official sponsors of events such as the World Cup, given the financial burden as well as the threat of 'ambush' sponsors. Let us look first at Korea Telecom (KT), which is one of the largest telephone companies in Asia and the mother company of KTF, a mobile communication service provider. Its motivation for being an official sponsor was to solidify its image within Korea as the chief 'player' in the communication and information technology industry. It coined the campaign slogan 'e-World Cup' to promote its dominant presence in broadband networks, its pioneering CDMA mobile service track record and its expansion into digital HDTV broadcasting services. To leverage its official sponsorship of the World Cup, KT also promoted the advertising tagline 'Korea Team Fighting', which was a playful use of its KTF subsidiary acronym. KT took full advantage of its many brand touch-points to maximize its exposure during the World Cup, such as its seemingly non-stop television advertising, newspaper advertising, store signs and so on. It distributed its own cell phones, programmed to receive SMS from fans, to players. It also telecast the games live on its giant outdoor advertising screens in key locations that contributed significantly to the 'street cheering' atmosphere that earmarked the Korean hosting of the World Cup.

Another official sponsor that deserves a closer look is Hyundai Motors. It could be argued that, as the unrivalled number one car company in Korea, Hyundai had no need for an aggressive marketing push. However, if you look at the bigger picture of Hyundai's past marketing and its future objectives, its sponsorship of the 2002 World Cup makes a great deal of business sense. Hyundai Motors was one of the sponsors for Euro 2000, and they used that event to reinvigorate their presence in the European market. Hyundai's brand was telecast to 26 cities in Europe with a total running time of over 153 hours with the advertising effect estimated to be worth about $240 million (News World, 2001). In short, Hyundai's association with FIFA 2002 was targeted more towards the global market as opposed to just domestic consumption. This was clearly evident in their English website, which extolled its position as one of the top five auto manufacturers in the world. Its global strategy was aided by its use of key 'brand ambassadors', such as football legend Johan Cruyff. Hyundai's strategy also included a grassroots effort epitomized by its sponsorship of the Hyundai Football World Championship, which is an amateur mini world cup that is played by five-a-side teams of people aged over eighteen. The finals were held on the eve of the 2002 FIFA World Cup.

A third interesting official sponsor was POSCO, the largest steel manufacturer in Korea. What made their participation in FIFA 2002 somewhat intriguing is that their market is decidedly a non-consumer one. As an industrial goods producer, their immediate targets are steel procurement managers within and outside Korea. In addition to their sponsorship of FIFA 2002, POSCO owns two teams in the Korean football league – the Pohang Steelers and the Chunnam Dragons. Moreover, POSCO, unlike other owners of football teams in Korea, owns its football stadiums and supports youth football. It could be argued that POSCO is not only a vertically integrated steel company but also a vertically integrated football supporter. It is against this backdrop that POSCO's support of FIFA 2002 can be more accurately understood. POSCO has undertaken an aggressive consumer-oriented marketing strategy over the last ten years that aimed to soften its image as being merely a successful industrial company. Its core campaign slogan has been 'we move the world without making much noise'. The campaign aims to make consumers aware that steel is incorporated into almost every aspect of daily life, such as automobiles, bicycles, building and so on. Through these efforts POSCO is showing itself to be a good corporate citizen that is contributing to the quality of life of Koreans. Since football is a vital part of Korean's leisure-related life, POSCO is making its presence felt here as well. Given these overall considerations, POSCO's FIFA sponsorship can be lumped into its marketing public relations effort.

The official sponsors cases cited above point to a number of key motivations for supporting events such as the FIFA World Cup. One key aspect is the competitive dimension. In the case of KT, they are in almost a duopolistic situation with SK Telecom. It was therefore important for KT to pre-empt their rival SK Telecom to become an official sponsor. Even though the competitive situation is not as severe for either Hyundai or POSCO, for them the competitive edge can be to improve their global position. As a 'new kid on the block' among the 'Global Five' auto manufacturers, Hyundai needs to be more aggressive than its more established competitors. POSCO, despite being a latecomer as compared to USX or Nippon Steel, has now become the world's largest (on a single-company basis) and most efficient steel producer. This fact is well known in Korea, but the company is virtually unknown outside of its home country, especially among consumers. It would not be cost-effective for POSCO to engage in the type of all-points marketing approach used in Korea in other countries. However, the sponsorship of a big impact event such as the World Cup brings instant global recognition across a wide range of audiences.

Another motivation for sponsoring the World Cup is incorporating it into the overall communication strategy. Integrated marketing communication requires a well coordinated effort on all fronts that could include advertising, public relations, sales promotion and sports sponsorship. Had Hyundai not had success in sponsoring Euro 2000, it may have not seriously thought about being involved with FIFA 2002. However, Hyundai judged that the brand awareness and general goodwill generated by its past efforts would go to waste if it did not also participate as an official sponsor. It would be missing a 'crown jewel' in its various associations with football, both within Korea and abroad. For KT, being an official sponsor would enable it to bombard its local audience with a *bona fide* '360-degree' brand touch-point execution, as identified above. For future World Cups, sponsors with access to such varied internal media will achieve similar success. Telecom companies like KT appear to be a natural selection as viable sponsors with such media resources. For POSCO, the story is much the same and, being an integrated supporter of football in Korea, its non-participation in FIFA 2002 would have drawn unwanted attention.

The third motivation for being a sponsor is to promote a company's social responsibility. That is a strong theme in many sports sponsorship situations in Asia. POSCO owns two football teams, despite the fact that these teams have not been financially viable for some time. These teams are located in the cities Pohang and Kwangyang, where POSCO has its two major steel plants. Many of the fans actually work for POSCO in these two cities. Since these cities are small cities, without the financial backing of POSCO, having a professional team in the top-flight football league would not be possible. The same can be argued for many other Korean football teams, such as Ulsan, supported by Hyundai, and Suwon, supported by Samsung. For a time Samsung supported the whole Korean football league, the Korean baseball league and Korean basketball league. KT commemorated its successful sponsorship of FIFA 2002 in the following year by holding a 'Football Meeting with the Guardian Angels' that aided orphans, children of immigrant labourers and other underprivileged classes in Korea.

Unofficial FIFA 2002 tie-ins

The unofficial marketing tie-ins in Korea have stirred as much interest as the official sponsors described above. The corporate tie-in created for sporting events such as the World Cup or the Olympics without becoming an official sponsor is called 'ambush marketing'. FIFA and the International Olympic Committee are meticulous about the rights and limitations afforded to official sponsors, and it is often the limitations as opposed to the sponsorship fees that turn away potential sponsors. The lack of an 'official partner' designation has not prevented many companies from taking advantage of FIFA 2002. Chief among the success stories were the cases of SK Telecom, Samsung and Nike.

SK Telecom is mentioned almost invariably as the biggest corporate success story of FIFA 2002. Perhaps the biggest reason for SK Telecom's reputation is its association with the 'Red Devils', which is the name of the supporters of Korea's national football team. SK Telecom contributed about $300 000 to the Red Devils, which of course is a small sum of money for the company. In return, they obtained the rights to many of the Red Devils' cheering chants and songs. The Red Devils is a non-profit organization, but their visibility, especially at national football games, was omnipresent. Their influence could be seen by the 'colour code'

Figure 17.1
The Red Devils conduct 'street cheering' during FIFA 2002 in Korea
Reproduced with permission

that was respected by almost all the local spectators, who wore red. Also, they conducted the cheering chants and songs (see Figure 17.1) as well as organizing the rolling out of the national flag and also giant place signs.

In many respects, the tie-up of SK Telecom with this organization had more meaning to the average Korean than any link to some foreign organization – even FIFA. SK Telecom began its 2002 World Cup campaign almost nine months earlier than the contest, in September 2001. It began innocently with SK Telecom's introduction of the Red Devils' cheer of *Dae Han Min Guk!* ('Republic of Korea! in Korean). The Korean national football team played a series of friendly matches with other national teams leading up to FIFA 2002. During these telecast games, the *Dae Han Min Guk!* chant became the most recognizable cheer (see Figure 17.2) and, by association, SK Telecom the most recognized brand. SK Telecom also hooked up with another ambush marketer, Samsung, by conducting a promotional campaign whereby new customers of Samsung cell phones and SK Telecom service were drawn to win cash prizes that increased with Korea's scoring of goals during the preliminary round. Once the World Cup

Figure 17.2
Foreigners get in on the act and join in the cheering of *Dae Han Min Guk!*
Reproduced with permission

started, SK Telecom telecast very timely advertisements that rallied Korean support for the national team by citing the other national team playing, such as 'Next up for Korea is the United States…'. Perhaps the most organized effort by SK Telecom was its staging of a rock concert in front of City Hall. It set up a massive LED electronic board on which the game against the US was telecast to about 100 000 supporters. Leading the cheer were a number of top Korean rock bands, including the Yoon Do Hyun band that had recorded one of the key cheering songs, *Victory Korea!*

Another notable case is that of Nike. It seems that Nike has a track record of participating more on the sidelines, especially as compared to adidas, which again was an official partner during FIFA 2002. Nike's two-pronged approach was to conduct a massive global advertising campaign that had many of its star players appearing in the spotlight. Many of these players of course appeared in the actual games. It is estimated that Nike-sponsored players were captured on television for a total of 8373 minutes and scored 20 goals, as compared to the 2136 minutes and 7 goals for adidas players (Kim, 2002b: 114–138). The same study showed that the player who was captured for the longest duration was

Korean Nike player Hong Myung Bo, followed by Ronaldo of Brazil – another Nike player. The other thrust by Nike was to sponsor the Korean national football team. The Nike 'Swoosh' was amply displayed on all the team uniforms sponsored by Nike. The Nike jersey worn by the Korean national team sold like hot-cakes, especially after the squad reached the semifinals.

These cases underscore the potential for success even without official sponsorship status. In both SK Telecom and Nike's strategies, the common denominator was that both companies were able to find a good proxy for the 'official' status. After all, both companies in fact 'sponsored' some symbolic organization that represented Korean football. In the case of SK Telecom it was the Red Devils, and for Nike it was the national football team. Here is where consumer perception and reality may differ – in many studies, SK Telecom appears as one of the most remembered 'official' sponsors of FIFA 2002 in Korea (Shin et al., 2003). For many Koreans, the Red Devils symbolized everything that was good about FIFA 2002 – such as national unity, national support and good behaviour. SK Telecom had the foresight to tie-in with this organization when it failed to become an official sponsor. Along similar lines, Nike's association with the national football team was another good strategy. When consumers' involvement is more intensely focused on the football game itself, their discrimination regarding who sponsors which part of the World Cup becomes naturally blurred and even trivial. It is precisely this 'low involvement' on the part of consumers regarding official sponsorship that 'ambush' marketers are relying upon (Kim, 2004).

Samsung's strategy was somewhat different, but no less effective. Samsung Credit Card scored an immediate awareness increase by using the national football team coach, Dutchman Guus Hiddink, in their advertising. Using Hiddink as another symbol of Korean football, Samsung was able to link many positive associations from the team and the man himself to the company. A memorable advertisement during their campaign was one that showed Hiddink being his usual tough self and celebrating the Korean team's scoring of a goal while Frank Sinatra's My Way played in the background. Samsung is trying to maintain its old link with Hiddink by using him and the coach for the 2006 team, another Dutchman, Dick Advocaat, in their FIFA 2006 Germany World Cup. Advocaat has experienced success during the Korean national team's test matches after taking the reins over from yet another Dutchman, Joe Bonfrere.

Unofficial tie-in marketing also points to the need for preparation by the ambush marketing companies. As noted above, SK Telecom's preparation began well in advance of the games. It's planning of the advertising campaign was perceived as being much more organized than that of KT. Being an unofficial sponsor may encourage such concerted efforts, but the strategy for ambush marketers should be to be perceived as being in the same category as that of official sponsors. Only then can the premium of the official sponsorship 'halo' be discounted. Of course it helps to be a famous brand, like Samsung, LG or Nike. It may be interesting to see in future studies whether high brand equity of non-sponsors negates the advantages of official sponsors. An interview with one of the creative brains of the SK Telecom campaign can be read in Appendix 17.1. What is most apparent from the author's discussion with Joonhyoung Park is that the planning of the ambush campaign was crafted and executed in an exceedingly well-organized manner.

SK Telecom, Nike and Samsung's success also should be tempered by specific execution considerations. In other words, the decision-makers in these companies' marketing departments and advertising agencies made many brilliant choices in executing their ambush campaigns. The onus to have a creatively sound marketing strategy is equally high, regardless of whether a company is an official sponsor or not. SK Telecom's choice of the Red Devils was a stroke of genius, but had it not followed up that with the innovative and spot-on advertising executions, it would not have been as effective in the end. The same, of course, can be said for the official sponsors, who have to exploit fully their FIFA connections and not rely just on them. If there is an invisible advantage for the non-sponsors, it may be their freedom to manoeuvre creatively. As mentioned at the outset, official sponsors are limited in terms of how they can use their association with FIFA. To counter the inevitable inroads made by ambush marketers, both the official sponsors and FIFA must accept that at the end of the day it will be creative and well-executed marketing strategies that will capture the attention and hearts of consumers. Being an official sponsor gives companies a leg-up inside the venues and to some extent in 'above the line' advertising media, but there is a limit to how much 'below the line' activity by non-sponsors FIFA can actually control. KT may have lost some attention for its brand because of SK Telecom, but it held its own because of its integrated marketing communication platform. That should be the key focus for an official sponsor: it must create leverage from its official sponsorship to its other marketing activities.

Corporate sponsorship and the Korean football league

As noted above, some clear differences in the structure of the Korean professional football league (called the K League) as compared to their counterparts abroad are the corporate sponsorship of the league and the individual teams. POSCO's support of two teams and in essence two cities was seen as their contribution to Korean society and the two municipalities. Perhaps an unintended consequence of such sponsorship by corporations is that in some circles it is seen as a key impediment to the growth of these teams and the league. Moreover, the wellbeing of the teams becomes tied to the profitability of the mother company. For example, the K League team in Daejon went bankrupt when its corporate sponsor suffered financial difficulties in the wake of the currency turmoil in the late 1990s. About $15–$20 million is pumped into these teams annually to pay for the players, staff and marketing of the teams. It is a paltry sum when compared to the expenditures of the top football leagues, such as the English Premier League or La Primera Liga of Spain. Some critics therefore argue that Korean professional teams and the league need to be more self-reliant and less dependent on corporate subsidies. The movement now is towards creating 'citizen' teams that have shared ownership by many interest groups, and most of all by its local communities. The first two of its kind are Inchon United and Daegu FC, teams created in the cities of Inchon and Daegu respectively with public ownership and partial support of some corporations like LG and Samsung. An interview with the marketing and PR Manager for Inchon United, Sung Jin Kwon, can be found in Appendix 17.2.

It is ironic that the success of FIFA 2002 has been a double-edged sword in terms of its effect on the K League. On the one hand, many world-class stadiums were built that are now being used for K League games. More importantly, the World Cup broadened the appeal of football to other demographic segments, such as young women. Football in Korea, as in many countries, is followed by young and middle-aged men, but during FIFA 2002 almost half of the Red Devils consists of young women who got caught up in the excitement of supporting the national team. Some of these young women now follow football to some extent in general, and perhaps more specifically for their hometown team. From a marketing and sponsorship perspective, this makes football a desirable medium to reach a key target market in Korea. Young women are often considered to be the most coveted group by marketers, since they are involved in the purchase of products for themselves, their husbands and boyfriends, and their family. Young men, in contrast, are not as interested in purchasing products or in brands. Thus, sponsorship of football in Korea heretofore has not previously been a good marketing vehicle. However, if the K League can induce more women to watch football on site or on television, then the economics of marketing will adapt to change in a positive way. The downside of the FIFA 2002 success was that for many Koreans nothing will match the euphoria of the 'Legend of the Semifinals'. The oft-used moniker refers to the Korean team's unexpected success on the pitch. The bar has now been set so high that watching domestic football seems tame and unexciting. Another windfall from Korea's football success was the recruitment of its key players by the top leagues in Europe. The most noteworthy transfer was that of Ji Sung Park, who first moved to PSV Eindhoven (coached by Guus Hiddink), helping the team reach the semifinals of the Champion's League, and then in 2005 to the desirable Manchester United side in the English Premiership. While the K League is struggling to get air time even on Korean cable television, ESPN MBC televises not only all of Manchester United's EPL games but also their various FA and Carling Cup games. Another cable channel, KBS Sports, televises other EPL games, especially those involving Chelsea – which is now sponsored by Samsung Electronics. An interview with Samsung's Sponsorship Marketing Manager, Jae Hoon Lee, can be read in Appendix 17.3. Even though Samsung's involvement with Chelsea is motivated by global marketing reasons, its ripple effects are felt all the way back in Korea. There is another player, Young Pyo Lee, who also played for PSV Eindhoven and now plays for Tottenham Hotspur. With Park and Lee playing in the EPL, it is easy to understand why many Koreans are now much more interested in the rivalries between Chelsea, Liverpool, Arsenal and Manchester United than they are in domestic competition. This is not to mention other Korean players, such as Doori Cha and Jung Hwan Ahn playing in Germany's Bundesliga, and Chun Soo Lee, who played for a while in Spain's La Primera Liga. When all of their televised games are taken into consideration, it leaves little room for the less 'sexy' domestic league.

The plight of the K League is neatly summarized in a scathing critique by Lee (2005), a supporter of the Inchon United team and a former Red Devil. Lee argues that there are virtually 'three leagues' in Korean football. The 'major league' is where the whole nation gets worked up about its players playing 'A' matches against other countries. A simple measure of the validity of that assertion is how the three main Korean television networks will often concurrently broadcast even friendly matches, let alone qualifying games and of course World Cup games. It seems there is no such thing as exclusive television coverage when national pride and interest is on the line. The next league is the 'Euro league', which signifies the supporters of the top European leagues, such as the EPL and Primera Liga. As noted above, the number of fervent followers of those leagues exploded exponentially with the signing of the top Korean players, like Park. The 'minor league' in this mix is the K League. It is a sad sight indeed to see venues like the magnificent 60 000 capacity Busan Asiad (the site of Korea's 2–1 defeat of Portugal in the World Cup 2002) filled with only about 1000 people for many of its K League games.

The challenge for Korean football is to integrate the 'three leagues' identified above. At present there is no apparent positive linkage between the 'major' and the 'minor' leagues, and moreover none between the 'Euro' and 'minor' leagues. Despite the financial hardships faced by the K League, the Korean football system is designed to help Korea be successful at the international competition level. The best example of this is how Guus Hiddink was allowed by the Korean Football Association essentially to pick the 2002 World Cup team and train them intact for over a year, often excusing them from K League commitments. When the K League teams baulked at the same request by the KFA for the 2006 Cup preparations, they were roundly criticized as being selfish and unpatriotic. When FC Seoul signed the football prodigy Ju Young Park, their coach was also criticized for not wanting him to train with the national side when it seemed against the team's best interests. In contrast to the Korean team, players like Zidane and Figo arrived for the World Cup 2002 games tired and lacking practice with their national teammates because their team, Real Madrid, finished its league and Champion's League very late. A collective mindset has to be established that a strong K League is a necessary condition for building a stronger national team. This support has to come not only from the KFA, but also from the general football-following public.

Many studies have shown that the primary motivation for following 'A' matches is a sense of patriotism rather than just being about loving football. In that regard, sports that Koreans have traditionally excelled at in the Olympics, such as field hockey, handball and so on, have suffered similar fates. Lee (2005) argues that, despite their winning record, the quality of the Korean side's 2002 matches were quite low. Nevertheless, what made the matches riveting and even seemingly well-played for most Koreans was that the fans were focused mostly on the result. Winning meant increased national pride, and losing meant loss of face. The fact that Japan was co-hosting the event only added to the high stakes involved for Korean matches. This kind of nationalism for 'A' matches is not unique to Korea. What is different, however, is that in Europe, South America and even Japan, a similar kind of fan attachment to winning and losing can be found for their local league teams. These allegiances are territorial, usually formed in a city or a sector within a city. In Korea, as noted frequently in this chapter, the teams have had more of a corporate identity stemming from corporate sponsorship. Lee (2005) notes that when Chun Soo Lee scored for Ulsan against Suwon in a K League game played in Suwon right after the World Cup, most Suwon fans cheered for

Lee because of his World Cup success. European leagues face security problems because of the intense and often mean-spirited emotional rivalries between supporters of opposing teams. The K League has the luxury of not having any such worry, but from a long-term standpoint of generating greater local supporter enthusiasm for its teams, it could benefit from more territorial rivalries. 'Territorial rivalries', the term itself, is a *faux pas* in Korean politics because of the historical tensions between the regions, and it is easy to understand why the KFA would shy away from making it an open policy. However, steps must be taken to instil a positive form of competitive spirit between the teams. The 'tribalism' that we find in European football, despite its negative side effects, is something that is sorely missing in the K League. There is still continued talk about creating a three-nation league that would have more inter-league games between the Japanese, Korean and Chinese football teams. Given the interest in national games in Korea, this could be a partial solution. However, in some respects this adds to the overemphasis on national level games, which is seen as part of the problem of the lack of interest in the K League.

The aforementioned 'citizen' teams in Inchon and Daegu are a very good first step. These teams are modelled on public teams like Manchester United or the 'socios' type of ownership of Real Madrid. Of course, both Manchester United and Real Madrid have transcended their regional appeal and have nationwide and international supporters; however, they both began as 'local' teams in the cities of Manchester and Madrid. The hard core supporters for both teams still hail from those cities or regions. That has not happened in the case of the K League, where there is only a very small nucleus of local supporters for many of its teams. Again, corporate sponsorship has added to this problem by sometimes locating teams in small communities where the sponsor has offices or factories. More teams are needed in bigger markets like Seoul, which only recently added a team but reasonably could support many more. London, a much smaller city, is home to Spurs, Fulham, West Ham, Chelsea, Arsenal and Charlton, just counting the top-flight teams. To put this into perspective, the population of Greater Seoul, including the satellite communities of Bundang and Ilsan, is about 14 million. The population of Kwang Yang, home to the Chunnam Dragons, is about 140 000. Thus Seoul is about 100 times as big as Kwang Yang, but each has just one team.

Another part of the problem for the K League as compared to European football is that it has a significantly underdeveloped infrastructure. For instance, there is no official second-tier professional league in Korea. The FA Cup in Korea is played by the K League and a semi-professional league of teams affiliated with corporations such as large banks. A more significant problem, perhaps, is the shortage of youth football in Korea. For instance, the number of primary school students playing football is less than 7000. The player entrusted with the future of Korean football is twenty-year old Ju Young Park, who was 'discovered' in the fourth grade by his school's football coach and spent a year in Brazil in his first year of high school supported by a scholarship from POSCO. Despite his apparent potential, most of his football, aside from his participation in the Korean junior national team, has been played at school level. He only became a professional in 2005, when he was signed by FC Seoul while he was still playing for Korea University. This is in stark contrast to another 20-year-old, Wayne Rooney, who was signed by Everton in 1994 when he was just nine years old. In many respects Wayne Rooney has played professionally sponsored and organized football for over ten years, as compared to Park's one. Ian Porterfield, a veteran coach of many professional football teams, including Chelsea, is the current coach of the Busan team in the K League. He argues that there is much to be done to improve the only Korean professional football league (Deurden, 2005):

> There's no production line, you have to set a policy in place to develop young players. You have to put the right people in place and it may take twenty to thirty years, but it will grow. There are thirteen K league teams in Korea and little else, so much talent gets wasted or never discovered. Korea has fantastic potential but football is not important here, it's only important when the national team plays.
>
> There are a lot of good players here that can do well. I think the big disadvantage that they've got here is that they develop very late in their career. In Korea, education is everything, university studies, so players develop a lot later than in the UK and I think it's a big disadvantage. You've got players of twenty-six, twenty-seven, who are babies as far as experience, compared with other people.

Much has been made of the contribution by the Red Devils toward the success of FIFA 2002. Again, the focus of the Red Devils has been on organizing support and cheering for the 'A' matches. It would seem somewhat obvious that a similar concerted effort might be needed to mobilize fan support for the K League. Corporate support for the Red Devils has become even greater and, ironically, for FIFA 2006 their sponsor is KTF and not SK Telecom. Perhaps corporations might consider supporting fan organizations at the local club level as well. Part of the 'tribalism' that characterizes football elsewhere includes symbols such as jerseys, team flags, facial adornment, cheering chants and songs. All of these devices helped the Red Devils to develop a distinct identity. That kind of intense involvement with the local teams has not been developed, but maybe with more organized efforts by the teams and supporting organizations it can be fostered. A study by Shin and Lee (2003) shows that supporters of the various K League teams differ in their level of involvement, and that it varies across sexes and ages, and by how long they have lived in a particular community. K League teams need to develop programmes that will appeal not only to the core target but also to a wider group of people in order to increase their fan base.

 Conclusion

This chapter has looked at the state of corporate sponsorship in Korean professional football. The chapter started out on a very optimistic note by talking about key successes, in particular Korea's co-staging with Japan of FIFA 2002, which resulted in commercial success as well as Korea's sporting success on the pitch. These efforts were in no small way enhanced by the sponsorship of both official corporate partners and ambush marketers. Notwithstanding all of these achievements, the future outlook for Korean professional football, especially for the K League, is more uncertain. Here, corporate sponsorship of the league and the individual teams has actually imparted some negative effects, such as not encouraging self-sustainable organizations. It might be almost blasphemous to suggest that the measure of footballing success should not be based on how the national team performs at the World Cup, but most experts would agree that Korea has overachieved on the international stage despite its local football shortcomings. To have Korean professional football develop along the lines of the European leagues, more concerted and broader efforts will be needed at the local level.

Acknowledgements

The author thanks Joonho Lee, Bokgi Min and Sanghyun Park for their research assistance.

Bibliography and references

Cho, J. S. (2006). Telecoms Ride World Cup Bandwagon. *Korea Times*, 9 January.

Deurden, J. (2005). *KFA Must Empower Young Soccer Talent* (available at http://english.ohmynews.com/articleview/article_view.asp?no=251461&rel_no=1).

Kim, A. (2001). *A Study on the Effects of Sports Sponsorship on Corporate Image: The Case of POSCO*. POSRI Report.

Kim, J. (2002a). *Sports Marketing Strategy after the World Cup: diagnosis of advertising strategy after the World Cup*. KOBACO Advertising Education Center.

Kim, J. (2002b). *Sports Marketing Strategy after the World Cup: changes in social attitudes*. Seoul YMCA Report.

Kim, Y. M. (2004). Comparative study on the effect of sponsorship activity and ambush marketing activity on corporate image for the 2002 FIFA World Cup Korea/Japan. *Korean Journal of Sport Management*, **9(3)**, 47–65.

Lee, J. H. (2005). Three types of football in Korea. *Inchon United Magazine*.

News World (2001). http://www.newsworld.co.kr/cont/0207/54.html.

Shin, D. Y., Sung, M. L. and Yong, C. C. (2003). The sport marketing strategy after the World Cup. *The Korean Journal of Physical Education*, **42(5)**, 527–538.

Shin, S. H. and Jong, H. L. (2003). A study of marketing strategies based on professional soccer team involvement. *Korean Journal of Sport Management*, **8(2)**, 213–230.

Appendix 17.1

Interview with Joonhyoung Park, Executive Director, Brand Marketing Consulting, at TBWA/Korea, the agency responsible for SK Telecom's 2002 advertising campaign

Q: What was the motivation behind SK Telecom's 2002 World Cup campaign?

JP: SK Telecom was the number-one mobile telephone service provider at the time of the FIFA 2002. SK did not feel the need to be that active in promoting the company, and actually passed up the offer to be an official sponsor of the World Cup. However, as the World Cup approached there was a consensus building within the company that it too had to be involved in at least some way to maintain its image as a number-one company. After much brainstorming, the conclusion was reached that some creative marketing and advertising could be done without being an official sponsor. The focal point of SK Telecom's campaign was its sponsorship of the Red Devils, the official supporting organization for the Korean national team – not to be confused with Manchester United or the Belgian national football team supporters, who share the same name. The Red Devils (*Bulgeun Akma* in Korean) symbolized what made the FIFA 2002 in Korea so memorably positive to almost the entire nation. The Red Devils brought together an entire nation with the collective purpose of supporting the national football team.

When SK Telecom formalized its relationship with the Red Devils, TBWA set out to change the mindset of Koreans concerning football and marketing. The first paradigm shift was that football was not only a game or sport, but also a 'festival.' The second change was that we were not just celebrating the sporting heroes but also ourselves as a country. The third conceptual change was to activate the involvement of people from being passive observers to active participants. So in essence this campaign was by design a form of 'experiential marketing'.

The campaign was planned about a year before the World Cup, to coincide with the 'A' matches leading right up to the actual games. The Red Devils' sponsorship allowed SK Telecom to use the official cheering chants and songs. The first stage of this campaign was entitled 'Be the Reds', where the advertisements advised people on how to look like a Red Devil. The second stage was entitled 'Learn the Reds', where the advertisements instructed people how to cheer for the team. The third stage was entitled 'Do the Reds', where people were induced to action right before and during the World Cup games. The fourth stage was never actually carried out because of Korea's unexpected success, but centred on consoling Koreans in the event that they failed in the early rounds. When TBWA realized that the national team was going to advance to the later rounds, we quickly shot an advertisement that celebrated our success.

Q2: What did the sponsorship of the Red Devils actually consist of?

JP: One must bear in mind that the Red Devils is a non-profit organization. Therefore, the key support was in the buying of shirts and related cheering equipment for the Red Devils. The people who made a lot of money during the games were actually the shirt manufacturers who printed the 'Be the Reds' logo without having to pay a licence fee.

Q3: What were some of the key measures of success of SK Telecom's marketing and advertising of FIFA 2002?

JP: In all internal market research studies, SK Telecom came out clearly as the number-one brand associated with FIFA 2002. In fact, many people mistakenly assume that SK Telecom was an official sponsor, whereas we only supported the Red Devils. Of course SK Telecom did end up spending about $30 million in advertising and media costs, but from a cost–benefit standpoint, SK Telecom's performance clearly surpassed that of KT, the official sponsor and SK's main rival. Aside from those tangible results, there are many other intangible contributions that can be attributed to SK Telecom's campaign. First, we demonstrated the power of advertising to help people 'learn' how to rally behind a national cause. Second, we moved people to action, to become active in their support of the team by going to the stadium or at least to the giant outdoor screens to experience the celebration as a 'people'. Third, this campaign is often cited as the first 'buzz marketing' success story, since many people contacted other people to follow their lead by using their cell phones and the Internet. We also understand that FIFA closely monitored SK Telecom's campaign to make sure we did not violate any sponsorship rules (we did not). SK Telecom's success was such that FIFA has now changed its regulations so ambush marketers can be better controlled in future World Cups.

Q4: What do you think is the role of sports marketing in integrated marketing communication?

JP: That is a very difficult question to answer in general, because it depends on a host of factors. I would say that sports marketing is becoming relevant in the sense that the focus of marketing and advertising is changing. In the past, especially in Korea, marketing was mostly centred on celebrities, especially as models and spokespersons. Now, the 'heroes' can be sports stars – as we saw with FIFA 2002. Guus Hiddink, the coach of the 2002 team, is still considered to be a major 'star' even though he has long since left Korea. Future stars will come from all walks of life, such as gamers like Yohwan Lim. So, the diversification of our focus of attention is definitely a very interesting trend.

Appendix 17.2

Interview with Sung Jin Kwon, Director of Marketing for Inchon United

Q1: What are the pros and cons of being a 'citizen' football team?
SJK: The major advantage is that Inchon United is not used primarily as a corporate PR vehicle, in which case there would be less concern about developing new and long-term marketing promotions for the team. As a 'citizen' football team we can try to build strong bonds with the local fans. The most significant disadvantage is the lack of a dependable source of financing for the various marketing activities that are needed by the team. So in essence the difficulty of the team's situation is that there is a big trade-off between being independent and not being financially self-sufficient.

Q2: Is the creation of 'citizen' football teams the long-term solution to many of the K League's problems?
SJK: First of all, a definition of what constitutes a 'citizen' team is in order. Despite the belief that such teams exist in other places, such as in Europe, the reality is that Korea and Japan are the only countries where 'citizen' teams have been created. In Korea, the term has been misrepresented for political purposes. The best benchmarks are the 'citizen' teams in Japan, which have the regional support of the local governments, corporations and communities. What is most critical is to have a well-balanced local supporting infrastructure.

Q3: What are some of the marketing strategies that Inchon United has used to create more a local emotional connection for the team?
SJK: At the moment, we are not deliberately undertaking any marketing activity to create more local emotional connection for the team. Of course, the best method would be to create 'enemies' or

arch (territorial) rivals, but that is something that the marketplace/system is not yet ready to accept, so we are taking a 'wait and see' approach as far as this matter is concerned.

Q4: What are some of the collective marketing and PR efforts that the K League must make to develop the K League?
SJK: The most important activity that is needed is to make the K League more accessible on television. In addition to the broadcasting of K League games, we need to increase the exposure of highlights and information about the K League on sporting programmes to existing and potential fans. There are many sporting programmes on Korean television, but their focus tends to be more on what happens with the national team. Last year was somewhat different because of the impact of the signing and playing of Ju Young Park by Seoul FC. That definitely had a positive impact on promoting the K League. The return and good form shown by Chun Soo Lee (formerly of the Primera Liga) received a lot of buzz. But these are only a drop in the bucket, and more such efforts are needed.

Q5: What are some of the marketing and PR plans for the near future?
SJK: The campaign slogan for this year for Inchon United is 'with the citizens'. As mentioned above, the team does not have the financial resources to pursue all of its marketing and PR plans. Last year we experimented with having 'community day' and other promotional events to fill Moonhak Stadium (another key venue of the World Cup 2002). Since over 80 per cent of the funding comes from various sponsors, we will have to maintain good relations with the local business community.

Q6: How did you personally get involved with the team? What are some of the joys of being in a 'citizen' team, and what are some of the challenges?
SJK: I joined the team from its inception. I joined the team with the conviction that Korean football must be defined by the K League and not by the national squad. My mission is to introduce modern marketing methods to gradually improve the state of and support for Korean professional football. My challenge is that the powers that be in Korean football have a different mindset in terms of the direction that needs to be taken. I therefore expect that the pace of change for the K League will be somewhat slow in coming.

Appendix 17.3

Interview with Jae Hoon Lee, Sponsorship Marketing Manager, Samsung Electronics

Q1: What are some of the motivations for sponsoring football teams abroad and at home?

JHL: There are three main motivations for sponsoring football teams such as Chelsea. The first reason is to have a differentiated communication approach as compared with traditional 'above the line' methods such as advertising. Advertising is effective for many communication purposes, but cannot achieve all of Samsung's objectives. We find that sports marketing and sponsorship are more effective in increasing the emotional connection and likeability of the Samsung brand with existing and potential consumers. The second reason for sponsorship is to improve the global presence of the brand. Samsung's sponsorship of Chelsea has significantly improved the awareness of the brand name in Europe. The third reason is related to the second, and involves making sure that Samsung gets into the consideration set of consumers who are in the market for electronic products such as cell phones. Sports marketing is very effective in broadening the number of brand touchpoints in that regard.

Q2: Why was Chelsea chosen as Samsung's partner for Europe?

JHL: The choice of Chelsea was an easy one since it has always been Samsung's policy to choose the number-one team in the country or region. For instance, in Brazil Samsung also sponsors the Corinthians team, which is the top-performing team in that country. Given the success of the Chelsea team in the 2004/05 season, Samsung deemed that associating with the team would increase Samsung's presence not only among the millions of Chelsea supporters worldwide but also among the followers of European football. The added bonus was that the corporate and team colours of Chelsea and Samsung both happened to be the same blue. So from an integrated marketing communications perspective, this turned out to be another benefit.

Q3: What are some interesting examples of Samsung's use of its Chelsea sponsorship?

JHL: Samsung's deal with Chelsea allows the company exclusive use of many different non-traditional media that can be classified as 'below the line'. Samsung receives a Skybox that can be used for the marketing of Samsung's many corporate clients. It also has the use of a Hospitality Box that complements the Skybox and is used to bring in other people as well as lottery-picked new consumers of Samsung products. These efforts increase the involvement of consumers at our innumerable retail sites. The Samsung brand is also prominently displayed on many of Chelsea's merchandise products, including various jersey kits. All of the large television monitors within the Stanford Bridge stadium are Samsung displays that show Samsung's logo. Also, on selected Sponsors' Days we can prominently show our new products. So it is more than just a 'shirt deal', and it enables Samsung to present the brand with multiple touch-points.

General conclusion

This book is the first step in the development of a sectorial form of marketing, i.e. marketing applied to football. It has shown that football is becoming more and more international in its economical and marketing dimension (we have known for decades that football is the most popular sport in the world regarding both amateur games and TV exposure). As we have seen, Europe is still the dominant model because of the size of its national championships (particularly on the 'Big Five market' but also on emergent markets) and because of the financial means available thanks to sponsorship, TV rights, ticketing and merchandising.

However, there is real potential for football (and the marketing related to it) to grow outside Europe. Korea and Japan showed in 2002 that the World Cup could be the opportunity to launch a new sport in countries where football had no history or legitimacy. However, the US experiences and the failure of football leagues underline how important it is to take into account the cultural differences when we talk about sport consumption. Brazil, on the other hand, is a huge potential market but needs real economic and marketing structures, as does Africa – which has enormous fan potential but also a lack of infrastructure to develop the economic and marketing dimensions of football.

Clearly, we can say that sport marketing applied to football is becoming more and more globalized and the diffusion of the international research (and hopefully the new trends evoked in this book) at an international level will permit the development of football in new markets. This is one of the goals of this book: to provide a state-of-the-art guide to what is done in soccer marketing all over the world by practitioners and academics.

We can be satisfied with what has been achieved in this book, but of course further research is needed on this topic. The present book can be considered to be 'exploratory study'; the next contributions will probably have to be more representative by using other methodologies – for example, ambitious quantitative surveys. Articles that were published in *International Journal of Sport Marketing and Sponsorship* special issue on marketing and football in 2006 provide good examples of what sport marketing applied to football might be in the future.

However, we should not consider this book only as a sectorial approach. This is a big debate in the community about applied research: should we consider marketing applied to sport, culture, aircraft industry, chemicals, etc. as 'real' theoretical marketing? Of course not, if it is just descriptive. However, sport marketing cannot be considered as a sectorial approach because sport services, for example, has enough specifics to be fertile. The coproduction of sport services by the consumer implies, for example, a particular marketing strategy among suppliers (events organizers or sport suppliers, such as federations or private companies). Therefore, sport marketing can lead to the development of new tools that concern the marketing mix (regarding facilities, consumers, communications, prices of tickets, for example) and provide new solutions for practitioners.

That is why new trends in marketing applied to football have occurred, thanks to this collective work, and I hope it will give us the chance to see much more work on this topic in the following year.

Michel Desbordes
5 May 2006

Index